Environmental Tax Reform (ETR)

Creating Sustainable Growth in Europe Series

Creating sustainable growth in europe (csge) was a policy research initiative launched and funded by the Anglo-German Foundation. It was designed to explore how—if at all—we can increase economic growth in Europe without tipping the balance against social justice and the environment. Four linked research programmes took up this challenge through original empirical research and by pooling and comparing data, experience, and ideas from the UK, Germany, and beyond. The initiative culminated in a series of publications, conferences and seminars in late 2009. For more information see www.agf.org.uk

Series Editors

A. B. Atkinson and Ray Cunningham

Books in the series

Environmental Tax Reform (ETR)
A Policy for Green Growth
Edited by Paul Ekins and Stefan Speck

Converging Worlds of Welfare?
British and German Social Policy in the 21st Century
Edited by Jochen Clasen

Environmental Tax Reform (ETR)

A Policy for Green Growth

Edited by
Paul Ekins and Stefan Speck

OXFORD
UNIVERSITY PRESS

OXFORD
UNIVERSITY PRESS

Great Clarendon Street, Oxford OX2 6DP

Oxford University Press is a department of the University of Oxford.
It furthers the University's objective of excellence in research, scholarship,
and education by publishing worldwide in

Oxford New York

Auckland Cape Town Dar es Salaam Hong Kong Karachi
Kuala Lumpur Madrid Melbourne Mexico City Nairobi
New Delhi Shanghai Taipei Toronto

With offices in

Argentina Austria Brazil Chile Czech Republic France Greece
Guatemala Hungary Italy Japan Poland Portugal Singapore
South Korea Switzerland Thailand Turkey Ukraine Vietnam

Oxford is a registered trade mark of Oxford University Press
in the UK and in certain other countries

Published in the United States
by Oxford University Press Inc., New York

© Oxford University Press 2011

The moral rights of the author have been asserted
Database right Oxford University Press (maker)

First published 2011

British Library Cataloguing in Publication Data

Data available

Library of Congress Cataloging in Publication Data

Data available

Typeset by SPI Publisher Services, Pondicherry, India
Printed in Great Britain
on acid-free paper by
MPG Books Group, Bodmin and King's Lynn

ISBN 978-0-19-958450-5

10 9 8 7 6 5 4 3 2 1

This book is dedicated to the search for an environmentally sustainable economy, to which its authors are committed.

Foreword

In 2004, the Trustees of the Anglo-German Foundation made a brave and important decision. They decided that the Foundation had largely fulfilled the objectives for which it was created in 1973 and that it should bring its work to a conclusion in 2009. This was a brave decision since few institutions have the courage to draw their activities to an end when they have served their purpose. It was an important decision, since they decided to spend the Foundation's final resources on a five-year major research project. It is the fruits of this research that are reported in the impressive volumes in this series.

The world has changed greatly since 1973, and so too have the two countries—Germany and the United Kingdom—which established the Foundation. At that time, the United Kingdom was just on the point of becoming a member of the European Communities, joining the six founder Member States. Germany was divided, as was the world, politically and economically. Today is very different. The European Communities have become the European Union, with 27 Member States, and more countries applying to join. China, Brazil, and India have become major economic powers. It is therefore not surprising that the Foundation decided that its founding purpose—in encouraging the exchange of knowledge, ideas, and best practice between two countries—had been served. These activities have now moved to a global plane. As it was put by Ray Cunningham, final Director, in his history of the Anglo-German Foundation, the two systems should now be seen, not just together, but 'rather as two linked entities within a much larger economic and political whole' (*The Anglo-German Foundation 1973–2009*, London: AGF, 2009).

Concern with the changing world context underlay the Trustees' choice of subject for the final major research initiative: Creating Sustainable Growth in Europe (csge). As they recognized, the key issue faced by policy makers, and by individual citizens, is the capacity to adapt to global developments in a way that preserves the essential qualities of our societies. This will involve institutional change—including, as they themselves have demonstrated, that institutions should come and go. Change is inevitably disruptive. It will necessitate major shifts in our future life styles, and the burden of adjustment needs to be shared fairly. In achieving the necessary change, a key role will be played by research. All of the four programmes that formed part of the csge initiative may be seen as contributing to our understanding of the problem of reconciling the desire for progress with environmental sustainability and social justice.

Indeed, in highlighting environmental and social sustainability several years ago, when the csge initiative was launched, the Foundation was ahead of the public debate. Regrettably, it remains, five years later, just as much the case that we need to bring together research on environmental sustainability with the mainstream debate about macroeconomic policy, employment, and growth. We have not really grasped the macroeconomic nettle. Nor is it sufficiently recognized that sustainability at a global level can only be achieved if we address at the same time the longstanding issue of securing more even global development. We need to remember the words of President Heinemann, when announcing the creation of the Foundation: 'all of us, young or old, face the necessity to halt the ravaging of the resources of nature and the poisoning of our environment and food, in order to counter the hunger of millions of people which can lead to world-wide conflict' (quoted in the history of the Anglo-German Foundation referred to above).

How can the research of the csge initiative, reported in these volumes, contribute to the policy debate? Here I will highlight just two themes. The first is the integration of economic and social policy. Too often these are treated as unconnected, and today, with government debt dominating policy discussion throughout the industrialized world, there is a serious risk that the positive functions of public spending will be ignored—to our long-term cost. But issues such as pensions have to be seen as an integrated whole. Pensions are not just relevant to macroeconomic stability, but affect the lives of most of us. Moreover, in the debate about future consumption levels, pensions form a key part of any intergenerational compact. As should investment in infrastructure. There are many other examples where research can facilitate joined-up policy-making. As the EU moves slowly towards a common immigration policy, the design of the policy has to take account of the implications for the labour market, for the macro-economy, for social cohesion, and of the environmental impact. When we discuss the introduction of environmental taxes, we have to consider their distributional burden. Sustainability is a social, as well as an environmental, concern.

The second theme is the identification of the *key actors*. The mission of the Foundation was to contribute to the policy process and to encourage exchange between researchers and practitioners. Over the past third of a century, the policy process has changed. Evidently, the EU is now a leading world player, and, for all the inherent difficulties in making decisions with so many Member States, is increasingly providing the locus for policy formation. Power has also shifted downwards, with increased responsibilities being assumed by regional or local governments. In this respect, the United Kingdom today looks more like the Federal Republic of Germany. But policy is not just made by politicians. Research on the csge initiative has emphasized the key role of managers, the role of social partners, and the role of families. We need to understand better the mechanisms by which change is determined and facilitated.

The csge initiative was steered by an Academic Advisory Board, which I chaired, and I would like to end by thanking the members of the Board for their helpful and constructive participation, and Ray Cunningham and his colleagues at the Foundation, with whom it was a great pleasure to work.

Tony Atkinson

September 2010

Preface

A key role in generating the material for this book was played by the PETRE research project of the Anglo-German Foundation. It is therefore only right that the book should begin with a statement of the purpose and structure of the project, together with the names of the project's partners and lead investigators.

Purpose and Structure of the PETRE Project

The PETRE project, standing for 'Resource Productivity, Environmental Tax Reform and Sustainable Growth in Europe', was a research project of the Anglo-German Foundation carried out by:

- Professor Paul Ekins, now at UCL Energy Institute, University College London (UCL), UK (Co-ordinator);
- Dr Terry Barker, Cambridge Econometrics (CE), UK;
- Professor Bernd Meyer, University of Osnabrück and GWS, Germany;
- Professor Martin Jänicke, Free University (FU), Berlin, Germany;
- Dr Stefan Giljum and Dr Stefan Speck, Sustainable Europe Research Institute (SERI), Austria;
- Professor Petr Šauer, University of Economics (UEP), Prague, Czech Republic;
- and colleagues from all institutions.

PETRE sought to explore the potential contribution of resource productivity, and of environmental tax reform (ETR) which may promote it, to sustainable growth in Europe. 'Sustainable growth' for the purposes of PETRE meant sustainable economic growth, which is not the same as a sustainable increase in human welfare because this depends on other factors than economic growth, importantly including the environment. 'Sustainable economic growth' was also interpreted as *environmentally* sustainable economic growth, abstracting from the myriad social and economic factors which may make economic growth unsustainable. This environmentally sustainable economic growth is also sometimes referred to in a shorthand form, in the book and in its subtitle, as simply 'green growth'.

The PETRE project linked the concepts of resource productivity and environmental tax reform (ETR), in order to contribute at a European level to the joint pursuit of the Lisbon Strategy, and to provide a new impetus to growth and competitiveness, and the EU Sustainable Development Strategy.

The key research questions of PETRE were:

1. What are the long-term relationships between energy and resource prices, and energy and resource use, environmental quality, economic growth, and competitiveness?

2. What have been the effects so far of European environmental tax reforms (ETRs) on employment, economic growth, and competitiveness? What are the medium-term implications of such reforms in the UK and Germany for the national, European, and global economies? Do they give any grounds for expecting that ETRs will be able to increase economic growth and employment while reducing local and global environmental impacts?

3. What implications follow from this analysis for the design of further environmental tax reforms for both old and new EU Member States?

The research undertaken in PETRE was divided into five linked 'work packages' (WPs), of which the first was divided into three parts (WP1A–C). Taken together the WPs investigated the major issues related to resource productivity and ETR, including both economic and environmental implications and impacts, in single countries, within the EU and in the global economy.

In relation to the research questions, the purposes of the WPs may be outlined as follows:

- WP1 explored the link between resource use, economic performance, and environmental quality, specifically seeking to characterize the relationship between trends in resource productivity, resource (especially energy) prices, environmental quality, economic growth, and competitiveness. WP1 was divided into three parts: WP1A focused on the productivity, prices, and growth issues; WP1B on growth, environmental quality, and well-being issues; and WP1C on the economic and environmental contribution of the environmental industries.

- WP2 focused on the resource and labour impacts of European ETRs to date, and sought to determine what have been the resource and labour impacts of the ETRs that have been implemented in Germany and the UK.

- WP3 used two EU-wide European macro-econometric models to model the single-country, European, and global economic and environmental effects of different ETR regimes, and to make projections to 2020, exploring what might be the impacts on labour and resource productivity, resource use and employment, and what might be the environmental impacts, of major ETRs in the UK, Germany, and the EU in the future, and what were the reasons for any differences in the models' projections.

- WP4 explored the implications of the analyses undertaken in WP1–3 for the new EU Member States in Central and Eastern Europe, and made recommendations for ETR design and implementation in these countries.

- WP5 focused on the global dimensions of sustainable growth in Europe, investigating the positive and negative implications of higher European resource productivity for European competitiveness, for worldwide patterns of natural resource extraction and of production, trade, and consumption, and for other (especially developing) countries, and the policy implications.

By exploring these issues in a specific, rigorous, and quantitative way, PETRE sought to make an innovative and durable contribution to one of the most important issues facing Europe and the world today: how to integrate environmental and economic objectives, reducing global environmental impacts while enhancing economic competitiveness and improving quality of life.

Acknowledgements

Our first acknowledgement, and grateful thanks, must go to the Anglo-German Foundation (AGF), which funded the three-year research project, 'Resource Productivity, Environmental Tax Reform and Sustainable Growth in Europe' (PETRE), from which all but one of the chapters in this book derive. This project was one of four in the AGF's final programme of research, entitled 'Creating Sustainable Growth in Europe', at the end of which, in December 2009, the AGF wound itself up. The four Final Reports from the programme may be found on the AGF's website (still functioning at the time of writing) at <http://www.agf.org.uk/>, and the PETRE Final Report may be found on the PETRE website (<http://www.petre.org.uk>). We would like specially to thank Ray Cunningham and Regina Vogel, the Director and Deputy Director, of AGF, its staff Ann Pfeiffer and Annette Birkholz, and its Academic Advisory Board, for all the help and advice they gave during the course of the research, and for the organization of the splendid mid-term and concluding events in London and Berlin which helped us to disseminate its conclusions.

The PETRE project also had its own Advisory Council, the members of which, all acting in their personal capacity, gave valuable advice throughout our three years of work. We would especially like to thank Nils-Axel Braathen (OECD), David Gee (European Environment Agency), Harry Lehmann (Federal Environment Agency, Germany), Nick Mabey (EE3G), Derek Osborn (then with the Sustainable Development Commission, UK), and Hermann Pieper. Of course, while they certainly improved the quality of our work, none of them is in any way responsible for its remaining shortcomings.

David Gee at the European Environment Agency (EEA) also commissioned extra research to fill in some of the gaps in the PETRE work, most notably on the implications of ETR for household income distribution. We are grateful to him and the EEA for allowing us to publish an edited version of the EEA's report in this area, which appears as Chapter 10 in the book.

We would like to thank our research colleagues for three years of most stimulating and congenial research activity, and for the efficiency with which they delivered their chapters for this book well after the project itself had terminated.

Acknowledgements

Finally our thanks go to the editorial and production staff at Oxford University Press, who showed faith in this book by accepting it and who have made its production a pleasure through their efficiency and good nature.

Paul Ekins and Stefan Speck

London and Vienna
December 2010

Contents

Part I. The Need and Rationale for Environmental Tax Reform

Part II. Experiences in Environmental Tax Reform

List of Figures

List of Tables

Abbreviations

ADEME	Agence de l'Environnement et de la Maîtrise de l'Energie
ADF	Augmented Dickey-Fuller
AIM	Asia-Pacific Integrated Model
BAU	business as usual
BEE	Bundesverband Erneuerbare Energien (German Renewable Energy Federation)
BERR	Department for Business Enterprise and Regulatory Reform
BGR	Bundesanstalt für Geowissenschaften und Rohstoffe (Federal Institute for Geosciences and Natural Resources, Germany)
BMU	Bundesministerium für Umwelt, Naturschutz und Reaktorsicherheit (Federal Ministry for the Environment, Nature Protection and Nuclear Safety, Germany)
CCA	Climate Change Agreement (UK)
CCL	Climate Change Levy (UK)
CCS	Carbon Capture and Storage
CDIAC	Carbon Dioxide Information Analysis Center
CDM	Clean Development Mechanism
CE	Cambridge Econometrics
CEEC	Central and Eastern European Countries
CES	constant elasticity of substitution
CFCs	chlorofluorocarbons
CGE	computable general equilibrium
CH4	methane
CHP	combined heat and power
CO	carbon monoxide
CO_2	carbon dioxide
COMETR	Competitiveness Effects of Environmental Tax Reforms
COMPASS	Comprehensive Model for Policy Assessment
CPI	Consumer Price Index

Abbreviations

csge	Creating Sustainable Growth in Europe
DE	Domestic Extraction
Defra	Department for Environment, Food and Rural Affairs (UK)
DETR	(former) Department for the Environment, Transport and the Regions (UK)
DIW	Deutsches Institut für Wirtschaftsforschung (German Institute for Economic Research)
DMC	Domestic Material Consumption
DMI	Direct Material Input
DOE	Department of Energy (US)
DTI	Department of Trade and Industry (UK)
E3ME	Energy-Environment-Economy Model for Europe
E3MG	Energy-Environment-Economy Model at the Global Level
EC	European Commission
ECM	error-correction model
EEA	European Environment Agency
EEG	Renewable Energy Resources Act (Germany)
EE IO	environmentally extended input-output
EEK	Estonian kroon
EEM	energy-emission model
EFR	environmental fiscal reform
EI	environmental industry
EKC	environmental Kuznets curve
EREF	European Renewable Energies Federation
ESA95	European System of Accounts 1995
ET	environmental tax (taxes)
ETC-WMF	European Topic Centre on Waste and Material Flows
ETR	environmental tax reform
ETS	emission trading scheme
FIT	feed-in tariff
FFU	Forschungszentrum für Umweltpolitik (Environmental Policy Research Centre, Germany)
FCCC	Framework Convention on Climate Change
FoE	Friends of the Earth
FoEE	Friends of the Earth Europe
GBG	Green Budget Germany
GDP	gross domestic product

GFR	green fiscal reform
GHG	greenhouse gas
GHK	consultancy in the UK
GINFORS	Global Interindustry Forecasting System
GMM	Generalized Method of Moments
GRAM	Global Resource Accounting Model
GTAP	Global Trade Analysis Project
GVA	gross value added
GWP	global warming potential
GWS	Gesellschaft für Wirtschaftliche Strukturforschung mbH (Institute for Economic Structures Research) (Germany)
HFC	hydrofluorocarbons
HG	homogeneous goods
IBRD	International Bank for Reconstruction and Development
IEA	International Energy Agency
IEEP	Institute for European Environmental Policy (UK, Belgium)
IFS	Institute for Fiscal Studies (UK)
IMCP	Innovation Model Comparison Project
IMF	International Monetary Fund
IO	input-output
IOM	input-output model
IPCC	Intergovernmental Panel on Climate Change
IRTS	increasing returns to scale
IUCN	International Union for Conservation of Nature
JI	Joint Implementation
KfW	Kreditanstalt für Wiederaufbau (Germany)
kg	kilogram
LM	Lagrange Multiplier
LP	Lumsdaine-Papell
LUM	land-use model
MBI	market-based instrument
MDG	Millennium Development Goal
MDM	Multi-sectoral Dynamic Model
MEA	Millennium Ecosystem Assessment
MFA	material flow accounting
MIM	material-input model

Abbreviations

MM	macro-model
MoE	Ministry of Environment (Czech Republic)
MoF	Ministry of Finance (Czech Republic)
MoSA	Ministry of Social Affairs (Czech Republic)
MRIO	multi-regional input-output
MS	Member States
mtC	million tonnes of carbon
N_2O	nitrous oxide
NACE	Statistical Classification of Economic Activities in the European Community
NBER	National Bureau of Economic Research
NGO	non-governmental organization
NOx	nitrogen oxides
OECD	Organisation for Economic Co-operation and Development
OEIM	Oxford Energy Industry Model
OLS	Ordinary Least Squares
ONS	Office of National Statistics (UK)
OPEC	Organization of Petroleum Exporting Countries
PETRAS	Policies for Ecological Tax Reform—Assessment of Social Responses
PETRE	Resource Productivity, Environmental Tax Reform and Sustainable Growth in Europe
PFC	perfluorocarbons
PM10	black smoke (particles of diameter 10 microns or less)
PMG	Pooled Mean Group
PP	percentage points *or*
PP	Phillips-Perron
ppm	parts per million
PPP	Polluter Pays Principle *or*
PPP	purchasing power parity
PV	photovoltaic
RMC	Raw Material Consumption
RME	Raw Material Equivalent
ROW	rest of the world
RTB	Raw Material Trade Balances
RWI	Rheinisch-Westfälisches Institut für Wirtschaftsforschung (Germany)
SEF	State Environmental Protection Fund (Czech Republic)

SERI	Sustainable Europe Research Institute (Austria)
SF_6	sulphur hexafluoride
SNA	System of National Accounts
SO_2	sulphur dioxide
SRU	Sachverständigenrat für Umweltfragen (German Advisory Council on the Environment)
SSC	social security contributions
SUR	seemingly unrelated regression
tC	ton of carbon
TMR	Total Material Requirement
toe	tonnes of oil equivalent
UBA	Umweltbundesamt (German Federal Environment Agency)
UNCTAD	United Nations Conference on Trade and Development
UNDP	United Nations Development Programme
UNEP	United Nations Environment Programme
UNESCAP	United Nations Economic and Social Commission of Asia Pacific
UNFCCC	United Nations Framework Convention on Climate Change
USGS	United States Geological Survey
VAR	Vector Autoregression
VAT	value-added tax
vzbv	Verbraucherzentrale Bundesverband (Federation of German Consumer Organisations)
WTO	World Trade Organization
WWF	World Wide Fund for Nature
ZA	Zivot & Andrews

Notes on Contributors

Paolo Agnolucci is an environmental/energy economist with a strong analytical and statistical background. He holds a Ph.D. in Economics from Birkbeck College, University of London. After working as environmental adviser for a corporate client and as consultant in the energy sector, he spent six years at the Policy Studies Institute, London. He is currently a Visiting Scholar in the Department of Land Economy, University of Cambridge, while working as a forecasting analyst in the energy industry. Paolo has authored several journal articles on renewable energy, hydrogen and fuel cells, and energy economics.

Terry Barker has a Ph.D. in Economics from the University of Cambridge and is the Chairman of Cambridge Econometrics, having founded the company in 1985. Since 2005 he has also been the Director of the Cambridge Centre for Climate Change Mitigation Research (4CMR), Department of Land Economy, University of Cambridge. He was a Co-ordinating Lead Author (CLA) for the Intergovernmental Panel on Climate Control (IPCC)'s Fourth Assessment Report, 2007, for the chapter on cross-sectoral mitigation. Previously he was CLA in the Third Assessment Report, 2001, taking responsibility for the chapter on the effects of greenhouse gas mitigation policies on the global energy industries. He was a member of the core writing team for the Synthesis Report Climate Change 2001.

Jennifer Barton works for Cambridge Econometrics (CE) as an applied economist, contributing to the econometric analysis of large and detailed data sets, and to using historical relationships to predict future trends. She contributes to the maintenance and development of CE's large-scale energy-environment-economy model of Europe (E3ME) and the global E3MG model. These responsibilities include regular data updates for the model and the econometric estimation of the models' equation sets. She also contributes to the regular economic analysis and commentary in CE's publications *Industry and the British Economy* and *Regional Economic Prospects*, which are published through the company's online Knowledge Base. She graduated from the University of Bath in 2009 with an upper-second class honours degree in Economics. She previously worked for an economics consultancy in London, providing a combination of research, analysis, and data collection for clients and senior colleagues.

Daniel Blobel is a Senior Analyst at the Ecologic Institute in Berlin. A thematic focus of his work is climate policies, including both mitigation and adaptation. In relation to mitigation policies, he has worked on several projects addressing concepts and impacts of environmental fiscal reform. Other themes of his work have included: indicators for sustainable development, impact assessment, and the interactions between environmental and social policies. Daniel Blobel holds a degree in geo-ecology from Karlsruhe University.

Martin Bruckner studied Business Informatics at the Vienna University of Technology and holds a Master's degree in Social and Human Ecology at the IFF, Vienna. He was visiting scholar at the Universitat Autònoma de Barcelona (Spain) in the master's programme of Ecological Economics and project assistant at the Trolls Upgrading Project, Bergen (Norway). Since 2005, he has worked at the Sustainable Europe Research Institute (SERI) in the research group 'Sustainable Resource Use'.

Thomas Drosdowski graduated in economics from the University of Hanover in Germany in 2002, his main interests being economic growth, income distribution, and economic policy. In 2007 he received his Ph.D. degree from the University of Hanover for his research work concerning the nexus of economy, environment, and distributional issues. Since February 2007 he has been working for the GWS mbH (Institute for Economic Structures Research, Germany) on projects on regional labour market development and socio-economic issues. He is one of the authors of the upcoming second report on the socio-economic development of Germany for the German Ministry of Education, analysing income distribution between households and their consumption structures, as well as the development of formal qualifications in the labour market.

Paul Ekins has a Ph.D. in economics from the University of London and is Professor of Energy and Environment Policy at the UCL Energy Institute, University College London. He is also a Co-Director of the UK Energy Research Centre. He has extensive experience consulting for business, government, and international organizations. In 1994 he received a Global 500 Award 'for outstanding environmental achievement' from the United Nations Environment Programme. His academic work focuses on the conditions and policies for achieving an environmentally sustainable economy, and he is an authority on a number of areas of energy-environment-economy interaction and environmental policy. He is the author of numerous papers, book chapters, and articles in a wide range of journals, and has written or edited twelve books, with two more forthcoming.

Holger Gerdes is a Fellow at the Ecologic Institute in Berlin, working as a policy analyst in the field of environmental economics. His work concentrates on the economic valuation of environmental goods and services, the evaluation and design of sustainability indicators, and the assessment of public policies. In this context, his research activities focus on the economic aspects of the global loss of biological diversity and on the design of market-based instruments for ecosystem services. He holds a Master's degree in Environment and Resource Management from the Free University of Amsterdam and is currently pursuing his doctoral studies at the Technical University of Berlin.

Stefan Giljum received an interdisciplinary Master's degree in 'Human Ecology and Environmental Economics' and a doctoral degree in 'Social Ecology' in Vienna. He was visiting scholar at the Universidad de Chile in Santiago and at the University of Keele,

UK. Since 1999, he has worked as a researcher at the Sustainable Europe Research Institute (SERI), and since 2007, he has been head of the research group 'Sustainable Resource Use'. He works and publishes in the areas of environmental accounting, economic-environment modelling, and the links between international trade, environment, and development.

Friedrich Hinterberger is the founding President of the Sustainable Europe Research Institute (SERI). He studied national economics at the Johannes-Kepler University Linz. From 1985 to 1991, he was a scientific member at the Justus-Liebig University Gießen. Since 1985 he has taught at universities both in Austria and abroad. From 1993 to 2000, he led the working group Ecological Economics and Ecological Economical Policy at the Wuppertal Institute for Climate, Environment and Energy. Since 1999, he has been the founding president of the Sustainable Europe Research Institute. He is a board member of the Austrian chapter of the Club of Rome. His work focuses on ecological economics, scenarios for sustainable economies and societies, and quality of life research.

Martin Jänicke has more than 35 years of experience as professor of comparative politics, scientific author, and senior policy adviser (e.g. on the planning staff of the Chancellor's Office, 1974–6, and the German Environmental Ministry, since 1999). He was a member of the Berlin State Parliament in the early 1980s and a member of the German UNESCO Commission. He was Director of the Environmental Policy Research Centre, Freie Universität Berlin (1986–2007) and Vice President of the government Expert Council on the Environment (2000–4). In 2007, he was Expert Reviewer of the Fourth IPCC Assessment Report. Today he is a member of the International Advisory Board of the Wuppertal Institut and of the Board of the Deutsche Bundesstiftung Umwelt. His books on state failure, ecological modernization, and best practice in environmental policy have been translated into several languages. In 1998 he received the Nature Protection Foundation Prize in Berlin.

Ariane Jungnitz studied economics at the Universities of Münster, Germany and Stockholm, Sweden majoring in 'Energy and Resource Economics', 'International Economics', and 'Econometrics', receiving her Master's in Economics in 2005. From 2005 to 2006 she worked as a consultant in the energy department of PriceWaterhouseCoopers in Düsseldorf, Germany. From June 2006 until July 2008 Ariane Jungnitz worked at GWS in Osnabrück, Germany. There she worked on several projects in the field of energy and resource economics using input-output modelling and analysis. Since August 2008 she has worked as project manager and strategic energy market analyst at HKM, Duisburg—one of Germany`s largest iron and steel works.

Jaroslav Klusák completed his Ph.D. at the University of Economics, Prague, Department of Environmental Economics in 2006, where he also teaches Environmental Economics courses. His specialization is economic growth and its relationship to the quality of the environment, environmental accounting, and the macroeconomic consequences of environmental protection policy. He is a member of the Environmental Accounting Working Group at the Ministry of the Environment of the Czech Republic. Since 2004 he has worked as an analyst in a consultancy company, where he is responsible for energy savings, renewable energy projects, and energy management. He has published papers and articles in both Czech and international magazines, mainly focused on municipal energy management, the relationship between economic growth and environmental quality, and environmental accounting.

Daniel Lee is an applied economist in CE's Energy and Environment team. He collaborates in the maintenance and development of MDM-E3, CE's integrated energy-environment econometric model of the UK. He manages the production of and contributes to the analysis in CE's twice-yearly publication *UK Energy and the Environment*, and contributes to the analysis and forecasts in CE's energy and environment projects. He also provides analysis for CE's other regular publications, including *Regional Economic Prospects* and *Industry and the British Economy*. He holds an honours degree in Economics from the University of Cambridge.

Christian Lutz is managing director and head of the research group 'energy and environment'at GWS, Institute for Economic Structures Research, in Osnabrück, Germany. He works in the field of construction and application of economy-energy-environment models. He has been a consultant to government, industry, and non-profit organizations. His research interests include sustainable development, energy and environmental policy, and the application of multi-regional input-output models for analysing global resource flows.

Bernd Meyer is Professor of Economics (macroeconomic theory) at the University of Osnabrück and director of the Institute for Economic Structures Research (GWS) mbH. His main research field is the development of sectorally disaggregated macroeconometric models and their application, especially in economic-environmental research. He is a member of several national and international organizations. In 1997 and 1998 he was chairman of the 'Evolutionary Economics' division of the Gesellschaft für Wirtschafts- und Sozialwissenschaften (Verein für Socialpolitik). Since 1996 he has been a member and since 1999 the chairman of the Council of Advisers for Economic-Environmental Accounting in the German Ministry for the Environment.

Hector Pollitt specializes in the application of econometric techniques to large, disaggregated data sets to interpret historical experience, to simulate the impact of alternative policy options, and for forecasting. He leads on the operation and development of Cambridge Econometrics' large-scale European econometric model, E3ME, and on the company's contribution to developing the global E3MG model. He also contributes the same expertise to the similar UK model, MDM-E3. These responsibilities include overseeing the maintenance and development of the models' extensive time-series and cross-section databases, with detailed sectoral and regional disaggregation, and the estimation and updating of the models' parameters. He leads on the application of E3ME in impact studies and forecasting exercises, notably for energy-environment-economy analysis and for detailed sectoral analysis.

Christine Polzin holds a degree in International Economics and Business Administration from the European University Viadrina and Reims Management

School, as well an M.Phil. in Development Studies from the University of Oxford. She gained critical insights into the field of International Development through various internships and as a Research Officer at the University of Oxford. In November 2008 she joined the research group 'Sustainable Resource Use'.

Petr Šauer is Associate Professor and Head of the Department of Environmental Economics, University of Economics Prague, Czech Republic. He has also worked at the Economic Institute of the Czechoslovak Academy of Sciences and at the Federal Commission (ministry) of the Environment of the Czech-Slovak Federal Republic. His present research orientation deals with environmental economics, policy, and management; and his latest projects have been on voluntary agreements in environmental policy, municipal solid waste management, regional sustainable development, and participatory approaches to environmental governance, optimization of expenses on environmental protection, methodology of ex-post analyses in environmental policy, environmental tax reform, and curricula development in the field of environmental economics and management. In his academic work he is well-known for innovative participatory teaching approaches— namely for using class lab experimenting and a case study approach. He is the author of the first textbook on environmental economics and policy in the Czech Republic and many scientific publications.

Stefan Speck is an environmental economist with a Ph.D. in economics from Keele University in England. Since April 2008 he has worked as a senior consultant at Kommunalkredit Public Consulting in Austria. Before that he worked as an independent consultant in the field of market-based instruments and environmental financing. In the past he was employed at the National Environmental Research Institute/University of Aarhus in Denmark as a part-time senior project scientist within the EU-funded project 'Competitiveness effects of environmental tax reforms' (COMETR). He also contributed to a study evaluating the effectiveness of environmentally related taxes and charges in European countries and published several articles in the field of environmental taxation and competitiveness. In addition, during 2004 he was part of a team working on a project funded by the European Environment Agency (EEA) analysing the use of economic instruments for environmental policy in Europe. Currently he is the project manager of another EEA-funded project, studying the distributional implications of environmental tax reforms.

Philip Summerton is an applied economist whose main specialization is in the application of CE's large-scale energy-environment -economy models to analyse E3 issues in the UK and the rest of Europe. He leads the modelling and data analysis for the maintenance and development of CE's large-scale econometric models, notably MDM-E3 (the Multisectoral Dynamic Energy-Environment-Economy model for the UK), and he also contributes to E3ME (Energy-Environment-Economy Model for Europe) and E3MG (Energy-Environment-Economy Global Model). He is a major contributor to CE's twice-yearly release of analysis and forecasts in *UK Energy and the Environment*.

Ondřej Vojáček graduated from the University of Economics, Prague in 2005. He has worked at the Department of Environmental Economics at the same university since 2005. He specializes in empirical research in the environmental economics field, especially in environmental policy, consumer choice modelling, discrete choice models, tradable emission schemes, environmental taxes and charges, and the broader context of environmental policy implementation. He is the author of several scientific studies, papers in Czech and foreign reviewed journals, and the co-author with J. Kreuz of the textbook *Firm and the Environment* (Oeconomica, 2007). He teaches courses on environmental economics, cases in environmental economic, policy and management, and the firm and the environment.

Kirsten Wiebe was born in 1982 and holds Bachelor and Master of Science degrees in Econometrics and Operations Research from Maastricht University. Her specialization track was Operations Research. During her Bachelor studies she spent one semester in Sweden at Handelhögskolan vid Göteborgs Universitet. During that semester she took courses in the field of international and environmental economics. In autumn 2006 she worked for three months as a volunteer in Kinshasa, Democratic Republic of Congo, where she was also an election observer. She has worked at GWSmbH (Gesellschaft für Wirtschaftliche Strukturforschung—Institute of Economic Structures Research) in Osnabrück, Germany, since January 2007. Her research there focuses on global economic modelling, environmental and resource economics, and sustainable development.

Marc Ingo Wolter studied economics at the University of Osnabrück (master in economics 1996). From 1996 to 2002, he was a research assistant at the University of Osnabrück, finishing his Ph.D. in economics in 2002. Since 1997, he has worked at GWS. He has gained a variety of experience in projects for ministries in Germany (the German Federal Ministries for the Economy, Environment, Finance, Research, and Education) and Austria (the Austrian Federal Ministry for Traffic, Innovation and Technology) and international organizations (Asian Development Bank and DGs of the EU Commission). His research interests include sustainable development, energy and environmental policy, labour markets, and the impacts of demographic change in Germany. Since 2003, he has built several country models for Eastern European countries, which describe the interrelations between energy balances and economic development. For the time being, he works on a 3E-Model for Austria, which is used for energy simulation studies.

Roland Zieschank studied political science and administrative sciences in Tübingen and Konstanz. Since 1990, he has been project manager at the Environmental Policy Research Centre (FFU) of the Freie Universität Berlin. His research interests include the following topics: (a) resource efficiency, the ETR and sustainable growth in Europe, (b) development of macro-indicators for monitoring the state of the environment, (c) the development of a 'National Welfare Index' for Germany as a contribution to the international 'beyond GDP' discussion, (d) the completion of regulatory politics by more communication-oriented policy elements, and (e) integration of socio-scientific knowledge into environmental communication in different knowledge transfer projects. He has also worked at the Federal Environmental Protection Agency (Umweltbundesamt) and the Science Centre Berlin.

Jarmila Zimmermannová works at the Ministry of the Environment of the Czech Republic, Department of Sustainable Energy and Transportation. She is responsible mainly for economic instruments in the transport and energy area, especially for environmental tax reform and environmental taxation in the Czech Republic. She represents the Ministry of the Environment at Joint Meetings of Tax and Environment Experts in the OECD and other meetings regarding environmental taxation issues. In September 2008, she completed her Ph.D. at the University of Economics, Prague. The theme of her Ph.D. thesis was the impact of taxation of electricity, natural gas, and solid fuels on particular sectors of NACE in the Czech Republic. She still cooperates with the University of Economics, Prague, Department of Environmental Economics.

Part I
The Need and Rationale for Environmental Tax Reform

1

Introduction to the Issues and the Book

Paul Ekins

Throughout industrial history, economic growth has been associated with increased use of energy and materials. As human populations and the extent of their economic activity have grown together, they have begun to exert a pressure on natural systems—of climate, water production, food supply—that is now widely regarded as unsustainable. The pressing question therefore emerges whether the link between economic growth, natural resource use, and environmental impact is ineluctable, or whether this link can be broken, such that the resulting economic growth may be described as 'green growth', and, if so, how.

This book explores the potential contribution of a particular public policy—variously called environmental tax reform (ETR), environmental fiscal reform (EFR) or green fiscal reform (GFR)—to reconciling economic growth and the environment. Its content derives largely from a three-year research programme, 'Resource Productivity, Environmental Tax Reform and Sustainable Growth in Europe' (PETRE), funded by the Anglo-German Foundation as part of its wider research programme 'Creating Sustainable Growth in Europe'.

The remainder of this Introduction outlines the substantive issues that provide the rationale for the more detailed analysis of ETR and its implications which follows in subsequent chapters: the nature of the environment/economy interaction, the relationship between the economy, the environment and human well-being; and the reasons for thinking that ETR might be able to make an important contribution to human well-being by both helping to protect the environment and conserve its resources, and increasing employment and economic output. If ETR can indeed achieve this, then it can certainly claim to be a contributor to sustainable economic growth, or 'green growth'.

3

1.1 The Nature of the Environment-Economy Interaction

A number of recent scientific reports (e.g. IPCC 2007; MEA 2005) have suggested that, as noted above, the level of human population combined with the scale and nature of human economic activities are putting excessive, unsustainable pressure on natural systems.

This is not the place to explore the physical science basis of these assessments in detail, but the basic problematique that they imply is, following Daly (1992), as set out conceptually in Figure 1.1.

Figure 1.1 suggests that the biosphere provides three kinds of functions to human populations and economic activities: source functions, through the provision of energy and material resources of different kinds; sink functions, whereby land, water, and air receive the waste materials and energy from

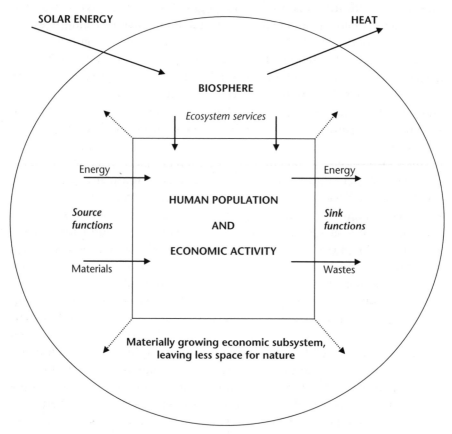

Figure 1.1 Conceptual model of relationships between the biosphere, human population, and economic activities

Source: Adapted from Daly (1992: 5).

human activities; and ecosystem services such as ozone shielding, climate stability, and many others, which together make the Earth, unlike other planets of which we are aware, habitable for humans. The biosphere is powered by solar energy, some of the heat from which is re-radiated into space. The human economy is currently mainly powered by fossil fuels.

Currently the human economic subsystem is growing both materially and in its use of energy and space. The greatly increased flows of materials and energy associated with this growth are disrupting the natural processes that provides the ecosystem services, resulting in such phenomena as climate change and the various climatic disruptions that go with it, the net effect of which is to make the Earth less accommodating of humans. In addition there is pressure on some of the source functions (especially in respect of some renewable resources, which are being exploited beyond their regeneration rate, but there are also fears about the ability of oil supplies to meet projected demands even in the short term, with worries about large oil price rises), and practically all countries are seeking to reduce the flows of wastes into the air, water, and land because of their effects on ecosystems and human health. Finally, the expansion of human population and activities in spatial terms is leading to less and less space for other species and the ecosystems they inhabit and a resulting mass extinction of other species (Myers 1989), with long-term effects that are still unknown.

Again the situation may be illustrated conceptually as in Figure 1.2. In the absence of humans, the process of evolution causes the biosphere and environmental functions to act normally in a mutually reinforcing way, with greater speciation, diversity, and complexity of ecosystems as the result. The functions bring benefits to human economies and populations, as shown, but the scale of human populations and activities is now causing negative feedbacks on the biosphere, reducing its ability to perform the environmental functions for both humans and other species. This has negative effects on

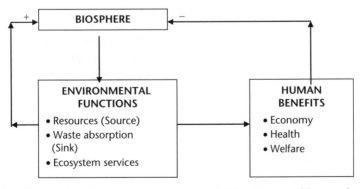

Figure 1.2 The relationship between environmental functions and human benefits

human populations and activities, but so far has not prevented them from continuing their growth, with stronger and stronger negative feedbacks. At some point, on current trends, the biosphere will cease to be able to provide the benefits that humans want and need. This is what is meant by unsustainability: humans are using the environment unsustainably such that it will at some point be unable to perform the functions on which human populations depend for their economy, health, and welfare.

In order to reduce the impacts of humans and their activities on the environment, humans will have to reduce their mobilization of materials and energy from the environment. This process is called 'dematerialization' or 'decoupling'.

1.2 The Need for Dematerialization

Dematerialization may be defined as a decrease in the quantity of resources, measured by mass, being used by an economy. It is clearly related to, but is distinct from, the concept of *decoupling*, which is a decline in the ratio of the amount used of a certain resource, or of the environmental impact, to the value generated or otherwise involved in the resource use or environmental impact. The unit of decoupling is therefore a weight per unit of value. *Relative* decoupling means that productivity/efficiency improvements have been realized, but total inputs, or pollution outputs, continue to increase as economic output increases. *Absolute* decoupling refers to the situation in which there is an overall reduction in required material inputs or pollution outputs, even while the economy grows, whether through productivity improvements or through a decrease in pollution, or a combination of the two.

If dematerialization occurs in a growing economy, then it is indicative of absolute decoupling. If it occurs in a shrinking economy, its relationship to decoupling is unclear. Decoupling may be defined in terms of emissions and other environmental impacts as well as resource use. Dematerialization is usually only defined in terms of resource use, although, especially in mass balance studies, there is no overriding reason why this should be so. Obviously both resource use and emissions may lead to environmental impacts, although these impacts are normally considered as an extension to, rather than as part of, the dematerialization concept.

Three kinds of materials may be defined in an economy. There are virgin resources, those which enter the economy for the first time after their extraction from the natural environment; recycled resources, which circulate in the economy through multiple uses; and materials for disposal (not resources at this stage because they have no economic value). The dematerialization concept may be applied to any or all of these stages of resource and material use, depending on whether it is the use of virgin resources, the circulation of resources in the economy, or the disposal of materials, that has been reduced. The distinction between these stages of resource and material use is important, because the policies to affect the different stages may be very different.

Dematerialization, as opposed to decoupling, is not a concept that has received much explicit policy attention. In fact it is not easy to think of any policies that have been introduced with the explicit purpose of 'dematerialization'. It is therefore important, in thinking about policies that might achieve dematerialization, to be clear about the purpose of dematerialization. This may include one or more of the following objectives, associated with the different stages of resource and material use:

1. to reduce the depletion, and therefore extend the period of availability, of a scarce resource;
2. to reduce the environmental impacts associated with the extraction, transport, processing, or use of the resource;
3. to reduce the environmental impacts of the disposal of the material at the end of its useful life.

As will be seen below, the main policy to achieve dematerialization which will be explored in this book is one which increases the prices associated with resource use and environmental impacts.

Clearly different materials have very different environmental impacts (Van der Voet et al. 2003). In order to reduce environmental impacts, dematerialization needs to focus on the materials producing the greatest impacts, as well as reducing their quantity mobilized by the economy. However, the mobilization of any material by the economy is the source of some environmental impact, especially its mobilization in bulk, and if the related energy use and the whole life cycle of the material is taken into account. For example, bulk aggregates may be inert in environmental terms, but their mining and transport can be energy intensive and result in very great environmental disturbance in the location of the mine (such shifting of materials is called 'hidden flows' by Bringezu and Bleischwitz 2009: 56 ff.). This is the rationale for calling for the dematerialization of the economy in general, as well as seeking special control of substances with particularly harmful impacts.

New methods for measuring materials flows have resulted in much information, organized through concepts such as Total Material Requirement (TMR, which includes 'hidden flows'), Domestic Material Consumption (DMC) and Direct Material Input (DMI). The OECD has recently published guidance on the measurement of material flows (OECD 2008). Through such studies as that for the UK by Bringezu and Schütz (2001), which utilizes these concepts, it is increasingly possible to characterize material flows, making it possible for the first time to assess whether or not dematerialization is taking or has taken place. For example, Bringezu et al. 2004 (p. 120) find that, for 26 countries and with the exception only of the Czech Republic, 'no significant absolute decline of direct material input per capita has been observed so far in the course of economic growth'.

Moll et al. (2005) provide a limited disaggregation of material flows into the four main materials by mass to flow through the economy (excluding water): biomass, construction minerals, industrial minerals and ores, and fossil fuels. The flow of these materials through the economies of the EU-15 countries since 1980 has been remarkably constant (Moll et al. 2005, Fig. 4-4, p. 35). This confirms that, while technical progress tends continuously to improve the efficiency or productivity with which resources are employed, the decoupling has in the main been relative rather than absolute. The productivity or efficiency gains have overall been outweighed by growth in the scale of the economy, and there has been a small absolute increase in a number of both resource inputs and emission and waste outputs. It is clear that if absolute decoupling (dematerialization) is required to reduce the physical scale of the economy such that it becomes environmentally sustainable, then either current environmental policies will have to be applied much more stringently, or new, more effective, policies will have to be found.

1.3 Policies for Dematerialization and Environmental Improvement

There are various types of policy instruments which a national government can employ in an attempt to improve the environment. Such instruments may be grouped under four generic headings (see Jordan et al. 2003), and the same categorization may be used for policies for dematerialization:

- market/incentive-based (also called economic) instruments (see EEA 2006, for a recent review of European experience). These instruments include 'emissions trading, environmental taxes and charges, deposit-refund systems, subsidies (including the removal of environmentally-harmful subsidies), green purchasing, and liability and compensation' (EEA 2006: 13);

- regulation instruments, which seek to define legal standards in relation to technologies, environmental performance, pressures or outcomes. These are probably still the most widely used kinds of environmental policies;

- voluntary/self-regulation (also called negotiated) agreements between governments and producing organizations (see ten Brink 2002, for a comprehensive discussion);

- information/education-based instruments (the main example of which given by Jordan et al. (2003) is eco-labels, but there are others), which may be mandatory or voluntary.

It has been increasingly common in more recent times to seek to deploy these instruments in so-called 'policy packages', which combine them in order to enhance their overall effectiveness. This book, however, is principally about the implementation of environmental taxes through the policy of environmental tax reform (ETR), which is defined and discussed in more detail below.

The rationale for environmental taxation is that markets often do not price in the damaging environmental impacts, with the result that they are excessive. The environmental tax increases the price of these environmental impacts both in absolute terms and relative to other prices in the economy. This tends to reduce the environmental damage. The amount of this reduction is an important indicator of the effectiveness of environmental taxation as an instrument of environmental policy, and is an important consideration in later chapters of this book.

1.4 The Environment, the Economy, and Human-Well-Being[1]

It is conventional to assume that the level of economic output is positively related to human well-being and that therefore the growth in that output, called economic growth and measured in money terms, will increase human well-being. Figures 1.1. and 1.2 already cast some doubt on the general validity of this assumption, because if economic growth results in the depletion of environmental resources and negative environmental impacts, as is the case in the absence of absolute decoupling, then any well-being increase from increased incomes may be offset by reductions in well-being from environmental damage.

However, substantial recent research on human happiness has also cast doubt on the presumed positive relationship between economic growth and human well-being for reasons apart from environmental impacts. This section will very briefly review this research, the results of which are important for the overall conclusions to be drawn at the end of this book.

The notion that human happiness is an important objective of human life goes back considerably further than the 1776 US Declaration of Independence which famously identified its pursuit as one of 'inalienable rights' given to humans by their Creator. As Nettle (2005) notes, the ancient Greek philosopher Aristippus argued in the fourth century BC that the goal of life is to

---

[1] This section draws substantially on Ekins and Venn (2009).

maximize the totality of one's pleasures. However it was not until the 1960s that psychologists began to investigate happiness in a scientific manner. Further it was not until the 1970s that economists looked into the notion of happiness and its relationship with economic growth.

One of the first conclusions from this work is that the concept of well-being/happiness is not easy to define. Often different words are used to try to explain the concept. Indeed Easterlin (2003: 11,176) states that he takes the terms 'happiness, utility, well-being, life satisfaction, and welfare to be interchangeable'. However, despite different definitions of well-being, McAllister (2005) argues that there does appear to be common ground between the different descriptions and resulting measurements of well-being, although these may be differentiated according to whether the measurements are subjective or objective. Most researchers agree about the elements that make up well-being: physical well-being; material well-being; social well-being; development and activity; emotional well-being. The elements can be paraphrased as physical health, income and wealth, relationships, meaningful work and leisure, personal stability and (lack of) depression. Mental health is increasingly seen as fundamental to overall health and well-being. These elements are sometimes viewed as 'drivers' of well-being. As is discussed further below, it is interesting and remarkable that the natural environment per se is absent from this list.

With regard to the influence on well-being of economic growth, one of the earliest and most influential papers was by Easterlin (1974), who found that, first, individual happiness appears to be the same across poor countries and rich countries, and secondly, economic growth does not appear to raise well-being. Rather Easterlin proposed that people compare themselves with their peers, and it is their relative income in respect of this group that delivers well-being, rather than its absolute level. Therefore, raising the income of all does not increase the well-being of all (Easterlin, 1995). Similar lines of investigation were taken up by Hirsch (1976), Scitovsky (1976), and Frank (1985), with similar conclusions, and although a later study (Oswald 1997) criticized the approach taken, it also found that 'it seems extra income is not contributing dramatically to the quality of people's lives' (Oswald 1997: 1818).

Income, relative or absolute, is however usually included in lists of factors which affect well-being. For example, Dolan et al. (2006: 33) reviewed 150 peer-reviewed papers and grouped their contributory factors to well-being under seven broad headings: (1) income; (2) personal characteristics—who we are, our genetic makeup; (3) socially developed characteristics—our health and education; (4) how we spend our time—the work we do, and activities we engage in; (5) attitudes and beliefs towards self/others/life—how we interpret the world; (6) relationships—the way we connect with others; and (7) the wider economic, social, and political environment—the place we live. Again, the natural environment is at best implicit in this list.

Although measurements of well-being tend to be one of two types, subjective or objective, empirical work has shown that economic conditions, like unemployment, inflation, and income, have a strong impact on people's subjective well-being. Clark and Oswald (1994) showed that unemployed people are significantly less happy than those with a job (see also Winkelmann and Winkelmann 1998; Di Tella et al. 2001; Ouweneel 2002). This is important for this book because of the impact of environmental tax reform (ETR) on levels of employment, identified later in the book (see Chapter 9).

At best, the relationship between happiness and income seems to be nonlinear, increases in income generating diminishing marginal happiness as incomes grow. Over time, happiness appears to be relatively unrelated to income. Layard's (2005) research has found, as shown for the US in Figure 1.3, that substantial real per capita income growth in developed countries over the last decades has led to no significant increases in subjective well-being—despite massive increases in purchasing power, people in developed nations seem to feel no happier than they did 50 years ago.

Figure 1.4 shows that once average income in a country exceeds $20,000 per head, increases in income are no longer associated strongly, if at all, with increases in self-reported happiness.

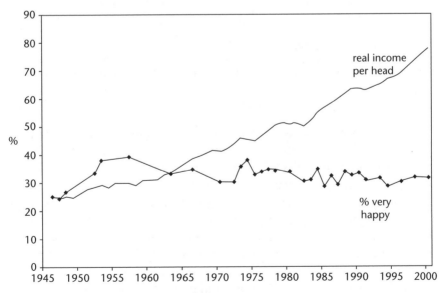

Figure 1.3 Income and happiness in the United States

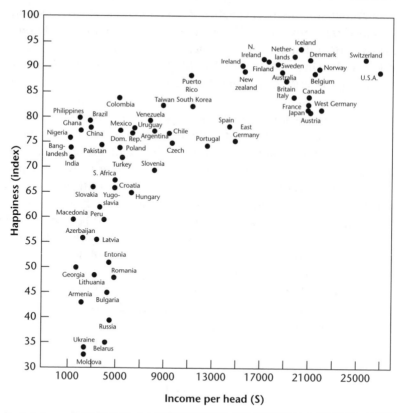

Figure 1.4 Income and happiness for different countries

Source: Layard (2005: 32). From *Happiness: Lessons from a New Science* by Richard Layard, copyright © 2005 by Richard Layard. Used by permission of The Penguin Press, a division of Penguin Group (USA) Inc.

Along with Easterlin, Layard (2005) argues that relative income is more important in explaining well-being than absolute wealth, explaining this through a process known as the 'hedonic treadmill'. As individuals and societies grow wealthier, they adapt to new and higher living standards and adjust expectations upwards. This means that aspirations are never satisfied, and that at higher income levels increases in income make less difference, as basic needs are satisfied but consumption desires remain. On the basis of his research, Layard also identifies seven main factors that influence the well-being of people: family relationships, financial situation, work, community and friends, health, personal freedom, and personal values (Layard 2005: 63). Again, the natural environment is conspicuous by its absence from this list.

However, the landmark study of the natural environment, the Millennium Ecosystem Assessment (MEA 2005) is in no doubt of the (intuitively fairly obvious) fact that human well-being is fundamentally dependent on the 'ecosystem goods and services', the production of which depends on the continued functioning of basic environmental processes.

Carried out between 2001 and 2005, the MEA sought to assess the consequences of ecosystem change for human well-being and to establish the scientific basis for actions needed to enhance the conservation and sustainable use of ecosystems, and resulted in one of the most comprehensive assessments to date, at the conceptual level, of the multiple inter-linkages between the environment and human well-being. Ecosystem services as defined by the MEA comprise *provisioning services* such as food, water, timber, and genetic resources; *regulating services* that affect climate, floods, disease, wastes, and water quality; *cultural services* that provide recreational, aesthetic, and spiritual benefits; and *supporting services* such as soil formation, pollination, and nutrient cycling. Supporting services are included as an overarching category as it is perceived that they are essential for sustaining each of the other three ecosystem services. The link between supporting services and human well-being is therefore crucial but indirect.

Human well-being is assumed to have multiple constituents (MEA 2005, p. v), including the *basic material for a good life,* such as secure and adequate livelihoods, enough food at all times, shelter, clothing, and access to goods; *health,* including feeling well and having a healthy physical environment, such as clean air and access to clean water; *good social relations*, including social cohesion, mutual respect, and the ability to help others and provide for children; *security*, including secure access to natural and other resources, personal safety, and security from natural and human-made disasters; and *freedom of choice and action,* including the opportunity to achieve what an individual values doing and being.

It is clear that the MEA approach to human well-being is close to those discussed above. Building on its classifications, the MEA (2005) maps ecosystem services onto human well-being as in Figure 1.5, with the arrows indicating the strength as well as the nature of the linkages, and their shading indicating the extent to which it is possible for socioeconomic factors to mediate the linkage (for example, if it is possible to purchase a substitute for a degraded ecosystem service, then there is a high potential for mediation).

The MEA argues that both the strength of the linkages and the potential for mediation differ in different ecosystems and regions. The MEA additionally identifies non-ecosystem factors which have the potential to influence human well-being (classified into economic, social, technological, and cultural factors), and notes that, as in Figure 1.2, these can feed back into the environment and affect ecosystem services, but these interactions are not shown in Figure 1.5.

It is clear from the review of Dolan et al. (2006) that there are remarkably few studies that investigate environment–well-being relationships, or seek

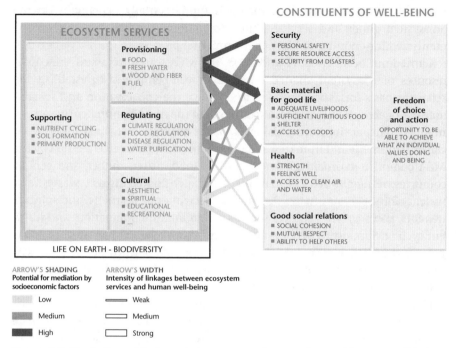

CONSTITUENTS OF WELL-BEING

ECOSYSTEM SERVICES

Provisioning
- FOOD
- FRESH WATER
- WOOD AND FIBER
- FUEL
- ...

Supporting
- NUTRIENT CYCLING
- SOIL FORMATION
- PRIMARY PRODUCTION
- ...

Regulating
- CLIMATE REGULATION
- FLOOD REGULATION
- DISEASE REGULATION
- WATER PURIFICATION
- ...

Cultural
- AESTHETIC
- SPIRITUAL
- EDUCATIONAL
- RECREATIONAL
- ...

LIFE ON EARTH - BIODIVERSITY

Security
- PERSONAL SAFETY
- SECURE RESOURCE ACCESS
- SECURITY FROM DISASTERS

Basic material for good life
- ADEQUATE LIVELIHOODS
- SUFFICIENT NUTRITIOUS FOOD
- SHELTER
- ACCESS TO GOODS

Health
- STRENGTH
- FEELING WELL
- ACCESS TO CLEAN AIR AND WATER

Good social relations
- SOCIAL COHESION
- MUTUAL RESPECT
- ABILITY TO HELP OTHERS

Freedom of choice and action
OPPORTUNITY TO BE ABLE TO ACHIEVE WHAT AN INDIVIDUAL VALUES DOING AND BEING

ARROW'S **SHADING**
Potential for mediation by socioeconomic factors

- Low
- Medium
- High

ARROW'S **WIDTH**
Intensity of linkages between ecosystem services and human well-being

- ⟹ Weak
- ⟹ Medium
- ⟹ Strong

Figure 1.5 Illustration of linkages between ecosystem services and human well-being
Source: MEA (2005: 50). MEA (Millennium Ecosystem Assessment) (2005), *Ecosystems and Human Well-being: Synthesis*, Island Press, Washington, DC.

empirically to assess the strength of the linkages identified in Figure 1.5. Both Dolan et al. (2006) and MEA (2005: 6) also note there is a limited amount of information available to assess the consequences of changes in ecosystem services for human well-being. However, the basic fact that the environment is an important influence on human well-being seems very well established, so that for the rest of this book it will be assumed that policies that improve the environment and its ability to deliver ecosystem goods and services are in that regard desirable, although their overall desirability will depend, as with any other policy, on the costs that their implementation incurs. The balance between the cost and environmental benefit of environmental tax reform (ETR) is a major theme of subsequent chapters of this book.

1.5 The Purpose of Environmental Tax Reform (ETR)

The European Environment Agency has defined ETR as 'a reform of the national tax system where there is a shift of the burden of taxes from conventional taxes such as labour to environmentally damaging activities, such as resource use or pollution' (EEA 2005: 84). ETR is therefore a particular kind of policy instrument, which seeks to apply revenue-raising economic instruments (which may be taxes or auctioned permits in an emissions trading scheme) to resource use and pollution, in order to increase the efficiency of resource use (resource productivity) and improve the environment, and reduce other taxes such that the policy is revenue neutral overall. ETR is therefore a tax *shift*, rather than a tax increase, whereby taxation is shifted from 'goods' such as labour (e.g. income taxes, social security contributions) or capital (e.g. corporation taxes) to 'bads' (pollution, resource depletion). ETR was implemented on a relatively small scale in a number of North European countries in the 1990s and early 2000s, with broadly positive results. One of the major purposes of the PETRE project on which this book is largely based was to explore the economic, environmental, and resource implications, for Europe and the rest of the world, of a large-scale ETR in Europe that could achieve the EU's greenhouse gas (GHG) reduction targets by 2020.

ETR is hypothesized to increase human well-being through the economic and environmental pathways illustrated in Figure 1.6.

This suggests that environmentally ETR will reduce pollution and resource use; economically it will increase output and employment directly, and stimulate green innovation that will do so further indirectly, as well as bringing about further environmental improvement. In themselves, both these economic and environmental impacts will increase human well-being; but the economic impact will be decoupled from environmental damage, so it is more likely to have a positive net impact on human well-being than much current economic growth.

There are good theoretical reasons for supposing that ETR will have the effects shown in Figure 1.6. These have been extensively covered in the environmental economics literature (see Ekins and Barker 2001 for a survey). Very briefly, because many environmental impacts are not priced, they do not enter into market decisions and they are therefore greater, and have a greater negative impact on human welfare, than is desirable. Environmental taxes

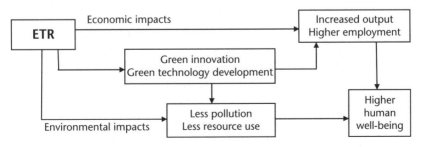

Figure 1.6 Hypothesized paths from ETR to higher human well-being

give a price (explicitly or implicitly), or a cost, to these impacts, therefore encouraging their reduction, which increases human welfare. This is the rationale for supposing that ETR will lead to increased human welfare from environmental benefits.

The environmental taxes also raise revenues which, for a given level of total tax revenue, allows other taxes to be reduced. Taxes on labour and profits are known to have disincentive effects and cause economic output to be lower than it would otherwise be. Reducing such taxes can therefore, other things being equal, increase output. However, increasing energy taxes, other things being equal, is likely to reduce output. The balance of these two effects (and a key strand of the academic literature explores how different kinds of taxes interact) will determine whether the tax shift will reduce or increase output overall.

A further effect on output may come from the impact of the tax shift on employment. If employers' labour taxes have been reduced as part of the tax shift (and this has often been the case where such shifts have been implemented), this may increase employers' labour demand. If there is unemployment in the economy, this may lead to more people being employed who were formerly unemployed. This would result in an increase in output.

Finally, the shift in the relative prices of carbon/energy and labour or profits will result in a shift in the relative benefits of labour-saving carbon/energy-saving technical change. Because carbon/energy is made relatively more expensive, more technological and innovation effort is likely to be directed to using less of it, thereby raising its productivity. If this process reveals opportunities for carbon/energy saving that were cost-effective even before the carbon/energy tax increase, or have become so (and there is substantial evidence of the existence of such opportunities, even in well-run and profitable firms), or if it channels innovation into directions that enable other resource savings and product improvements, then the tax shift could also lead to increases in output and employment through this route (the middle pathway in Figure 1.6).

Identifying the existence and size of these effects requires a model of the economy and detailed modelling of the tax shift and its effects on different economic sectors. Chapters 8–11 inclusive describe such modelling in some detail. It should be borne in mind in this context that models of this sort deliver insights and broad indications of outcomes, rather than 'truth', and that to some extent the outcomes are dependent on modelling assumptions made and the model structure that is chosen. Having said that, the two models employed in PETRE are both well grounded in both economic theory and actual data about the European economy and energy system, and there is no reason for thinking that their results are not robust. Key issues related to the modelling are discussed in Chapter 8.

If indeed ETR turns out to be able to achieve absolute environmental improvements in a context of economic growth (or 'decoupling' in the language used above), then this growth may be described as 'green growth'. It is an empirical question to which later chapters return as to whether this 'green growth' will be at a higher or lower rate than the 'brown growth' currently experienced, which results in further environmental deterioration. What will become clear is that there is no suggestion in the chapters that follow, or in any of the substantial literature reviewed, that achieving absolute decoupling requires economic growth to cease completely, or even for the economy to decline. On the evidence of this project, 'green growth' may turn out to be slower than 'brown growth', at least until the environmental destruction such as climate change associated with the latter starts destroying some of the basic conditions for economic growth, which may slow down rates of 'brown growth'. But there is no evidence that 'green growth' at some level is unachievable, and achieving it seems likely to become increasingly important for human well-being.

1.6 Methodologies Employed in the PETRE Project

The PETRE project used a range of methodologies, including micro-econometric analysis, decomposition analysis, literature review, desk-based analysis and synthesis of data, macro-econometric modelling, questionnaires, surveys and interviews, and physical input-output modelling. The chapters go into these methodologies in some detail where this is necessary to understand their results, but here they are briefly described together to give an overall sense of why they were used and the kind of work that was undertaken.

Micro-econometric analysis

ETR operates by raising the prices of resource use and pollution through taxing the relevant resource or pollutant. To raise enough revenues for a significant tax shift, taxation should apply broadly to a range of sectors in the economy. An issue which affects the appropriateness of energy-related policy is whether the differences in energy use between sectors are *deterministic* (that is, they derive from particular characteristics of the sector, and will persist over time in a fashion which can be forecast relatively accurately) or *stochastic* (that is, they are affected by random processes within or between the sectors, and although they persist over time, they fluctuate in an unpredictable way making any forecast particularly difficult and potentially inaccurate). Determining whether sectoral energy use is deterministic or stochastic requires the use of quite complex econometric analysis of the sectors concerned, which takes account of any radical changes (*structural breaks*) in energy use within the sectors which may have occurred during the period under analysis. Results of this analysis are reported in Agnolucci and Venn (forthcoming).

Again focusing on energy use in industrial subsectors (this time in the UK and Germany), econometric analysis was carried out to explore how this varies with price and sectoral gross value added (reported in Agnolucci 2009).

Fairly complex econometric analysis was also used (see Agnolucci 2008a) to investigate the *environmental Kuznets curve*, or EKC, hypothesis (that, while economic growth might indeed cause negative environmental effects in the early stages of economic development, as incomes rise at some point the negative impacts will cease and the environment will begin to improve) for ten British and German industrial subsectors over 1978–2004.

Finally, econometrics was also used to investigate the impacts of the British and German ETRs, implemented in 2001 and over 1999–2003 respectively, on the economy and on the labour market. This produced estimates of the energy reductions caused by the ETRs which are similar to those obtained from more complicated multi-sectoral econometric models (see Agnolucci 2008b).

All these pieces of econometric work are described to some extent in Chapters 3, 4, 7, 8, and 9.

Decomposition analysis

Decomposition analysis seeks to divide the changes in any use of energy between the various factors which are causing them. Three such factors are commonly identified as affecting energy use: economic growth (the *scale* effect), which produces an increase in energy use; the technology used (the *technical* effect), and because new technology tends to be more energy efficient than the technology it replaces, this normally reduces energy use; and the structure of the economy or sector (the *composition* effect)—economies that are becoming more oriented towards services, which use less energy than manufacturing, will tend to have a negative composition effect, tending to reduce their energy use. These three effects were investigated for the German economy over 1994–2004, as reported in Jungnitz (2008).

Literature review, desk-based research, and data analysis

These methodologies were used in relation to the previous implementation of ETRs (Chapters 5 and 10), the extent and growth of the environmental industries (Chapter 12), and the relationship between economic growth, the environment, and human well-being (see above and Venn 2007a, 2007b: Ekins and Venn 2009).

Macro-econometric modelling: the E3ME and GINFORS models

The two models used in the PETRE project are well documented—the GINFORS[2] model in Meyer et al. (2007), Giljum, Behrens et al. (2008), Lutz et al. (2010), and the E3ME[3] model in Cambridge Econometrics (2009). The models are compared in Barker et al. (2007a). Chapter 8 summarizes these descriptions of the models.

Qualitative research

Qualitative research was used for the analysis of the ETR preparation and implementation in the Czech Republic, reported in Chapter 6.

Physical input-output modelling

The project constructed the Global Resource Accounting Model (GRAM), to illustrate European trade patterns from the perspective of material flows and analyse how the introduction of an ETR in Europe would impact the economies and the environment in other world regions. GRAM is a multi-regional input-output material flow model (Giljum, Lutz et al. 2008). The GRAM model was constructed to calculate comprehensive material consumption and resource productivity indicators and to determine the resource base of the European economy in a comprehensive manner, fully including the international trade dimension. Results of this work are reported in Chapters 2 and 11.

1.7 Overview of this Book

This chapter has made the case that the global economy as a whole is environmentally unsustainable, i.e. it is using global resources and ecosystems at a rate and in a manner that cannot be sustained indefinitely into the future. The rest of Part I explores various other dimensions of the rationale and need for ETR. Chapter 2 shows that Europe's economy is to a significant and growing degree dependent on imports of natural resources from other world regions. While the overall level of resource use in Europe has stabilized in the past 20 years, a shift of environmental burden through international trade can be observed, with growing physical imports and associated indirect material flows and increasing substitution of domestic material extraction, in particular with regard to fossil fuels and metal ores. Based on the results of a new

---

[2] **G**lobal **In**terindustry **For**ecasting **S**ystem.
[3] Energy-Environment-Economy Model for Europe.

trade-material flow model, this chapter analyses the physical dimension of European trade relations with other world regions and the implications for EU policies aiming to increase resource productivity.

Chapter 3 assesses the determinants of carbon dioxide (CO_2) emissions in different German and UK industrial sectors by adopting two approaches well established in the economic literature, i.e. the estimation of energy demand and of an Environmental Kuznets Curve. The first approach focuses on the effect of the energy price alongside economic activity. By estimating industrial energy demand, the effect of future energy taxes and price increases on the consumption can be assessed. In the second approach, the focus is more on economic activity and the shape of the relationship between economic activity and CO_2 emissions. The effect of a number of variables in this relationship is assessed, namely the energy price, the consumption of capital, materials, labour and services, and the intensity of energy use.

Energy intensities of industrial subsectors differ widely due to differences in the final product and ultimately in the production process. The aim of Chapter 4 is to assess whether these differences are stochastic or deterministic. The analysis is implemented for a number of UK industrial subsectors over the 1970–2004 and 1978–2004 time periods. It turns out that it is only when modelling structural breaks that one can conclude that the evidence in favour of the long-term differences being deterministic outbalances the evidence pointing to their nature being stochastic. This supports the adoption of policy instruments, such as environmental taxation, which are applied across productive sectors in a way which is not affected by the short-run evolution of the sectors.

Part II moves on to some description and analysis of the theory behind and outcomes of ETRs that have already been implemented in several of the old EU Member States, such as Denmark, Germany, Finland, Netherlands, Sweden, and the UK. Chapter 5 very briefly identifies the key characteristics of these green tax reform packages, with a special focus on Germany and the UK. It notes that recent years have seen a growth in support for ETRs in the new EU Member States, with Estonia and the Czech Republic introducing this policy instrument, and the chapter discusses the prospects for ETR in these new EU Member States, on the basis of the experience of the Estonian ETR, highlighting some differences in the overall revenue structure between old and new EU Member States. The chapter then reviews the theoretical literature on ETR and the 'double dividend' hypothesis (the idea that ETR can yield economic as well as environmental benefits, as shown in Figure 1.6), before moving on to a review of the empirical modelling literature that assesses the effects of the ETRs on the environment and the economy through estimates of changes in emissions, sectoral effects, such as changes in output, employment, and trade, and macroeconomic variables such as GDP and total employment.

Chapter 6 looks in more detail at the experience of ETR in the Czech Republic, which has a long history of environmental payments and charges, and of interest in ETR for some years, with some implicit tax shifts during the 1990s. The chapter describes the first explicit ETR in 2008, in the context of the implementation of the EU Energy Tax Directive, and uses this policy as the basis for detailed qualitative research into different stakeholders' understanding of and support for ETR. The chapter ends with some lessons and recommendations from the Czech experience which could be useful to other Central and Eastern European countries contemplating ETR.

Finally in Part II, Chapter 7 estimates the effect of the implemented UK and German ETRs on the demand for energy and the level of unemployment. Employing a novel methodology for this field, by estimating a specification based on a translog cost function that permits the modelling of the cross-price elasticities among capital, labour, energy, material, and services, it comes to similar conclusions to those of more complex modelling assessments of ETR, some of which were discussed in Chapter 5.

Part III of the book is devoted to a detailed analysis of a major ETR for Europe, projected out to 2020. Chapter 8 begins by describing the models that have been used for projecting this ETR. This chapter is crucial for interpreting the modelling results because, as with any modelling exercise, the underlying assumptions and simplifications made in the models play a large role in determining the magnitude and direction of the results. With these models, the model parameters for behavioural relationships are estimated empirically over historical time-series data. The treatment of technological progress and labour-market responses influences the results. The chapter describes the main modelling tools, E3ME and GINFORS, that were used to provide a quantitative analysis of the effects of ETR. It outlines the similarities between the two, for example their basic structure following the national accounts and long-run econometric equations, while also discussing the differences between the models and relative advantages in each case, such as E3ME's ability to model short-run dynamic effects in Europe, and GINFORS' global coverage. The chapter also identifies areas in which the models' results are likely to differ, particularly with regard to the intended impacts of ETR. It also considers how the treatment of revenues from environmental taxes and charges affects the results of modelling ETRs. The chapter then moves on to describe how the models are applied in the project to model ETR, essentially outlining the lines of causality without quantifying the results. For example, higher energy prices lead to a reduction in energy demand and lower output in the energy industries; however, higher prices erode real incomes and may have an adverse effect on other household expenditure, particularly on luxury goods. This in itself has knock-on effects for other industry sectors and, when combined with tax decreases elsewhere (so government balances remain unchanged), there are many potential indirect impacts. It is important that such interactions are understood before trying to interpret the detailed results.

Chapter 9 then describes the modelling of an ETR for Europe, using the models described in Chapter 8. The chapter starts by describing the role of the baseline in the analysis and why it is important to choose an appropriate baseline. It then describes the main scenarios undertaken, with a discussion of the taxes implemented and the relationship between the EU Emission Trading Scheme (ETS) and the carbon tax applied to the rest of the economy, the role of revenue recycling in the different scenarios, and the spending of some of the tax revenues on eco-innovation. The major part of the chapter describes the results of the modelling, including:

- aggregate energy/environment results (i.e. reduction in emissions and energy demand);
- aggregate economic results;
- sectoral energy/environment results;
- sectoral economic results.

One of the major issues that has arisen in connection with ETRs in the past has been their implications for the distribution of household income, and this is the subject of Chapter 10. It starts with a literature review, which shows that ETR in principle can be regressive (i.e. it can have a disproportionate negative impact on low-income households), especially when it applies to household energy use, but that there are various ways in which this regressive effect can be mitigated. It then proceeds to analyse, using the E3ME model, the ETR scenarios described in Chapter 9. Because in this case the ETR increases household income, the income for all household groups increases, but in general those for middle quintiles increase by a smaller proportion than for the top and bottom quintiles. A rather different pattern emerges from a distributional analysis of an ETR for German households, when clearly regressive effects are apparent, but these are small, and could therefore be largely removed using revenues from the ETR.

As noted in Chapter 2, the European economy is intricately connected with the wider global economy, in terms of material flows as well as through economic activity. Chapter 11 explores the implications of the European ETR modelled in Chapter 9 for the rest of the world, using the results of the global GINFORS model. Changes of competitiveness of different European industries in global markets are analysed through the development of European trade relations with other world regions, and the economic consequences (in terms of economic growth, investment, international trade, etc.) of the implementation of an ETR in Europe for other world regions are also described. Finally, the chapter also provides a quantitative analysis of changing global patterns in natural resource extraction, energy use, and CO_2 emissions in all world regions due to the implementation of a European ETR.

Processes of innovation and technological change are not easy to model in a macroeconomic context because they depend so much on actions at the microeconomic (firm) level. Chapter 12 presents evidence about the evolution in Europe of the fast-growing group of activities that is collectively called the Environment Industry, and its contribution to European economies, especially that of Germany. Because it mitigates damaging environmental effects of other economic activity, and because its growth (which is under-estimated for definitional and statistical reasons) means that it is an increasingly important generator of economic output and source of employment, this industry may be viewed as both a *condition* for, as well as a key *contributor* to, sustainable growth. The Environment Industry is essentially policy driven. Recent developments in Germany in four important subsectors of the Environment Industry—renewable energy, eco-construction, fuel-efficient diesel cars, and waste management/recycling—are analysed in order to get insights into the effect on them of policy drivers in general and relative price changes, such as those introduced through ETR, in particular.

The final chapter, Chapter 13, pulls together the findings described in the book, draws conclusions, and makes recommendations for an ETR in Europe. It treats specifically the implications of ETR in Europe for the new Member States of Central and Eastern Europe, for Europe as a whole, and for the rest of the world. The book concludes with recommendations for ETR design in Europe, based on the conclusions of the PETRE project.

References

Agnolucci, P. (2008a), 'The Relationship between CO2 Emissions and Economic Growth in the British and German Industrial Sectors', PETRE Working Paper, Policy Studies Institute, London.

——(2008b), 'The Effect of The German and British Environmental Taxation Reforms: A Simple Assessment', PETRE Working Paper, Policy Studies Institute, London.

——(2009), 'The Energy Demand in the British and German Industrial Sectors: Heterogeneity and Common Factors', *Energy Economics*, 31: 175–87.

——and A. Venn (forthcoming), 'Industrial Energy Intensities in the UK: Is there a Deterministic or Stochastic Difference among Sectors?', *Applied Economics*.

Barker, T., B. Meyer, H. Pollitt, and C. Lutz (2007a), 'Modelling Environmental Tax Reform in Germany and the United Kingdom with E3ME and GINFORS', PETRE Working Paper.

Bringezu, S., and R. Bleischwitz (2009), *Sustainable Resource Management: Global Trends, Visions and Policies*, Sheffield: Greenleaf Publishing.

Bringezu, S., and H. Schütz (2001), 'Total Resource Flows of the United Kingdom', Report for DEFRA, Wuppertal Institute, Wuppertal.

———S. Steger, and J. Baudisch (2004), 'International Comparison of Resource Use and its Relation to Economic Growth: The Development of Total Material Requirement, Direct Material Inputs and Hidden Flows and the Structure of TMR', *Ecological Economics*, 51: 97–124.

Cambridge Econometrics (2009), 'E3ME Manual', available at <http://www.camecon-e3memanual.com/cgi-bin/EPW_CGI>.

Clark, A. E., and A. J. Oswald (1994), 'Unhappiness and Unemployment', *Economic Journal*, 104: 648–59.

Daly, H. E. (1992), 'From Empty World to Full World Economics', in R. Goodland, H. E. Daly, and S. El Serafy (eds.), *Population, Technology and Lifestyle: The Transition to Sustainability*, Washington, DC: Island Press.

Di Tella, R., R. J. MacCulloch, and A. J. Oswald (2001), 'Preferences over Inflation and Unemployment: Evidence from Surveys of Happiness', *American Economic Review*, 91(1): 335–41.

Dolan, P., T. Peasgood, and M. White (2006), 'Review of Research on the Influences on Personal Well-Being and Application to Policy Making', University of Sheffield. Report commissioned by Defra and available at <http://collections.europarchive.org/tna/20080530153425/ http://www.sustainable-development.gov.uk/publications/pdf/WellbeingProject2.pdf> (accessed 29 November 2010).

Easterlin, R. (1974) 'Does Economic Growth Improve the Human Lot? Some Empirical Evidence', in P. A. David and M. W. Reder, (eds.), *Nations and Households in Economic Growth: Essays in Honour of Moses Abramowitz*, New York and London: Academic Press.

——(1995), 'Will Raising the Incomes of All Increase the Happiness of All?' *Journal of Economic Behavior and Organization*, 27: 35–47.

——(2003), 'Explaining Happiness', *Proceedings of the National Academy of Sciences*, 100: 11176–83.

EEA (European Environment Agency) (2005), *Market-Based Instruments for Environmental Policy in Europe*, EEA Technical Report No. 8/2005, Copenhagen, Denmark.

——(2006), *Using the Market for Cost-Effective Environmental Policy: Market-Based Instruments in Europe*, EEA Report No. 1/2006, Copenhagen.

Ekins, P., and T. Barker (2001), 'Carbon Taxes and Carbon Emissions Trading', *Journal of Economic Surveys*, 15(3): 325–76.

——and A. Venn (2009), 'Economic Growth, the Environment and Well-Being', PETRE Working Paper, University College London.

Frank, R. (1985), *Choosing the Right Pond: Human Behaviour and the Quest for Status*, Oxford: Oxford University Press.

Giljum, S., A. Behrens, F. Hinterberger, C. Lutz, and B. Meyer (2008), 'Modelling Scenarios towards a Sustainable Use of Natural Resources in Europe', *Environmental Science & Policy*, 11(3), May: 204–16.

——Lutz, C., A. Jungnitz, M. Bruckner, and F. Hinterberger (2008), 'Global Dimensions of European Natural Resource Use: First Results from the Global Resource Accounting

Model (GRAM)', SERI Working Paper 7, Sustainable Europe Research Institute, Vienna.

Hirsch, F. (1976), *Social Limits to Growth*, Cambridge, Mass.: Harvard University Press.

IPCC (Intergovernmental Panel on Climate Change) (2007), *Climate Change 2007—The Physical Science Basis*, contribution of Working Group I to the Fourth Assessment Report of the IPCC, IPCC, <http://www.ipcc.ch/ipccreports/ar4-wg1.htm>.

Jordan, A., R. Wurzel, and A. Zito (eds.) (2003), *'New' Instruments of Environmental Governance?: National Experiences and Prospects*, London: Frank Cass.

Jungnitz, A. (2008), 'Decomposition Analysis of Energy, Material and Greenhouse Gases in Germany', PETRE Working Paper, GWS (Institute for Economic Structures Research, Germany), Osnabrück.

Layard, R. (2005), *Happiness*, London: Penguin Books.

Lutz, C., B. Meyer, and M. I. Wolter (2010), 'The Global Multisector/Multicountry 3-E Model GINFORS: A Description of the Model and a Baseline Forecast for Global Energy Demand and CO_2 Emissions', *International Journal of Global Environmental Issues*, 10(1–2): 25–45.

McAllister, F. (2005) 'Wellbeing Concepts and Challenges', Discussion paper prepared by Fiona McAllister for the Sustainable Development Research Network. Available at <http://www.sd-research.org.uk/wp-content/uploads/sdrnwellbeingpaper-final_000.pdf> (accessed 29 November 2010).

MEA (Millennium Ecosystem Assessment) (2005), *Ecosystems and Human Well-Being: Synthesis*, Washington, DC: Island Press.

Meyer, B., C. Lutz, P. Schnur, and G. Zika (2007), 'National Economic Policy Simulations with Global Interdependencies: A Sensitivity Analysis for Germany', *Economic Systems Research*, 19(1): 37–55.

Moll, S., S. Bringezu, and H. Schütz (2005), *Resource Use in European Countries: An Estimate of Materials and Waste Streams in the Community, Including Imports and Exports using the Instrument of Material Flow Analysis*, Wuppertal Report No. 1, Wuppertal Institute, Wuppertal, <http://www.wupperinst.org/en/publications/entnd/index.html?beitrag_id=386&bid=80> (accessed 29 November 2010).

Myers, N. (1989), 'Extinction Rates Past and Present', *BioScience*, 39(1), January: 39–41.

Nettle, D. (2005), *Happiness: The Science behind Your Smile,* Oxford: Oxford University Press.

OECD (Organisation for Economic Co-operation and Development) (2008), *Measuring Material Flows and Resource Productivity: Synthesis Report*, Paris: OECD. Available at <http://www.oecd.org/dataoecd/55/12/40464014.pdf> (accessed 30 June 2010).

Oswald, A. J. (1997), 'Happiness and Economic Performance', *Economic Journal*, 107: 1815–31.

Ouweneel, P. (2002), Social Security and Wellbeing of the Unemployed in 42 Nations', *Journal of Happiness Studies*, 3: 167–92.

Scitovsky, T. (1976), *The Joyless Economy: The Psychology of Human Satisfaction*, Oxford: Oxford University Press.

ten Brink, P. (ed.) (2002), *Voluntary Environmental Agreements: Process, Practice and Future Use*, Sheffield: Greenleaf Publishing.

Van der Voet, E., L. Van Oers, and I. Nikolic (2003), 'Dematerialisation: Not Just a Matter of Weight', CML Report 160, CML, University of Leiden, Netherlands. Available at <https://openaccess.leidenuniv.nl/dspace/handle/1887/11907> (accessed 29 November 2010).

Venn, A. (2007a), 'Bibliography on Happiness, Economic Growth and the Environment', PETRE Working Paper, Policy Studies Institute, London.

——(2007b), 'Review of Data on Environment/Well-Being Relationships', PETRE Working Paper, Policy Studies Institute, London.

Winkelmann, L., and R. Winkelmann (1998), 'Why are the Unemployed So Unhappy? Evidence from Panel Data', *Economica*, 65: 1–15.

2

European Resource Use and Resource Productivity in a Global Context

Stefan Giljum, Christian Lutz, Ariane Jungnitz,
Martin Bruckner and Friedrich Hinterberger

2.1 Introduction

European production and consumption activities are increasingly dependent on material and energy resources from other world regions and therefore have significant economic and environmental impacts on other regions of the world. While the overall level of resource use in Europe has stabilized over the past 20 years, the sources of these resources are increasingly located abroad. Today, around one-third of the material and energy resources used by Europe are imported (Schütz et al. 2004; Weisz et al. 2006; Giljum et al. 2008b). This substitution of domestic material extraction through international trade in physical imports also shifts part of Europe's environmental burden abroad, with a corresponding shift of environmental and social impacts from the local to the global level (SERI et al. 2009).

The main reserves of the most important resources, especially fossil fuels and metal ores, are located outside Europe, causing a critical dependence on other countries and regions. For example, the EU-27 countries possess only 3% of global iron ore reserves, 1% of global oil reserves, and 1% of global uranium reserves (USGS 2006). For many rare metal ores, a very high dependency on imports can be observed. For platinum and tantalum the import rate is 100%, for iron ores 83%, and for bauxite 74% (European Commission 2006).

Recognizing the impacts that production and consumption activities within the EU have on other world regions, the European Commission has called for a more sustainable management of natural resources, along with a decoupling of resource consumption and related negative environmental impacts from economic growth in Europe (European Commission 2005). This strategy should reduce the environmental impact the EU has on the rest of the world and thus contribute to global sustainable development.

In light of Europe's high and growing dependence on resource imports, the European Union has also taken a number of policy measures to address resource security, resource productivity, and related environmental concerns. Among these are the Raw Materials Initiative (2008), the Sustainable Consumption and Production Action Plan (2008), the trade strategy Global Europe (2006), as well as the Thematic Strategy on the Sustainable Use of Natural Resources (2005). In these policy documents, the issues of access to resources and resource security are highlighted as key issues for the future success of the European economy.

Based on the results of a new economy-material flow model, the Global Resource Accounting Model (GRAM; see Giljum et al. 2008a), this chapter analyses the physical dimension of Europe's economic interrelations with other world regions and the implications for EU policies aiming to increase resource productivity. The GRAM results permit the calculation of comprehensive indicators of raw material consumption, which are required to assess to what extent a country's consumption patterns are dependent on natural resource inputs from abroad.

The findings are also an important input to the current discussion on producer versus consumer responsibilities regarding environmental impacts associated with production of goods and services (see, for example, Lenzen et al. 2007). Whereas most accounting frameworks (such as the Kyoto Protocol in the case of carbon emissions) follow a production or territory accounting principle, a consumption-oriented accounting approach is required when discussing concepts such as the allocation of a 'fair share' of the world's resources to all inhabitants of the planet (see also Lenzen et al. 2007; Peters 2008).

This chapter is structured as follows. Section 2.2 explains how international trade relocates the environmental burden. In Section 2.3 different kinds of material consumption indicators are introduced. Section 2.4 provides a methodological summary of input-output-based approaches to calculating indirect material flows and introduces the Global Resource Accounting Model (GRAM). Section 2.5 contains a description of the results, which are discussed from the perspective of European trade and environmental policy in Section 2.6.

2.2 International trade and resource flows

Globalization has been characterized by increasing volumes of international trade and the integration of different world regions into the global market. Between 2000 and 2007, world export volumes grew by 5.5% annually, while production only increased by 3.0% a year. The highest growth in trade occurred for manufactured products (6.5%), followed by agricultural products (4.0%), and fuels and mineral products (3.5%) (WTO 2008).

The inclusion of the natural resource requirements of traded products therefore receives growing importance when domestic production and consumption patterns are evaluated from the perspective of global sustainable development. In addition to direct imports and exports, all material requirements necessary to produce the traded goods (these are also termed indirect material flows associated with or embodied in imports and exports) have to be considered in the analysis. Thereby, possible shifts of environmental burden associated with extraction and processing of materials can be illustrated. Such shifts may result from changing global patterns of production, trade, and consumption.

A number of studies applied methods of physical accounting and environmental-economic modelling to examine the distribution of environmental burdens between different world regions due to their specific economic specialization. They found empirical evidence of increasing externalization of environmental burden by industrialized countries through trade and increasing environmental intensity of exports of non-OECD countries (for example, Nijdam et al. 2005; Peters and Hertwich 2006, 2008; see also Tukker and Jensen 2006 for an overview). Some studies revealed that this shift is also accompanied by an absolute increase in environmental pressures at the global level, as production technologies in developing regions often have a greater material, energy, and emission intensity than those in industrialized countries (Shui and Harriss 2006).

2.3 Indicators of resource consumption

In the methodological framework of material flow accounting and analysis (MFA), indirect material flows associated with imports and exports describe the upstream material requirements necessary to produce a traded product. This upstream process includes resource extraction, processing and manufacturing, and transportation to the border of the analysed country. As explained in the OECD/EUROSTAT guidebook on material flow accounting (OECD 2007), trade flows including indirect material flows should be measured in terms of 'Raw Material Equivalents' (RME), which express the amount of raw materials required along the whole production chain of an imported or exported product.

In terms of RME, the weight of an imported car would not only include its own weight (for example, 500 kg of steel, 300 kg of other metals, and 200 kg of plastics), but also the weight of all the materials that were required to produce its components. In other words, the total weight in RMEs of a car includes not only the steel, plastic, etc. in the finished product, but also the weight of the rest of the raw materials that were used to make the steel, plastic, etc., plus the weight of the crude iron ore and the coal which were processed in a furnace to produce the steel, plus the construction minerals and metals that were used to build the processing facilities, plus the metals and other materials needed for the mining machines, etc.

From an environmental point of view, analysing international trade in terms of RME is therefore better suited for international comparisons of countries and world regions than the application of indicators which only consider international trade in terms of direct imports and exports, in other words, the weight of products crossing the border. In terms of RMEs, the material consumption indicators do not improve if a country dislocates the extraction and processing of raw material from its own territory to other countries (Moll and Bringezu 2005).

If RMEs of traded products are available, comprehensive MFA-based consumption indicators can be calculated. This chapter presents the calculations of the indicator 'Raw Material Consumption' (RMC), which includes all economically used material extraction (of domestic and foreign origin) consumed by final demand in the country analysed. Physical trade balances in terms of raw material equivalents (Raw Material Trade Balances, RTB) of countries and world regions are also illustrated here. These trade balances include the directly imported and exported natural resources and products, as well as all the upstream (or embodied) resources which were accumulated along the production chains.

2.4 The Global Resource Accounting Model (GRAM)

Environmentally extended input-output (EE IO) models have been used for some decades now for the purpose of calculating ecological rucksacks of the foreign trade of countries (for example, Leontief and Ford 1970). These models permit the analysis of the implications for natural resource use of structural changes in the economy, as well as of changes in technology, trade, investments, consumption, and lifestyles.

The input-output (IO) approach avoids imprecise definitions of system boundaries, as the scope of analysis comprises the entire economic system. Furthermore, its high consistency eliminates the possibility of double-counting. However, applying the IO approach also has disadvantages. These arise in particular from the high level of aggregation of economic sectors in the IO tables, which impedes analysis of specific materials (such as single metals or single agricultural products) and leads to problems of inhomogeneities within (theoretically homogeneous) sectors.

In order to analyse global issues, multi-regional IO (MRIO) models are used. They link national economies via bilateral trade data to the global economy and thus create a consistent global economic model. A number of studies have been published in recent years which applied MRIO modelling to assess environmental pressures embodied in international trade (for an overview see Wiedmann 2009; Wiedmann et al. 2007).

The Global Resource Accounting Model (GRAM), a MRIO model extended by material extraction data from global MFA accounts, was constructed in the course of the PETRE project (a detailed description can be found in Giljum et al. 2008a). The model links monetary input-output (IO) tables for 50 countries, the OPEC region, and the region 'Rest of the world' via bilateral trade data for the year 2000. The data come from the OECD, which provides the most comprehensive, reliable, and transparent international data set. The tables of the 2006 edition are based on the year 2000 (Yamano and Ahmad 2006). Therefore, most of the data presented in this chapter focus on the year 2000. This monetary model is then extended by a global data set on material inputs in physical units (SERI 2008), which is attached to the IO tables in the form of additional vectors.

The allocation of the material extraction data to economic sectors in the IO tables is not a trivial task. In contrast to emissions of greenhouse gases, for example, which originate from many economic sectors (Ahmad and Wyckoff 2003; Peters and Hertwich, 2008), raw materials are only extracted by a very limited number of industries. Therefore, the very detailed material input data, covering more than 200 raw materials, need to be aggregated in order to link material input data to the sectors available in the IO tables. The OECD IO tables only disaggregate three economic sectors of primary extraction: agriculture, forestry, fisheries; mining and quarrying/energy; and mining and quarrying/non-energy. In order to obtain a level of detail that is higher than that, material data are linked to those industries which are the main recipients of certain raw material inputs at the first stage of further processing; in other words, iron ores are allocated to the iron and steel sector. However, to avoid distortions caused by this assumption, exports of unprocessed raw materials are separated first and directly linked to the exports of the three extracting sectors. For more details on the technical implementation of the model relationships, see Giljum et al. (2008a).

2.5 Results

The GRAM model permits analysis of the resource consumption of countries and world regions from a global perspective, including international trade and related raw material extraction along international production chains. This section presents global resource extraction data from the Global Material Flow Database (SERI 2008) and then shows, based on the results which were generated by the GRAM model, how materials are traded and consumed in different world regions. Finally, the resource efficiency of different economies is discussed.

2.5.1 *Extraction of resources*

As the world economy grows, humans extract and harvest increasing amounts of natural resources from ecosystems and mines—around 60 billion tonnes annually (Behrens et al. 2007). These natural resources comprise renewable and non-renewable resources. Renewable materials include agricultural products and fish for food and animal feedstock, and timber to produce furniture and paper. Non-renewable resources include fossil fuels that provide energy, metal ores used for example in the manufacture of cars and computers, and industrial and construction minerals used in buildings and other physical infrastructure.

Additional materials are extracted or removed from the soil surface in order to get access to valuable resources, but are not used in production processes themselves. Overburden from mining activities is the most prominent example of this. These materials account for a further annual extraction of 40 billion tonnes. Altogether, over 100 billion tonnes of material are moved worldwide each year. This annual extraction of natural resources is steadily increasing. As more goods and services are produced each year, more natural resources are required. In 1980, the world economy extracted almost 40 billion tonnes. By 2005, this number had grown to 58 billion tonnes, an increase of almost 50% (Figure 2.1).

Resource extraction has increased in all major categories: biomass from agriculture and forestry, fossil fuels, metal ores, and industrial and construction minerals. Between 1980 and 2005, the extraction of natural gas, sand, and gravel almost doubled, and nickel ore extraction tripled. For some of the biotic resources, such as fish, the signs of overuse can already be observed—catch rates have been declining over the past ten years.

In contrast to the global increase, European extraction of natural resources has nearly stabilized at the 1980 level. Europe's extraction of natural resources increased by less than 10% over the past 30 years. Only extraction of construction minerals and biomass increased, by about 20%, while the extraction of metal ores remained constant, and the extraction of industrial minerals decreased by 25%. The production of coal and oil in Europe peaked in 1987. Since then, the production of these fossil fuels has dropped by 35%. In 1980, Europe accounted for 19% of the global extraction of natural resources. This share sank in all of the eight resource categories in Figure 2.1 to a total of 13%

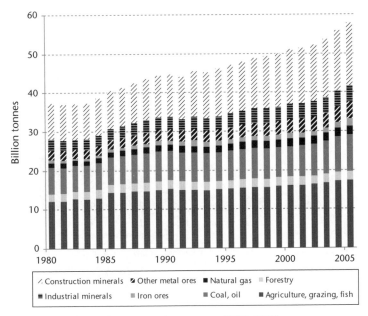

Figure 2.1 Global extraction of natural resources, 1980–2005
Source: SERI Global Material Flow Database. 2008 Version. See <http://www.material flows.net>.

in 2005. This is particularly the case for coal, oil, metal ores, and industrial minerals, where Europe's share of global production decreased by about 50%.

The extraction and processing of natural resources is often very intensive in the use of materials, energy, water, and land. These activities therefore often entail environmental problems, such as the destruction of fertile land, water shortages, or toxic pollution. Social problems are also often linked to extraction activities, including human rights violations, poor working conditions, and low wages. These negative environmental and social impacts are most strongly felt in poor developing and emerging countries with low environmental and social protection standards (SERI et al. 2009).

THE GEOGRAPHY OF RESOURCE EXTRACTION
Each person on the planet (indirectly) extracts on average over 8 tonnes of natural resources per year, or 22 kg per day. If we include the unused extraction of materials (for example, overburden and erosion), each inhabitant of the planet mobilizes almost 15 tonnes of materials per year.

Resource extraction is very unevenly distributed across the world. How many natural resources are extracted on a continent depends on several factors, notably the size of the continent, the availability of resources, and the size of the population, as well as the level of affluence. In 2005, by far the largest share

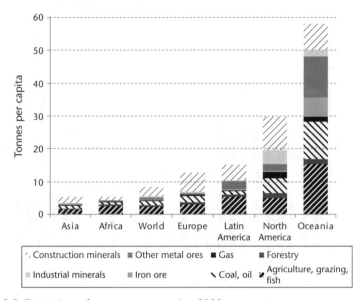

Figure 2.2 Extraction of resources per capita, 2000
Source: SERI Global Material Flow Database. 2008 Version. See <http://www.materialflows.net>.

of resource extraction took place in Asia (48%), where more than half of the world's population lives. North America ranked second with 19%, followed by Latin America and Europe (13% each), Africa (9%), and Oceania (3%).

There is also a big variation globally in the amounts and types of natural resources extracted per capita (see Figure 2.2).

As a continent, Oceania has the smallest share of extraction, but the biggest extraction of resources per capita: in 2000, 58 tonnes per year were extracted per person, dominated by metal ores with a share of one-third. Australia is the biggest economy in Oceania and has significantly expanded its mining industries in recent years. North America ranked second with 30 tonnes extracted per person per year, followed by Latin America. As with Australia, large amounts of the resources extracted in Latin America are exported to other countries; in particular metal ores, timber, and agricultural products such as soya. The average per capita extraction of resources in Europe in 2000 was around 13 tonnes per year. The smallest amounts per capita were extracted in Africa and Asia, each with only 5.5 tonnes per year.

2.5.2 Trade in resources

While the extraction of natural resources is very unevenly distributed across the world, international trade redistributes resources across the globe, allowing some countries to export resources and to raise revenues and other countries to increase their supply of raw materials and products.

Since international exchange requires goods to be transported between the countries of extraction and production to countries of consumption, growth in trade has significantly increased greenhouse gas emissions from transport activities. Around a quarter of global energy-related greenhouse gas emissions originate from transport activities (WTO and UNEP 2009). Trade also contributes to increased land and material requirements for transport infrastructure, such as roads, harbours, and airports.

THE STRUCTURE OF WORLD TRADE

Current patterns of trade are largely determined by the availability of resources in different world regions and the economic position of countries in the world system (Eisenmenger and Giljum 2006). Industrialized countries in Europe and North America, but also in Asia, largely export manufactured products with a high value added. Many developing countries, on the other hand, continue to rely strongly on the export of raw materials such as agricultural products, minerals, and fossil fuels (WTO 2008).

Exporting manufactured products usually generates higher profits compared to export of commodities. Furthermore, environmental pressures related to extraction and processing of resources are high. However, some resource-exporting countries do earn significant income from their exports, for example prices of many resources increased sharply between 2003 and 2008. Examples include the OPEC countries for oil exports, or Chile and Australia for exports of metal ores.

If managed with high environmental and social standards and under effective local governance structures, exports of natural resources can have positive impacts on regional development in poorer countries. However, the massive growth of the global trade system in the latter half of the 20th century has had significant impacts on the way we use natural resources and poses some severe environmental and social threats.

TRADE REINFORCES INEQUALITIES IN RESOURCE CONSUMPTION

Global trade of natural resources allows countries and world regions with high purchasing power to increase resource consumption beyond their own national resource capacities. In recent years, more and more countries have become net importers of natural resources and products and thus consume more than would be possible based on domestic resources only. These countries run an 'ecological trade deficit'.

It may not be regarded as problematic that countries with poor natural endowments have net resource imports. However, the inequalities in resource use facilitated by the current patterns of world trade raise concern as they may jeopardize sustainable and equitable development in all world regions.

In order to ensure material welfare for all people, trade could help by redistributing resources from countries with a high extraction to countries with lower extraction. Regionally, this is the case for Oceania, which has by far the highest per capita extraction of resources and reveals also the highest per capita net exports. However, the opposite is the case for North America and Europe. These continents both have a per capita extraction above the global average and consume more than what is locally available. They have the highest net imports of natural resources, with 2.5 and 1.6 tonnes per capita per year, respectively. Developing and emerging economies with a low level of per capita extraction, especially in Africa and Latin America, are mostly net exporters of natural resources (see Figure 2.3).

Oceania constitutes an exception as it has high per capita material extraction and consumption levels, but still the highest net exports in a continental comparison (21 tonnes per person per year). For the Asian continent, imports and exports of direct and embodied resources virtually balance out. Asia is a net importer, particularly in the case of biomass and metal ores, and a net exporter for fossil fuels. Shifts are likely to have taken place since the year 2000, especially in China and India which, according to the World Bank's World Development Indicators database, have doubled their GDP (in PPP) between 2000 and 2006 (World Bank 2009). It can be expected that Asia has expanded its net imports significantly since then, given China's huge increase in demand for natural resources.

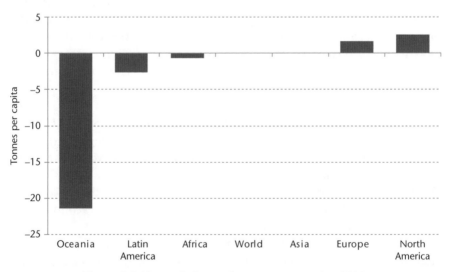

Figure 2.3 Net trade flows of resources per capita, 2000

Europe is a net importer in nearly every material category, particularly of biomass (420 million tonnes), fossil fuels (320 million tonnes), and metal ores (more than 210 million tonnes), with only small net exports of industrial and construction minerals (-11 million tonnes). A comparison of single countries including some regions (European Union, OPEC, and the 'Rest of the world' region) shows that imports of the EU-25 countries as a whole are surpassing their exports of embodied natural resources by 1.3 billion tonnes (Figure 2.4). Worth mentioning also is the fact that the EU-15 countries even exceed the net imports of the EU-25; in other words, the new EU member countries are net exporters of embodied natural resources, particularly due to the high net exports of fossil fuels, metals, and minerals from Poland and the Czech Republic.

Looking at individual countries, the United States (989 million tonnes) and Japan (963 million tonnes) are the biggest net importers, followed by Western European and some highly industrialized Asian countries (Germany, South Korea, Italy, Great Britain, France, Spain, and Singapore). At the other end of the spectrum are located the biggest net exporters, in other words the countries and world regions with the highest surpluses of exports of raw and embodied materials. The biggest net exporter is the group of OPEC countries

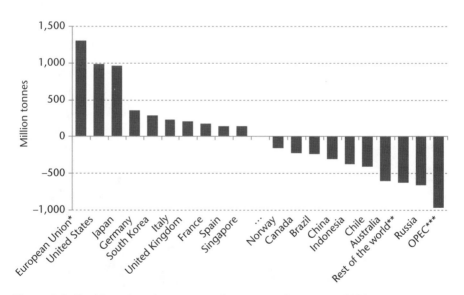

Figure 2.4. Ranking of net importers and exporters of resources, 2000

Notes: * EU-25 region was included in this ranking. ** Rest of the world is a region comprising mainly Latin American, African, and Asian countries where no IO data were available. The population of this region adds up to about 1.5 billion people. *** The OPEC region includes the countries Algeria, Iran, Iraq, Kuwait, Libya, Nigeria, Qatar, Saudi Arabia, United Arab Emirates, and Venezuela.

(962 million tons), followed by Russia (653 million tons), the region 'Rest of the World' (626 million tons), and Australia (601 million tonnes).

The illustration shows that resources are shifted (both in the form of raw materials and as materials embodied in products) from resource-rich countries or regions (such as OPEC, Russia, and Australia) and/or economically less developed countries (for example, in the 'Rest of the world'), to countries with lower raw material reserves and/or high consumption levels, notably in Europe and North America.

2.5.3 Consumption of resources

There are huge differences in per capita consumption of natural resources between different countries and world regions. People in rich countries consume up to ten times more natural resources than those in the poorest countries. In Europe, around 13 tonnes of resources are extracted per person per year (Domestic Extraction, DE), excluding unused resource extraction, whereas 14.5 tonnes are consumed per person per year (Raw Material Consumption, RMC; see Figure 2.5). Europeans therefore need imported resources from other world regions to maintain their level of consumption.

Consumption is even higher in other world regions. On average, a North American consumes around 32 tonnes per year; an inhabitant of Oceania

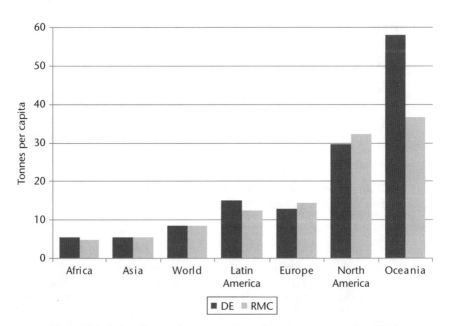

Figure 2.5 Extraction and consumption of resources per capita, 2000

about 37 tonnes per year. On average, in comparison to Europe, people in these continents have larger houses, eat more meat, and drive bigger cars. These differences in lifestyle increase resource consumption. Far fewer resources are consumed in other world regions. In Asia, resource consumption is about equal to resource extraction at around 5.5 tonnes per person per year. The average resource consumption of an African is lower than 5 tonnes per year (compared to the extraction of 5.5 tonnes per year).

CONSUMPTION OF RESOURCES AND GLOBAL
RESOURCE DEPENDENCIES

In many countries local resource availabilities cannot meet the demand for all the products that are consumed domestically. Setting resource consumption in relation to the domestic extraction of resources illustrates to what extent different world regions are outsourcing material and energy-intensive production processes abroad. Figure 2.6 thus shows to what extent resource consumption in the six continents is in line with or above their potential self-sufficiency.

Consumption of natural resources exceeds the continental supply in North America (9%) and Europe (13%), while Oceania, Africa, and Latin America consume fewer resources than they extract (37%, 17%, and 13%, respectively). Europe (and the EU in particular) combines relatively low endowment of resources, in particular regarding fossil fuels and metal ores, with high population density and high GDP per capita. It therefore reveals the highest differences between domestic extraction and consumption. In particular, for metal ores, consumption exceeds domestic extraction by 75%. But also for

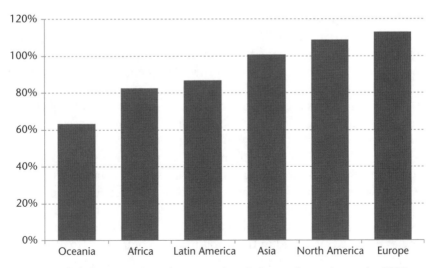

Figure 2.6 Consumption of resources in relation to domestic supply, 2000

fossil fuels (24%) and biomass (20%), the European lifestyle depends significantly on imports.

2.5.4 *Resource efficiency*

Resource efficiency, which measures the economic value produced per unit of natural resources, has continuously improved over past decades. As described earlier, worldwide resource extraction grew by around 50% between 1980 and 2005. Growing resource extraction was closely correlated with global growth in population (see SERI et al. 2009). World economic output (GDP) increased by 110% in the same time period. As GDP growth was higher than growth in resource extraction, a 'relative decoupling' of resource extraction from economic growth was achieved. Thus, the world economy today uses around 30% fewer natural resources to produce one euro or dollar of GDP than 30 years ago. As a consequence, the resource intensity, the reciprocal value of resource efficiency, of the global economy is declining.

This is a positive trend and shows that we are improving our resource efficiency in relative terms. However, the absolute amount of resource extraction and resource use is still rising at a global level (see Figure 2.1). Economic growth is outweighing the gains in resource efficiency. A similar trend can be observed for Europe, where resource productivity increased by more than 30% between 1990 and 2004. However, GDP also grew by the same order of magnitude and no absolute reduction of resource use was achieved (EUROSTAT 2007).

RESOURCE EFFICIENCY IN DIFFERENT WORLD REGIONS
World regions use very different amounts of resources to produce their GDP. How many resources are required depends on several factors: the types and amounts of resources available in the different world regions, the imports and exports of resources, and the production technologies, as well as the structure of an economy; in other words, which economic activities contribute most to GDP.

Figure 2.7 illustrates the resource intensity of each continent in 2000. On average, around 1.6 kg of natural resources (not including unused resources) were needed in the year 2000 to produce one dollar of GDP.

Africa is the continent with the highest resource intensity. On average, African countries need almost 8 kg of domestic resources to produce one dollar of GDP. Two of the main reasons for the high resource intensities are the dominance of resource-intensive economic activities, such as mining and agriculture, in many African economies and the relatively less efficient technologies that are being used in these countries in comparison to other world regions. However, Africa is a net exporter of resources (see Figures 2.3, 2.5, and 2.6), so many of the resources Africa extracts are consumed in other countries.

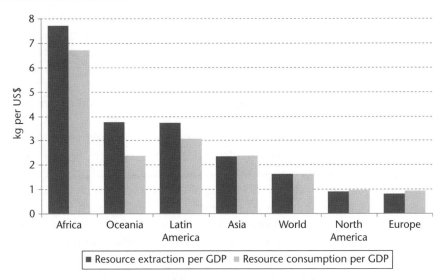

Figure 2.7 Resource intensity of production and consumption, 2000

Therefore, resource consumption in Africa is less resource intensive than resource extraction (less than 7 kg).

Natural resources also play an important role in the economies of Latin America and Oceania (in particular, Australia). Consequently, their resource intensity is also above the world average. These countries also have high exports of resources to other world regions. Consequently, resource intensity of extraction (3.7 kg per dollar) is higher than resource intensity of consumption (2.4 kg per dollar).

The reverse trends can be observed for Europe and North America. With 0.8 and 0.9 kg of resource use per dollar respectively, these economic regions are relatively more resource efficient, as service sectors are the largest component of GDP. Services, such as banking or health care, are less resource intensive than mining, agriculture, or manufacturing. However, Europe and North America need resources from other world regions to maintain their economic system. Resource intensity is therefore higher for resource consumption than for resource extraction (0.9 kg per dollar for Europe and 1 kg per dollar for North America).

2.6 Discussion and conclusions

This chapter has presented data and indicators on resource trade, resource consumption, and resource efficiency for the year 2000. The results illustrate that global patterns of resource extraction are reinforced through international trade. Although European and North American countries already have the highest levels of per capita resource extraction (with the exception of Oceania), international trade increases the gap and, from the perspective of world regions, allocates additional natural resources from extraction in developing and emerging countries to consumption in the industrialized countries. However, as the physical trade balances of single countries revealed, some OECD countries are among the most significant net exporters of embodied materials, most notably Australia and Canada.

This trade pattern of net imports to the North is particularly visible for the EU-25, which faces the strongest dependence on resource imports of all investigated world regions, in particular regarding agricultural products, fossil fuels, and metal ores. In current EU trade policy documents, such the EU trade strategy ('Global Europe') from 2006, these issues of increasing import dependency are explicitly addressed and the access to resources and resource security highlighted as a key to the future success of the European export economies: 'More than ever, Europe needs to import to export. Tackling restrictions on access to resources such as energy, metals and scrap, primary raw materials including certain agricultural materials, hides and skins must be a high priority. Measures taken by some of our biggest trading partners to restrict access to their supplies of these inputs are causing some EU industries major problems' (European Commission 2006: 7).

Furthermore, the EU-25 as a whole shows higher (direct and indirect) net imports of natural resources than any other single economy, including the USA and Japan. Material consumption in Europe thus is to the largest extent not met by domestic resources alone; a result that confirms calculations of European resource use according to other indicators, in particular the 'Ecological Footprint' (WWF et al. 2005).

The results also illustrate that resource efficiency should not be the key indicator informing about the environmental performance of a country. As Figure 2.7 has shown, resource efficiency is highest for the continents with the highest levels of resource extraction and consumption, except for Oceania, whose economy is much more dominated by resource-intensive activities. Based on resource efficiency, one might assume that Europe and North America are the most sustainable continents in terms of resource use. However, total levels of resource extraction and consumption per capita (Figure 2.5) show that the contrary is the case. The most efficient countries in the world are in most cases also the ones which extract and consume the most.

Resource efficiency alone, therefore, is not suitable to indicate the environmental sustainability of a national economy. Total levels of extraction and consumption are crucial additional indicators in this context, providing information not only about relative improvements, but also about the absolute levels of environmental pressures.

The data thus illustrate that the technological progress we have witnessed in Europe and other industrialized countries over past decades, which has allowed us to use raw materials and energy ever more efficiently, will not solve the environmental problems related to resource use. One key reason for this is the 'rebound effect' (Jackson 2009). When enterprises use less energy and fewer materials to produce their products and services, production costs decrease. Lower production costs, in turn, lower the price of the relevant product or service. And lower prices for consumers mean that—with the same budget—consumers can purchase more of the cheaper product or other products. Rising resource efficiency therefore often increases overall demand and consequently the overall consumption of natural resources.

Resource policies that focus solely on increasing resource efficiency are therefore not sufficient in the context of European sustainable development and sustainable growth. Europe should set an international example and formulate targets not only for resource productivity (which are also still lacking), but also regarding absolute levels of European resource use. The world faces increasing competition for natural resources, and there are increasing concerns about the potential limits of resource availability and use. In this situation, an absolute reduction of per capita resource consumption in the high-consuming industrialized countries is the precondition for allowing further growth in developing and emerging economies without overusing the resource capacities of the planet.

References

Ahmad, N., and A. Wyckoff (2003), *Carbon dioxide emissions embodied in international trade*, Paris: OECD.

Behrens, A., S. Giljum, J. Kovanda, and S. Niza (2007), 'The Material Basis of the Global Economy: Worldwide Patterns of Natural Resource Extraction and their Implications for Sustainable Resource Use Policies', *Ecological Economics*, 64: 444–53.

Eisenmenger, N., and S. Giljum (2006), 'Evidence from Societal Metabolism Studies for Ecologically Unequal Trade', in A. Hornborg and C. L. Crumley (eds.), *The World System and the Earth System: Global Socio-environmental Change and Sustainability since the Neolithic*, Walnut Creek, Calif.: Left Coast Press Inc.

European Commission (2005), *Thematic Strategy on the Sustainable Use of Natural Resources*, Brussels: European Commission.

——— (2006), *Global Europe: Competing in the World: A Contribution to the EU's Growth and Jobs Strategy*, Brussels: EC, DG External Trade.

EUROSTAT (2007), *Measuring Progress towards a More Sustainable Europe: 2007 Monitoring Report of the EU Sustainable Development Strategy*, Luxembourg: Statistical Office of the European Communities.

Giljum, S., C. Lutz, and A. Jungnitz (2008a), 'The Global Resource Accounting Model (GRAM): A Methodological Concept Paper', Vienna: Sustainable Europe Research Institute, available at <http://seri.at/wp-content/uploads/2009/08/SERI-Working-Paper-7.pdf>.

————M. Bruckner, and F. Hinterberger (2008b), 'Global Dimensions of European Natural Resource Use: First Results from the Global Resource Accounting Model (GRAM)', Vienna: Sustainable Europe Research Institute, available at <http://seri.at/wp-content/uploads/2009/09/SERI_Studies_81.pdf>.

Jackson, T. (2009), *Prosperity without Growth: Economics for a Finite Planet,* London, Earthscan.

Lenzen, M., J. Murray, F. Sack, and T. Wiedmann (2007), 'Shared Producer and Consumer Responsibility—Theory and Practice', *Ecological Economics*, 61: 27–42.

Leontief, W., and D. Ford (1970), 'Environmental Repercussions and the Economic System', *Review of Economics and Statistics*, 52: 262–72.

Moll, S., and S. Bringezu (2005), *Aggregated Indicators for Resource Use and Resource Productivity: Their Meaning, Cross-Country Comparability, and Potential Driving Factors,* Copenhagen: European Environment Agency.

Nijdam, D. S., H. C. Wilting, M. J. Goedkoop, and J. Madsen (2005), 'Environmental Load from Dutch Private Consumption: How Much Damage Takes Place Abroad?', *Journal of Industrial Ecology*, 9: 147–68.

Organisation for Economic Co-operation and Development (OECD) (2007), *Measuring Material Flows and Resource Productivity: The OECD Guide*, Paris: Environment Directorate.

Peters, G. (2008), 'From Production-Based to Consumption-Based National Emission Inventories', *Ecological Economics*, 65: 13–23.

——and E. Hertwich (2006), 'Structural Analysis of International Trade: Environmental Impacts of Norway', *Economic Systems Research*, 18: 155–81.

————(2008), 'CO$_2$ Embodied in International Trade with Implications for Global Climate Policy', *Environmental Science & Technology*, 42: 1401–7.

Schütz, H., S. Bringezu, and S. Moll (2004), *Globalisation and the Shifting Environmental Burden: Material Trade Flows of the European Union*, Wuppertal: Wuppertal Institute.

SERI (Sustainable Europe Research Institute) (2008), Global Material Flow Database. 2008 Version. Available at <http://www.materialflows.net>.

SERI, GLOBAL 2000 and FRIENDS OF THE EARTH EUROPE (2009), *Overconsumption? Our Use of the World's Natural Resources*, Vienna and Brussels.

Shui, B., and R. C. Harriss (2006), 'The Role of CO$_2$ Embodiment in US-China Trade', *Energy Policy*, 34: 4063–8.

Tukker, A., and B. Jensen (2006), 'Environmental Impacts of Products: A Detailed Review of Studies', *Journal of Industrial Ecology*, 10: 159–82.

USGS (2006), *Minerals Yearbook 2006*, Washington: United States Geological Survey.

Weisz, H., F. Krausmann, C. Amann, N. Eisenmenger, K.-H. Erb, K. Hubacek, and M. Fischer-Kowalski (2006), 'The Physical Economy of the European Union: Cross-Country Comparison and Determinants of Material Consumption', *Ecological Economics*, 58: 676–98.

Wiedmann, T. (2009), 'A Review of Recent Multi-Region Input-Output Models Used for Consumption-Based Emission and Resource Accounting', *Ecological Economics*, 69: 211–21.

——Lenzen, M., K. Turner, and J. Barrett (2007), 'Examining the Global Environmental Impact of Regional Consumption Activities—Part 2: Review of Input-Output Models for the Assessment of Environmental Impacts Embodied in Trade', *Ecological Economics*, 61: 15–26.

World Bank (2009), World Development Indicators 2009, available at <http://data.worldbank.org/indicator>.

WTO (2008), *International Trade Statistics 2008*, Geneva: World Trade Organization.

WTO and UNEP (2009), *Trade and Climate Change*, WTO-UNEP Report. Available at <http://www.wto.org/english/res_e/booksp_e/trade_climate_change_e.pdf>.

WWF, Global Footprint Network, and IUCN (2005), *Europe 2005: The Ecological Footprint*, Brussels: WWF European Policy Office, available at <http://www.footprintnetwork.org/images/uploads/Europe_2005_Ecological_Footprint.pdf>.

Yamano, N., and N. Ahmad (2006), *The OECD's Input-Output Database—2006 Edition*. Paris: OECD, Directorate for Science, Technology and Industry, Economic Analysis and Statistics Division.

3

Energy Consumption and CO_2 Emissions in the German and British Industrial Sectors

Paolo Agnolucci[1]

3.1 Introduction

The relationship between CO_2 emissions and economic growth has been analysed extensively in the literature. From a policy point of view, the motivations
for estimating this relationship have become more and more important in the
last couple of decades. Emissions of greenhouse gases (GHGs) and the recent
surge in the oil price have increased the attention devoted to the role of energy
in modern economies. Assuming that inter-fuel substitution is limited in the
short term, GHG reductions will require lower energy consumption.

In the literature, two approaches to the analysis of the relationship between
CO_2 emissions and economic growth can be found. In the first approach, one
can estimate energy and fuel demands and then apply emission coefficients to
determine the amount of CO_2 emissions. The advantage of this approach is
that the relationship between energy consumption, price, and economic
activity is very well grounded in economic theory. In the second approach,
the profile of CO_2 emissions can be assessed in the framework of environmental Kuznets curves (EKCs). According to this hypothesis, CO_2 emissions
increase in the early stages of economic growth, but the trend reverses
beyond some level of economic activity.[2] More broadly, the justification for

---

[1] The author would like to thank Ron Smith of Birkbeck College, University of London, for the
encouragement received during the preparation of this chapter, and Paul Ekins of University
College London and Kirsten Wiebe of GWS for feedback on a previous draft.
[2] The presence of an inverted U relationship between pollution and economic growth was
originally advanced in Grossman and Krueger (1993) for SO_2 and smoke. Since then, several
studies have estimated this relationship across indicators of environmental quality or pollution,
countries, and time periods. A number of surveys have been published, notably Copeland and
Taylor (2004), de Bruyn and Heintz (1998), Dinda (2004), Ekins (1997), and Stern (1998).

a non-linear relationship between pollution and economic activity is related to the fact that economic growth affects environmental quality through a number of effects, namely, the scale, technological, and composition effects[3] (Grossman and Krueger 1993).

Considering that it accounts for about a third of total global consumption (Greening et al. 2007), the fact that industrial energy consumption attracts considerable academic interest should not come as a surprise. However, most of the studies of industrial energy demand follow the seminal work of Berndt and Wood (1975) and concentrate on factor and inter-fuel substitution models. Recently, only a few published articles have estimated the energy demand in the industrial sector, which is assumed to have a log-linear specification. Two examples are Enevoldsen et al. (2007) and Adeyemi and Hunt (2010). Enevoldsen et al. (2007) estimate energy and fuel demands for about 15 sectors in Denmark, Norway, and Sweden. Energy price elasticities vary between −0.44 and −0.38. Adeyemi and Hunt (2010) model industrial demand in 15 OECD countries over the period 1962–2003, while exploring the issues of energy-saving technical change and asymmetric price responses. When assuming energy-saving technical change, the not statistically significant price elasticity is −0.22, while when assuming an asymmetric price effect, the elasticities of price maxima, recoveries, and cuts are −0.52, −0.68, and −0.30, respectively. In their literature survey, Adeyemi and Hunt (2010) listed only seven recent publications which estimate a log-linear specification for the energy consumption of industrial sectors in OECD countries.[4]

Similarly, not many contributions based on EKCs seem to have assessed CO$_2$ emissions from industrial sectors, as studies tend to focus on emissions from countries as a whole. This study aims to tackle this apparent gap in the analysis of industrial energy consumption and CO$_2$ emissions. Section 3.2 deals with the estimation of energy demand. We first present the estimation strategy, we then discuss the results from the estimation, and finally we draw conclusions. In Section 3.3, we discuss the approaches used to estimate CO$_2$

---

[3] Other things being equal, economic growth is expected to have a negative scale impact on the environment but as the economy develops, cleaner activities may increase their contribution to total GDP, i.e. the composition effect. In addition, polluting technologies can be replaced by cleaner ones, i.e. the technological effect. One can also distinguish between proximate causes, i.e. the three effects above, and underlying causes. These include positive income elasticities for environmental quality, international trade, openness of political systems, environmental regulation, and increased levels of awareness and education—see de Bruyn et al. (1998), Dinda (2004), Selden and Song (1994), and Stern (2004) for a thorough discussion.

[4] This could be due to the fact that other approaches have proved more successful in estimating energy demand. However, this is at odds with the remark in Pesaran et al. (1998), according to whom the log-linear specification generally outperforms more complex specifications across a large variety of settings. A reason for the relatively low number of studies found in academic journals could be the success of the log-linear approach. As mentioned in Adeyemi and Hunt (2010), this procedure has become standard and, it can be argued, its application is probably not considered worthy of academic publication, as it does not innovate on current mainstream practice.

EKCs in the literature and assess the impact of a number of factors on the results from the empirical studies. It is worth mentioning that this discussion is carried out only by comparing results from studies which have adopted more than one methodological approach. The reason for this choice is related to our desire to control for the presence of multiple factors which might affect the final result. Building on the conclusions from the literature survey, empirical results for ten industrial sectors are presented. Section 3.5 sets out the conclusions of this chapter. A Technical Appendix contains more complex explanation about the econometrics and estimation strategy employed.

3.2 Energy Demand of Industrial Subsectors

This section estimates the energy demand of the British and German industrial sectors for 1978–2004 and 1991–2004 samples, respectively. In the case of Germany, data are available only for the shorter sample. Energy demands are estimated for a panel consisting of ten industrial subsectors in the case of Germany and eight sectors in the case of the UK. In the energy literature there is quite an established tradition of studies estimating energy demands across economic sectors or countries. One might mention Adeyemi and Hunt (2010), Baltagi et al. (2002), Baltagi and Griffin (1983), Baltagi and Griffin (1997), Garcia-Cerrutti (2000), Pesaran et al. (1998), and Pock (2007).

As in the papers mentioned above, the main economic motivation of this study is the estimation of energy demand. However, in the case of the UK industrial sectors, we also aim to tackle the uncertainty regarding the scale of economic activity and the size of price elasticities of industrial energy demand. In particular, three recent contributions have provided different estimates, despite using the same modelling approach, i.e. the Structural Time Series Models of Harvey (1989). Agnolucci (2010) obtained a long-run income and price elasticity of 0.45 and −0.59 on the 1973–2005 sample; Hunt et al.'s (2003) estimates were 0.72 and −0.16 for the 1972–1995 sample, while Dimitropuolos et al.'s (2005) estimates were 0.70 and −0.15 for the 1967–1999 sample.[5] It goes without saying that the policy implications of the parameters in Hunt et al. (2003), Dimitropuolos et al. (2005), and Agnolucci (2010) are remarkably different. High price elasticities enable policy makers to constrain energy consumption through moderate price increases which can be brought about through energy taxes or tradable permit systems. High elasticities of

---

[5] It is worth mentioning that this dichotomy seems rather entrenched in empirical studies. In fact, Hunt and Lynk (1992) reported elasticities for economic activity and price equal to 0.70 and −0.29, i.e. similar to Hunt et al. (2003) and Dimitropuolos et al. (2005), while Lynk (1989) reported values of 0.44 and −0.69, i.e. similar to those in Agnolucci (2007).

economic activity, on the other hand, make reducing energy consumption a much harder task, as the increase in energy consumption due to economic growth will be sizeable.

This chapter hopes to cast some light on the size of the coefficients for UK industrial energy demand by using a panel approach. The estimation strategy, and the variety of estimators used, are set out in more detail in a Technical Appendix at the end of this chapter.

3.2.1 Estimation Strategy

The panel for the British and German industrial sectors is composed of the subsectors presented in Table 3.1.

The basic model is given by the equation:

$$e_{it} = f(\alpha, p_{it}, y_{it}, time\ trend)$$

where e stands for energy demand, α for the intercept, p for the energy price, and y for the gross value added (GVA) of the industrial sector. The index points out that observations are tracked across time t for each sector i assessed in the study. The use of the expression $e_{it} = f(\bullet)$ indicates that the exact specification of the equation above will depend on the estimator used.

The energy price for these sectors has been obtained by weighting the industrial fuel prices by sector-specific fuel consumption. Indices of real fuel prices, including taxes, were obtained from IEA (2006a). Data on the consumption of fuels, namely Coal and Coal Products (including blast furnace gases), Electricity, Natural Gas and Petroleum Products, and energy consumption, were obtained from IEA (2007). Gross value added for the sectors assessed in this chapter was taken from DeStatis (2006), ONS (2006a), and ONS (2006b). Data on the GVA of the German sectors are available only for the 1991–2004 time period, while for the UK, data are available for the 1978–2004 time period. The British Transport and Mining sectors are not modelled, due

Table 3.1. Industrial sectors assessed in Section 3.2

Sector	ISIC Taxonomy
Mining and Quarrying	13–14
Food and Tobacco	15–16
Textile and Leather	17–19
Pulp, Paper and Printing	21–22
Chemicals	24
Non-Metallic Minerals	26
Machinery	28–32
Transport Equipment	34–35
Construction	45
Metals	27

to limitations in the data on fuel consumption. For the sake of brevity, we do not report the discussion of the data, although this is available upon request. More detail on the econometrics of the estimation strategy is given in the Technical Appendix.

3.2.2 Results

Figure 3.1a displays the coefficients from the statistically significant estimators in Table A3.1a in the Technical Appendix, with the exception of those from the Anderson-Hsiao (AH) estimator. This estimate is discarded on the basis of the heterogeneous bias. Note the similarity among the estimates, the average for which is 0.47. As shown in Figure 3.1a, the confidence intervals of the estimators overlap over the 0.25–0.60 range.

In the case of the elasticity for economic activity in the UK, all the statistically significant estimates (apart from the AH and Demeaned Mean Group (DMG) estimators—see Technical Appendix) show very similar confidence intervals and point estimates, as shown in Figure 3.1b. If one wanted to fix a point estimate for the elasticity of economic activity on energy consumption, a value near 0.52, i.e. the average from all statistically significant estimators, would seem a sensible candidate. The range of the confidence intervals shared by all estimators is 0.35–0.75. It is interesting to note that the value 0.52 is very similar to the value obtained for the German sectors.

In the case of British energy demand, the number of estimators with price coefficients which conform to economic theory is markedly higher. Figure 3.1c shows that the averages from the estimators in the first and second group

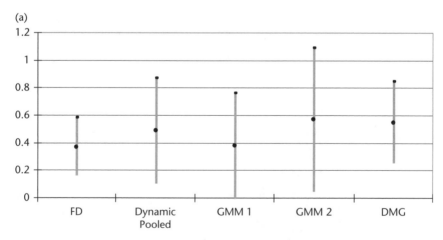

Figure 3.1a Point estimate and 95% confidence intervals of the statistically significant coefficients on economic activity in the sample of German energy demand

(b)

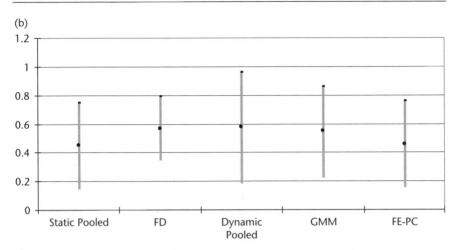

Figure 3.1b Point estimate and 95% confidence intervals of the statistically significant coefficients on economic activity in the British energy demand estimated over the 1978–2004 sample

(c)

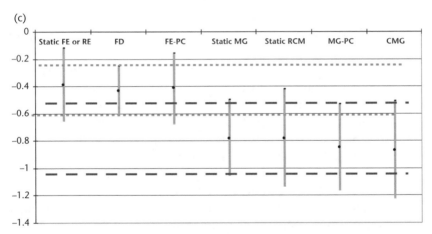

Figure 3.1c Point estimate and 95% confidence intervals of the statistically significant price coefficients in the British energy demand estimated over the 1978–2004 sample

Note: The broken line delimits the range of the confidence intervals shared by the heterogeneous estimators while the dotted line delimits the range of the confidence intervals shared by the homogeneous estimators.

are -0.41 and −0.82, respectively; the average from all estimates is −0.64, which is our preferred choice of price elasticity estimate.

The point estimates discussed above are helpful in reconciling the results from Agnolucci (2010), Dimitropoulos et al. (2005), and Hunt et al. (2003) for the UK industrial sector. In the case of income elasticity, our point estimate of 0.52 falls between the values of 0.70 from Hunt et al. (2003) and

Dimitropoulos et al. (2005), and 0.45 from Agnolucci (2010). Both values fall in the confidence interval shared by all estimators in Figure 3.1b, i.e. 0.35–0.75. In the case of price elasticity, −0.59 from Agnolucci (2010) falls rather close to our estimate of −0.64. Conversely, the price elasticities from Hunt et al. (2003), −0.20, and from Dimitropoulos et al. (2005), −0.17, fall in the confidence interval for the Fixed Effect (FE) and Fixed Effect with Principal Components (FE-PC) estimators only. In other words, Agnolucci (2010), Dimitropoulos et al. (2005), and Hunt et al. (2003) produced results which are not statistically significantly different from those obtained in this chapter with regard to income elasticity. In the case of price elasticity, however, the estimates from Dimitropoulos et al. (2005) and Hunt et al. (2003) are rejected by all estimators used in the study, with the exception of FE and FE-PC. The value of price elasticity from Dimitropoulos et al. (2005) and Hunt et al. (2003) seems appropriate only when one is ready to assume that energy demand across subsectors is homogeneous.

3.2.3 Conclusions

A number of conclusions can be drawn from the research presented in this chapter. With regard to the coefficients from pooled estimators, only in the 1978–2004 sample could we obtain a number of statistically significant estimates for both economic activity and price. Our preferred choice for the long-run elasticities of economic activity and price are 0.52 and −0.64. Similar values are found in the case of the shorter sample. The estimates from this chapter increase confidence in the role of energy taxes and trading permits in climate change policy. Policy instruments influencing the energy price are likely to be rather effective in constraining energy demand. To the extent that inter-fuel substitutability is limited in the short term, reductions in energy consumption are also likely to deliver GHG reductions, but this is a complex issue, especially when electricity may be involved in the substitution, because this has zero carbon emissions at the point of use. These considerations become important in relation to the results of Section 3.3.

In relation to the contrasting estimates from Agnolucci (2010), Dimitropoulos et al. (2005), and Hunt et al. (2003), this study validates the results from the three papers in the case of income elasticity. However, in the case of price elasticity, the results here are much more similar to those from Agnolucci (2010). A similar price elasticity to Dimitropoulos et al. (2005) and Hunt et al. (2003) is obtained in this study when assuming static energy demand which is homogeneous across subsectors. These rather stringent assumptions somewhat limit the relevance of the estimates from Dimitropoulos et al. (2005) and Hunt et al. (2003).

Heterogeneity was discovered to be an important factor in explaining the variation of price elasticity in the UK. As discussed above, all heterogeneous estimators in Figure 3.1c produced higher estimates than those from homogeneous estimators. Finally, in the case of the data set used in this chapter, a number of estimators which do not take into account cross-sectional dependence produced similar estimates to the estimators which do so; compare, for example, the estimates for price elasticity from the Static Mean Group (MG) and the Mean Group with Principal Components (MG-PC). This is a reassuring result as estimators allowing for cross-sectional dependence have never been applied in the energy literature. However, as there is no guarantee that this result will hold for other sectors and/or countries, future research would benefit from implementing estimators allowing for cross-sectional dependence, in order to assess the robustness of the estimates to factors which simultaneously affect more than one sector and/or country.

3.3 Environmental Kuznets Curves (EKCs) for Industrial Sectors

3.3.1 *Evidence from EKC CO$_2$ Studies*

From a number of surveys on EKCs, one can conclude that the initial enthusiasm for this hypothesis now seems to be turning into growing scepticism—the title of Stern (2004) is a case in point. Several authors have concluded that the statistical analysis on which EKCs are based is not robust, for example, Galeotti et al. (2006) and Stern (2004). Copeland and Taylor (2004) doubt the existence of a simple and predictable relationship between pollution and per capita income. According to Ekins (1997), unequivocal empirical evidence for EKCs is very scant. However, other authors take a more positive view. The World Bank Development Report (IBRD 1992) shows that the de-linking implied by EKCs has emerged for several pollutants in OECD countries. Similar conclusions have been reported by a number of empirical studies quoted in de Bruyn et al. (1998).

Leaving aside the uncertainty on the validity of the EKC hypothesis, a number of issues impede a clear policy conclusion. Ekins (1997) points out that despite increases in economic activity in developed countries, reviews of overall environmental quality show continuing and serious environmental degradation on all fronts. In addition, even when growth is likely to have reduced emissions, there is no reason to assume that this process will continue in the future (Bruvoll and Medin 2003), as it could be a temporary phenomenon due to abatement opportunities becoming exhausted or too expensive (Pezzey 1989). The result would be an 'N'-shaped curve which has been estimated for a number of pollutants—see summary table in Ekins (1997).

Table 3.2. Functional relationships and parameter restrictions in EKC studies

Functional Relationship	Parameter Restrictions
No relationship	$\beta_1=\beta_2=\beta_3 0$
Monotonically increasing or decreasing relationship	$\beta_1>0, \beta_2=\beta_3 0$ and $\beta_1<0, \beta_2=\beta_3 0$
Inverted U-shaped relationship	$\beta_1>0, \beta_2<0$
U-shape relationship	$\beta_1<0, \beta_2>0$
N-shaped relationship	$\beta_1>0, \beta_2<0$ and $\beta_3>0$
Inverted N-shaped relationship	$\beta_1<0, \beta_2>0$ and $\beta_3<0$

Source: Ekins (1997).

A reduced form single equation is normally used to test the relationship between pollution or environmental degradation and economic growth in the EKC framework. Most studies adopt a parametric approach, i.e. quadratic and cubic polynomials, using variables in levels or after taking logarithms

$$y_t = \alpha + \beta_1 x_t + \beta_2 x_t^2 + \beta_3 x_t^3 + \gamma z_t + \varepsilon_t \tag{3.1}$$

where y_t is an environmental indicator, x_t is a measure of economic activity, and z_t a vector of variables expected to influence the measure of environmental quality. When using a panel data set, the index i is added to all variables in the specification. Table 3.2 shows the parameter restrictions needed to obtain a certain functional relationship between economic activity and environmental quality. However, any conclusions on the relationship cannot be limited to an analysis of the parameters as they have to take into account the location of turning points. For example, an N-shaped functional form could describe an EKC relationship, if the second turning point occurs for values which are so far outside present and possible future values as to be of no practical relevance.

As an alternative to parametric specifications, one could estimate spline functions, i.e. linear functions allowed to have different parameters for different groups of observations, as in Aldy (2005), Schmalensee et al. (1998), Dijkgraaf and Vollebergh (2005), or use a non-parametric specification, i.e. a method estimating the regression locally, as in Taskin and Zaim (2000), Bertinelli and Strobl (2005), or Millimet et al. (2003). While on the one hand these approaches impose fewer restrictions on the shape of the empirical relationship, their disadvantages are related to data requirements and the so-called curse of dimensionality which comes into play when more than one explanatory variable is considered (Galeotti and Lanza 2005).

Carbon dioxide is a non-toxic gas, i.e. its emissions are not immediately damaging to health, and it causes global warming only in the long run. While some local pollutants can be reduced through end-of-pipe technologies, very little apart from fuel switching can be done at present to abate CO_2 without reducing fossil energy use (Yaguchi et al. 2007). In addition, widespread awareness of climate change is relatively recent and, being a global problem, its costs are borne externally. All these reasons cast doubt on why a CO_2 EKC should exist. However, Lantz and Feng (2006) quote about 15 studies supporting the existence of a CO_2 EKC and about ten which failed to do so, but they themselves find a U-shaped, rather than an inverted-U, relationship. The following subsections assess how the results from studies analysing the relationship between economic activity and CO_2 are influenced by the regressors included in the regression, the functional form, and the treatment of heterogeneity.

3.3.2 *The Impact of the Included Regressors*

Depending on the emission of interest, several additional explanatory variables have been inserted in (3.1) such as trade, political rights, and civil liberties, the contribution to national GDP of individual sectors, energy prices, and the amount of national natural resources. Additional variables in estimated EKCs might produce a better model, taking into account proximate and underlying causes of emissions (Stern 2004). In empirical studies, the estimation of the relationship between CO_2 and economic activity is greatly affected by the variables used in (3.1). Additional regressors seem to have a considerable impact on either or both of the value of the estimated parameters and the shape of the functional relationship between CO_2 and economic activity. For example, by extending quadratic and cubic terms to the population density and time trend, the finding of a U-shaped relationship in Lantz and Feng (2006) disappears. The functional form becomes U-inverted, although the coefficient on the second degree is not significant. Also in Aldy (2005) the shape is sensitive to the variables in the regression. In fact, taking into account the effect of trade casts doubts on whether per capita emissions fall appreciably with income during any part of the sample. The EKC appears to have higher peaks and much higher post-peak emissions. In some other instances, adding other variables affects only the value of the parameters but not the shape of the functional relationship, at least in a qualitative way. In Neumayer (2002), the turning point decreases from about \$850 million to about \$20 million per capita when introducing variables describing the endowment of natural resources and the weather conditions.

The addition of variables to (3.1) seems particularly justified when there is a clear link between the additional regressors and CO_2 emissions, as in the case of the energy price (Agras and Chapman 1999) or trade (see Aldy 2005 and Talukdar and Meisner 2001). On the other hand, more attention should be paid to the issue of exogeneity of the variables. Very few studies perform statistical tests, which can be implemented in a Vector Autoregression (VAR) or in a one-equation setting (see e.g. Azomahou et al. 2006; Cole et al. 1997; or Pesaran et al. 2001). Weak exogeneity of the regressors can also indirectly be tested by using a Chow test or by assessing the stability of the coefficients of the equation when estimated on a recursive sample (Ericsson et al. 1991).

Another issue which has not attracted much attention in the literature is the derivative nature of CO_2. As emissions are caused by burning fossil fuels, it seems interesting to control for the effect of energy consumption in (3.1). Sun (1999) argues that CO_2 EKCs derive mainly from the peak theory of energy intensity, i.e. energy intensity first increases in the period of industrialization, reaches a maximum, and then decreases. This reflects the structural shifts from heavy to light industry and the increased importance of the service sectors. In Sun (1999), the CO_2 EKC is just a reflection of an historical pattern of energy intensity. By introducing energy consumption as an independent variable, one can assess how the relationship between CO_2 and economic activity is influenced by factors other than energy consumption.

3.3.3 *The Impact of Functional Forms*

The results from CO_2 EKC studies in the literature do not tend to be qualitatively affected by using variables in levels or in logs. Holtz-Eakin and Selden (1995) and Cole et al. (1997) estimate an in-sample monotonous relationship in both a quadratic model in logs and the same model in levels. For both developed and developing countries, Galeotti and Lanza (2005) estimated an inverted U-shaped relationship in both the linear and the log-linear model, with rather similar turning points. However, in the case of the OECD countries, a turning point can be estimated only for the log-linear specification. Also the adoption of a piecewise linear function seems to have only a moderate influence on the results of the studies—see, for example, Aldy (2005), Moomaw and Unruh (1997), and Vollebergh et al. (2005).

In Azomahou et al. (2006), the non-parametric estimator and the first-difference estimator applied on a cubic functional form agreed on CO_2 emissions being monotonously increasing. However, according to the fixed effect estimator applied on a cubic functional form, the relationship has an inverted U shape, with its peak well within the sample range. In Vollebergh et al. (2005), for values of economic activity higher than 1990 $20,000, CO_2 emissions increase when using a semi-parametric estimator but decrease when using a two-way pooled estimator applied on a cubic function. However, Vollebergh et al. (2005) point out the very wide confidence bands of the non-parametric estimator for the observations in the upper tail of the distribution. The authors rely on the (in this instance) more accurate parametric method to assess the existence of within-sample turning points which could be estimated for 16 out of the 24 countries.

Overall, the functional form does not seem very influential on the qualitative outcome of the studies assessing the relationship between economic activity and CO$_2$ emissions. This statement is particularly accurate in the case of the choice between linear and log-linear models, and between standard polynomials and spline functions. The use of non-parametric estimators tends to produce different results from those obtained from standard polynomial models. However, it is not clear whether the performance of parametric estimators is negatively influenced by the number of observations in the sample.

3.3.4 *The Impact of Heterogeneity*

A final issue which affects empirical studies using panel data sets is the treatment of heterogeneity. Pooled estimators, for example, the fixed or the random effect model, impose a common shape and slope on the relationship between environmental quality and economic activity, thus implying the same pattern of development with respect to emissions (Leifman and Heil 2005). The hypothesis of homogeneity has been rejected in Dijkgraaf et al. (2005) for CO$_2$ in a panel of OECD countries, in List and Gallet (1999) for nitrogen oxides (NO$_x$) and sulphur dioxide (SO$_2$) in the USA, and in Aldy (2005) for CO$_2$ emissions in the USA. In a parametric setting, heterogeneity can be taken into account by using heterogeneous estimators such as those applied in Section 3.2. From a theoretical point of view, if EKCs are the product of a Solow model incorporating progress in abatement technologies, the emission path, the peak emission level, and the turning point will all be country specific (Brock and Taylor 2004).

A number of authors have found substantial heterogeneity in their estimated CO$_2$ EKCs (Aldy 2005; Martínez-Zarzoso and Bengochea-Morancho 2004; and Vollebergh et al. 2005). However, differences between the results from heterogeneous and homogeneous estimators have not always been as marked as one would expect—see, for example, Aldy (2005) and Vollebergh et al. (2005). This could be due to the fact that the fixed and random effect estimators are consistent if applied to a heterogeneous static model (Pesaran and Smith 1995). On the other hand, evidence from Martínez-Zarzoso and Bengochea-Morancho (2004) denies this asymptotic result, as the MG and Pooled Mean Group (PMG) estimate an N-shaped relationship, while the fixed effect corroborates the EKC hypothesis.

3.3.5 *EKC CO$_2$ Estimations for Industrial Sectors*

In this study, the relationship between CO$_2$ and economic activity is assessed at the sectoral level, more precisely for ten British and German industrial subsectors over the period 1978–2004. A number of authors, for example, Millimet et al. (2003) and Vollebergh et al. (2005), have stressed the importance of the modelling strategy adopted in the estimation of EKCs. On the basis of the conclusions from the previous section, the focus of this chapter is on the variables used in the estimation. In particular, we assess the influence of energy price and of the consumption of four production inputs, namely, materials, labour, service, and capital, on the relationship between economic activity and CO_2 emissions. We also verify whether economic activity has a role to play in explaining CO_2 emissions when controlling for energy consumption. In a panel context, Aldy (2005) and Perman and Stern (2003) have stressed the importance of estimating the EKC relationship for each panel member as well as for the whole panel (Aldy 2005; Perman and Stern 2003). Following this advice, we estimated the relationship between CO_2 and economic activity for each sector assessed in the study, and for the panel as a whole. However, the panel estimation implemented through the estimators in Section 3.2.1 is not discussed here, as it tended to produce non-statistically significant results.

Table 3.3 displays the industrial sectors modelled in this study. As mentioned above, the sample spans the 1978–2004 time period. Data for CO_2 consumption were sourced from IEA (2006b).[6] This database contains information on a number of sectors which have not been assessed in this study, mainly because the CO_2 consumption time series presents a number of breaks which are probably due to limitations in the data collection process. Therefore estimations are carried out for only four German and six British sectors. Data on gross output, and on the consumption of materials, labour, services, and capital were taken from the EU KLEMS database. For most of the sectors used in this study, these data are available only from 1978 onwards. Timmer et al. (2007) provide a succinct overview of the methodology used to build the database. All models have been estimated using the logarithms of the indices of the variables mentioned above. The base year is 1995.

Table 3.3. Industrial sectors modelled in Section 3.3

Identifier	Sectors	ISIC Taxonomy	Germany	UK
FT	Food and Tobacco	15–16	√	√
PPP	Pulp, Paper and Printing	21–22	√	√
MAC	Machinery	28–32	√	√
TRA	Transport Equipment	34–35	√	
CHE	Chemicals	24		√
NMM	Non-Metallic Minerals	26		√
CON	Construction	45		√

[6] As discussed in Galeotti et al. (2005), the IEA data set is likely to be more precise than the data set from the Carbon Dioxide Information Analysis Center (CDIAC) of the Oak Ridge National Laboratory, which has been used in a number of empirical studies.

According to Millimet et al. (2003) and Vollebergh et al. (2005), the modelling strategy adopted has a considerable effect on the results from EKC studies. On the basis of the findings from Section 3.3, and following the predominant practice in the literature, this study uses only cubic and quadratic specifications, with and without a linear trend. In Section 3.3, the variables used in the regression were found to be the most important factors influencing the shape of CO$_2$ EKCs. For this reason we estimated the basic EKC specification (3.1), and specifications with additional variables taking into account factors which are believed to influence the relationship between CO$_2$ emissions and the economic activity of industrial sectors. As CO$_2$ emissions are produced from fossil fuels, energy price seems likely to affect the relationship between economic activity and CO$_2$ emissions (Agras and Chapman 1999). By comparing the results from (3.1) and from

$$y_t = \alpha + \beta_1 x_t + \beta_2 x_t^2 + \beta_3 x_t^3 + \beta_4 p_t + \varepsilon_t, \tag{3.2}$$

where p_t is the energy price, we can assess the importance of the energy price in CO$_2$ EKCs.

Sun (1999) argues that 'the CO$_2$ EKC is just a reflection of a historical pattern of energy intensity [. . . . as the] CO$_2$ emission Kuznets curve merely reflects the peak-theory of energy intensity', i.e. energy intensity first increases, reaches a maximum, and then decreases. If CO$_2$ EKCs are simply caused by the historical pattern of energy consumption, economic activity should not be statistically significant after controlling for the effect of energy consumption, e_t, in

$$y_t = \alpha + \beta_1 x_t + \beta_2 x_t^2 + \beta_3 x_t^3 + \beta_4 e_t + \varepsilon_t \tag{3.3}$$

By comparing the results from (3.1) and from (3.3), we can assess whether the argument in Sun (1999) is supported by the data set used in this chapter.

A considerable number of studies have assessed the relationship among production inputs, with inputs normally divided into capital, labour, energy, and materials (Berndt and Wood 1975). A recent review can be found in Broadstock et al. (2007). Considering this well-established literature branch focused on input substitution, it seems desirable to assess the effect of adding the consumption of production inputs to an ordinary CO$_2$ EKC, which can be rewritten as

$$y_t = \alpha + \beta_1 x_t + \beta_2 x_t^2 + \beta_3 x_t^3 + \beta_4 mat_t + \beta_5 lab_t + \beta_6 ser_t + \beta_7 cap_t + \varepsilon_t \tag{3.4}$$

where mat_t, lab_t, ser_t, and cap_t indicate the consumption of materials, labour, services, and capital. By comparing the results from (3.1) and (3.4), we can assess whether the CO$_2$ EKC is robust to the inclusion of variables, taking into account the inputs used in the production process.

Each of the equations above was estimated using a cubic and a quadratic functional form, with and without a linear time trend. Model selection has been implemented on the basis of the minimization of the information criteria. For each selected model, the relationship between CO_2 emissions and economic activity was plotted for the values of economic activity observed in the sample. In order to facilitate comparison, plotted functional forms have been shifted so that CO_2 emission is zero at the average of economic activity observed in the sample. This does not affect the shape of the functional form, simply its location in a Cartesian system.

Tables 3.4a and 3.4b and the EKC curves in Figures 3.2a and 3.2b present the results from the estimation of (3.1), i.e. the EKC model incorporating economic activity only. As one can see from the EKC curves in Figure 3.2a, the relationship between economic activity and CO_2 emissions in the German industrial sectors tends to have an N shape. In the case of the Pulp, Paper and Printing sector, CO_2 emissions are about to reach the second turning point, while in the case of the Machinery and Transport sectors, they are decisively heading upwards. In the case of the Food and Tobacco sector, the relationship between economic activity and CO_2 emission has an inverted N shape. Emissions are beyond the second turning point and are heading downwards. As one can see in Table 3.4a, all coefficients are statistically significant at the 90% level or above. A negative linear trend is present in all sectors except the Pulp, Paper and Printing sector.

In the case of the British sectors, considerable variation can be observed in the relationship between CO_2 emissions and economic activity (see Table 3.4b). Comparing the coefficients in Table 3.4b and the criteria in Table 3.3, an N shape is estimated in the Food and Tobacco sector, an inverted N shape in the Pulp, Paper and Printing, the Machinery, and the Non-Metallic Mineral sectors, an inverted U shape in the Chemical sector and a U shape in the Construction sector. The EKC curves in Figure 3.2b show that, among the three inverted N curves, the recent level of economic activity in the Pulp, Paper and Printing sector is near the level at which the second turning point

Table 3.4a. Estimated coefficients and t-statistics (in parentheses) of the relationship between economic activity and CO_2 emissions for the German industrial sectors

	FT	PPP	MAC	TRA
Constant	9253.73	−1802.04	−1325.28	−238.28
	(3.10) [**]	(−2.75) [**]	(−1.68) [+]	(−4.85) [**]
Economic Activity	−5920.60	1192.01	860.44	158.52
	(−3.07) [**]	(2.75) [**]	(1.67) [+]	(4.97) [**]
(Economic Activity)^2	1263.12	−261.86	−185.52	−34.30
	(3.06) [**]	(−2.74) [**]	(−1.65) [+]	(−4.98) [**]
(Economic Activity)^3	−89.81	19.15	13.34	2.47
	(−3.04) [**]	(2.73) [**]	(1.64) [+]	(4.98) [**]
Time Trend	−0.03		−0.07	−0.05
	(−19.22) [**]		(−4.56) [**]	(−4.29) [**]

Note: The symbols [+], [*] and [**] denotes statistical significance at the 90%, 95% and 99% confidence levels.

Table 3.4b. Estimated coefficients and t-statistics (in parentheses) of the relationship between economic activity and CO$_2$ emissions for the British industrial sectors

	FT	PPP	MAC	CHE	NMM	CON
Constant	−1789.31	4251.39	2296.21	−11.59	946.66	61.27
	(−1.59)	(2.52) $^{(*)}$	(1.63)	(−0.61)	(0.56)	(3.69) $^{(**)}$
Economic Activity	1256.06	−2847.61	−1541.09	9.07	−601.42	−26.68
	(1.65) $^{(+)}$	(−2.48) $^{(*)}$	(−1.61)	(1.05)	(−0.53)	(−3.40) $^{(**)}$
(Economic Activity)^2	−292.69	635.96	345.87	−1.21	127.38	3.16
	(−1.71) $^{(+)}$	(2.45) $^{(*)}$	(1.60)	(−1.24)	(0.50)	(3.40) $^{(**)}$
(Economic Activity)^3	22.70	−47.30	−25.90		−8.93	
	(1.76) $^{(+)}$	(−2.41) $^{(*)}$	(−1.60)		(−0.47)	
Time Trend	−0.03	−0.03	−0.03		−0.07	−0.05
	(−9.01) $^{(**)}$	(−2.65) $^{(**)}$	(−3.56) $^{(**)}$		(−8.90)	(−4.63) $^{(**)}$

Note: See note to Table 3.4a.

occurs; in the Machinery sector, emissions are steadily heading downwards; in the Non-Metallic Mineral sector, emissions are in the increasing portion of the curve. Given the levels of economic activity observed in the sample, emissions are also increasing in the case of the Food and Tobacco and the Construction sectors. In the Chemical sector, emissions are in the decreasing portion of an inverted U curve. As one can see in Table 3.4b, the coefficients of the curves are not statistically significant in the Chemical and Non-Metallic Minerals sectors. In the Machinery and the Food and Tobacco sectors, the coefficients are significant at the 10% level only.[7] One can conclude that in about half the sectors assessed in this study, CO$_2$ emissions have most recently shown an overall decreasing trend, although in some instances periods of increasing emissions in the presence of increasing sectoral output can be observed. This can be observed in the German and British Pulp, Paper and Printing sectors, the German Food and Tobacco sector and the British Chemical and the Machinery sectors. In the last two sectors, however, coefficients are not statistically significant.

From Figures 3.2a and 3.2b, one can also observe the effect of energy price on the relationship between economic activity and CO$_2$ emissions. The curve labelled EKC P is obtained by estimating model (3.2), which includes the energy price among the regressors, while the EKC curve plots the relationship obtained from the estimation of (3.1). The most striking difference between models (3.1) and (3.2) can be observed in the case of the UK Chemical sector. According to (3.2), CO$_2$ emissions are now increasing as output increases, while according to (3.1), CO$_2$ emissions decrease with economic activity. A change in the functional form can also be observed in the case of one of

---

[7] More precisely, the coefficients in the Machinery sector are not statistically significant, although all t-statistics fall very close to the 10% critical value, i.e. 1.64.

the two specifications selected for the British Non-Metallic Mineral sector, although the within-sample profile of emissions does not change. A slight change in the plot of the Pulp, Paper and Printing sector is also observed. In the German Transport sector and in the UK Food and Tobacco and Machinery sectors, the effect of adding the energy price in the model is virtually nil. With regard to the coefficients, a slight decrease in statistical significance can be observed in the UK Food and Tobacco, and Pulp, Paper and Printing sectors. Introducing the energy price makes the coefficients in the German Machinery sector not statistically significant. Conversely, the coefficients in the UK Chemical and Non-Metallic Minerals sectors become statistically significant. One can also notice that in half of the sectors, the energy price coefficient fails to be statistically significant; hence the small difference between some of the plots in Figures 3.2a and 3.2b.

In contrast to Agras and Chapman (1999), the relationship between economic activity and CO_2 emissions does not seem to be very influenced by the energy price, despite this variable being statistically significant in half the industrial sectors. The British Chemical and the German Pulp, Paper and Printing sectors are two noticeable exceptions. Considering that CO_2 emissions are produced by burning fossil fuels and that energy consumption is affected by price, energy price would be expected to affect CO_2 emissions. However, when using quadratic and cubic functional forms normally employed in EKC studies, a marked effect of price on the relationship between economic activity and CO_2 emissions cannot be detected in the data set analysed in this chapter (Tables 3.5a, 3.5b). This is a reassuring conclusion with regard to the validity of the results from the EKC literature, as most of the

Table 3.5a. Estimated coefficients and t-statistics (in parentheses) of the relationship between economic activity and CO_2 emissions for the German industrial sectors when controlling for the energy price effect

	FT	PPP		MAC	TRA
Constant	8604.47	−1604.33	−1247.76	−1596.50	−225.91
	(3.53) [**]	(−2.69) [**]	(−2.21) [*]	(−1.52)	(−3.78) [**]
Economic Activity	−5506.42	1049.15	808.63	1041.24	150.31
	(−3.50) [**]	(2.66) [**]	(2.16) [*]	(1.51)	(3.88) [**]
(Economic Activity)^2	1175.27	−227.32	−173.22	−225.39	−32.55
	(3.48) [**]	(−2.61) [**]	(−2.09) [*]	(−1.49)	(−3.94) [**]
(Economic Activity)^3	−83.59	16.39	12.34	16.27	2.35
	(−3.46) [**]	(2.55) [*]	(2.02) [*]	(1.48)	(4.00) [**]
Energy Price	−0.43	−0.51	−0.70	−0.34	0.10
	(−2.18) [*]	(−2.32) [*]	(−2.58) [**]	(−0.60)	(0.33)
Time Trend	−0.03		−0.01	−0.07	−0.05
	(−19.18) [**]		(−1.54)	(−4.16) [**]	(−4.46) [**]

Note: see note to Table 3.4a.

Table 3.5b. Estimated coefficients and t-statistics (in parentheses) of the relationship between economic activity and CO_2 emissions for the British industrial sectors when controlling for the energy price effect.

	FT	PPP	MAC	CHE	NMM	CON
Constant	-1828.57 (-1.52)	3515.70 (1.95) (+)	2307.57 (1.65) (+)	-2847.54 (-4.02) (**)	-2544.02 (-1.85) (+)	55.66 (3.38) (**)
Economic Activity	1281.81 (1.58)	-2355.01 (-1.92) (+)	-1546.89 (-1.64)	1938.66 (4.02) (**)	1735.20 (1.88) (+)	-23.13 (-2.88) (**)
(Economic Activity)^2	-298.29 (-1.63)	526.46 (1.90) (+)	346.66 (1.62)	-438.04 (-4.01) (**)	-393.32 (-1.90) (+)	2.70 (2.81) (**)
(Economic Activity)^3	23.11 (1.69) (+)	-39.20 (-1.87) (+)	-25.92 (-1.61)	32.97 (4.00) (**)	29.73 (1.93)	
Energy Price	-0.03 (-0.18)	-0.45 (-0.99)	0.12 (0.48)	-1.17 (-4.51) (**)	-0.73 (-2.96) (**)	-0.24 (-1.53)
Time Trend	-0.03 (-8.10) (**)	-0.03 (-2.45) (*)	-0.03 (-3.21) (**)	-0.05 (-3.89) (**)	-0.08 (-10.11) (**)	-0.04 (-3.19) (**)

Note: See note to Table 3.4a.

63

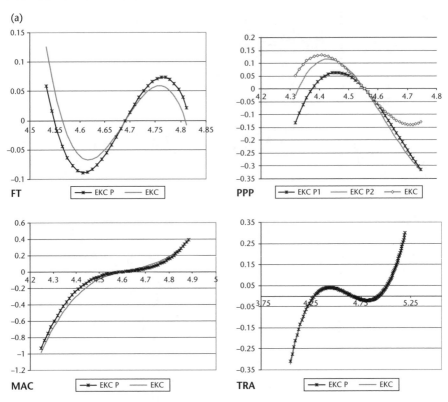

Figure 3.2a The relationship between economic activity and CO_2 emissions in the German industrial sectors

Notes: The plot labelled EKC P is obtained from the estimation of (3.2), i.e. taking into account the effect of the energy price, while the plot labelled EKC is obtained from the estimation of an EKC not controlling for the effect of the energy price. Two models (EKC P1 and EKC P2) are presented when the information criteria could not agree on the specification that fits the data best.

studies do not incorporate price but, for reasons to be given later, it says little about the likely effect on the sectors of an environmental tax reform (ETR).

Figures 3.3a and 3.3b and Tables 3.6a and 3.6b display the results from estimating model (3.3). For ease of comparison, the figure reports also the plot from model (3.1) (which is of course the same as in Figures 3.2a and 3.2b). In one instance, the Transport sector in Germany, the qualitative results from models (3.1) and (3.3) do not differ much, although the range of the emissions imputable to economic activity is somewhat reduced. In all other sectors, the effect of introducing energy consumption among the regressors is much more marked. In the British Construction sector, due to a change in the functional form, emissions imputable to economic activity still increase, but at a much lower rate. In the Pulp, Paper and Printing, the Non-Metallic

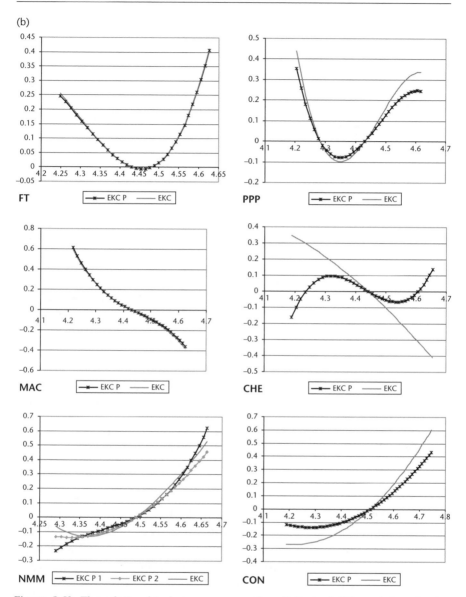

Figure 3.2b The relationship between economic activity and CO_2 emissions in the British industrial sectors

Note: See note to Figure 3.2a.

Minerals, and the Machinery sectors in the UK, and the Pulp, Paper and Printing sector in Germany, the relationship between CO_2 and economic activity shows a within-sample inverted U shape, although economic activity is approaching a second turning point in the last sector. After adding energy consumption, the CO_2 emissions of the UK Chemical sector increase with

(a)

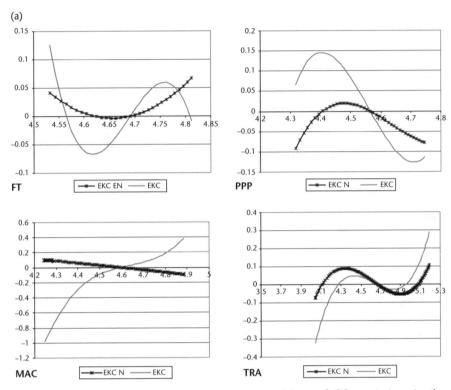

Figure 3.3a The relationship between economic activity and CO_2 emissions in the German industrial sectors

Notes: The plot labelled EKC N is obtained from the estimation of (3.3), i.e. taking into account the effect of energy intensity, while the plot labelled EKC is obtained from the estimation of an EKC not controlling for the effect of energy intensity.

economic activity, while emissions decrease with economic activity according to an ordinary CO_2 EKC model. A similarly drastic change in the pattern of emissions imputable to economic activity in (3.1) and (3.3) can also be observed in a number of other sectors, for example, the German Machinery sector and in Food and Tobacco sector of both countries. In terms of the coefficients of the regressions, economic activity is not significant in the German Pulp, Paper and Printing and the Machinery sectors, although the t-statistics fall rather close to the 90% critical value in the former sector. As should be expected, all coefficients on energy consumption are statistically significant.

One can conclude that our results do not support the view that CO_2 EKCs derive mainly from the peak theory of energy intensity (Sun 1999). In fact, after controlling for energy consumption, economic activity fails to have a statistically significant effect on CO_2 emissions only in three out of the ten sectors assessed in this chapter, namely the German Pulp, Printing and Paper

(b)

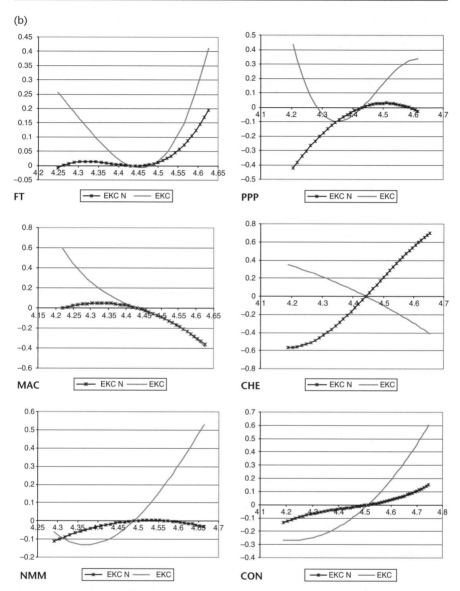

Figure 3.3b The relationship between economic activity and CO_2 emissions in the British industrial sectors.

Note: See note to Figure 3.3a.

and Machinery sectors, and the British Non-Metallic Minerals sector.[8] In addition, as in the case of the ordinary CO_2 EKCs, an inverted U shape in

---

[8] In this sector, however, economic activity was not statistically significant even in the specification which did not incorporate energy consumption.

Table 3.6a. Estimated coefficients and t-statistics (in parentheses) of the relationship between economic activity and CO_2 emissions for the German industrial sectors when controlling for the effect of energy intensity

	FT	PPP	MAC	TRA
Constant	61.71	−685.03	−1.17	−160.46
	(2.29) (*)	(−1.59)	(−0.41)	(−6.49) (**)
Economic Activity	−27.10	444.35	0.05	104.86
	(−2.36) (*)	(1.55)	(0.04)	(6.43) (**)
(Economic Activity)^2	2.91	−96.03	−0.04	−22.79
	(2.35) (*)	(−1.52)	(−0.28)	(−6.50) (**)
(Economic Activity)^3			6.91	1.64
			(1.48)	(6.52) (**)
Energy consumption	1.35	1.17	1.38	1.21
	(15.81) (**)	(6.79) (**)	(44.12) (**)	(7.26) (**)
Time Trend	−0.01	−0.02		−0.04
	(−7.95) (**)	(−6.01) (**)		(−6.14) (**)

Note: See note to Table 3.4a.

Table 3.6b. Estimated coefficients and t-statistics (in parentheses) of the relationship between economic activity and CO_2 emissions for the British industrial sectors when controlling for the effect of energy intensity

	FT	PPP	MAC	CHE	NMM	CON
Constant	−1390.92	−102.22	−85.04	1308.25	−40.66	−257.49
	(−3.74) (**)	(−2.78) (**)	(−6.53) (**)	(2.67) (**)	(−0.91)	(−3.84) (**)
Economic Activity	952.58	44.33	39.37	−883.38	17.73	173.85
	(3.76) (**)	(2.71) (**)	(6.98) (**)	(−2.64) (**)	(0.89)	(3.89) (**)
(Economic Activity)^2	−217.36	−4.92	−4.55	197.99	−1.96	−39.13
	(−3.78) (**)	(−2.66) (**)	(−7.23) (**)	(2.59) (**)	(−0.86)	(−3.94) (**)
(Economic Activity)^3	16.53			−14.73		2.94
	(3.80) (**)			(−2.54) (*)		(4.00) (**)
Energy consumption	0.98	1.64	1.11	1.16	1.16	0.98
	(8.81) (**)	(8.86) (**)	(11.52) (**)	(7.13) (**)	(4.94) (**)	(17.17) (**)
Time Trend	−0.02	−0.04	−0.01	−0.07	−0.02	−0.02
	(−9.06) (**)	(−12.35) (**)	(−4.83) (**)	(−7.44) (**)	(−1.35)	(−9.60) (**)

Note: See note to Table 3.4a.

the relationship between economic activity and CO_2 emissions can be observed only in about half of the sectors assessed in this study. Some doubts about our results are related to the fact that the parameters on energy consumption are well above unity. However, when estimating a panel relationship, the coefficient on energy consumption takes values closer to unity. These results are available upon request.

Including consumption of capital, labour, material, and services in the EKC relationship, i.e. estimating (3.4), has a considerable impact on the relationship between CO_2 emissions and economic activity. As one can see in Figure 3.4a, in all German sectors apart from the Machinery sector, the relationship between economic activity and CO_2 emissions is upward sloping. With regard to the results from the estimation (see Table 3.7a) in the Food and Tobacco and Machinery sectors, the correlation between labour consumption and CO$_2$ emissions is positive. As the consumption of labour has steadily decreased over the sample, this implies a decrease in CO$_2$ emissions. Coefficients on the consumption of services and materials are always negative, with the exception of the coefficient on services in the Transport sector. As the consumption of these two production factors has increased over the sample, this implies a reduction in CO$_2$ emissions. A reduction in CO$_2$ emissions is also caused by the increase in capital observed in the sample; with the exception of the transport sector, the estimates on the consumption of capital are negative and statistically significant. The consumption of the other production inputs does not tend to produce statistically significant coefficients.

The impact of adding production inputs to the regression is much smaller in the British industrial sectors, especially in the Food and Tobacco (FT), Chemical (CHE), Machinery (MAC), and Construction (CON) sectors (see Figure 3.4b). In the Pulp, Paper and Printing (PPP) and Non-Metallic Minerals (NMM) sectors, adding production inputs to the regression causes CO$_2$ emissions to decrease for the observations in the upper tail of the distribution of economic activity. As one can see in Table 3.7b, all coefficients on economic activity are statistically significant. When compared to Table 3.4b, one can notice the change in the significance levels of the coefficients on economic activity in the Chemical and Non-Metallic Mineral sectors. With regard to the coefficients

Table 3.7a. Estimated coefficients and t-statistics (in parentheses) of the relationship between economic activity and CO$_2$ emissions for the German industrial sectors when controlling for the effect of materials, labour, services and capital

	FT	PPP	MAC	TRA
Constant	92.93	−1443.86	−69.43	−198.33
	(3.54) [***]	(−2.25) [*]	(−2.18) [*]	(−1.83) [+]
Economic Activity	−35.27	952.18	34.05	134.66
	(−3.01) [***]	(2.23) [*]	(2.01) [*]	(1.87) [+]
(Economic Activity)^2	3.82	−207.40	−3.60	−28.95
	(2.97) [***]	(−2.19) [*]	(−2.22) [*]	(−1.89) [+]
(Economic Activity)^3		15.07		2.10
		(2.16) [*]		(1.92) [+]
Materials	−0.25	−0.44	−0.79	−1.65
	(−0.63)	(−0.95)	(−0.33)	(−3.41) [***]
Labour	0.24	−0.82	3.44	−0.40
	(0.55)	(−2.01) [*]	(1.59)	(−1.15)
Services	−0.04	−0.41	−0.45	0.31
	(−0.14)	(−1.00)	(−0.57)	(1.23)
Capital	−1.37	−0.42	−4.11	0.21
	(−4.81) [***]	(−1.72) [+]	(−2.41) [*]	(0.26)
Time Trend	−0.02		0.14	−0.05
	(−4.02) [***]		(1.85) [+]	(−1.77) [+]

Note: see note to Table 3.4a.

Table 3.7b. Estimated coefficients and t-statistics (in parentheses) of the relationship between economic activity and CO_2 emissions for the British industrial sectors when controlling for the effect of materials, labour, services and capital

	FT	PPP	MAC	CHE	NMM	CON
Constant	−3035.24	4287.55	2015.40	−76.94	3029.83	−1320.36
	(−2.54)	(1.71) (+)	(2.05) (*)	(−2.85) (**)	(2.57) (**)	(−2.33) (*)
Economic Activity	2093.15	−2910.68	−1355.16	39.62	−2058.36	916.71
	(2.59) (**)	(−1.71) (+)	(−2.03) (*)	(3.39) (**)	(−2.55) (**)	(2.34) (*)
(Economic Activity)^2	−480.50	658.37	304.29	−4.64	466.50	−211.20
	(−2.63) (**)	(1.71) (+)	(2.02) (*)	(−3.53) (**)	(2.53) (*)	(−2.34) (*)
(Economic Activity)^3	36.73	−49.63	−22.82		−35.17	16.21
	(2.68) (**)	(−1.70) (+)	(−2.01) (*)		(−2.51) (*)	(2.35) (*)
Materials	−0.02	0.08	−0.35	0.55	−0.17	0.51
	(−0.14)	(0.11)	(−4.51) (**)	(2.34) (*)	(−0.62)	(2.22) (*)
Labour	−0.24	0.43	−0.08	−0.50	0.34	0.31
	(−1.05)	(0.33)	(−0.26)	(−0.61)	(1.16)	(0.89)
Services	0.02	−0.13	−0.02	0.31	0.15	−0.04
	(0.22)	(−0.46)	(−0.22)	(0.72)	(1.76) (+)	(−0.37)
Capital	1.15	1.11	1.87	−0.91	−1.22	−0.80
	(2.51) (*)	(2.22) (*)	(3.35) (**)	(−2.68) (**)	(−2.14) (*)	(−1.94) (+)
Time Trend	−0.05	−0.05	−0.08		−0.03	−0.03
	(−5.38) (**)	(−1.45)	(−3.72) (**)		(−2.15) (*)	(−1.83) (+)

Notes: See note to Table 3.4a.

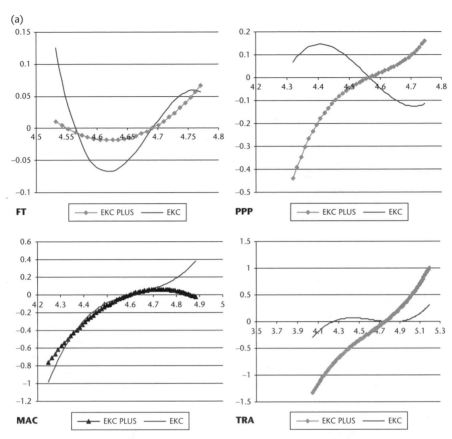

Figure 3.4a The relationship between economic activity and CO$_2$ emissions in the German industrial sectors

Notes: The plot labelled EKC PLUS is obtained from the estimation of (3.4), i.e. taking into account the effect of the consumption of capital, labour, materials, and services, while the plot labelled EKC is obtained from the estimation of an EKC not controlling for the effect of these production inputs.

on the production inputs, the consumption of labour is never statistically significant, while consumption of services is statistically significant at the 90% level only in the Non-Metallic Minerals sector. The consumption of materials is significant only in the Machinery, Chemical and Construction sectors, while the coefficients on capital are always statistically significant. Both production factors produce coefficients with positive sign in half the sectors, which implies an increase in CO$_2$ emissions as the consumption of capital and materials strongly increases in the sample.

By comparing the plots obtained from the estimation of (3.1) and (3.4), one can conclude that the shape of the relationship between economic activity and CO$_2$ emissions is affected by the consumption of materials, labour,

(b)

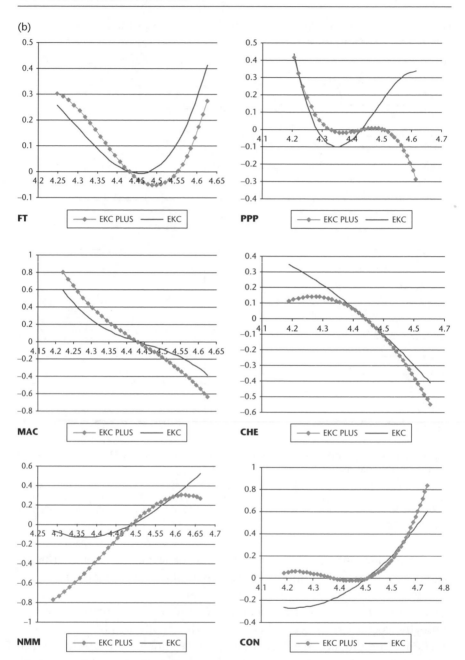

Figure 3.4b The relationship between economic activity and CO_2 emissions in the British industrial sectors

Notes: See note to Figure 3.4a.

services, and capital in about half the sectors assessed in this chapter. One sector (German PPP) displays a negative relationship between economic activity and CO$_2$ emissions when model (3.1) is estimated, but produces a positive relationship when the four input factors are added to the regression. In three sectors, estimating (3.4) causes a fall in CO$_2$ emissions for a high level of economic activity (German MAC, British PPP, NMM). In three other cases (German FT, Transport (TRA), British CON), however, the relationship between economic activity and CO$_2$ emissions takes a more upward shape when the effect of materials, labour, services, and capital is taken into account.

A number of conclusions can be drawn from the analysis presented above. First of all, the relationship between CO$_2$ and economic activity was found to differ widely across the sectors assessed in this chapter. In no instance could we find unequivocal evidence of a CO$_2$ EKC for all specifications used in this chapter. In about half the sectors, CO$_2$ emissions have shown an overall decreasing trend as output from the sector has increased, while in the remaining sectors CO$_2$ emissions have increased with the level of economic activity. Secondly, contrary to our expectations, energy price did not have much effect on the shape of the relationship between CO$_2$ and economic activity. This is a reassuring result, as most studies estimate CO$_2$ EKCs without controlling for energy price. Thirdly, not much evidence could be found supporting the hypothesis in Sun (1999), i.e. that CO$_2$ EKCs are mainly a by-product of the historical pattern of energy intensity. In fact, after controlling for energy consumption, economic activity was still significant in the EKC regression. We also discovered that the consumption of capital, materials, services, and labour in CO$_2$ emissions has a considerable influence on the shape of the relationship between CO$_2$ and economic activity.

3.4 Conclusions

According to the research presented in this chapter, one can conclude that the importance of the factors driving CO$_2$ emissions depends very much on the analytical framework. In the traditional energy demand setting in Section 3.2, we discovered that both economic activity and energy price have an important role in determining energy consumption. In the UK industrial sectors, our preferred choice for the long-run elasticity of economic activity and price are 0.52 and −0.64. Similar values are found in the case of the German sectors. This estimate for price elasticity leads us to conclude that policy instruments influencing the energy price are likely to be rather effective at constraining energy demand. Considering that in the short term inter-fuel substitutability is limited, CO$_2$ reductions are likely to be delivered through decreases in energy consumption. In other words, the estimates from this chapter increase confidence in the role played by energy taxes and trading permits in climate change policy.

Our literature review of CO_2 Environmental Kuznets Curves (EKCs) discussed the methodological approaches which have been adopted in the literature. Overall, the variables used in the regression—in addition to economic activity (x, say) and its powers (x^2, x^3 etc.)—were found to be the most important factor influencing the results of the studies. For this reason, the empirical estimation of CO_2 EKCs in this chapter has focused on the effect of additional regressors in the EKC framework. When estimating an ordinary CO_2 EKC, *i.e.* CO_2 *emissions regressed on economic activity and its powers*, the relationship between CO_2 and economic activity was found to differ widely across the ten industrial subsectors we assessed. Only in one sector, could we estimate a CO_2 EKC. In about half the sectors, CO_2 emissions have decreased as a function of increasing economic activity. In the remaining sectors, increasing output levels cause increasing levels of emissions. In addition, we discovered that energy price does not have a strong effect on the shape of the relationship between CO_2 and economic activity. We also could not find much evidence supporting the hypothesis in Sun (1999), that CO_2 EKCs are mainly a by-product of the historical pattern of energy intensity. After controlling for energy consumption, economic activity was still significant in the EKC model. Finally, similar to the case of ordinary CO_2 EKC, we concluded that the industrial subsectors we assessed show a great diversity in terms of the effect of the consumption of capital, materials, services, and labour in CO_2 emissions, and in terms of the shape of the relationship between CO_2 and economic activity when these factors are taken into account.

With regard to the determinants of CO_2 emissions, it is interesting to notice that our results on the effect of the energy price from the EKC estimation differ markedly from those obtained in the estimation of the energy demand. These contrasting results have a relatively simple, but important, explanation. In the CO_2 EKC estimation, we used the energy price as a proxy for CO_2 price. However, this will only be valid if the sectoral CO_2 intensity of energy use does not change. In fact, however, inter-fuel substitution caused by changing relative prices of fossil fuels, or by technological changes, may alter the CO_2 intensity of energy use considerably. In particular, any shift in fuel use towards electricity (the emissions from which are accounted to power stations rather than the sectors which consume the electricity) will greatly change a sector's apparent CO_2 emissions. These considerations largely invalidate the use of the energy price as a proxy for the CO_2 price. The contrasting results from CO_2 EKC and energy demand estimation can also be explained by the fact that the economic rationale for EKCs is not as strong as that for a demand function. Overall, our findings in relation to the role of energy price in CO_2

EKCs do not seem robust. Considering that the results from the energy demand estimation are confirmed by the results presented in Agnolucci (2010), overall we lean towards those results and we conclude that energy price is likely to have a strong effect on CO$_2$ emissions through reduction in the use of energy.

In the case of economic activity, the estimation of energy demand confirmed the role of this factor in the profile of energy consumption. In the CO$_2$ EKC estimation, we discovered that the relationship between economic activity and emissions cannot be easily generalized, as this relationship differs across sectors, and also across countries. This confirms the insights from Shafik (1994), who argues that the relationship between pollution and economic activity is the result of a number of factors, the importance of which can depend on institutional settings and available technologies. This conclusion has normally been drawn for national CO$_2$ emissions. In our study, we discovered that the same conclusion can be reached at the sectoral level.

Technical Appendix

In the panel approach employed in this chapter, in particular, we implement the fixed and random effect model, in both a dynamic and a static model, the First-Difference (FD) estimator, the Anderson-Hsiao (AH) estimator, the GMM (Generalized Method of Moments) estimator, as well as a number of estimators allowing for heterogeneity and for cross-sectional dependency. Among the former, we implement the Mean-Group (MG) estimator of Pesaran and Smith (1995) and the Random Coefficient Model of Swamy (1970). The main advantage of using heterogeneous estimators is related to the fact that homogeneous estimators are inconsistent if the parameters are heterogeneous and the model is dynamic (Pesaran and Smith 1995). Heterogeneity may stem from omitted common variables or global shocks which causes cross-sectional dependency in the data set. When not taken into account, the parameters are estimated inconsistently if the common factors in the data set are correlated with the regressors in the model. In order to assess the effect of common factors on the coefficients, this study uses a number of estimators where energy demand is estimated after removing cross-sectional dependence. These approaches comprise both homogeneous and heterogeneous estimators.

The estimation uses data in logarithms. For all models, specifications with and without a linear time trend have been estimated. Model selection has been carried out using information criteria among the models with coefficients which conform to economic theory. All estimators have been computed with robust standard errors when tests of serial correlation and heteroskedasticity were significant. The significance of the long-run parameters has been assessed by estimating the model after applying the Bewley transformation (Bewley 1979).

Among the static pooled estimators normally used in the literature, this study uses the Fixed (FE) and the Random (RE) Effect estimators,[9] and the First Difference (FD) estimators.[10] In the case of dynamic models,

$$y_{it} = \alpha_i + \rho y_{it-1} + x'_{it}\beta + \varepsilon_{it} \tag{3.5}$$

this study uses the FE and RE estimators, the Anderson-Hsiao (AH), and the GMM estimator.[11] As the lagged dependent variable in (3.5) is correlated with the disturbances, the FE estimator is no longer consistent if the panel is observed over a short period (Nickell 1981). The Anderson and Hsiao (AH) estimator is consistent, although not efficient, when t or n tends to infinity (Anderson and Hsiao 1982). However, when t tends to infinity, the FE estimator is also consistent. The GMM approach (Arrelano and Bond 1991) increases efficiency by using additional instruments. The one-step and two-step GMM estimators differ with respect to the weighting matrix used in the estimation.

Another bias in the estimation of (3.5) arises when parameters are heterogeneous. In this setting, pooled estimators are inconsistent even with large t (Pesaran and Smith 1995). Heterogeneity can be allowed by the Mean Group estimator (Pesaran and Smith 1995) and the Random Coefficient estimator (Swamy 1970). The Mean Group (MG) estimator, which is computed by estimating one regression for each cross-section and averaging the parameters, has the drawback of being rather sensitive to outliers in the estimates[12] (Smith and Fuertes 2004). It is worth mentioning that the difference between the MG and the RC estimator goes to zero as t goes to infinity.

Unobserved heterogeneity can be introduced by common shocks influencing all units, possibly to a different degree. These shocks also introduce cross-sectional dependence in the errors. If shocks are correlated with the regressors, estimators which do not take common factors into account will be inconsistent. Some of the estimators which can be used in this setting are the Fixed Effect with Principal Components (FE-PC) of Coakley et al. (2002), the Mean Group with Principal Components (MG-PC), the Demeaned Mean Group (DMG), and the Common Correlated Effect Mean Group

---

[9] Three specifications have been estimated, i.e. one assuming a cross-section specific intercept and linear trend (two-way model), another maintaining a cross-section specific intercept but imposing a common linear trend, and the last with a cross-section specific intercept only. The last two models are examples of the one-way model. Following common practice in the literature, the choice between the FE and the RE estimators has been implemented through the Hausman test.

[10] The FD estimator has been estimated in models with an intercept and without an intercept, i.e. corresponding to the one-way model with and without a common linear trend.

[11] Like every other estimator, the one- and two-step GMM estimator has been computed in both the model with intercept and trend, and the model with intercept only. As the intercept can be eliminated either by first-differencing or through the orthogonality conditions, the sensitivity of the estimates has been assessed by running models based on both transformations. In the case of the one-step estimator, robust estimators have been used in the presence of serial correlation in the disturbances. In the case of the two-step estimators, only the weights described in Arellano-Bond (1991) have been used.

[12] In the case of the static model, MG elasticities are equal to the average of the parameters of each cross-section. In the case of the dynamic model, the long-run MG elasticities are computed from the long-run elasticities of each cross-section.

(CMG) (Pesaran 2006). A thorough discussion of these estimators can be found in Coakley et al. (2006). In the FE-PC estimator, common factors are extracted through principal components from the residuals of the static regressions run for each cross-section in the panel.[13] The pooled estimator is run after adding the principal components to the model for the panel. The assumption of homogeneity can be relaxed by estimating the MG-PC estimator. Another approach to the estimation of models affected by common factors requires the use of demeaned data. The DMG estimator is an MG estimator run on data obtained after subtracting the cross-sectional average from the original observations. Finally, the CMG estimator (Pesaran 2006) is obtained by adding the cross-sectional average of the dependent and independent variables to the model for the whole panel.

Tables A3.1a and A3.1b present the values and the 95% confidence intervals of the parameters obtained from the panel estimators used in this study. Only estimates of coefficients which conform to economic theory are reported in the tables. Detailed results for all estimators are available upon request. In the tables a number of coefficients are not statistically significant, particularly when using the short sample (see Table A3.1a). In the German sector, the price coefficient is never significant, while the coefficient on economic activity is significant in a number of instances, its value ranging between 0.37 (FD and the GMM estimators) and 0.88 (AH estimators). It is worth pointing out that the AH estimator is poorly determined—as shown by the wide confidence intervals. Note too that the coefficient is markedly smaller than those obtained from the other estimators. Pesaran and Smith (1995) show that the application of homogeneous estimators in dynamic heterogeneous models causes overestimation of the long-run effect. This bias can explain the greater size of the AH coefficient, although the parameters from the GMM and the dynamic pooled

Table A3.1a. Long-run parameters and 95% confidence intervals (in parentheses) from the estimators discussed in Section 3.2

	Germany (1991–2004)		
	GVA	Price	Trend
FD	0.37 [(*)] (0.17 – 0.58)	– 0.12 (–0.30 – 0.07)	
Dynamic FE or RE	−0.49 [(*)] (0.11 – 0.87)	– 0.31 (–0.88 – 0.27)	
AH	0.88 [(*)] /0.76	−1.05/−0.84	
	(0.18 – 1.59) / (–0.05 – 1.57)	(–2.76 – 0.67) / (–2.78 – 1.11)	
GMM	0.38 [(*)] / 0.57 [(*)]	−0.31 / −0.23	−0.01 (–0.03 – 0.00)
	(0.00 – 0.76) / (0.05–1.09)	(–0.99 – 0.37) /(–0.96 – 0.49)	
Dynamic RCM	0.23 (–5.06 – 5.52)	−0.04 (–7.66 – 7.75)	
MG–PC	0.22 (–0.25 – 0.69)	−0.06 (–0.32 – 0.21)	
DMG	0.55 [(*)] (0.26 – 0.85)	−0.42 (–1.23 – 0.38)	
CMG	0.33 (–0.10 – 0.75)	−0.36 (–0.97 – 0.26)	0.01 (0.00 – 0.02)

Note: (*) denotes statistical significance at the 95% level.

[13] When using principal components to model cross-sectoral dependence, specifications with one and two principal components were estimated.

Table A3.1b. Long-run parameters and 95% confidence intervals (in parentheses) from the estimators discussed in Section 3.2

	UK (1978–2004)		
	GVA	Price	Trend
Static FE or RE	0.45 [*] (0.15 – 0.75)	−0.39 [*] (−0.65 – −0.12)	−0.02 (−0.03 – −0.02)
FD	0.57 [*] (0.35 – 0.79)	−0.43 [*] (−0.61 – −0.25)	
Dynamic FE or RE	0.58 [*] (0.19 – 0.96)	−1.18 [*] (−1.88 – −0.48)	−0.03 (−0.04 – −0.02)
AH	1.03 (−1.47 – 3.53)	−1.34 (−4.42 – 1.74)	
GMM	0.42 / 0.55 [*] (−0.12–0.96) / (0.23–0.86)	−0.98 [*] − −1.02 [*] (−1.61 – −0.34) / (−1.61 – −0.43	−0.01 / −0.01 (−0.02 – −0.01) / (−0.01 – 0.00)
Static MG	0.01 (0.06) (−0.51 – 0.54)	−0.78 [*] (−1.05 – −0.50)	−0.03 (−0.05 – −0. 01)
Dynamic MG	0.01 (−1.31 – 1.34)	−1.65 [*] (−2.63 – −0.67)	−0.02 (−0.03 – 0. 00)
Static RCM	0.05 (−0.53 – 0.63)	− 0.78 [*] (−1.13 – −0.42)	−0.03 (−0.05 – −0.01)
Dynamic RCM	0.37 (−3.55 – 4.28)	−1.03 (−5.16–3.31)	−0.01 (−0.03 – 0.00)
FE–PC	0.46 [*] (0.16 – 0.76)	−0.41 [*] (−0.67 – −0.16)	−0.02 (−0.03 – −0.02)
MG–PC	0.02 (−0.54 – 0.59)	−0.85 [*] (−1.16 – −0.53)	−0.03 (−0.04 – −0.02)
DMG	0.76 [*] (0.13 – 1.38)	−0.80 (−1.36 – 0.24)	
CMG	0.43 (−0.32 – 1.18)	−0.87 [*] (−1.22 – −0.51)	− 0.002 (−0.01 – 0.01)

Note: [*] denotes statistical significance at the 95% level.

estimators,[14] which should also be affected, are more similar to those from the DMG estimator.

In the case of the elasticity for economic activity in the UK, in Table A3.1b one can notice the high standard error of the estimate from the AH estimator, which despite the high value is not statistically significant, and the standard error of the estimate from the DMG estimator, which is caused by two series having coefficients around two. All the other statistically significant estimates in the table show very similar confidence intervals and point estimates, as shown in Figure 3.1b.

In the case of British energy demand, more than half of the estimates for the price coefficient are statistically significant. In the case of six estimators, i.e. the static and the dynamic pooled, the FD, the GMM, and the FE-PC, both coefficients on price and economic activity are statistically significant. Among the statistically significant estimates in Table A3.1b, the price coefficient produced by the dynamic MG estimator is clearly an outlier. One can also notice its very wide confidence interval. For these two reasons, the value obtained from this estimator is discarded.[15] In the table one can also notice that the absolute value of the price coefficient from the dynamic homogeneous estimators, i.e. the dynamic pooled, the AH, and the GMM estimators, tends to be lower than the values obtained from the other estimators. As this is probably due to the

---

[14] In this section the term 'pooled' is used to indicate the fixed effect and random effect model. The selection between the two models has been carried out on the basis of the Hausman tests mentioned above.

[15] The result from the dynamic MG estimator is probably due to the fact that, when the coefficient on the lagged dependent variable is high, the size of relatively small outliers among the short-run coefficients is magnified by the small denominator used to compute long-run coefficients.

heterogeneity bias mentioned above, these estimators are also discarded. The other statistically significant coefficients cluster into two groups, one comprising the static pooled, the FD, and the FE-PC estimators, the other comprising the static MG and RCM, the MG-PC, and the CMG estimators (see Figure 3.1c). The averages from the estimators in the first and second groups are -0.41 and -0.82, respectively; the average from all estimates is -0.64. Considering this bimodal distribution, it is not surprising that the confidence intervals overlap for a very small range, more precisely -0.61 to -0.53, the average of the range being -0.58. This value is clearly a good candidate for a point estimate of price elasticity. However, if one is willing to maintain the hypothesis of homogeneity across subsectors, -0.41 should be adopted as the estimate for price elasticity. Similarly, -0.82 would be a reasonable estimate if one wanted to stress heterogeneity across sectors. Our preferred choice, -0.64, is the average from all estimates in Figure 3.1c. In fact, considering the sample used in this study, both the static homogeneous estimators and the heterogeneous estimators are likely to present some shortcomings. Static homogeneous estimators are only affected by the heterogeneous bias asymptotically, a result which is unlikely to hold considering the time span in this study. Similarly, Hsiao et al. (1999) have shown that the MG estimators are unlikely to perform well when n or t are small, because the outlier estimates obtained from the panel components are not sufficiently smoothed out when creating an average for the whole panel.

References

Adeyemi, O. I., and L. C. Hunt (2010), 'Modelling OECD Industrial Energy Demand: Asymmetric Price Responses and Energy-Saving Technical Change', *Energy Economics*, 32(5): 1157–64.

Agnolucci, P. (2010), 'Non-Transport Energy Consumption in the UK: A Comparison of Alternative Approaches', *Energy Journal*, 31(4): 111–36.

Agras, J., and D. Chapman (1999), 'A Dynamic Approach to the Environmental Kuznets Curve Hypothesis', *Ecological Economics*, 28: 267–77.

Aldy, J. E. (2005), 'An Environmental Kuznets Curve Analysis of U.S. State-Level Carbon Dioxide Emissions', *Journal of Environment and Development*, 14: 48–72.

Anderson, T. W., and O. C. Hsiao (1982), 'Formulation and Estimation of Dynamic-Models Using Panel Data', *Journal of Econometrics*, 18: 47–82.

Arellano, M., and S. Bond (1991), 'Some Tests of Specification for Panel Data: Monte Carlo Evidence and an Application to Employment Equations', *Review of Economic Studies*, 58(2): 277–97.

Azomahou, T., F. Laisney, and P. N. Van (2006), 'Economic Development and CO$_2$ Emissions: A Nonparametric Panel Approach', *Journal of Public Economics*, 90: 1347–63.

Baltagi, B. H., G. Bresson, and A. Pirotte (2002), 'Comparison of Forecast Performance for Homogeneous, Heterogeneous and Shrinkage Estimators—Some Empirical Evidence from US Electricity and Natural-Gas Consumption', *Economics Letters*, 76: 375–82.

Baltagi, B. H., and J. M. Griffin (1983), 'Gasoline Demand in the OECD: An Application of Pooling and Testing Procedures', *European Economic Review*, 22: 117–37.

—— —— (1997), 'Pooled Estimators vs. their Heterogeneous Counterparts in the Context of Dynamic Demand for Gasoline', *Journal of Econometrics*, 77: 303–27.

Berndt, E. R., and D. O. Wood (1975), 'Technology, Prices, and Derived Demand for Energy, *Review of Economics and Statistics*, 57: 259–68.

Bertinelli, L., and E. Strobl (2005), 'The Environmental Kuznets Curve Semi-parametrically Revisited', *Economics Letters*, 88: 350–7.

Bewley, R. A. (1979), 'The Direct Estimation of the Equilibrium Response in a Linear Model', Economic Letters, 3: 357–61.

Broadstock, D., L. Hunt, and S. Sorrell (2007), *Elasticity of Substitution Studies: UKERC Review of Evidence for the Rebound Effect*, London: UK Energy Research Centre.

Brock, W. A., and M. S. Taylor (2004), *The Green Solow Model*, NBER Working Paper No. 10557, Cambridge, Mass.: National Bureau of Economic Research (NBER)

Bruvoll, A., and H. Medin (2003), 'Factors Behind the Environmental Kuznets Curve: A Decomposition of the Changes in Air Pollution', *Environmental and Resource Economics*, 24: 27–48.

Coakley, J., A. M. Fuertes, and R. P. Smith (2002), 'A Principal Components Approach to Cross-Section Dependence in Panels', Mimeo, London: Birkbeck College, University of London.

—— —— —— (2006), 'Unobserved Heterogeneity in Panel Time Series Models', *Computational Statistics and Data Analysis*, 50: 2361–80.

Cole, M. A., A. J. Rayner, and J. M. Bates (1997), 'The Environmental Kuznets Curve: An Empirical Analysis', *Environment and Development Economics*, 2: 401–16.

Copeland, B. R., and M. S. Taylor (2004), 'Trade, Growth and the Environment', *Journal of Economic Literature*, 42: 7–71.

de Bruyn, S. M., J. C. J. M. van den Bergh, and J. B. Opschoor (1998), 'Economic Growth and Emissions: Reconsidering the Empirical Basis of Environmental Kuznets Curves', *Ecological Economics*, 25: 161–75.

Dijkgraaf, E., and H. R. J. Vollebergh (2005), 'A Test for Parameter Heterogeneity in CO2 Panel EKC Estimations', *Environmental and Resource Economics*, 32: 229–39.

Dimitropoulos, J., L. C. Hunt, and G. Judge (2005), 'Estimating Underlying Energy Demand Trends Using UK Annual Data', *Applied Economics Letters*, 12: 239–44.

Dinda, S. (2004), 'Environmental Kuznets Curve Hypothesis: A Survey', *Ecological Economics*, 49: 431–55.

Ekins, P. (1997), 'The Kuznets Curve for the Environment and Economic Growth: Examining the Evidence', *Environment and Planning A*, 29: 805–30.

Enevoldsen, M. K., A. V. Ryelund, and M. S. Andersen (2007), 'Decoupling of Industrial Energy Consumption and CO_2-Emissions in Energy-Intensive Industries in Scandinavia', *Energy Economics*, 29: 665–92.

Ericsson, N. R., J. Campos, and H. Tran (1991), 'PC-Give and David Hendry's Econometric Methodology', *Revista de Econometria*, 10: 7–117.

Galeotti, M., and A. Lanza (2005), 'Desperately Seeking Environmental Kuznets', *Environmental Modelling and Software*, 20: 1379–88.

—— —— and F. Pauli (2006), 'Reassessing the Environmental Kuznets Curve for CO$_2$ Emissions: A Robustness Exercise', *Ecological Economics*, 57: 152–63.

Garcia-Cerrutti, L. M. (2000), 'Estimating Elasticities of Residential Energy Demand from Panel County Data Using Dynamic Random Variables Models with Heteroskedastic and Correlated Error Terms', *Resource and Energy Economics*, 22: 355–66.

Greening, L. A., G. Boyd, and J. M. Rooprise (2007), 'Modeling of Industrial Energy Consumption: An Introduction and Context', *Energy Economics*, 29: 599–608.

Grossman, G. M., and A. B. Krueger (1993), 'Environmental Impacts of the North American Free Trade Agreement', in P. Garber (eds.), *The U.S. –Mexico Free Trade Agreement*, Cambridge, Mass.: MIT Press, 13–56.

Holtz-Eakin, D., and T. M. Selden (1995), 'Stoking the Fires? CO$_2$ Emissions and Economic Growth', *Journal of Public Economics*, 57: 85–101.

Hsiao, C., M. H. Pesaran, and A. K. Tahmiscioglu (1999), 'Bayes Estimation of Short-Run Coefficients in Dynamic Panel Data Models', in C. Hsiao, K. Lahiri, L.-F. Lee, and M. H. Pesaran (eds.), *Analysis of Panels and Limited Dependent Variable Models: A Volume in Honour of G.S. Maddala*, Cambridge: Cambridge University Press.

Hunt, L. C., G. Judge, and Y. Ninomiya (2003), 'Underlying Trends and Seasonality in UK Energy Demand: A Sectoral Analysis', *Energy Economics*, 25: 93–118.

—— and E. L. Lynk (1992), 'Industrial Energy Demand in the UK: A Cointegration Approach', in D. Hawdon (ed.), *Energy Demand: Evidence and Expectations*. Guildford, UK: Surrey University Press, 143–62.

International Bank for Reconstruction and Development (IBRD) (1992), *Development and the Environment World Development Report* (World Bank), Oxford: Oxford University Press.

International Energy Agency (IEA) (2006a), *Energy Prices and Taxes*, Paris: IEA.

—— (2006b), *CO$_2$ Emissions from Fuel Combustion 1971–2004*, Paris: IEA.

—— (2007), *Energy Balances of OECD Countries*, Paris: IEA.

Lantz, V., and Q. Feng (2006), 'Assessing Income, Population, and Technology Impacts on CO2 Emissions in Canada: Where's the EKC?' *Ecological Economics*, 57: 229–38.

Leifman, M., and M. Heil (2005), Guest Editors' Note, *Journal of Environment and Development*, 14: 7–26.

List, J. A., and C. A. Gallet (1999), 'The Environmental Kuznets Curve: Does One Size Fit All?' *Ecological Economics*, 31: 409–23.

Lynk, E. L. (1989), 'The Demand for Energy by UK Manufacturing Industry', *Manchester School*, 57: 1–16.

Martínez-Zarzoso, I. and A. Bengochea-Morancho (2004), 'Testing for Environmental Kuznets Curves for CO$_2$ Evidence from Pooled Mean Group Estimates', *Economics Letters*, 32(1): 121–6.

Millimet, D. L., J. A. List, and T. Stengos (2003), 'The Environmental Kuznets Curve: Real Progress or Misspecified Models?' *Review of Economics and Statistics*, 85: 1038–47.

Moomaw, W. R., and G. C. Unruh (1997), 'Are Environmental Kuznets Curves Misleading Us? The Case of CO$_2$ Emissions', *Environment and Development Economics*, 2: 451–64.

Neumayer, E. (2002), 'Can Natural Factors Explain any Cross-Country Differences in Carbon Dioxide Emissions?' *Energy Policy*, 30: 7–12.

Nickell, S. (1981), 'Biases in Dynamic-Models with Fixed Effects', *Econometrica*, 49: 1417–26.

Office of National Statistics (ONS) (2006a), *Detailed Index of Production Database*, available electronically at ⟨http://www.statistics.gov.uk⟩, London: ONS.

—— (2006b), *Economic Trends Annual Supplement*, 32, London: ONS.

Perman, R., and D. I. Stern (2003), 'Evidence from Panel Unit Root and Cointegration Tests that the Environmental Kuznets Curve does Not Exist', *Australian Journal of Agricultural and Resource Economics*, 47: 325–47.

Pesaran, M. H. (2006), 'Estimation and Inference in Large Heterogeneous Panels with a Multifactor Error Structure', *Econometrica*, 74(4): 967–1012.

——Y. Shin, and R. J. Smith (2001), 'Bounds Testing Approaches to the Analysis of Level Relationships', *Journal of Applied Econometrics*, 16: 289–326.

——and R. P. Smith (1995), 'Estimating Long-Run Relationships from Dynamic Heterogeneous Panels', *Journal of Econometrics*, 68: 79–113.

—— —— and T. Akiyama (1998), *Energy Demand in Asian Developing Economies*, Oxford: Oxford University Press.

Pezzey, J. (1989), *Economic Analysis of Sustainable Growth and Sustainable Development*, World Bank Environment Department Working Paper No. 15, Washington: The World Bank.

Pock, M. (2007), 'Gasoline and Diesel Demand in Europe: New Insights', Mimeo, Vienna: Institute for Advanced Studies.

Schmalensee, R., T. M. Stoker, and R. A. Judson (1998), 'World Carbon Dioxide Emissions: 1950–2050', *Review of Economics and Statistics*, 80: 15–27.

Selden, T., and D. Song (1994), 'Environmental Quality and Development: Is there a Kuznets Curve for Air Pollution Emissions?', *Journal of Environmental Economics and Management*, 27: 147–62.

Shafik, N. (1994), 'Economic Development and Environmental Quality: An Econometric Analysis', *Oxford Economic Papers*, 46: 757–73.

Smith, R. P., and A. Fuertes (2004), *Panel Time Series*, London: Cemmap, IFS.

Statistiches Bundesamt (DeStatis) (2006), *Volkswirtschaftliche Gesamtrechnungen Inlandsproduktsberechnung Detaillierte Jahresergebnisse*, Wiesbaden: DeStatis.

Stern, D. I. (1998), 'Progress on the Environmental Kuznets Curve?' *Environment and Development Economics*, 3: 175–98.

—— (2004), 'The Rise and Fall of the Environmental Kuznets Curve', *World Development*, 32: 1419–39.

Sun, J.W. (1999), 'The Nature of CO_2 Emission Kuznets Curve', *Energy Policy*, 27: 691–4.

Swamy, P. A. V. B. (1970), 'Efficient Inference in a Random Coefficient Regression Model', *Econometrica*, 38: 311–23.

Talukdar, D., and C. M. Meisner (2001), 'Does the Private Sector Help or Hurt the Environment? Evidence from Carbon Dioxide Pollution in Developing Countries', *World Development*, 29: 827–40.

Taskin, F., and O. Zaim (2000), 'Searching for a Kuznets Curve in Environmental Efficiency Using Kernel Estimation', *Economics Letters*, 68: 217–23.

Timmer, M., M. O'Mahony, and B. van Ark (2007), 'The EU KLEMS Growth and Productivity Accounts: An Overview', University of Groningen and University of Birmingham.

Vollebergh, H. R. J., E. Dijkgraaf, and B. Melenberg (2005), 'Environmental Kuznetz Curves for CO_2: Heterogeneity versus Homogeneity', Discussion Paper No. 2005–25 Tilburg: Tilburg University.

Yaguchi, Y., T. Sonobe, and K. Otsuka (2007), 'Beyond the Environmental Kuznets Curve: A Comparative Study of SO_2 and CO_2 Emissions between Japan and China', *Environment and Development Economics*, 12: 445–70.

4

Is Environmental Tax Reform an Appropriate Policy for Industrial Sectors with Different Energy Intensities? An Analysis of UK Industrial Sectors

Paolo Agnolucci

4.1 Introduction

Energy consumption, like the consumption of any productive factors, is determined by the final product and the technology used in the production process. It is therefore clear that the energy intensity, i.e. the ratio between energy consumption e_t and economic activity y_t, of, say, the chemical sector will be different from that of, say, the construction sector. The existence of long-term differences among the energy intensities of different sectors is simply a fact.

The properties of long-term differences, i.e. differences which persist across time, are related to the properties of short-term random differences. If these are transitory, long-term differences will be *deterministic* (i.e. they derive from particular characteristics of the sector, and will persist over time in a fashion which can be forecast relatively accurately). If short-term random differences are persistent, they accumulate across time and long-term differences will be *stochastic* (i.e. they are affected by random processes within or between the sectors, and although they persist over time, they fluctuate in an unpredictable way, making any forecast difficult and potentially inaccurate).

This chapter aims to assess whether the uniform application of policies like ETRs in the industrial sector, without taking into account differences in the production process of industrial sectors, is justified by the dynamic properties of the economic variables which are influenced by the policy. As the ultimate aim of ETRs is to influence the labour and energy intensity of production processes, we perform this analysis by assessing whether the long-term differences among the energy intensities of the British industrial sectors are deterministic or stochastic, as defined above.

The nature of the long-term differences between sectors has important implications for policy because it affects the timing and frequency of policy interventions, and the choice of policy instruments. When long-term differences among time series of a variable like energy intensity are stochastic, random shocks to the series persist indefinitely. If policy makers have an interest in the series following a certain time pattern (declining, in the case of energy intensity), they will need to intervene any time a random shock is leading the series in a direction opposite to the one aimed at. When long-term differences among the series are deterministic, random shocks to the series are transitory. Therefore, policy makers do not need to intervene at any single minor departure of the series from the desired time pattern, as random shocks will naturally dissipate across time. In fact, if they want to affect the time evolution of the series, policy makers will need to implement prolonged policy measures able to affect the deterministic difference between the series.

Another policy implication is related to the type of instruments which can be used by policy makers. When long-term differences are stochastic, policy mechanisms affecting economic actors in a uniform fashion would seem a rather blunt instrument. In such cases, policy instruments should seek to address the different sectors individually, with more targeted, one-off (perhaps sector-specific) interventions, taking into account the specific conditions and evolution of the sectors. On the other hand, when long-term differences are deterministic, a uniform policy instrument is suited to policy makers' objectives. In this case, with regard to energy intensity, taxes on energy across industrial sectors would be an appropriate way to seek to reduce energy use.

This chapter is structured as follows. Section 4.2 briefly discusses the significance of energy intensity and policy. Section 4.3 identifies the sources of data of energy intensity and reviews the trends in energy intensity in a number of different sectors of UK industry. Section 4.4 describes the methodology to be used in the analysis of the long-term differences in energy intensity in these sectors and presents results. Section 4.5 presents the chapter's conclusions.

4.2 The Significance of Energy Intensity

Given the importance of energy in the policy discourse about climate change, resources, and the environment, it is not surprising that energy intensity has received considerable attention in the academic and policy-making community. From a policy point of view, energy intensity is related to energy efficiency, which, according to DTI (2006), is increasingly recognized as a priority by the European Commission and all member countries and has become the focus of a number of policies adopted in several countries (World Energy Council 2004).

Energy efficiency is the ratio between energy services and energy consumption. As energy services are difficult to measure, and in some cases even to define, energy intensity is normally used in policy-making. Sets of indicators on energy intensity are regularly produced by a number of governments. Energy intensity indicators can be used to assess changes in the intensity of energy use; help raise public awareness; complement other inputs to policy and programme analyses; and improve the role of efficiency improvements in energy markets.

There is a general downward trend in energy intensity in UK industry and, as noted above, policy makers need to know whether to intervene frequently sector by sector to seek to maintain this, or to adopt a more long-term approach with a more uniform policy instrument across sectors. In this section, we focus on the energy intensity properties of British industrial sectors in order to assess whether policies applied uniformly across sectors can be justified on the basis of the dynamic properties of the series.

4.3 Description of the Data

Annual data on energy consumption is taken from IEA (2005), which provides information for the sectors listed in the first column of Table 4.1 for the 1970–2004 time span. Data on gross value added (GVA) have been sourced from ONS (2006). As shown in the third and fourth columns of Table 4.1, GVA data are available at two different levels of detail. The more aggregate GVA time series matches the time span of the energy data for 1970–2004, but requires aggregation of the last five sectors in column 1. On the other hand, the most disaggregated GVA time series (matching the energy taxonomy with the exception of Iron and Steel and Non-Ferrous metals, which needs to be aggregated) is only available over a shorter period, 1978–2004, requiring the dropping of eight observations in the estimation. While using the longer sample is preferable for the power of the statistical tests to be used, concerns arise related to the difference among the sectors which need aggregation, i.e. the sectors in the last five rows of Table 4.1.[1] For this reason, the differences among industrial sectors were assessed in both samples, i.e. by using the taxonomy in column 3 for the longer sample and that in column 4 for the shorter sample.

---

[1] In fact, as shown in Figure 4.1b, the Metal sector has by far the highest energy intensity, i.e. twice as big as the second highest sector. When the metal sector is aggregated with the other three sectors in OTH1 (see Figure 4.1a), the energy intensity is similar to that for Food and Tobacco.

Table 4.1. Industrial sectors modelled in the 1970–2004 sample and in the 1978–2004 sample

Industrial sectors	ISIC code	Acronym	
		1970-2004	1978-2004
Mining and Quarrying	13 and 14	MIN	MIN
Food and Tobacco	15 and 16	FT	FT
Textile and Leather	17, 18 and 19	TXT	TXT
Wood and Wood Products	20	WPP	WPP
Paper, Pulp, and Printing	21 and 22		
Chemical and Petrochemical Industry	24	CHE	CHE
Non-Metallic Minerals	26	NMM	NMM
Construction	45	CON	CON
Iron and Steel	27.1 + 27.31	OTH1	MET
Non-Ferrous Metals	27.2 + 27.32		
Transport Equipment	34 + 35		TRA
Machinery	28, 29, 30, 31 and 32		MAC
Non Specified Industry	25, 33, 36 and 37		OTH2

The energy intensities for the two samples can be observed in Figures 4.1a and 4.1b. As can be seen, the Construction, Wood, Pulp, Paper and Print, Food and Tobacco, Textiles, Machinery and Transport Equipment have lower energy intensities than the average for the industrial sector. The Chemical, Non-Mineral Metal, and Metal sectors have the highest energy intensities. Figure 4.2 displays the difference between the sectoral energy intensities and the average for the industrial sector. The time series for some subsectors presents a number of spikes, mainly caused by sudden changes in the sub-sectors. Those occurring in 1970–2 and 1984 in the Textile sector and in 1989 and 2003 in the Mining sector are all caused by sudden changes in energy consumption, unmatched by changes of the GVA. A sudden decrease in energy consumption is also the cause of the marked decrease in the Construction sector in the last two years of the sample. In the Food and Tobacco sector, the increase between 1980 and 1990 is due to energy intensity in the sector decreasing at a lower rate than in the other industrial sectors. The increase in the Textile sector at the end of the sample is caused by the fact that a decrease in GVA is not matched by a corresponding change in energy consumption. Like the Food and Tobacco sector, the time series for the Chemical sector in Figure 4.2 switches between two levels, namely the pre-1982 and the post-1989 levels. Energy intensity in this sector almost halves between 1982 and 1989—see Figures 4.1a and 4.1b. As this reduction exceeds the decrease in the industrial sector as a whole, the time plot in Figure 4.2 presents a downward trend. Finally, the decrease in the time series for the Non-Metallic Mineral sector observed in the first few years and in the last ten years of the sample is mainly due to changes in energy consumption in the sector.

(a)

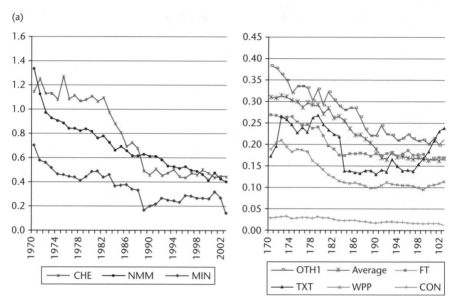

Figure 4.1a Energy intensity of industrial sectors, 1970–2004
Note: See Table 4.1 for the list of sectors referred to by acronyms in the key to the figure.

(b)

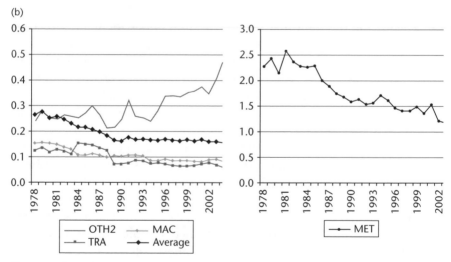

Figure 4.1b Energy intensity of industrial sectors, 1978–2004
Note: See note to Figure 4.1a.

(a)

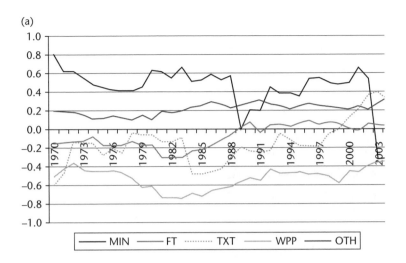

(b)

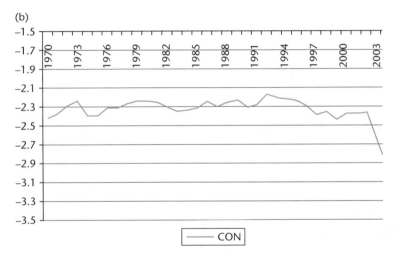

(c)

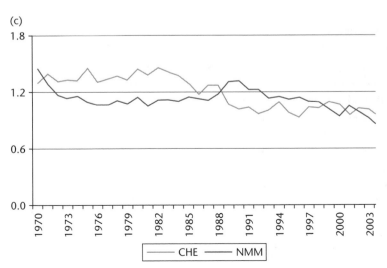

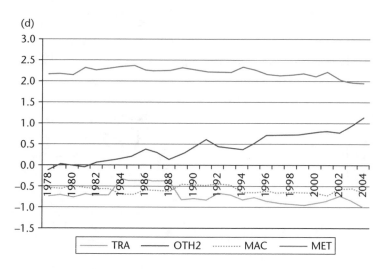

Figure 4.2 Difference between the energy intensity of the sectors assessed in this study and the energy intensity of the industrial sector as a whole

Note: Figures 4.2a, 4.2b, and 4.2c show the time series for the sector assessed for the 1970–2004 1970–2004 sample,while Figure 4.2d shows the time series for the additional sectors assessed for the 1978–2004 sample. See Table 4.1 for the list of sectors referred to by acronyms in the key to the figure.

Figures 4.2a, 4.2b, and 4.2c show the time series for the sector assessed for the 1970–2004 sample, while Figure 4.2d shows the time series for the additional sectors assessed for the 1978–2004 sample. The list of sectors described by the acronyms in the key to the figure can be seen in Table 4.1.

With regard to the sectors aggregated together into the Other Industry sector in the 1970–2004 sample (see Figure 4.2d), the Metallic, Transport Equipment, and Machinery sectors are relatively flat until 1995. A decrease in the Metallic sector can be observed thereafter. In the Transport Equipment sector, the sudden increase in 1984 and the decrease in 1988 in the relative energy intensity are caused by sudden changes in energy consumption. Quite interestingly, the non-specified industrial sector (OTH2) shows increasing energy intensity over the whole observation sample.

While gradual changes in the level or trend of long-term difference could be explained by structural change in the sectors or by changes in the level or trends of factors affecting the energy intensity (e.g. energy price), a number of the sudden changes described above are likely to be caused by measurement errors and other limitations in the data set. While bearing this point in mind, using a data set published by international institutions seems more advisable than embarking on a subjective data adjustment process, the criteria for which would be likely to be uncertain and somewhat arbitrary.

4.4 Methodological Approach

The methodology to be applied is relatively common in a number of economic fields, but, as far as we know, it has so far found little application in the energy field. The study follows the approach of Carlino and Mills (1993), where a series $Y_{i,\,t}$ is assessed relative to a benchmark $Y_{b,\,t}$. The dependent variable is therefore $y_{i,t}^d = Y_{i,t} - Y_{b,t}$ rather than the level $Y_{i,\,t}$. It is normally assumed that the difference from the benchmark consists of a time-invariant component x_i, a linear trend t, and a random short-run difference v_t. Breaks in the deterministic components can also be accommodated by the variable m_i. Long-term differences between a series and its benchmark can be written as

$$y_{i,t}^d = x_i + \beta_i t + \delta_i m_i + v_t \tag{4.1}$$

The nature of the differences is assessed by testing for the presence of unit roots in $y_{i,t}^d$. If there is a unit root, long-term differences are stochastic, as short-term random differences accumulate across time. If there is no unit root, short-term random differences dissipate and long-term differences are deterministic. Sections 4.4.1 and 4.4.2 deal with the details of this analysis. Readers interested only in the policy implications of our work can go straight to the conclusions in Section 4.5.

4.4.1 Unit Root Testing for Structural Breaks

The presence of unit roots has been tested by running the Augmented Dickey-Fuller (ADF), the Phillips-Perron (PP), the DF^{MAX} (Leybourne 1995), the DF^{RMA} (Shin and So 2001), the DF^{GLS} (Elliott et al. 1996), and the M^{GLS} tests (Ng and Perron 2001). Overall, these tests point to the long-term differences being stochastic. Only in a few instances, namely in the Construction sector according to the M^{GLS} tests, and in the Metal and the Machinery sectors according to a number of tests, can the long-term differences be considered deterministic. Detailed results are available upon request. In order to discern whether this conclusion is caused by the relatively low power of unit root tests, one could run panel unit root tests, as in Chen and Lee (2007), Lee (2005), Narayan and Smyth (2007), and Tauchmann (2006). This approach is not followed here due to the limitations of panel unit root testing. These are related to the fact that the power of the univariate and panel unit root tests cannot be compared (see Maddala and Wu 1999) and to the fact that the alternative hypothesis in homogeneous tests is very restrictive, while in the case of heterogeneous tests, the results are inconclusive if the null hypothesis is rejected (see Breitung and Pesaran 2008). Other limitations are related to the treatment of cross-sectional dependence. This can be handled by demeaning the data (Im et al.

2003), by using a feasible generalized method or by implementing the test in Maddala and Wu (1999). However, all these approaches have shortcomings, which are discussed by Breitung and Pesaran (2008) among others. In another approach to dealing with cross-sectional dependence (see e.g. Bai and Ng 2004; Moon and Perron 2004; and Phillips and Sul 2003), cross-sectional correlation can be removed after estimating common factors. However, considering the limited number of sectors in our data set, it seems unlikely that common factors can be estimated at an acceptable level of precision.

4.4.2 Testing for Structural Breaks

Rather than using panel unit root tests, we preferred to implement univariate tests allowing for structural breaks. In fact, the results from unit root tests can be misleading when a structural break goes unaccounted for: the so-called Perron effect (Perron 1989). We report the results from the Lagrange Multiplier (LM) tests, and not from the more common Zivot & Andrews (ZA) and Lumsdaine-Papell (LP) tests (which may be found in Agnolucci and Venn forthcoming), because of the limitations of these two tests when a break occurs under the null—see Lee and Strazicich (LS) (2001). The main advantage of the LM tests—see LS (2004) and LS (2003)—is that breaks are allowed under the null hypothesis, while in the ZA and the LP tests, no break is assumed under the null.

Results from the LM tests differ markedly from those obtained from the tests not allowing for structural breaks. As can be seen in Table 4.2 regarding the industrial sectors, in about 55% of cases with one break, and 75% of cases with two breaks, the LM test is statistically significant and therefore the long-run differences can be considered deterministic. When the selection of the model (intercept only vs. intercept and trend) on the basis of the information criteria is inconclusive, two statistics are presented in the table, although this does not

Table 4.2. Results for the Lagrange Multiplier (LM) test with one break and two breaks

	LM 1 break	Breakdate	Model	LM 2 breaks	Breakdates		Model
MIN	−3.43	1999	C	−5.73 [*]	1988	1999	CC
FT	−3.83 [*]	1990	A	−3.96 [+]	1990	1998	AA
TXT	−2.43	1983	C	−2.86	1983	1997	AA
WPP	−3.44	1999	C	−3.10	1984	1991	AA
CHE	−3.29 [+]	1988	A	−4.57 [**]	1985	1988	AA
NMM	−4.89 [+]	1987	C	−6.10 [*]	1987	1993	CC
CON	−4.63 [+]	1998	C	−6.93 [**]	1990	1998	CC
MET	−5.14 [**] / −6.33 [**]	1991 / 1985	A / C	−6.62 [**]	1985	1991	CC
TRA	−2.62 / −3.46	1995 / 1987	A / C	−5.75 [*]	1983	1999	CC
MAC	−4.97 [+]	1993	C	−5.43 [+]	1993	1998	CC
OTH	−2.46 / −4.41	1985 / 1993	A / C	−2.96	1983	1988	AA

influence the properties of the long-term differences. In these cases both models have been reported in the table. With regard to the break dates, in eight instances the LM with one and two breaks select a common break date. With regard to the properties of the long-term differences, the two tests disagree only in the case of the Mining and the Transport Equipment sectors.

The breakpoints selected by the models in the table can be grouped into three clusters, from 1983 to 1988, from 1990 to 1993, and from 1997 to 1999. The first group of breaks can be imputed to the recession of the 1980s—the real GVA of the manufacturing sector went back to its 1979 value only in 1987 (ONS 2007). It is also worth remembering that energy prices have been rather unstable over this period, reaching their peak in 1985 and crashing the following year (BERR 2008). Also the breaks in the second group, i.e. from 1990 to 1993, might be influenced by the milder and shorter recession of the early 1990s, when the real GVA of the manufacturing sector went back to its 1990 value only in 1994. However, energy prices in this period were rather stable. The 1997–9 time period, over which the last group of breaks occurred, was not very remarkable in terms of economic conditions, with the GVA growing at a rate comparable to that observed in the previous couple of years (ONS 2007). The trend in the energy price, however, changed suddenly in 1996 when the decline that started in 1986 came to an end; energy prices stayed stable until 2003 before heading upwards in 2004 (BERR 2008). It should also be borne in mind that breaks in the series used in this study could be caused by the limitations of the data set. However, as mentioned above, it remains unclear how the data should be adjusted. Overall, using official data seems preferable to embarking on a somewhat arbitrary revision of the data set. If breaks are due to the limitations of the data, modelling structural breaks is one way in which such limitations may be accommodated.

4.5 Conclusions

This chapter has assessed whether long-term differences among the energy intensities of industrial sectors are stochastic or deterministic. By applying a limited selection of tests when compared to those presented in the literature, it has shown how the conclusions from the tests can be contradictory. The spirit of our conclusions is therefore similar to Gaffeo et al. (2005) where inference appears to be strongly dependent on the types of test used, so that conclusions reached at early stages of the testing procedure can be discarded at subsequent stages. In the case of this chapter, if the analysis had terminated with the implementation of panel unit root tests, we would have concluded that long-term differences in energy intensities among industrial sectors were stochastic. However, after allowing for structural breaks in the series, the opposite conclusion can be reached. With few exceptions, long-term differences are deterministic after one takes the occurrence of breaks into account. As in Chen and Lee (2007), Altinay and Karagol (2004), and Altinay and Karagol (2005), the modelling of structural breaks was found to be the determining factor in judging the stationarity of the time series modelled in this study.

The policy implications of this study are related to the timing and frequency of policy interventions and to the types of instrument. As long-term differences among industrial sectors are mainly deterministic, short-term random differences dissipate over time. For this reason, policy makers with an interest in the series following a certain time pattern do not need to intervene whenever there is a single minor departure of the series from the desired trend. As pointed out by Chen and Lee (2007) and Narayan and Smyth (2007), in this case government should not be concerned with short-term fluctuations when implementing energy policies. In fact, if they want to affect the evolution of the series, policy makers will need to implement prolonged policy measures able to affect the deterministic components. In addition, bearing in mind the deterministic nature of the long-term differences across industrial sectors, future movements of the series can be predicted on the basis of past behaviour. However, this is true only if one is ready to assume that the series will be structurally stable over the forecast horizon.

In relation to the type of instruments which can be used by policy makers, we can conclude that policies taking into account the evolution of the series and the peculiarity of the economic actors cannot be justified on the basis of the analysis discussed here. In fact, the presence of long-term deterministic differences among the series supports the adoption of policy instruments which are applied across productive sectors without frequent changes. Among the policies in the energy sector, energy and CO_2 taxes applied to all industrial sectors would be an example of this type of instrument. While the analysis discussed in this chapter does not consider the effects on the competitiveness of the industrial sectors, we can conclude that it is not possible to dismiss the introduction of these taxes on the basis of the peculiarity of some industrial sectors. In addition, if there is a relationship between the supposed adverse effects of these taxes and the difference in energy intensities across sectors, the importance of these effects is likely to reflect the deterministic nature of the series assessed in this study and its long-term pattern. Caution is needed when drawing conclusions from the use of a narrow set of statistical methodologies. As discussed above, the results from tests allowing for breaks are opposite to univariate and panel tests assuming structural stability. Policy advice from the latter would be completely different from the conclusions drawn from this chapter and would ignore the importance of structural breaks.

In this study, modelling breaks has turned out to be a rather important issue. Breaks in the long-term differences may be due to time-varying and sector-specific factors which are not directly taken into account in this study. Alternatively, structural breaks may be caused by a change in the importance of subsectors contained in the industrial sectors assessed in this study, provided that these subsectors have different energy intensities (e.g. pharmaceuticals and base chemicals in the chemical sector). Estimated break dates seem to have been influenced by changing economic conditions, i.e. the recessions in the 1980s and early 1990s, and fluctuations in the energy price, notably the 1986 crash and the levelling off of the energy price in 1996. It is also possible that some of the breaks in the series are caused by limitations in the data set, as discussed in Section 4.3. If this argument is right, modelling structural breaks may be considered a convenient approach to taking into account limitations in the quality of data available to researchers.

References

Agnolucci, P., and A. Venn (forthcoming), 'Industrial Energy Intensities in the UK: Is there a Deterministic or Stochastic Difference among Sectors?' *Applied Economics*.

Altinay, G., and E. Karagol (2004), 'Structural Break, Unit Root, and the Causality Between Energy Consumption and GDP in Turkey', *Energy Economics*, 26: 985–94.

————(2005), 'Electricity Consumption and Economic Growth: Evidence from Turkey', *Energy Economics*, 27: 849–56.

Bai, J., and S. Ng (2004), 'A PANIC Attack on Unit Roots and Cointegration', *Econometrica*, 72: 1127–77.

BERR (Department for Business Enterprise and Regulatory Reform) (2008), *Quarterly Energy Trends*, London: BERR.

Breitung, J., and M. H. Pesaran (2008), 'Unit Roots and Cointegration in Panels', in L. Matyas and P. Sevestre (eds.) (2008), *The Econometrics of Panel Data*, 3rd edition, Berlin: Kluwer Academic Publishers.

Carlino, G. A., and L. O. Mills (1993), 'Are U.S. Regional Incomes Converging?' *Journal of Monetary Economics*, 32: 335–46.

Chen, P. F., and C. C. Lee (2007), 'Is Energy Consumption per Capita Broken Stationary? New Evidence from Regional-Based Panels', *Energy Policy*, 35(6): 3526–40.

DTI (Department of Trade and Industry) (2006), *Energy: its impact on the environment and society – 2006* London: DTI.

Elliott, G., T. J. Rothenberg, and J. H. Stock (ERS) (1996), 'Efficient Tests for an Autoregressive Unit Root', *Econometrica* 64(4): 813–36.

Gaffeo, E., M. Gallegati, and M. Gallegati (2005), 'Requiem for the Unit Root in per Capita Real GDP? Additional Evidence from Historical Data', *Empirical Economics*, 30: 37–63.

Im, K. S., M. H. Pesaran, and Y. Shin (2003), 'Testing for Unit Roots in Heterogeneous Panels', *Journal of Econometrics*, 115: 53–74.

International Energy Agency (IEA) (2005), *Energy Balances*, Paris: OECD/IEA.

Lee, C. C. (2005), 'Energy Consumption and GDP in Developing Countries: A Cointegrated Panel Analysis', *Energy Economics*, 27: 415–27.

Lee, J., and M. C. Strazicich (2001), 'Break Point Estimation and Spurious Rejections with Endogenous Unit Root Tests', *Oxford Bulletin of Economics and Statistics*, 63(5): 535–58.

————(2003), 'Minimum Lagrange Multiplier Unit Root Tests with Two Structural Breaks', *Review of Economics and Statistics*, 85(4): 1082–9.

————(2004), 'Minimum LM Unit Root Test with One Structural Break Boone', Department of Economics, Appalachian State University, NC.

Leybourne, S. J. (1995), 'Testing for Unit Roots Using Forward and Reverse Dickey-Fuller Regressions', *Oxford Bulletin of Economics and Statistics*, 57(4): 559–71.

Maddala, G. S., and S. Wu (1999), 'A Comparative Study of Unit Root Tests with Panel Data and a New Simple Test', *Oxford Bulletin of Economics and Statistics*, 61, Special Issue: 631–52.

Moon, H. R., and B. Perron (2004), 'Testing for a Unit Root in Panels with Dynamic Factors', *Journal of Econometrics*, 122: 81–126.

Narayan, P. K., and R. Smyth (2007), 'Are Shocks to Energy Consumption Permanent or Temporary? Evidence from 182 Countries', *Energy Policy*, 35: 333–41.

Ng, S., and P. Perron (2001), 'Lag Length Selection and the Construction of Unit Root Tests with Good Size and Power', *Econometrica* 69(6): 1519–54.

Office for National Statistics (ONS) (2006), *Detailed Index of Production* London: ONS.

——(2007), *Detailed Index of production (series CKYY)*, London: ONS.

Perron, P. (1989), 'The Great Crash, the Oil Price Shock, and the Unit-Root Hypothesis', *Econometrica*, 57(6): 1361–401.

Phillips, P. C. B., and D. Sul (2003), 'Dynamic Panel Estimation and Homogeneity Testing under Cross Section Dependence', *Econometrics Journal*, 6: 217–59.

Shin, D. W., and B. S. So (2001), 'Recursive Mean Adjustment for Unit Root Tests', *Journal of Time Series Analysis*, 22(5): 595–612.

Tauchmann, H. (2006), 'Cost of Electric Power Sector Carbon Mitigation in India: International Implications', *Energy Policy*, 34: 1619–29.

US Department of Energy (DOE) (2006), *Indicators of Energy Intensity in the United States*, Washington: US Department of Energy Energy Efficiency and Renewable Energy.

World Energy Council (2004), *Energy Efficiency: A Worldwide Review*, London: World Energy Council.

Part II
Experiences in Environmental Tax Reform

5

Environmental Taxes and ETRs in Europe: The Current Situation and a Review of the Modelling Literature

Stefan Speck, Philip Summerton, Daniel Lee and Kirsten Wiebe

Significant tax reforms were undertaken in European countries during the 1990s and the early 2000s. Their main objectives were to broaden the overall tax base leading to an increase in general consumption taxes, such as VAT and environmental taxes, and to reduce labour costs (Eurostat 2009).

During this period, and as part of such substantial tax and fiscal reform efforts, the Nordic governments adopted the concept of an environmental tax reform (ETR), later followed by the governments of the Netherlands, the UK, and Germany. The strategy taken by those countries was to launch new environmental taxes, in the majority of cases, taxes levied on the consumption of energy and CO_2 emissions, and to revise already existing energy taxes. The other component of the tax-shifting programmes was mainly implemented by reducing income taxes as well as non-wage labour costs, such as social security contributions, and by raising tax-free allowances with regard to incomes.

The main characteristics of these ETRs are discussed in the next section, followed by an analysis of the development in the new EU member states. The rest of this chapter reviews the literature and reports on the projected effects of the ETRs on the environment and the economy through modelled estimates of changes in emissions, sectoral effects (such as changes in output, employment, and trade), and macroeconomic variables such as GDP and total employment.

5.1 ETR experiences in Europe

5.1.1 Western Europe

Although the fundamental reasons for implementing ETRs in EU member states are similar, the design of the programmes varies. Design issues contrast in terms of the economic sectors affected, as well as the recycling mechanisms adopted. Taxes on energy consumption or CO_2 emissions are the most common instruments of ETR, although the UK has also introduced landfill and aggregate taxation, while Denmark and the Netherlands have increased existing taxes on waste disposal. Often, ETR design is modified by concerns over the effect of unilateral environmental taxation on international competitiveness (Ekins and Speck 2008). This has led to a variety of exemptions for certain industries, often in contradiction to the Polluter Pays Principle (PPP), the value judgement that the burden of taxation should fall on those who directly produce environmental costs. The following overview and discussion of ETRs in Western European countries is brief, because they have already been extensively described elsewhere (see, for example, Speck and Jilkova 2009 and Cambridge Econometrics 2009a, which provide the basis for the following country descriptions).

SWEDEN

Sweden became the first EU-15 country to introduce ETR in 1991, and went on to develop a rather complex environmental tax system. Specific charges for CO_2, SO_2, and NO_X were introduced in the early 1990s. However, the most striking feature was the introduction of the CO_2 tax in 1991. Special tax provisions were not granted to Swedish industry at that time, so the ETR led to a significant increase in the overall tax rate, in particular for energy products other than transport fuels. The introduction of the CO_2 tax was slightly compensated by a reduction in the energy/excise taxes, and a refund mechanism limiting the total energy tax burden paid by industry has been put in place. The tax scheme revision in 1993 completely exempted the manufacturing industry which paid only a fraction of the CO_2 tax rates, thus reducing its tax burden quite dramatically.

The introduction of environmental taxes was part of a major fiscal reform process with the main aim of reducing personal income taxes. The shortfall in total revenue caused by the cut in income taxes was partly compensated by the newly introduced SO_2 and CO_2 taxes. Further tax-shift programmes were introduced during the last ten years: the green tax shift between 2001 and 2006 and a fiscal policy programme during 2007 and 2009. The former programme shifted about 1.5 billion euro via an increase in environmental taxes and the simultaneous reduction in income taxes. Revenues amounting to around 0.5 billion euro were generated by increasing environmental taxes and taxes on labour were reduced by approximately 7 billion euro, aiming to increase labour supply and employment. The earmarking of revenues was never established in Swedish fiscal policy shifts.

The different levels of taxation for heating fuels (as per ton CO_2) were not modified by the two fiscal policies implemented during the last decade. Households and services are facing higher rates (27 euro in 1991 increasing to 108 euro per ton of CO_2 in 2009) than other economic sectors which are subject to international competition and carbon leakage, i.e. industry, agriculture, and combined heat and power plants (CHP). The tax rate was set at 7 euro in 1991 and increased to 23 euro for the sectors which are outside of the EU emission trading scheme (ETS) and to 16 euro for sectors within the EU ETS in 2009. However, the Swedish government proposed the re-design of the energy and CO_2 taxation schemes of fossil heating fuels for all economic sectors (households, services, agriculture, industry outside EU ETS, and industry within EU ETS).

The first policy reform is to re-calculate the energy tax rates of different heating fuels by setting tax rates in accordance with the energy content of the fuels. The basis of this reform process is the current energy tax rate for heating oil. The tax rates as of 2011 for different energy products are presented in Table 5.1.

Apart from the modification of energy tax rates, a re-design of the overall energy and CO_2 tax regime is proposed for 2011 as shown in Table 5.2., i.e. revising the tax provisions for those economic sectors which are eligible for CO_2 tax reduction. A key aspect of this revision policy is a complete re-design of the tax burden for industries as the complete energy tax exemption will be abolished and all industrial sectors (inside and outside the EU ETS) are liable to pay a reduced energy tax (30% of the full energy tax rate). The CO_2 tax for industries outside the EU ETS will be increased over time and set to zero for industries which are part of the EU ETS.

DENMARK

The Danish tax-shifting programmes were implemented in three phases between 1994 and 2002. While the first and third ETRs primarily targeted households, the second was aimed at industry. These differences are also

Table 5.1. Proposal of the Swedish Government for a reform of the energy tax

Energy product	Current energy tax rates	Energy tax rates in 2011
Heavy fuel oil (€/litre)	0.086	0.086
Coal and coke (€/kg)	0.037	0.065
Natural gas (€/m³)	0.028	0.095

Source: Åkerfeldt (2009).

Table 5.2. Development of taxation of fossil heating fuels in Sweden

Economic sectors	2009	2011 (Government proposal)
Households and service	• 100% energy tax — not based on energy content (0.1–0.8 Eurocent/kWh) • 100% CO_2 tax	• 100% energy tax — based on energy content (0.8 Eurocent/kWh) • 100% CO_2 tax
Industry outside EU ETS + agriculture	• 0 energy tax • 21% CO_2 tax • 0.8% rule — further tax reductions	• 30% energy tax = 0.25 Eurocent/kWh • 30% CO_2 tax (60% in 2015) • 0.8% rule more strict (abolished in 2015)
Installations within EU ETS (responsible for about 50% of Swedish CO_2 emissions)	*Industry + heat production in CHP*: • 0 energy tax • 15% CO_2 tax *Other heat plants*: • 100% energy tax • 94% CO_2 tax	*Industry*: • 30 % energy tax = 0.25 Eurocent/kWh • 0 CO_2 tax *Heat production in CHP*: • 30% energy tax = 0.25 Eurocent/kWh • 7% CO_2 tax *Other heat plants*: • 100% energy tax • 94% CO_2 tax

Source: Åkerfeldt (2009).

reflected in the recycling mechanisms adopted. For example, during the second phase industry faced a higher energy/CO_2 tax burden, but this was relieved by a reduction of employers' social security contributions. A rather unique system of special tax provisions for industry was introduced in 1995 because of concerns about competitiveness, whereby there is differentiation between industrial energy consumption for space heating and process purposes. Process energy is generally exempt from any energy taxes and only a reduced CO_2 tax rate applies.

THE NETHERLANDS

The Netherlands has recycled increased energy tax revenues into both lower income tax and employers' contributions, alongside a 3% reduction in corporate taxes, greater tax credits for small businesses, and increases in tax-free allowances. Varying levels of energy consumption of electricity and natural gas are taxed at different rates.

FINLAND

Finland became the first country in Europe to implement an ETR when in 1990 it introduced a CO_2 tax levied on all energy products with the exception of transport fuels. The Finnish ETRs, as implemented in 1997 and 1998 respectively, never aimed to be revenue neutral. The intention of the tax-shifting programme was to reduce general tax revenues but to offset some of the losses caused by the reduction of labour taxes by increases in environmental taxes and by broadening the tax base.

Widespread special energy tax provisions, such as tax reduction for industry, are not part of the Finnish energy taxation scheme, with the exception of electricity taxes, which discriminate between households and industry in the sense that industry faces a lower tax rate. However, the context of this policy of not granting special tax provisions to industry is that nominal energy tax rates in Finland are generally lower than those implemented in neighbouring countries.

GERMANY

The potential of an environmental tax reform in Germany had already been discussed in the early 1990s but it took until April 1999 before the ETR was finally implemented. When launching the ETR the clearly defined objectives of the German government were:

• to improve environmental protection and in particular to reduce greenhouse gas emissions as a means of climate change mitigation (an environmental objective); and

• to reduce employers' and employees' statutory pension fund contributions (social security contributions) in order to reduce labour costs and to increase employment (economic/employment objective).

The ETR was very broad as all economic sectors were affected. The key ETR policies were to increase transport fuel taxes in five stages and to introduce a tax on electricity. The recycling mechanism of the ETR package, the reduction of both employers' and employees' pension fund contributions, aimed to lower Germany's non-wage labour costs, which are among the highest in the world (OECD 2009). The politicians expected an increase in employment from the reduction in these costs as the contribution to the pension fund was reduced from 20.3% in 1998 to 19.5% in 2004.[1]

No energy taxes were imposed on hard coal and non-energetic use of energy carriers. Special regulations (tax reduction and compensation measures) apply to energy-intensive industries and agriculture only, to avoid a too high financial burden on these sectors. The ETR-induced energy tax increases ceased in 2003 and since then tax rates have not changed in nominal terms, meaning that the real value of the tax rates dropped during the period 2004–9. This is in contrast to policies adopted in Sweden and the Netherlands where the tax rates are indexed to inflation.

[1] The pension fund contribution rate was even lower in 2001/2 at 19.1%. Due to economic and demographic developments, the rate was increased again to 19.9% in 2008.

THE UK

The two main ETR schemes in the UK were associated with the Landfill Tax and the Climate Change Levy (CCL).[2] The Landfill Tax, introduced in 1996, is charged on businesses and local authorities that dispose of waste using land-fill, and the revenue was recycled through reduced employers' social security contributions. The CCL, introduced in 2001, is an energy tax on commercial and industrial use of energy (household energy use is exempt), aimed at providing incentives to increase energy efficiency and reduce consumption of dirty fuels. Electricity generated from renewable sources or from CHP is exempt from the CCL. A potential 80% discount from the levy for energy-intensive industries provides an incentive to agree formal targets for improv-ing energy efficiency or reducing emissions by signing up to Climate Change Agreements (CCAs).

The revenues from these environmental taxes have been used to reduce employers' social security contributions and, in addition, a fraction of the generated revenues is used for special funds. However, rises in the rates of landfill tax since 1996, and of CCL since 2006, have not been recycled into any further tax reductions. The UK is the only ETR country not to reduce employees' taxes, which is not surprising as all ETR schemes target industries.

The ETR packages all have in common that the same recycling measure has been applied, i.e. a reduction of the employers' social security contributions. This policy approach should guarantee that the total tax burden of industry as a whole remains almost the same. However, this policy clearly means that the tax liability of different industrial sectors is affected differently, i.e. some sectors are net winners and others are net losers.

Apart from these two ETR schemes, the UK government launched a small-scale ETR in 2002 by introducing an aggregates tax. The revenue was also used to compensate the reduction in employers' social security contribution and to establish a special fund ('Sustainability Fund'). The tax rate was set at £1.60 per tonne (2.35 euro), which was around 20% of the average price per tonne of material. An analysis undertaken by HM Revenue and Customs revealed that this instrument can be effective in reducing the sale of aggregates as well as encouraging a small shift to alternative 'untaxed' secondary waste materials (EEA 2008). These results are of great interest as they show that the use of economic instruments can support the process of the dematerialization of the economy.

The scope of the ETRs differs in particular when compared with the German ETR as not only energy taxes have been introduced as part of the packages. In addition, the size of all three ETRs together is rather small as the total tax

[2] In 2002, the UK launched a third ETR scheme by introducing an aggregates tax package. The same recycling programme as in the case of the two other schemes applies.

revenues of the three taxes amounts to about 0.15% of GDP during 2005 compared to the German case where the total tax-shifting programme amounted to about 0.8% of GDP in 2003.

5.1.2 The situation in the new EU member states

The use of environmental taxes and charges in environmental policy has a long tradition in the new EU member states (Speck et al. 2001a; Nordic Council 2006). An often rather complex scheme of air and water pollution charges has been in place in some of these countries since the 1970s. It is important to bear in mind when assessing these schemes that the generated revenues are earmarked for environmental funds (Speck et al. 2001b).

Environmental funds played a significant role in co-financing environmental investment infrastructure as part of the transposition of the requirements for joining the EU laid down in the environmental *acquis*. These funds are still in operation as a tool for co-financing investments as the new EU member states are still facing a backlog in environmental infrastructure investments. All countries have revised their tax policies as well as implemented changes in the overall public finance systems during the last few years. These changes were often linked to and a consequence of the requirements of the EU accession process. For example, all countries have to transpose the 2003 Energy Taxation Directive[3] into national law during the coming years. This Directive restructuring the Community framework for the taxation of energy products widened the scope of the pre-existing EU energy taxation framework, which had previously been addressed by the Mineral Oils Directive (Directive 1992/82/EEC) by setting minimum excise tax rates only on mineral oil products. The new framework for the taxation of energy products extends the number of energy products, as minimum tax rates are set for all energy products including natural gas, coal, and electricity, as well as increasing the minimum rates for transport fuels. All EU member states, including the new EU member states from Central and Eastern Europe, are obliged to comply with fiscal structures and the levels of taxation laid down in the 2003 Taxation of Energy Products Directive. However, the new EU member states negotiated temporary exemptions and transitional periods for full compliance with the regulations, as straight transposition could have created serious economic and social difficulties in view of their ongoing economic transition. The transitional periods granted to the new EU member states are in some cases up to 2009/10.[4] This development opens up the possibility of launching an ETR as the revenues

---

[3] Council Directive 2003/96/EC of 27 October 2003 restructuring the Community framework for the taxation of energy products and electricity.
[4] Council Directives 2004/74/EC and 2004/75/EC.

raised by either increasing existing energy taxes or by introducing new energy taxes can be used for tax-shifting programmes. Countries, such as Estonia and the Czech Republic, made use of this opportunity as they launched ETRs.[5]

In July 2005, the Estonian government launched an ETR which will be implemented in two phases during 2006 and 2013. The first phase started in 2006, lasting until the end of 2008, with the second phase following in 2013. The main principle of the Estonian ETR is to shift the tax burden from income to taxes and charges levied on energy, natural resources, and environmental pollution (Lelumees 2007).

In 2006, the Estonian government gradually increased the rates of pollution charges and natural resources taxes, thereby increasing the revenues from around 600 million Estonian kroon (EEK) (39 million euro) in 2005 to about 900 million EEK (58 million euro) in 2009 (Kraav and Lüpsik 2007a and 2007b).[6] More important is the energy tax policy as these taxes are the main revenue-raising source. Table 5.3 shows the increases of tax rates levied on oil products.

The rise in tax rates is also reflected in energy tax revenues as they grew from 863 million EEK in 2003 to 1,869 million EEK in 2007.

The additional revenues accrued were used to offset tax reductions, with the marginal personal income tax rate being reduced from 23% in 2006 to 20% in 2009. In addition, some tax exemptions, such as an increase in the basic allowance and further exemptions for pensioners and families with more than two children, are part of the overall policy package. This tax-shifting programme is following the tradition of the Swedish ETRs, where the revenues from energy and CO_2 taxes were used to reduce marginal income tax rates.

This rather low personal income tax rate is not unusual in the new EU member states as many of them have already introduced, or will be introducing, a flat-rate tax on personal income as well as on corporate income. However, the share of non-wage costs as part of overall labour costs is higher

Table 5.3. Development of energy tax rates in Estonia

	July 2003	July 2006	January 2009	% change: July 2003–January 2009	% change: July 2006–January 2009
	€ per 1,000l	€ per 1,000l	€ per 1,000l	in %	in %
Petrol Unleaded	224	285	359	60	26
Diesel	163	245	330	103	35
gas oil	27	44	61	127	39

Source: EC, excise duty tables, different years.

[5] This chapter does not discuss the Czech ETR as it is the focus of Chapter 6.
[6] This development has to be seen in the context that the revenues from pollution charges amounted to 35 million EEK in 1995.

Table 5.4. Structure of tax revenues by major type of taxes (in % of the total tax burden—situation as of 2007)

	Czech Republic	Denmark	Estonia	Germany	UK	EU
Indirect tax	30.5	37.1	43	32.7	35.4	34.8
Direct tax	25.3	61.2	23.7	28.7	46.3	34.3
Personal income	11.7	51.8	18.5	23.4	28.9	23.5
Social contribution	44.2	2.0	33.3	38.5	18.4	31.2
employers	27.9	0	32.4	16.6	10.1	18
employees	9.8	2.0	0.5	15.5	7.7	9.6
Total tax	100	100	100	100	100	100
Total tax % of GDP	36.9	48.7	33.1	39.5	36.3	39.8
Environment tax (energy tax)	6.8	12.1	7.0	5.7	6.7	6.2
	(6.3)	(4.6)	(5.7)	(4.7)	(5.0)	(4.5)

Note: EU=weighted EU.27 average.
Source: Eurostat (2009).

in Estonia than the EU average, as social security contributions (the so-called social tax in Estonia) are fully paid by employers and amount to 33% of the taxable amount (Ministry of Finance 2007).

The principal policy objectives of the Estonian ETR are in line with those of old EU member states: the ETR should improve the competitiveness of the Estonian economy; support economic development; and reduce unemployment. However, the policy tool involved in achieving the last objective in particular is rather interesting as other recycling mechanisms, such as the reduction of employers' social security contributions (SSC), are in general assessed as being more effective in reducing unemployment than the reduction of personal income taxes as implemented in Estonia (see, for example, OECD 2001). However, the adoption of a recycling mechanism aiming to reduce employers' and employee's SSC—as was done in Germany for example—is not an option for the Estonian government as the social security contribution paid by employees is rather negligible (see Table 5.4) and therefore the only way of offsetting the increase in energy costs caused by energy tax increases that households are facing is to reduce the marginal income tax rate and increase the basic allowance.

5.1.3 ETR – the latest development in Europe

Several interesting developments concerning the wider application of ETR and CO_2 taxes have occurred in European countries in the last two years.

SWITZERLAND
In 2008, Switzerland introduced a CO_2 tax levied on fuels—exempting transport fuels—with revenues of the CO_2 tax recycled back to companies and

households. The CO_2 tax package has a number of aspects worth highlighting. First, the tax rate was set at 12 CHF per ton CO_2 (7.8 euro) in 2008. An automatic mechanism of increasing the CO_2 tax rates if predetermined emission reduction targets are not achieved is part of the tax bill. As the latest reduction target[7] has not been achieved, the CO_2 tax rate will be increased to 36 CHF per ton (23.4 euro) at the beginning of 2010, while companies committed to reducing CO_2 emissions can be exempted. The revenues are recycled back to companies and households as a lump-sum, i.e. the health insurance premium payable by the individual citizen will be reduced by a fixed amount. Parts of the increased revenues resulting from the higher CO_2 tax from 2010 onwards will be used to fund the renovation/insulation of buildings.

IRELAND

The latest country to introduce a carbon tax was Ireland. The rate of the carbon tax was set at 15 euro and all energy products with the exception of electricity are subject to the tax. However, economic entities which are participating in the EU ETS are exempt from the carbon tax. It is forecast that the tax leads to an increase in end-user prices of between 3.5% (petrol) and 11% (coal) and should generate 330 million euro in a full year. However, the revenues are not deemed to be recycled back to the economy, implying that Ireland is not following the approach of other countries when implementing an ETR. This policy has also to be seen in the context of the huge financial crisis Ireland is currently facing.

FRANCE

By far the most attention-grabbing development occurred during September 2009 in France when the French Government spelt out plans to introduce a CO_2 tax set at 17 euro per ton CO_2 at the beginning of 2010 and levied on the consumption of oil, gas, and coal, but not on electricity, increasing progressively during the following years. The political discussion surrounding the implementation of this fiscal instrument is of great interest as the tax follows the recommendation of an expert panel commissioned by the government and chaired by a former prime minister. However, the tax rate suggested by the expert panel was 32 euro per ton of CO_2, making sure that the tax would be effective in changing consumer behaviour. However, this proposal was ignored and instead the tax rate was set based on the average price of CO_2 on the carbon market since February 2008. The link to the EU ETS is important

---

[7] The target was to reduce CO_2 emissions by more than 13.5% in 2008 as compared to 1990. However, the reduction was only 11.2%, meaning that the clause triggering an increase in the CO_2 tax rate comes into effect.

as ETS sectors were exempt from the tax. During negotiation processes which took place during autumn 2009, the government announced further tax discounts and exemptions for economic sectors, such as truckers, farmers, and also the fishing sector. The planned CO_2 tax is part of a fiscal-neutral scheme as the revenues generated are planned to be recycled back to the economy in form of repayments to taxpayers through reductions in income tax or in the form of 'a green cheque'.

On 29 December 2009, the Constitutional Court annulled the CO_2 tax because of the many loopholes in the form of tax exemptions and discounts. The Constitutional Court concluded that the tax was designed in such a way that some 93% of industrial emissions were exempt. This was not justified in the view of the Constitutional Court as CO_2 allowances for installations under the EU ETS are given for free at least until 2013. Another point of criticism was that the tax will lead to an unfair burden on households, in particular, those living in rural areas, and therefore the tax bill will breach the constitutional requirements for equality. The French government announced almost immediately, i.e. only a couple of days after the bill was annulled, that the tax bill would be revised during the coming weeks and a revised tax bill would be brought before parliament in February 2010 and could come into force in April 2010.

The final decision made by the French government in March 2010 turned the whole tax discussion upside down as the French prime minister stated that France would not go ahead with the carbon tax because of the fear of damaging competitiveness if French industry were subject to the tax. Furthermore, it was stated that the tax proposal was put on hold, as it could be adopted only if the revision of the energy taxation directive were adopted at EU level.

5.1.4 ETR—a policy tool for EU member states

Experience shows that ETR is a potential policy tool for all EU member states. However, it is clear that the design of an ETR must correspond to each country's specific conditions. The two aspects of a tax-shifting programme, namely how additional revenues are raised and how revenues are recycled, are crucial, in particular with regard to the question of whether the principal political objectives will be achieved. An analysis of the taxation structure of selected EU member states (see Table 5.4) reveals large differences between EU member states, implying that recycling schemes adopted in the countries must reflect this diversity.

First, it has to be stated that the overall tax ratio, i.e. the sum of total tax and social security contributions, lies within the range of 33.1% and 48.7% of the selected EU member states with an EU-wide average of 39.8%. However, larger variations are visible with regard to the direct tax to total tax revenue ratio as countries like the UK and in particular Denmark (with 61.2%) are heavily reliant on these taxes. This is in contrast to the share of social security contributions (SSCs), as these charges are essential in terms of their revenue-raising potential in countries such as the Czech Republic, Estonia, and Germany (while Denmark hardly levies any SSCs at all). Furthermore, the split between SSCs paid by employers and employees respectively displays large differences. This finding makes it a clear requirement to consider carefully the prevailing taxation structure when designing an ETR and that the transfer of experience between countries must be treated with some caution.

It is also of interest to assess the revenue-raising potential of energy taxes as an important feature of launching an ETR in the coming years. This aspect is highlighted in Table 5.5 by comparing the revenues raised by transport fuel taxes compared with other energy taxes.

This comparison reveals some interesting facts as EU member states mainly raise revenues from transport fuel taxes, and the share of other energy taxes is often negligible, with the exception of Denmark and Sweden. It is worth emphasizing that the revenues from transport fuels—when expressed as the transport fuel-to-total tax ratio—are higher in the new EU member states compared to the old. It can therefore be surmised that, with regard to the potential for launching ETRs, there may be more scope for generating revenues through energy taxes levied on energy products other than transport fuels. Other existing energy tax rates are often rather low and sometimes still zero rated, as in the UK, where households' natural gas and electricity use is completely exempt from any energy tax and also subject to a reduced

Table 5.5. Transport fuel and other energy taxes as a percentage of total taxes (situation as of 2007)

	Transport fuel tax % of total taxes	Other energy tax % of total taxes
Old EU member states		
Denmark	2.5	2.3
Germany	3.5	1.0
Sweden	2.5	2.1
UK	4.7	0.3
	Transport fuel tax % of total taxes	Other energy tax % of total taxes
New EU member states		
Czech Republic	6.0	0.3
Estonia	5.4	0.3
Latvia	5.6	0.0
Poland	5.5	1.4

Source: EC (2009).

consumption tax (VAT) rate. Furthermore, there exist ample options for re-cycling the additional revenues generated. In addition, funds generated from the auctioning of emission allowances under the EU ETS could be another revenue source.

5.2 Expected effects of an ETR

5.2.1 Theory-based literature

There is a clear theoretical case for environmental taxation going back to Pigou (1920), on the basis that environmental taxation can be used to correct for market-based negative externalities. A negative externality occurs when the price to the consumer of a good or service is less than the cost of that good or service to society as a whole.

For example, in Figure 5.1, the efficient allocation of pollution is where the marginal benefit of pollution intersects the marginal social cost, but without intervention, the market would be at equilibrium where marginal benefit intersects the marginal private cost. The efficient Pigouvian tax is the differ-ence between the marginal social and private costs at the efficient allocation of pollution.

In theory, when the correct Pigouvian tax is in place, the market can efficiently allocate goods without any need for further intervention. However, there are some difficulties with Pigouvian taxation: not least that it is no easy task to identify the optimal level of pollution in many practical contexts. It is to address such difficulties that Baumol and Oates (1971) proposed an alterna-tive approach to implementing environmental taxes, which has come to be called the standards and pricing approach after their article. The approach

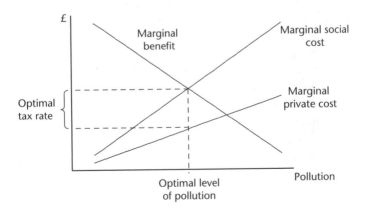

Figure 5.1 The efficient allocation of pollution

involves choosing environmental standards on the basis of their desired effects on, for example, human health, or on quality of life more generally, and then using environmental taxes on an iterative basis to bring levels of environmental damage down to the standards. Baumol and Oates showed that such environmental taxation had the property that it would achieve the desired environmental improvement at minimum cost to society at large. This has now become the principal approach to, and justification of, environmental taxes, including carbon taxes. Certainly all the carbon taxes that have been implemented to date have been put in place in order to contribute to defined programmes of CO_2 emission reduction, rather than on the basis of any optimality calculations.

ETR differs from basic environmental taxation because it recycles revenue into reductions in distortionary taxation, which gives rise to the possibility of a so-called 'double dividend' (Oates 1995). Labour taxes, for example, are considered to be distortionary because they put a gap between wages, which is the valuation an employer places on an employee, and take-home pay. The result is that employment is at less than the efficient optimum, and welfare is reduced. If the revenue from an ETR were used to reduce labour taxes, employment and welfare would increase because of the lack of distortions in the market. Strictly speaking, the double dividend is an improvement in welfare, but it is often interpreted as an increase in labour and economic growth.

At face value, the double dividend looks like a free lunch: environmental outcomes are improved at no cost to, and even a benefit to, the economy. Unfortunately, the 'tax interaction effect' can offset or even cancel out the double dividend (Oates 1995). This effect occurs when environmental taxes raise prices in the economy and thereby reduce the real wage, so that workers reduce their labour supply.[8] This in turn reduces taxes from labour taxation, which requires tax rates to be raised to maintain revenues, thereby offsetting, and perhaps dominating, the cuts in labour taxes and boost to employment caused by the reduction in labour taxes as part of an ETR. It is therefore possible that the distortionary effect of labour taxes could be increased, rather than reduced, by the tax shift. The outcome will depend first on the extent to which the revenue-recycling mechanism reduces the price rises from environmental taxes (e.g. through cuts in employers' SSCs, which reduce business costs and could be passed on in lower prices) and, secondly, on the response of labour supply to any residual price increases.

In response to such considerations, the double-dividend concept has been split into weak and strong versions (Goulder 1995). The former simply claims

---

[8] Under certain assumptions: workers may increase the labour supply if, for example, they need to work more hours to make up the fall in income (the 'income effect').

that the costs of environmental taxation will be reduced if the revenue is recycled into reducing existing tax distortions, which is relatively uncontroversial. The strong double dividend is the much more controversial argument that revenue recycling will actually improve welfare outcomes, through increased employment and/or economic output, even if environmental benefits are disregarded.

Numerous researchers have investigated the theoretical conditions under which the double dividend does or does not exist, and whether it is strong or weak. For example, Schöb (1996) demonstrates the importance of the tax system that exists before an ETR, and the revenue-recycling mechanism that is employed. If the polluting good on which taxes are increased is a strong complement for the clean good on which taxes are reduced, then a revenue-neutral tax shift could increase pollution and wipe out the double dividend. Bovenberg and van der Ploeg (1998) use a general equilibrium model with involuntary unemployment to show that ETR is more likely to result in an increase in employment if it shifts the tax burden from workers in the formal sector to those in the informal sector. The wage-setting mechanism in the labour market is also important, particularly if trade union membership prevents the market from clearing (Heady et al. 2000). Considering taxes other than on labour, Bovenberg and de Mooij (1997) show that shifting the tax burden from capital can produce a strong double dividend, depending on how internationally mobile capital is.

The theoretical literature has raised a number of other crucial issues surrounding ETR, and in particular unilateral ETR, where only one country or region enacts an ETR while others continue to sell untaxed dirty goods. One might expect this to reduce competitiveness in the ETR region's industries compared to those of the non-ETR region, since the costs of energy inputs will be higher. However, this is disputed by the Porter hypothesis (Porter and van der Linde 1995), which proposes that environmental regulation can induce increased efficiency and innovation and improve competitiveness as efficiency gains offset the costs of complying with the regulation. Originally, the hypothesis was applied to environmental standards, but it has since been applied to environmental taxation by other researchers (for example, Kriechel and Ziesemer, 2007). If the Porter hypothesis holds true, then firms must be failing to exploit efficiency-saving opportunities due to some market failure, and are only jolted into doing so by environmental regulation. This also increases the chances of there being a double dividend.

A related issue to the competitiveness effects of unilateral ETR is that of 'carbon leakage' (IPCC 2001; IPCC 2007, Working Group 3, Technical Summary, 8.8). Carbon leakage occurs when emissions in a non-ETR economy rise as a result of ETR being introduced in another economy, thereby offsetting the environmental improvement in the ETR region. This can happen if the prices of domestically produced emissions-intensive goods in the ETR economy are raised by environmental taxes, and consumers respond by switching to goods produced in non-ETR economies. In addition, industries in the ETR economy that themselves produce few or no emissions may be subject to 'indirect' carbon leakage if they are reliant on an emissions-intensive input, such as electricity (Sato and Mohr 2008). Matthes (2008) argues that the extent of carbon leakage depends on a number of highly sector-specific factors, including: the impact of environmental taxation on production costs; the ability to pass through costs to customers; the barriers to relocation to an economy without environmental taxation; and the stability of the factors favouring carbon leakage.

However, Grubb et al. (2002) argue that, as well as carbon leakage, which they call a negative spillover, environmental taxation and regulation also give rise to positive spillovers that will act to decrease emissions across all economies and not just those that take unilateral action. The most important of these is technological spillover. This occurs when developments in carbon-saving and energy-efficient technologies in an economy with environmental controls proliferate across the world. This concept is related to the Porter hypothesis. Technological spillovers to developing economies may be particularly significant. Grubb et al. also argue that there will be political and policy spillover, whereby unilateral action in some countries will encourage similar action in other countries due to political pressure and precedent.

In order to study the existence and extent of effects like carbon leakage and the double dividend, it is necessary to use integrated energy-economy models, which capture the economy-wide interactions and effects resulting from changes in taxation. Modelling studies of this kind form the subject of the next section.

5.2.2 Modelling-based literature

There have been many studies of the possible effects of ETRs in different countries, using integrated energy-economy models to investigate the interactions between the macro-economy and the sectors that are subject to environmental taxes. Such models combine economic theory with data about the economy, and can be broadly separated into computable general equilibrium (CGE) models and macro-econometric estimation models.

COMPUTABLE GENERAL EQUILIBRIUM MODELS
Analysis of the impact of ETR has often employed a computable general equilibrium (CGE) modelling framework of the economy and energy systems.

Examples of CGE models with a focus on integrated economy-energy-environment analysis include GEM-E3,[9] AIM,[10] and GTAP.[11]

CGE models are rooted in neoclassical and general equilibrium theory, in which the circular flow of goods and services in the economy is always in equilibrium. That is, demand and supply between consumers and producers must be equal and all markets must clear. CGE models usually impose this condition as an assumption, with prices set to ensure market clearing, and also the related assumptions that firms and households are profit and utility maximizers. The functional form of the equations in a CGE model must be defined in detail by the modeller, based on theoretical considerations. In order to guarantee the existence of equilibrium and to ensure that it is computable, CGE models often include restrictive assumptions in these functional forms. For example, production functions usually have constant elasticities of substitution and constant returns to scale.

CGE models are designed to include a high degree of disaggregation, by modelling different sectors and regions in the economy. Typically, the economy is disaggregated into sectors consisting of a single representative firm or household, and the flows of goods and services between these sectors are linked by an input-output (IO) approach. As discussed above, the firms and households are maximizers, and the flows between them are in equilibrium.

The main data inputs to CGE models are input-output databases for a single year. IO data are not the basis for the behavioural and technological parameters of the model however. Instead, these are chosen by the modeller, in large part on the basis of micro-level estimates of elasticities, and then the model is calibrated to match the IO data in the base year. This is in contrast to an econometric approach, where the model's equations are estimated to fit the data.

CGE modelling is most naturally suited to long-run analysis; that is, a static comparison between an economy's initial equilibrium and its new equilibrium under each test scenario. The need to always be in equilibrium means that the technique is less well suited to a dynamic analysis of short-run (e.g. transition) effects and how the economy reaches a new equilibrium.

While market-clearing assumptions are the starting point for a CGE model, most modern models include a number of specific exemptions. Investigations into the effects of ETR using CGE modelling tend to alter one or two variables or assumptions of interest in order to isolate their effects. For example, Bovenberg and van der Ploeg (1998) consider how the existence of structural unemployment affects the operation of the double dividend. To do this, they relax

[9] <http://www.gem-e3.net/>.
[10] Asia-Pacific Integrated Model, available at <http://www-iam.nies.go.jp/aim>.
[11] Global Trade Analysis Project, available at <http://www.gtap.agecon.purdue.edu/models>.

the assumption of market clearing in their model. Jaeger (2002) makes the assumption that pollution damage reduces welfare by lowering factor productivity. In contrast, previous CGE model-based research has assumed that environmental damage enters consumer utility directly (Jaeger 2002).

MACRO-ECONOMETRIC MODELS

The main alternatives to CGE modelling are time-series-based macro-econometric models. Examples include: Cambridge Econometrics' MDM-E3[12] (Barker and Peterson 1987), E3ME[13] (Cambridge Econometrics 2009b), and E3MG[14] models (which model the UK, European, and global economies respectively); the global model GINFORS[15] (Meyer et al. 2008) and the PANTA-RHEI[16] model of the German economy. Two of these models (E3ME and GINFORS) are used in the modelling of a large-scale ETR reported in Chapter 9.

Macro-econometric models originally came from an aggregated 'top-down' background, but now also use 'bottom-up' modelling by industry and sector, and an input-output approach, to achieve substantial disaggregation. In a macro-econometric model, the parameters are fitted to the data using statistical techniques, instead of calibration as in a CGE model. In addition, macro-econometric models need fewer and less strict assumptions than CGE models. In particular, as they are demand driven, demand and supply for all factors might not always be in equilibrium (although typically the model will include some safeguard to prevent them diverging too far). As a result, these models are quite well suited to analysing short-run dynamics and transition effects that are typically out of equilibrium. Generally, a macro-econometric model will also make less restrictive assumptions on the functional form of equations and on behaviour.

The main data inputs to macro-econometric models are time series, over which estimation takes place. This may also be combined with IO data in order to build a high sectoral disaggregation.

COMPARISON OF CGE AND ECONOMETRIC APPROACHES

CGE models produce forecasts that are strongly consistent with, and indeed dependent upon, neoclassical economic theory. This has the advantage that the forecast is based upon a large body of economic research and knowledge.

---

[12] Multi-sectoral Dynamic Model.

[13] Energy-Environment-Economy of Europe, available at <http://www.camecon.com/ModellingTraining/suite_economic_models/E3ME.aspx>.

[14] Energy-Environment-Economy (E3) Model at the Global Level , available at <http://www.camecon.com/ModellingTraining/suite_economic_models/E3MG.aspx>.

[15] Global Inter-industry Forecasting System.

[16] <http://www.gws-os.de/downloads/meyer-tokyo2005ppt.pdf>.

However, it also forms a constraint: a CGE model produces a forecast only as credible as the theory underpinning it. Neoclassical theory incorporates many strong assumptions about economic behaviour, as noted above, and tends to rely on equilibrium relationships that many would judge to hold only in the long run, if at all.

In contrast, a macro-econometric model is better matched to the data than it is to strict economic theory. This has the advantage that its equations are generated to a greater extent by real-world observations, and less by axiomatic and unproven assumptions. However, it also means that these models are subject to the famous Lucas critique (Lucas 1976): the past is not necessarily a good predictor of the future. In this context, the key Lucas critique of macro-econometric modelling would be that the parameters that are estimated may not be invariant to policy changes, and therefore they may change when an ETR is introduced. A CGE model is not so subject to this critique, since its predictions are based on theories and data on fundamental microeconomic characteristics, such as preferences and resource constraints, that are more likely to be invariant to policy changes.

Pissarides (2008) compares the merits of a number of examples of CGE and macro-econometric models for the analysis of carbon-reduction policies. Specifically, he examines Oxford Economics' CGE model OEIM (Oxford Energy Industry Model) and econometric Generalized Method of Moments (GMM) model, HM Revenue and Customs' CGE model, and Cambridge Econometrics' MDM-E3 model. He argues that econometric modelling is better suited to the analysis of short-run dynamics, but that in the long run the lack of equilibrium discipline could allow errors to cumulate. He also points out that econometric modelling is subject to the Lucas critique. Pissarides suggests that CGE modelling is generally superior in the long run and is also better at handling disaggregation into sectors: econometric models may be more subject to statistical errors when dealing with smaller data sets. However, he concedes that CGE modelling is not well suited to either short-run or dynamic analysis. The OEIM model includes some adjustment dynamics based on the aggregated GMM model, but Pissarides sees several weaknesses in the approach. Overall, he concludes that the differing modelling techniques should be viewed as complements, rather than alternatives, in policy analysis.

EFFECTS ON THE ECONOMY

There have been many empirical modelling-based studies on the impacts of both actual and hypothetical ETRs. This section concentrates on the macroeconomic effects of ETR, as opposed to the environmental effects, and on the effect of revenue recycling.

Strictly speaking, the double dividend entails an improvement in the welfare, or well-being of individuals in the economy (in addition to that resulting from the environmental benefits of the ETR). In empirical modelling, this is usually replaced with more measurable macroeconomic variables such as GDP and employment. The literature concentrates on whether revenue recycling generates either a strong (GDP and or/employment rise) double dividend or a weak (GDP and or/employment fall by less than would have occurred without revenue recycling) double dividend. Generally, the literature rarely finds evidence for the former, and nearly always finds evidence for the latter.

THE RESULTS OF META-ANALYSIS STUDIES

A good way of synthesizing the results of a large number of empirical studies on ETR is through a meta-analysis. A meta-analysis subjects the results of numerous studies to statistical analysis: the idea is to explain the differences in results between studies and to generate a general result. In this context, models of the energy-economy and their results under different scenarios are collected. The first such analysis for climate change mitigation was by Repetto and Austin (1997), who collated 16 models of the US economy and 162 scenarios. The regression analysis explained macroeconomic cost as a percentage reduction in GDP and used as explanatory variables the CO_2 reduction target, the number of years to meet the target, the assumed use of carbon tax revenues, and several model characteristics. The resulting regression gave the worst-case scenario (which did not include revenue recycling) for reducing carbon emissions by 30% by 2020 at a cost of 3% of GDP, and the best-case scenario (which did include revenue recycling), resulting in an increase of 2.5% in GDP (results reported in Barker et al. 2006). When revenue recycling was included in a scenario, the impact of environmental taxation on GDP was improved by an average of 1.2 percentage points, for a 30% reduction target.

Barker et al. (2006) provide a more recent example of meta-analysis. They use results from the nine international models in the Innovation Model Comparison Project (IMCP), together with three additional models from other sources and earlier IMCP studies. In all, there are 924 observations for the percentage change in Gross World Product (GWP). A major advantage of the IMCP data is that many of the models have been put through identical scenarios: the stabilization of the atmospheric carbon concentration at 550 parts per million (ppm), 500 ppm, and 450 ppm by the year 2100, through the use of ETR. The additional models are included because the IMCP models are similar in type and scope, and it is difficult to distinguish between them statistically. In the analysis, active revenue recycling is found to increase GWP in the case of the 450 ppm target by 2–3% in 2030. However, many of the models in the data set did not include a treatment of fiscal policy and therefore could not analyse revenue recycling. This meant that it was difficult for meta-analysis to distinguish between the effect of revenue recycling and the general characteristics of the models. Model characteristics were very important: CGE models tended to feature lower macroeconomic costs because they are constrained to quick and efficient equilibrium solutions. Just as important is the extent of emissions in a model's baseline: a model that required a greater ETR effort to reach the emissions targets tended to incur a greater macroeconomic cost or benefit.

Barker et al. (2006) find that the overall effect of ETR on GDP is generally small, whether positive or negative, particularly when the model incorporates 'induced technological change'. A model incorporates induced technology change when it treats technological progress as an endogenous variable that can be affected, for example, by government policies. In this case, an ETR can induce improvements in energy efficiency that offset, partially or fully, the rise in energy costs (this is an example of the Porter hypothesis). These improvements in energy efficiency may also have other economic benefits, for example spillovers to other regions or production of a higher-quality product.

OTHER STUDIES OF HYPOTHETICAL ETRS

These meta-studies are based on hypothetical ETRs, rather than ones that have actually been planned or carried out. There are many examples of studies of hypothetical ETRs. Meyer and Lutz (2002) model the impact of a uniform coordinated carbon tax across the G7 countries using the macro-econometric model COMPASS (Comprehensive Model for Policy Assessment). Other countries are not included in the analysis, so changes in trade patterns with countries not introducing ETR are not considered. Each government introduces a tax of $1 per ton of carbon (tC) in 2001, and raises it linearly to $10/tC by 2010. All revenue raised from this is recycled into reductions in social security contributions. The results of the simulation show that countries with high existing social security contributions, such as France and Italy, lose less than 0.5% of GDP while gaining around 1% in employment each. However, countries where social security contributions are already low do not fare so well. The US, for example, sheds 1.72% of GDP for a small rise in employment of 0.08%.

Hoerner and Bosquet (2001) surveyed 45 studies and 104 simulations of the introduction of ETR in several European countries, as well as at the European level. A slim majority (54%) estimated a zero or positive impact (i.e. a strong double dividend), but the overall conclusion is that the impact on GDP is likely to be small (no firm conclusions can be drawn, since the size of the modelled ETRs varied between each study). Recycling revenues into reducing employers' social security contributions was the most likely way of generating an increase in GDP; two-thirds of the simulations that recycled revenue in this way reported an increase. There were also indications that recycling revenue into promoting energy-efficient technologies tends to increase GDP, but too few studies included this for firm conclusions to be drawn.

Hoerner and Bosquet's survey suggests that the double dividend is more likely to be seen in increased employment than in increased output: 74% of the studies predicted that there would be an employment increase as a result of ETR, particularly when revenues are recycled into reductions in employers' social security contributions. There were also indications that the effect is particularly pronounced when the cut is targeted at low-income jobs. Of the studies where revenues were recycled into reduced income or corporate taxes, only about half reported a rise in employment. However, for employment to increase, it was generally necessary for the labour market model to be flexible; otherwise the ETR simply resulted in a wage-price spiral.

MODELLING STUDIES OF GERMANY

For the case of Germany's ETR of 1999, Bach et al. (2001) use the LEAN model to analyse three scenarios: the reference scenario; the introduction of the 1999 ETR; and additionally a decomposition analysis in which either energy taxes are introduced or social security contributions are lowered. LEAN is a sequential-dynamic CGE model that differentiates between 13 sectors, five of which are energy sources, and two regions, Germany and the remaining EU-12. The sectors are represented by constant-elasticity-of-substitution (CES) production functions. In the analysis, the ETR does not succeed in attaining all the desired results: the revenue from environmental taxes rises slower than the social security contributions decrease and the growth in employment is not sufficient to close this gap. GDP first increases in the short run due to high investment rates (for energy substitutes) and employment increases, since it is substituted for capital, but the effect on GDP and in turn also on employment is negative in the long run.

The extension of Germany's ETR in 2003 was also modelled using LEAN by Kohlhaas (2005). One important part of this analysis was dedicated to the isolated treatment of the impacts of changes in the special regulations for energy-intensive industries: this was found to be negligible. The effect on energy consumption of households was also found to be rather low compared to the effects on industrial sectors, since the energy consumption of industry is much more price elastic than that of households.

Bach et al. (2001) also used the macro-econometric input-output model PANTA-RHEI to carry out their analysis. PANTA-RHEI is an environmentally extended version of the econometric simulation and forecasting model IN-FORGE developed by GWS (see Lutz et al. 2005). It contains a deeply disaggregated energy and air pollution module, which distinguishes 30 energy sources and their inputs in 121 production sectors and households, as well as the related CO_2 emissions. Energy demand is fully integrated into the intermediate demand of firms and the consumption demand of households.

The short-run results from PANTA-RHEI were a little more pessimistic than those from LEAN. Germany's GDP is about 0.6% lower in 2003, although the gap closes slightly in the following years. Employment is higher by about 0.4%, which corresponds to approximately 140,000 more jobs. The reduction of social security contributions for employees does not completely offset the increased tax burden, which leads to a lower disposable income for households and hence to less private consumption and to lower production and investments in all sectors. LEAN was more optimistic than PANTA-RHEI since investment to reduce energy intensity occurred immediately, due to the efficient equilibrium tendency in the CGE model.

MODELLING STUDIES OF THE UK

For the UK case, Cambridge Econometrics (CE) et al. (2005) investigated the initial effects of the Climate Change Levy (CCL) on UK energy use and carbon emissions, in a report to HM Revenue and Customs. Alongside the actual CCL rates and exemptions (assumed to rise in line with inflation after 2005), climate change agreements (CCAs) were explicitly modelled as part of the analysis. The model used in the study was MDM-E3, an econometric time-series estimation model with a detailed treatment of short-run dynamics. The economic model is disaggregated into regions and industrial, consumption, and investment sectors, with the sectors linked by input-output coefficients. This is combined with a sub-model to estimate energy demand, which itself features a number of sub-models, and an environmental sub-model to estimate emissions.

The analysis compared dynamic simulations of the UK economy over 1998–2010 under different specifications. The scenarios included: a counterfactual case with no CCAs or CCL; the case where actual CCL rates and CCAs are introduced; and cases where there are no CCA exemptions. The results show a very small positive effect on GDP; in 2010 it was projected to be 0.06% higher than it would have been without the CCL, with the UK's trade performance slightly diminished. It was also projected that less would be raised from the CCL than is returned in the form of social security reductions. Even in scenarios where there was no revenue recycling, the impact on GDP was only very marginally negative. Removing the exemptions for CCA sectors improved GDP very slightly. The modest impacts are partly a reflection of the small size of the CCL, as well as of the operation of the double dividend.

MODELLING STUDIES OF THE EU

For the overall European Union case, Barker et al. (2009) investigated the macroeconomic implications of the actual ETRs that have been introduced in the EU, based on analysis done for the 2004–7 COMETR project[17] (see Andersen and Ekins 2009 for the detailed results of this project). The report used the E3ME model, which covers Europe. Like MDM-E3, E3ME uses macro-econometric time-series analysis combined with input-output tables and is highly disaggregated. Twenty-seven regions were covered in the analysis: the EU-25 plus Norway and Switzerland. A key feature of the analysis was that the six EU-15 countries that have introduced ETRs were included (surveyed in Section 5.1), and their actual ETRs were explicitly modelled in as much detail as possible, including: actual tax rates; the coverage of taxes across industry and households; the channels through which revenue was recycled; and the actual revenue raised by the taxes (which differed from simple calculations like 'taxes * fuel consumption' due to exemptions). However, some gaps in the data prevented some of the ETRs being modelled in the fullest possible detail.

The project combined an ex-post analysis of the period from 1994–2004, estimating the contribution that ETR had made to economic and environmental outcomes, with an ex-ante projection through to 2012. The projections included four scenarios: a counterfactual scenario with no reforms; the case where the actual ETRs are introduced; a case with no exemptions; and a case with no revenue recycling. It was found that, in the EU countries adopting ETR, GDP was increased by between 0.1% and 0.5% in 2012 compared to the reference scenario, which is equivalent to a small increase of 0.1% in the EU-25 as a whole. The scenario analysis suggested that these results were due to a small double-dividend effect in every country where there is revenue recycling. When there is no revenue recycling, ETR was found to lead to a net loss of output in all countries examined except Finland (which is heavily dependent on imports for supplies of fossil fuels, so that a shift away from fossil fuels improves the trade balance). Effects at the aggregate level were dominated by Germany, due to the size of its economy and importance in trade and, as a result, little happened at the European level until Germany introduced its reforms in 1999.

It was also estimated that ETR implementation causes employment in some of the adopting countries to increase by as much as 0.5% in 2012. Employment increases the most when revenue from the ETR is used to reduce employers' social security contributions, as was done in Denmark, Germany, and the UK. In Denmark, the ETR was found to have an immediate effect on the level of employment, which remained nearly 0.5% higher throughout the modelling period. In Germany, a modest increase in employment was recorded of approximately 0.2% against the reference case. In the UK, however, the change in employment is negligible, as the revenue recycled to reduce social

[17] Competitiveness Effects of Environmental Tax Reforms.

security contributions was much smaller. For each country, the increases in labour were partly attributable to the indirect effects of higher GDP, not just the reduction in labour costs.

THE IMPACT ON COMPETITIVENESS

Finally, on the issue of the effects of ETR on competitiveness, Zhang and Baranzini (2004) review the empirical literature on the effects of environmental regulation and taxation on international competitiveness. The studies they examine suggest that the effect has been modest. For example, Baron and ECON-Energy (1997) perform a static analysis of the cost increases to four energy-intensive industries in the OECD countries arising from a $100/tC tax on carbon emissions. Generally, the cost increases are found to be lower than 2%, with some exceptions in Australia and Canada. Zhang and Baranzini conclude that the effect of carbon taxes on competitiveness has to date been insignificant, but that this may change if future environmental policies are greater in scope and size.

EFFECTS ON ENERGY DEMAND AND THE ENVIRONMENT

While the search for a double dividend draws attention to the macroeconomic impacts, the main purpose of ETR is, of course, to improve environmental outcomes. Most studies are focused on reducing emissions of carbon dioxide and other greenhouse gasses. This section concentrates on the environmental impacts of ETR.

STUDIES OF HYPOTHETICAL ETRS

There is considerable evidence to suggest that ETR will be successful in reducing emissions to at least some extent, but a rise in emissions is possible. Hoerner and Bosquet (2001), in their survey of models of hypothetical ETRs in Europe, conclude that economic modelling bears out the environmental effectiveness of ETR. Almost 80% of the models they survey report that carbon emissions show a fall from the baseline simulation. However, this leaves 20% of these models showing an increase in carbon emissions from the baseline, albeit usually one of less than 5%. According to Hoerner and Bosquet, this occurs when the reduction in dirty energy demand due to its price increase is offset by a rise in demand due to a rise in economic growth, caused by revenue recycling.

Even so, most of the studies whose macroeconomic results were discussed in the previous section reported a positive environmental impact. Meyer and Lutz (2002), in their simulation of ETR introduction in the G7 countries, derive reductions in carbon emissions of around 5% in most countries, even though the macroeconomic impacts vary. The exception is Japan, which has a far lower emissions reduction, because its energy productivity has historically been unresponsive to price.

MODELLING STUDIES OF GERMANY

Bach et al. (2001), in their analysis of the 1999 German ETR using LEAN and PANTA-RHEI, report similar results for both models. In LEAN, CO_2 emissions decrease sharply in the short run and continuously stay at this new lower level, while in PANTA-RHEI CO_2 emissions decrease until 2003 and increase thereafter, due to a decrease in the relative prices of energy. The difference reflects the more rapid adjustment to a new equilibrium that occurs in a CGE model such as LEAN.

MODELLING STUDIES OF THE UK

Cambridge Econometrics et al. (2005) found a significant but modest fall in carbon emissions arising from the UK's CCL. Compared to the case where no CCL is introduced, total carbon emissions are reduced by 3.1 per million tonnes of carbon (mtC) in 2002, rising to 3.7 mtC by 2010. Total greenhouse gas emissions are reduced by 1.7% in 2002, increasing to 2.0% by 2010. However, it was also found that the existence of exemptions limited the environmental benefits. In the full-rate scenarios, where CCA sectors are charged the full CCL, fuel use in the CCA sectors is reduced by an additional 3–6% and CO_2 emissions by an additional 0.5 mtC.

The analysis reported that the bulk of the reductions in carbon emissions would arise from a sharp fall in energy demand. However, there would also be some switching between fuels: it was found that good-quality combined-heat-and-power capacity would increase by 1.2 GW by 2010 in comparison to the reference case. A particularly interesting result from this analysis was that a statistically significant 'announcement effect' on energy demand was found in 1999 for some fuel users, two years before the full CCL rates were intro-duced. By 2000, the energy demand from 'other final energy users' (chiefly comprising commerce and the public sector) had already fallen by 1.2% compared to the reference scenario.

MODELLING STUDIES OF THE EU

In its analysis of ETR at the European level using E3ME, Barker et al. (2009) found that there were reductions in greenhouse gas emissions in all six ETR countries in the 1990s compared to the baseline scenario, and projected that there would be falls through to at least 2012. The expected reduction averaged 3% by 2012, which results in a 1.3% reduction for the EU-25 as a whole. Unsurprisingly, the scale of emissions reduction is related to the scale of taxation on fuels: Finland and Sweden exhibit the largest reductions, with Sweden's emissions falling by around 7%. The smallest effects are in the

Netherlands and the UK. Exemptions were found generally to have a small but negative effect on the success of ETR, but the effect was large in the case of the Netherlands, because the tiered energy tax rates were considered to be exemptions, and so removing the exemption involved shifting all industry onto the highest tax rate.

Again, it was found that the main source of reductions in emissions would be a fall in demand for all fuels. In most cases, the reduction in fuel demand is in the region of 1–3%, although, as with the results for emissions, it is slightly larger in Sweden and Finland. Despite this, fuel demand recovers slightly over time as environmental taxes are not raised in line with fuel prices. However, in most cases, the fall in emissions was projected to be larger than the fall in fuel demand, indicating that tax policies prompt users to switch to cleaner fuels, as well as reducing overall energy demand.

THE IMPACT OF CARBON LEAKAGE

Barker et al. (2009) also considered the important issue of carbon leakage between EU countries arising specifically from ETR as part of the COMETR project. Leakages outside Europe were not captured. It was found that there was very little evidence that serious carbon leakage had occurred and that in some cases, due to induced technological change across borders, it may even have been negative. Furthermore, there was little change in trade patterns between ETR and non-ETR countries, indicating that there was a limited shift in competitiveness (although carbon leakage was slightly more prevalent in export-driven industries). These findings are attributed to the fact that energy costs are a small proportion of total industrial costs, and to technology spill-over from ETR to non-ETR countries.

However, many other studies find that there will be at least some carbon leakage arising from ETR. The Intergovernmental Panel on Climate Change's (IPCC) *Third Assessment Report* (2001) surveyed the literature on carbon leakage and found much variation in the estimates of its prevalence, but concluded that most estimates were in the range of 5–20%. This figure was repeated in the *Fourth Assessment Report* (2007), but it was felt that the effects from the EU ETS had been minimal, and were largely outweighed by such issues as transport costs, local market conditions, product variety, and incomplete information, which favoured local production. Matthes (2008) finds that, while it is not very noticeable at the overall level, carbon leakage can be a significant problem in certain energy-intensive manufacturing sectors, and that, consequently, any policies to ameliorate carbon leakage need to be precisely tailored to each affected sector.

The impact of meeting the Kyoto protocol targets on carbon leakage is assessed by Babiker (2005). He uses a global CGE model with seven regions, seven goods, and three industries and expands it so that there can be increasing returns to scale and strategic behaviour in the energy-intensive industries. He models the introduction of the Kyoto Protocol in the OECD countries and finds that there is extensive carbon leakage under certain assumptions:

- 20% for constant returns to scale and differentiated products;
- 25% for increasing returns to scale (IRTS) and differentiated products;
- 60% for constant returns and homogeneous goods (HG, i.e. commodities);
- 130% for the HG-IRTS combination.

All of these scenarios produce more carbon emissions than in most other studies, and in the last scenario, environmental regulation actually leads to increases in global emissions. However, Babiker's findings should be treated with some caution as they are heavily influenced by the assumptions used in the model. In particular, the basic CGE model assumes perfect competition, perfect information, and low or zero transaction or transport costs. These assumptions make it very easy for the producers of goods and services to cross borders and deliver output anywhere in the world at little or no extra cost. In addition, Babiker allows for increasing returns to scale in the energy-intensive industries only. The presence of increasing returns to scale in an industry drives its concentration into few producers in a single location, since large-scale production yields the highest returns. This effect is exaggerated when it is the case, as Babiker assumes, that increasing returns to scale exist in only one industry, because resources are drawn into that industry at the expense of others.

These assumptions are, of course, not entirely realistic. Therefore, what Babiker shows is that carbon leakage could potentially be very great under a certain set of circumstances. However, other studies have highlighted the importance of, for example, differentiated products, transport costs, and other barriers to relocation across borders.

5.2.3 Summary and Conclusions

Environmental tax reform has attracted a high level of interest in the theoretical and modelling environmental policy literature because the revenue-recycling mechanism raises the possibility of a double dividend, whereby welfare is increased by both a reduction in environmentally harmful activity and a reduction in conventional taxation. However, this apparent free lunch has been disputed, primarily on the grounds that ETR generates more tax distortions than it removes through the tax-interaction effect. In addition, there are concerns about carbon leakage and the impact of ETR on sectoral competitiveness.

A survey of the literature reveals, overall, a more qualified view between these two extremes. On the theoretical side, many factors have been identified that increase the chance that a double dividend can be achieved, including the existence of involuntary unemployment and the reduction of taxes on goods that are not complementary to emissions-intensive goods. On the empirical modelling side, the broad consensus appears to be that a weak double dividend is the most likely outcome of ETR. Perhaps more importantly, the modelled effects on total economic output, employment, competitiveness, and carbon leakage tend to be quite small, whatever their direction, although they can be larger at the sectoral level.

However, there is considerable uncertainty in the results, not least because the models that have been used to analyse ETR vary so much in their design and underlying assumptions, which makes it difficult to reach any precise conclusions and to declare in favour of any particular design of ETR.

References

Åkerfeldt, S. (2009), 'How Did We Do It? What Have Been the Effects? The Future?', Paper presented at the Forum Finanz, 'Ecological Tax Reform I: A Key to Sustainability and Competitiveness', organized by the Austrian Ministry of Finance and Eco Social Forum Europe, 29 October 2009, Vienna, Austria.

Andersen, M. S., and P. Ekins (eds.) (2009), *Carbon-Energy Taxation: Lessons from Europe*, Oxford: Oxford University Press.

Babiker, H. (2005), 'Climate Change Policy, Market Structure, and Carbon Leakage', *Journal of International Economics*, 65: 421–45.

Bach, S., C. Bork, M. Kohlhaas, C. Lutz, B. Meyer, B. Preatorius, and H. Welsch (2001), *Die ökologische Steuerreform in Deutschland: Eine modellgestützte Analyse ihrer Wirkungen auf Wirtschaft und Umwelt*, Heidelberg: Physica-Verlag.

Barker, T., S. Junankar, H. Pollitt, and P. Summerton (2009), 'The Macroeconomic Effects of Unilateral Environmental Tax Reforms in Europe, 1995–2012', in J. Cottrell, J. E. Milne, H. Ashiabor, L. Kreiser, and K. Deketelaere (eds), *Critical Issues in Environmental Taxation*: Volume VI, Oxford: Oxford University Press, 73–100.

—— and A. W. A. Peterson (1987), 'The Cambridge Multisectoral Dynamic Model of the British Economy', Cambridge: Cambridge University Press.

—— M. Qureshi, and J. Köhler (2006), 'The Costs of Greenhouse Gas Mitigation with Induced Technological Change: A Meta-Analysis of Estimates in the Literature', Tyndall Centre for Climate Change Research Working Paper 89.

Baron, R., and ECON-ENERGY (1997), 'Economic/Fiscal Instruments: Competitiveness Issues Related to Carbon/Energy Taxation', in UNFCCC and Annex I Expert Group on the FCCC (eds.) *Policies and Measures for Common Action Working Paper 14*, Paris: OECD/IEA.

Baumol, W., and Oates, W. (1971), 'The Use of Standards and Prices for the Protection of the Environment', *Swedish Journal of Economics*, 73, March: 42–54.

Bovenberg, A. Lans, and Ruud A. de Mooij (1997), 'Environmental Levies and Distortionary Taxation: Reply', *American Economic Review*, 87(1): 252–3.

Bovenberg, Lans, and Frederick van der Ploeg (1998), 'Tax Reform, Structural Unemployment and the Environment', *Scandinavian Journal of Economics*, 100(3), September: 593–61.

Cambridge Econometrics (2009a), Review of Literature on Environmental Tax Reform from Version 5.5 dated 23 April 2009.

—— (2009b), 'E3ME Manual', available at <http://www.camecon.com/ModellingTraining/suite_economic_models/E3ME/E3MEManual.aspx>.

—— Department of Applied Economics, University of Cambridge; and the Policy Studies Institute (2005), 'Modelling the Initial Effects of the Climate Change Levy'.

Ekins, P., and S. Speck (2008), 'Environmental Tax Reform in Europe: Energy Tax Rates and Competitiveness', in L. Kaiser, J. Milne, and N. Chalifour (eds.), *Critical Issues in Environmental Taxation: Volume V*, Oxford: Oxford University Press, 77–105.

European Commission (2009), *Excise Duty Tables*, DG Taxation and Customs Union, different years.

European Environment Agency (EEA) (2008), 'Effectiveness of Environmental Taxes and Charges for Managing Sand, Gravel and Rock Extraction in Selected EU Countries', EEA Report No. 2/2008, Copenhagen, Denmark.

Eurostat (2009), *Taxation Trends in the European Union: Data for the EU Member States and Norway*, 2009 Edition, Luxembourg: Eurostat.

Goulder, L. (1995), 'Environmental Taxation and the "Double Dividend": A Reader's Guide', *International Tax and Public Finance*, 2(2): 157–83.

Grubb, M., C. Hope, and R. Fouquet (2002), 'Climatic Implications of the Kyoto Protocol: The Contribution of International Spillover', *Climatic Change*, 54: 11–28.

Heady, C. J., A. Markandya, W. Blyth, J. Collingwood, and P. G.Taylor (2000), 'Study on the Relationship between Environmental/Energy Taxation and Employment Creation', report published by the European Commission, DG Environment, at <http://ec.europa.eu/environment/enveco/taxation/index.htm>.

Hoerner, J., and B. Bosquet (2001), *Environmental Tax Reform: The European Experience*, Washington, DC: Center for a Sustainable Economy.

IPCC (2001), *Third Assessment Report of the Intergovernmental Panel on Climate Change*, Cambridge and New York: Cambridge University Press.

—— (2007), *Fourth Assessment Report of the Intergovernmental Panel on Climate Change*, Cambridge and New York: Cambridge University Press.

Jaeger, William K. (2002), 'Carbon Taxation When Climate Affects Productivity', *Land Economics*, 78(3): 354–67.

Kohlhaas, M. (2005), 'Gesamtwirtschaftliche Effekte der ökologischen Steuerreform: Band II des Endberichts für das Vorhaben "Quantifizierung der Effekte der Ökologischen Steuerreform auf Umwelt, Beschäftigung und Innovation" ', Forschungsprojekt im Auftrag des Umweltbundesamts, Berlin.

Kraav, E., and S. Lüpsik (2007a), 'Estonian Ecological Tax Reform', Presentation at the COMETR Workshop, 22 May 2007, Prague, Czech Republic.

—— —— (2007b), 'Ecological Tax Reform in Estonia and Innovation Perspectives in the Energy Sector', Paper presented at the Eighth International Environmental Taxation Conference, 17–19 October 2007, Munich, Germany.

Kriechel, Ben and Thomas Ziesemer (2007), 'The Environmental Porter Hypothesis: Theory, Evidence, and a Model of Timing of Adoption', *Economics of Innovation and New Technology*, 18(3): 267–94.

Lelumees, L. (2007), 'Carrying out the Ecological Tax Reform in Estonia', Unpublished paper.

Lucas, R. (1976), 'Econometric Policy Evaluation: A Critique', in K. Brunner and A. Meltzer (eds.), *The Phillips Curve and Labor Markets*, Amsterdam: North-Holland: 19–46.

Lutz, C., B. Meyer, C. Nathani, and J. Schleich (2005), 'Endogenous Technological Change and Emissions: The Case of the German Steel Industry', *Energy Policy*, 33(9): 1143–54.

Matthes, F. C (2008), 'What Makes a Sector with Significant Cost Increase Subject to Leakage', in K. Neuhoff and F. C. Matthes (eds.), *The Role of Auctions for Emissions Trading*, Climate Strategies, Cambridge, available at <http://www.climatestrategies. org>, 29–34.

Meyer, B., and C. Lutz (2002), 'Carbon Tax and Labour Compensation—A Simulation for G7', in K. Uno (ed.), *Economy-Energy-Environment Simulation: Beyond the Kyoto Protocol*, London: Kluwer Academic Publishers, 185–90.

—— —— and M. I. Wolter (2008), 'The Global Multisector/Multicountry 3-E Model GINFORS: A Description of the Model and a Baseline Forecast for Global Energy Demand and CO2 Emissions', *Journal of Sustainable Development*, special issue on global models.

Ministry of Finance (2007), 'Estonian Tax and Tax Structure', Presentation.

Nordic Council of Ministers (2006), *The Use of Economic Instruments in Nordic and Baltic Environmental Policy 2001–2005*, TemaNord 2006: 525, Copenhagen, Denmark.

Oates, W. E. (1995), 'Green Taxes: Can We Protect the Environment and Improve the Tax System at the Same Time?' *Southern Economic Journal*, 61: 914–22.

Organisation of Economic Co-operation and Development (OECD) (2001), *Environmentally Related Taxes in OECD Countries: Issues and Strategies*, Paris: OECD.

—— (2009), *Taxing Wages 2007–2008*, Paris: OECD.

Pigou, A. C. (1920), *The Economics of Welfare*, London: Macmillan.

Pissarides, C. (2008), 'Assessment of Macro Economic Transmission Mechanisms of Carbon Constraints through the UK Economy', A Report for the Committee on Climate Change.

Porter, M. E., and C. van der Linde (1995), 'Towards a New Conception of the Environment-Competitiveness Relationship', *Journal of Economic Perspectives*, 9(4): 119–32.

Repetto, R., and D. Austin (1997), *The Costs of Climate Protection: A Guide for the Perplexed*, Washington: World Resources Institute.

Sato, M., and L. Mohr (2008), 'Leakage Concerns: A Small Number of Sectors are Potentially Affected', in K. Neuhoff and F. C. Matthes (eds.), *The Role of Auctions for Emissions Trading*, Climate Strategies, Cambridge, available at <http://www. climatestrategies.org>, 21–8.

Schöb, R. (1996), 'Evaluating Tax Reform in the Presence of Externalities', *Oxford Economic Papers*, 48(4): 537–55.

Speck, S., and J. Jilkova (2009), 'Design of Environmental Tax Reforms in Europe', in M. S. Andersen and P. Ekins (eds.) (2009), *Carbon-Energy Taxation: Lessons from Europe*, Oxford: Oxford University Press.

—— J. McNicholas, and M. Markovic (2001a), 'Environmental Taxes in an Enlarged Europe', Regional Environmental Center, Szentendre, Hungary.

—— —— —— (2001b), 'Environmental Funds in Accession Countries', Regional Environmental Center, Szentendre, Hungary.

Zhang, Z., and A. Baranzini (2004), 'What Do We Know About Carbon Taxes? An Inquiry into their Impacts on Competitiveness and Distribution of Income', *Energy Policy*, 32 (2004): 507–18.

6

Introducing Environmental Tax Reform: The Case of the Czech Republic

Petr Šauer, Ondřej Vojáček, Jaroslav Klusák and Jarmila Zimmermannová

6.1 Introduction

In terms of environmental tax reform (ETR), the Czech Republic can be considered a typical example of the Central and Eastern European Countries (CEEC) that have become EU Member States, despite differences in their previous and current environmental policies.

The analysis of the Czech Republic case demonstrates that despite convincing modelling results showing a positive economic impact of the introduction of ETR (in terms of both GDP and employment growth), there are still significant obstacles to its implementation. In our view, in addition to using the results of economic analyses in support of decision-making, a deeper analysis of the political economy in the CEEC is required to address the obstacles to ETR introduction in a country like the Czech Republic.

The goal of this chapter is to generate understanding of how ETR has been perceived in the Czech Republic, including the history of its preparation and barriers to its implementation in the country.

ETR is put into the context of the specifics of the Czech Republic, particularly the development of its environmental and economic policy and tax system since the mid-1990s. The chapter also briefly shows how some concepts of environmental taxes (ET) and ETR were designed, but not implemented, in this period.

The chapter investigates the first experience of practical implementation of ETR in the Czech Republic, presenting results of qualitative research conducted with key stakeholders. It shows the attitudes of these stakeholders to ETR's implementation and tries to formulate some conclusions related to its further progress. The main focus is on the political-economy and institutional settings for the preparation of ETR in the Czech Republic. The main goals of the research were: to learn about the differences in different stakeholders' understanding of ETR; to find out the key relations between the interests of the stakeholders and ETR, and the relationship between ETR and innovation processes (especially in industries); and to try to learn whether ETR promotes integration of environmental policy into other policies and what the impact of ETR has been on the development of governance.

6.2 ETR in the context of the Czech tradition in environmental charging and taxation

6.2.1 Brief history of the introduction of environmental charges and taxes

There is a long tradition of implementing economic tools of environmental policy in the Czech Republic (for more detail on this issue, see Šauer 2007; Hadrabová 2002; Sladovník and Rybářová 1990).

Air emission charges were first introduced in 1967. Charges for discharging wastewater into surface waters were first levied in 1979. In order to arrive at the rates to be charged, calculations of marginal abatement costs, the trial-and-error procedure, and the internalization of negative externalities from environmental degradation were considered as theoretical bases. The use of revenues for funding environmental protection projects via various environmental protection funds also dates from that period.

The current system of economic tools used in Czech environmental policy was introduced shortly after 1990 during the process of establishing a new state environmental policy and relevant legislation. Air emission charges, sewerage charges, water pollution charges, charges on municipal waste, charges on solid waste disposal, water extraction charges, charges on dispossession of agricultural and forest land, and mining charges (including aggregate materials charges—sand, gravel, and rock) all feature in the current system of environmental charges.

Although environmental charges have been regarded as working towards environmental protection, their narrow focus on particular components of the environment has worked against a broader approach to such protection. Also, as the emissions of most of the key pollutants have significantly decreased, the revenue from the respective charges is now relatively low compared to the administrative costs of their collection. The above-mentioned charge on aggregate materials is among the charges generating very small amount of revenue and having almost zero impact on environmental and landscape protection (for more details, see EEA 2008).

The changes in the whole tax system that occurred in the first half of the 1990s opened a space for the introduction of new taxes. The introduction of ET was discussed as part of the debate on public finance reform. A specific section on ET was incorporated into the Tax Act in 1993. The initial idea was that environmental charges and ET could work in parallel. The ET was supposed to focus on environmental problems not covered by the charges (e.g. taxation of particular products such as paints).

6.2.2 History of the ETR debate

An intellectual shift from ET to ETR can be observed in the latter half of the 1990s, when the concept of the ET started to be perceived in the context of lowering labour taxation. At this stage, the first calculations of potential ETR impacts were made. In those days, ETR was—with a certain simplification—regarded by politicians and experts (namely those from the Ministry of the Environment) as a really strong instrument of environmental policy. Theoretical disputes about ET rates were mostly based on the idea of Pigouvian taxation and internalization of externalities, but revenue generation was also discussed.

The first explicit official proposal of an environmental tax reform was prepared jointly by the Ministry of the Environment (MoE) and the Ministry of Finance (MoF) in the year 2000, and was discussed by the Czech government in the first half of 2001.

After elections in 2002, the new governmental Coalition Agreement (signed in June 2002) declared ETR as one of the goals and priorities of the new government. The Agreement explicitly incorporated a commitment to 'start working on a revenue-neutral ETR in the Czech Republic'. The intention was also introduced into the 'Proposal of a Public Finance Reform' in 2002. However, no explicit ETR was included in the first phase of the Reform in 2003.

A draft ETR was prepared in November 2003 and has been updated several times since then. For example, there was a commitment to prepare a proposal of fiscally neutral environmental tax changes in accordance with EU laws in the Government Program Statement in August 2004. Working materials developed by the Ministry of the Environment on implementing ETR (MoE 2005) were intensively discussed. Impact studies of the ETR proposals were developed, but none of the ETR proposals was finally implemented.

6.2.3 The practical introduction of ETR

Some progress on this agenda came at the beginning of 2007, when the Czech Prime Minister's cabinet acknowledged a scheme of ETR implementation in the Czech Republic. According to this schedule, the ETR implementation would consist of three phases: Phase I has been implemented since 2008 (see below). The goal of Phase II is to transform the system of air emission charges and evaluate the impacts of Phase I. Phase II should be implemented between 2010 and 2013. Phase III should be prepared by the end of 2012 and implemented between 2014 and 2017. According to current governmental materials, the ETR should be deepened and extended to cover additional natural resources, natural services, etc.

The exemption for the Czech Republic from EC Directive No. 2003/96 expired at the end of 2007. It has become necessary to implement the Directive at least at its minimal rates as of 1 January 2008. Because of that, the final version of a proposal for an ETR was discussed by the Czech government in January 2007 and the new energy taxation legislation approved in May 2007. This new energy taxation legislation did not initially include the revenue-neutrality element of ETR, but was in line with the EC Directive (No. 2003/96), current Czech legislation, a Government Assignment, the official State Environmental Policy of the Czech Republic, and the official State Energy Policy of the Czech Republic. However, revenue neutrality was implemented later. The legislation was prepared by the Ministry of Finance. Three new taxes were introduced (see Table 6.1).

Several exemptions were agreed at this stage of the ETR, for example household heating with natural gas, district heating (but only if the heat is generated from combined heat and power technology and delivered to households), power and heat from renewable energy sources, methane, and hydrogen fuel cells. The government has retained zero excise duty on the use of compressed natural gas in vehicles; electricity used in rail and road transport and fuels used for electricity production are not subject to the excise duty either.

The taxation neutrality principle was implemented after 2008 in the form of a lowering of income taxation for both corporations and individuals as a part of the governmental tax reform (from 24% to 21% in 2008 for companies and a 15% flat rate for individuals), which was part of the government tax reform approved in 2007 and coming into force in 2008. In Phase II (since 2009), contributions to the social security system paid by both employees and

Table 6.1. ETR in the Czech Republic—Phase I

	Tax rate	Household price increase
Solid fossil fuels	EUR 0.3/GJ	10 %
Natural gas for heating purposes	EUR 1.1/MWh	Exempted
Electricity	EUR 1/MWh	1%

Source: Act no. 261/2007 Coll.

employers were lowered by 1.5%, with an anticipated reduction in governmental revenues for 2009 of CZK 11 billion, i.e. 0.4 billion euros.

Despite the fact that the story of explicit ETR introduction in the Czech Republic before the year 2008 might not seem very successful (many drafts were developed and none of them was applied), it is interesting to note some examples in Czech economic policy of what might be regarded as the introduction of an implicit ETR, in that some environmental taxes were introduced or increased, and some labour taxes were reduced, but there was no political connection made between the two kinds of changes, nor was there any discussion or justification of a tax shift as such. As is evident from Table 6.2, ETR aspects have been present in Czech taxation policy since the 1990s, despite the fact that they were not understood or presented as an ETR.

6.3 A review of Czech ex-ante quantitative analyses

In the Czech Republic, attention has traditionally been paid to projects attempting to quantify the economic and social implications of the various ETR models considered. Their objective has been to improve the decision-making process used in public administration, in particular the Ministry of the Environment. Nearly every government proposal was connected with a study analysing the impacts on various stakeholders.

Three relevant ex-ante analyses (Ščasný and Brůha 2007; Zimmermannová 2008; Pur 2007) carried out since 2005 are reviewed here. By then, it was already almost clear what taxes would be implemented but the revenue-recycling model was not clear. The purpose of all the studies was to analyse the future impacts of the first ETR phase derived from the implementation of Directive 2003/96/ES within the Czech legal framework.

In reviewing the studies, the focus is on identifying possible changes in the costs of selected stakeholders (especially households) due to the

Table 6.2. Examples of implicit ETR in Czech taxation policy

Year	Environment-related tax (CO_2 related)	Reductions in other taxes
1995	Increase in motor fuel excise tax rates	Decrease in profit and labour taxation
1998	Increase in motor fuel excise tax rates and many fuels moved to the standard VAT rate	Significant profit tax rate cuts (from 39% to 35%)
1999	Excise tax rates on gasoline increased	Labour income tax brackets widened
2004	Excises on motor fuels increased	Profit taxation decreased
2008	New energy taxes introduced	Cuts in personal income tax and profit tax

implementation of ETR, and the redistributional aspects of the ETR implementation in the Czech Republic. Attention is also paid to the impacts on industry.

6.3.1 Impacts on households

Concerning distributional impacts, the studies (Ščasný and Brůha 2007; Pur 2007) come to the following conclusions.

Ščasný and Brůha, who take into consideration price and income elasticities, i.e., households' response to the tax introduction, conclude that an environmental tax reform disregarding the revenue neutrality principle (mere introduction of environmental taxes) would increase energy expenditures the most for households using solid fuels for heating and those connected to a central heat supply and using gas for heating. For households using gas for heating, the authors predict a reduction in the energy expenditures due to their changing behaviour; the same applies to households using electricity for heating and gas for cooking. The welfare reduction was most significant in households using gas or solid fuels for heating (CZK 800–900 per annum). Households in smaller municipalities would suffer a similar impact from the energy taxation. Pensioner households in smaller municipalities would suffer relatively the worst welfare impacts.

Pur's study does not take into account any household response to the introduction of new taxes. The author predicts a direct impact on household budgets in the form of an annual expenditure increase of CZK 607–845, depending on the household type. To compensate for those expenditures, the disposable income would have to increase for old-age pensioners and other (economically active, non-maintained, or unemployed) persons. Incomplete families with children would be affected more severely regarding their expenditures than the average population.

In general, we can say that based on the results of both the studies, the low-income household groups—pensioners and incomplete families with children —would be the most affected by the new taxation.

6.3.2 Impacts on industry

Concerning impacts on industry, the studies (Ščasný and Brůha 2007; Pur 2007; Zimmermannová 2007, 2008) come to the following conclusions.

Brůha and Ščasný examine first-order impacts, i.e., they do not take into account effects among sectors. We can say that the impacts on industry and its constituent sectors are low and that most of the calculations are at the statistical error level. According to the authors, we can even say that autonomous price fluctuations on global markets (oil and gas price volatility) have a greater impact on the national economic sectors than the analysed ETR.

Pur also examines first-order impacts. He concludes that even if the exemptions for energy-intensive industries were non-existent or only partial, the impact on the expenditures of companies operating in the industries would be low. First, the potential increase in certain expenditures could be compensated for by reducing labour costs, and secondly, the additional costs could be transferred to consumers without any significant threat to competitiveness. The annual expenditure increase would not pose a significant risk to the competitiveness of the Czech economy.

Zimmermannová employs an I-O model for the Czech Republic based on Leontief's methodology: she includes second-order impacts, i.e. cross-industry linkages. Her analysis employing a short-term price model shows that the solid fuel tax contributes the most to increased prices in industry sectors, particularly those with high solid fuel consumption. Consumption of solid fuels for electricity generation and coke production makes up approximately two-thirds of total solid fuel consumption in the Czech Republic, and if such a significant proportion of consumption is tax-exempt, this would certainly be reflected in the overall impact on the industries, compared to an alternative where just coal for electricity generation is taxed. According to information available to the author, no EU country has applied so-called double taxation, i.e. taxation on both fuels for electricity generation and electricity itself. The analysis shows that such taxation would have a significant impact on costs, particularly in some energy-intensive industries.

In general, we can say that based on the results of the reviewed studies, the impacts of the environmental taxes on industry are not very significant, chiefly due to the institution of tax exemptions.

6.4 Qualitative research on ETR implementation in the Czech Republic

6.4.1 PETRE project survey: methodology and research questions

Qualitative survey methods were chosen as the predominant way of addressing our research questions concerning the knowledge, attitudes, and opinions of the principal stakeholders, as well as the broader context of the stakeholders' understanding of ETR.

Knowledge of the theoretical background of ETR, findings from the quantitative studies concerning the potential impacts on particular stakeholders, and knowledge gathered from frequent working contacts with people representing various stakeholders were taken into consideration at the beginning of the preparation for the research. Findings from foreign literature presenting results of projects applying qualitative analyses were also used to formulate the research questions; especially those concerning the institutional background and understanding the true interests of relevant interest subjects.

The paper by Dresner et al. (2006), which reports the results of the PETRAS project (Policies for Ecological Tax Reform—Assessment of Social Responses), seems to be the most relevant to the Czech situation. According to this study, a lack of trust concerning the use of revenues, difficulty in understanding the purpose of a tax shift, and a desire for incentives for good behaviour, as well as perceived 'penalties' for bad behaviour, seem to be the most relevant barriers to ETR implementation. Dresner et al. have also formulated specific recommendations in order to increase acceptance of ETR, for example, administration of the levies by an independent body, explicit identification of the reduction in direct taxes, or earmarking of ETR revenues for energy-efficiency programmes or other environmental projects.

The study by the EEA (1996) also identifies important political barriers to the introduction of environmental, particularly energy, taxes. The most important are as follows: the perceived impacts on competitiveness and employment (particularly in some sectors and regions), impacts on low-income groups, perceived conflicts between national tax systems and EU or world trade rules, the EU unanimity rule when voting on fiscal measures, perceptions that the taxes have to be high if they are to work, the perceived conflict between changing behaviour (i.e. less tax) and maintaining revenues, existing subsidies, and regulations that provide environmentally perverse effects; and other policies and cultures which negate or inhibit environmental taxes.

Dunne and Clinch's (2004) research focused on the attitudes of the business sector to ETR in Ireland. They found that, although businesses were well-informed about day-to-day environmental issues and requirements, their awareness of ETR was generally very low. Knowledge of ETR and environmental taxes was generally better in bigger companies. The obstacles to the implementation of market-based instruments (MBIs) identified by Pearce (2001) were also relevant in investigating the implementation of ETR in the Czech Republic.

The survey conducted in the Czech Republic used in-depth interviews with the key stakeholders. The interviews were conducted by means of a structured questionnaire with open-ended questions. These were recorded, transcribed, and analysed. The questionnaire was progressively amended, based on the findings of the previous interviews.

A total of 25 interviews were conducted with a total of 17 subjects (some of the subjects were interviewed twice). Six of them were government representatives (from ministries responsible for the ETR); six were representatives of key relevant businesses (economic chamber, energy, heat and metallurgy); two were non-governmental representatives (organizations playing an important role in ETR preparation); one was a representative of labour unions (taking part in the ETR preparation group); and two were academic consultants taking part in the ETR preparation discussions.

The interviews were conducted in several rounds. In the first round, three key persons who had participated in the entire history of the Czech ETR preparation were interviewed, based on the first version of the questionnaire. In the second round, representatives of all key stakeholders were approached. In the third phase, the specific focus was on business stakeholders. In the fourth phase, respondents from the previous phases were asked additional questions based on previous research which enabled us to identify attitudes and facts changing over time. The research comprises the most detailed ETR qualitative national research case study of which the authors are aware.

The main research findings of the qualitative research are presented below, set in the context of the more general findings of previous qualitative ETR research done elsewhere. The findings show the specific political and stakeholders' relations and robust attitudes which influence the environmental policy in the country to a surprisingly great extent. There is no reason to suppose that the situation in other (especially new) EU Member States is different.

6.4.2 Empirical findings among stakeholders: public administration bodies, labour unions, and NGOs

The key public administration bodies that took part in the ETR preparation were as follows: the Ministry of the Environment (MoE) and its State Environmental Fund (SEF), the Ministry of Finance (MoF), and the Ministry of Social Affairs (MoSA).

Public administration bodies have different attitudes to ETR and its implementation in the Czech Republic. There was no agreement in the Ministry of the Environment (MoE) on the main objective of the ETR in the Czech Republic. Understandings of the objective varied from taxation of externalities to improvements in energy efficiency and also to public health protection. The MoE also had exaggerated expectations about ETR. The ETR concept was most popular in the latter half of the 1990s, and was very often viewed as a powerful and all-purpose instrument, for example, the ETR was mentioned in the proposals for a Waste Management Plan of the Czech Republic.

From the Ministry of Finance (MoF) point of view, ETR is only a fiscal instrument helping reduce the state budget deficit, so the MoF sees the main objective of ETR in terms of additional income for the state budget.

The public administration bodies agreed that the ETR was not supported by any significant PR campaigns explaining the positive impacts of the ETR process (lower wage costs, decreasing energy dependency, etc.). Also, only a few stakeholders were invited to cooperate in the public hearings process.

The idea that ETR is implemented for its own sake was mentioned several times by public administration representatives, meaning that the idea behind the ETR was lost during the implementation process. This corresponds to the finding of inconsistent opinions on the main objective of ETR.

Some of the public administration representatives also worried about the transformation of the existing system of environmental charges to environmental taxes, and this seems to be a key to understanding better the different positions of the MoE and the SEF on the one hand, and the MoF on the other hand. Traditionally, part of the environmental charges generates revenues for the State Environmental Fund, which is under the jurisdiction of the MoE. It is intended that the SEF will fund environmental protection projects, including co-financing Structural Fund projects until 2013. The revenue from environmental taxes, however, is a source of finance for the State Budget, i.e. under the jurisdiction of the MoF. The threat to the SEF of losing revenues has resulted in the MoE shifting from its initially declared support for the ETR towards advocating the previous system of charges, using, among other things, the argument of co-funding EU environmental protection projects.

The MoSA is not very enthusiastic about current ETR implementation, since recycling the actual ET revenue of CZK 3 billion would in practice mean lowering employers' social security contributions by 0.3%, which runs counter to the main concern of the MoSA, which is to ensure sufficient resources to cover mandatory expenditures (retirement pensions, etc.), especially in the context of an ageing population.

The labour unions also reject ETR for different reasons—mainly due to concerns about rising household expenditures on energy, especially for low-income and retired inhabitants particularly those in the countryside. The labour unions representative also emphasized that there had been no relevant discussion with representative stakeholders over Phase I of the ETR in the Czech Republic. Czech political bodies were also criticized for making no effort to utilize the transitional period under Directive 2003/96/EC on taxation of energy products and electricity implementation, implementation of which could have been postponed until 2012. Before the new taxes came into force, the labour unions were afraid of the parallel effects of new energy taxation under Directive 2003/96/EC and a VAT rate increase on heat produced in central heating plants, both of which came into force as of 1 January 2008 and were about to increase the living costs of households. They also agreed that Phase I of the ETR would have no significant impacts on the industry sector.

For the sake of completeness, it should be mentioned that the academics and non-governmental organizations (NGOs) that took part in the ETR preparation are very well informed about the principles of ETR. Some NGOs have been developing ETR proposals which go far beyond the governmental proposals in terms of their environmental goal ambitions. For proposed ETR models that are quite ambitious, see Němcová and Kotecký (2008).

6.4.3 Empirical findings among stakeholders: businesses

This section presents the principal findings derived from interviews with business representatives.

The individual business representatives did not differ substantially in their understanding of the objectives of ETR. They were mostly in agreement in believing that the chief objective was to stimulate businesses to conserve energy. The respondents largely identified with that objective. Environmental protection was also mentioned as one of their objectives; however, it always ranked second. They were critical in the sense that they felt ET should affect all polluters, i.e., not only industrial businesses and energy providers, but also transportation and households, which emit significant volumes of pollutants. Most of the respondents mentioned the European Union's attempt to reduce consumption of primary resources with respect to the EU's energy independence.

There was a problem with understanding the term 'environmental tax reform' as such, as it does not quite capture the essence of the changes in the Czech Republic. One of the typical answers in this sense was, 'You can only reform what you have; as long as you don't have something, you can only introduce it'.

It transpired that the respondents were not very well informed about the factual, comprehensively understood objectives of the ETR theoretical framework, which intends to shift the tax burden from 'goods' like human labour, to 'bads' like the use of natural resources and pollution, with a view to obtaining a 'double dividend'. However, even after they learnt about the double-dividend idea during the course of the interviews, respondents largely failed to identify with it. Instead, they were quite seriously considering various other models for recycling ET revenues, for example, to promote environmental protection via the State Environmental Fund. The idea of revenue utilization for solutions to environmental problems seemed to be of special importance for business, and was sometimes mentioned as a point which could change their position on ETR. The businesses also expressed opposition to 'environmental engineering' (by which they meant strict state planning in the fields of energy and the environment) and their belief in strong market forces as the best solution. Some of the business representatives from labour-intensive sectors supported the idea of making labour in businesses cheaper. A common feature of the business attitudes was their scepticism about the public administration's ability to return the revenues to businesses in some form.

The responses regarding awareness of ETR and communication with other stakeholders were not uniform in terms either of the degree of awareness of the ETR preparation process, or of the communication of the MoE with other stakeholders. Some expressed their satisfaction with the degree of awareness and communication with other stakeholders; and contrariwise, others were totally dissatisfied in this respect.

Business responses to the economic and other implications of the introduction of ET expressed concerns about the impacts on profitability and competitiveness, not only at the national level but also at the European level. They criticized the short interval between the elaboration of the final draft of the ET rates and their implementation. At the same time, however, they were obviously pleased to have pushed through practically minimal ET rates for Phase I.

Regarding the ETR and long-term expectations, the business respondents were in accord in that it was not clear from recent developments which way EU and Czech environmental policy would go. A little surprisingly, most business stakeholders mentioned the need for the concept of a long-term framework for energy and environmental policy. Businesses in the power industry mentioned their need to know the direction of energy and environmental policy development for at least 30 years, referring to the innovation cycle and the life span of their current technologies. In light of the above, it is no wonder that the Czech Republic's ETR, which should be phased in over three-year cycles according to the government-approved schedule, has not elicited a very positive response among stakeholders. The stakeholders interviewed agreed in thinking that the effect of the current ETR does not play a major role in their strategic and investment decisions. They often mentioned developments in prices and stocks of primary energy sources as a more important factor. On the other hand, the difficulties of certain sectors (e.g. the textile industry) that are on the edge of profitability were mentioned in the sense that any increase in the prices of their inputs would pose problems for them.

Stakeholders were asked whether increasing energy prices, partly also due to the ETR implementation, might be an important trigger of environmental innovation and businesses' efforts to conserve energy. The responses were not unanimous, and largely corresponded with those to the question about long-term expectations. There was agreement that increasing prices of primary energy sources would lead to efforts to introduce various efficiency measures (thermal insulation of buildings, replacement of boilers, etc.). On the other hand, the great uncertainty about the direction of future developments in primary energy source prices and environmental policy regulation results in businesses delaying long-term and costly innovations which are of crucial importance if the intended environmental goals are to be met. In this context, the businesses often mentioned the need for a long-term outlook in environmental policy. To invest more intensively, a ten-year time horizon was mentioned as a minimum requirement by almost all stakeholders (some of them mentioned even longer horizons, as already noted).

In this context, the innovation-motivating function of administrative instruments (mainly limits and their tightening) was mentioned favourably, but the motivating function of ET was not appreciated. The argument was that ET may be motivating for rich companies, which have good prospects, but not for sectors which cannot afford to pass on 100% of the input price increase in their product prices (because of competitiveness). The philosophy of ET as an environmental policy instrument was thus doubted, because according to some businesses, the philosophy that the more expensive a thing is the more will be spent on efficiency and innovation may not always be true—some sectors simply cannot afford investments.

Regarding the integration of ETR into other environmental policy instruments, business representatives were of the opinion that environmental regulation is not opposed to ETR in principle, but that its instruments lack interconnection and integration. Their responses contained broader reflections on national environmental policy. They made frequent references to the issue of emission limits and charges. Emission limits and other administrative instruments were frequently quoted as effective tools. The responses addressed other environmental policy instruments too, such as support mechanisms motivating businesses to environmental protection. The respondents spoke about financial mechanisms, as well as the need for infrastructure building and investment in education. Voluntary environmental agreements were also mentioned as a possible effective instrument.

To sum up, the results of the research among businesses showed that they view ET and the ETR in the broader context of the entire system of environmental policy instruments. On the other hand, a low level of awareness of the actual principles and objectives of ETR was discovered. Businesses also tend not to trust in the environmentally stimulating function of ET. Big concerns were revealed about the effect of deepening environmental regulation on economic competition.

The research also showed that business representatives felt no hostility towards environmental protection. Quite to the contrary, they perceived it as part of their social responsibilities. It became evident, nonetheless, that the business sphere does not wish to be a mere 'passive victim' of environmental regulation, but wants to be actively involved in the definition of environmental policy, which is currently not the case in the Czech Republic. In order to encourage their efforts in environmental protection and particularly when paying ET, the businesses implicitly inclined to the idea of using ET revenues to support their innovation processes. In their view, such support can be organized institutionally in various forms, be it as a regime of voluntary agreements or through the introduction of subsidy and other schemes.

Sometimes businesses were suspicious in that they viewed ET as an attempt to raise more funds for the state. They were willing to accept this as long as revenues from such taxes were utilized in resolving the real priorities in environmental protection (particulate air pollution, regional projects, etc.). However, they would be most satisfied if the funds were used to support business innovation, which is subject to certain cycles during which businesses need to invest. The businesses also said that they were struggling with the bad timing of the environmental regulation and the state authorities' failure to understand and respect investment cycles.

6.5 Conclusions and recommendations

Contemporary efforts and discussions concerning the introduction of ETR have to be seen in light of the long tradition of the use of environmental charges in the field of environmental policy in the Czech Republic. A new system of environmental policy tools was implemented in the early 1990s. The system covers air emission charges, sewerage charges, water pollution charges, and many others. The system follows the previous tradition in many respects.

Environmental taxes started to be discussed in the first half of the 1990s as part of the process of transition to a market economy. At that time, changes to the entire taxation system provided space for the introduction of new taxes. In 1993, the Act on Public Finance Reform legally introduced ET, but no concrete ET were implemented in practice.

The latter half of the 1990s was characterized by an intellectual shift from ET to ETR, that is, the concept of the ETR started to be discussed in the context of lowering labour taxation. At that time, some experts from the Ministry of the Environment (MoE) and some academics and NGOs regarded the ETR as a strong instrument in the environmental field. The policy drafts of the ETR that were regularly developed after 2000 were very diverse and none of them was implemented because of a lack of political agreement.

As has already been said, the ETR was finally introduced as of the beginning of 2008 because of the necessity to implement Directive 2003/96/EC. Fiscal neutrality was part of the government policy. ETR revenues in 2008 amounted to around CZK 3 billion (0.12 billion euros). According to the MoE, the taxation neutrality principle was achieved after the beginning of 2008 in the form of income taxation reductions for households and companies that were part of the government tax reform. However, the decrease in the social security contributions of 1.5% since 2009, with an anticipated reduction in governmental revenues paid by employers and employees for 2009 by CZK 11 billion (0.4 billion euros) was also declared by some MoE and MoF representatives to be a part of the ETR neutrality principle. Here, it is evident that revenue neutrality was neither properly deliberated nor unanimously announced by the public authorities. This will necessarily lead to the impression among the stakeholders—except the public administration itself—that there are two separate governmental policies—ET introduction and tax lowering (no matter whether in the form of income tax or social allowances). In fact, the real motivation for social-allowance lowering had nothing in common with the ETR. Its goal was mainly to help the economy to combat financial recession.

It is interesting that, despite the official (explicit) ETR preparation and implementation, it is possible to observe aspects of the Czech economic policy that could be called 'implicit ETR implementation'—on the one hand, there have been increases in or introductions of various environmentally sound taxes, and on the other hand, there has been a reduction in the labour taxation burden.

The current draft of Phase II of the ETR consists of a mix of environmental policy instruments focusing on local environmental problems. The following tools are on the agenda: increased charges on particulate matter, NO_x, SO_2, volatile organic compounds; tax deduction in the case of environmental investments; charging of households with high-emission boilers, etc.

The ETR is generally understood by respondents as being the introduction of (additional) environmental taxes or charges with the purpose of generating additional revenues for funding environmental improvement measures. The double-dividend idea is known only to those who have particpated in its preparation. Even after respondents had learned about the double-dividend idea during the interviews, they largely failed to identify with the objective. Business respondents were still considering various models for recycling ET revenues to promote environmental protection, which could be explained by the long tradition of environmental charges in the Czech Republic.

There is a question which is difficult to answer: what would have become of the ETR idea in the Czech Republic if there were no EU Energy Tax Directive? Most likely, the Czech Republic would have continued with its environmental charging policy, which is more complex and does not cover only the CO_2 emission problem. This is in fact continuously happening nowadays (see Phase II of the ETR above). Also, it is important to mention the implicit ETR, which has been introduced since the 1990s.

The main research question underlying the work presented here was formulated as follows: 'What are the implications of the analysis for the new EU

Member States in Central and Eastern Europe, and for the design and implementation of ETRs in these countries?' We believe that our research results provide a few recommendations, which can be helpful to other CEE countries in the process of planning and designing their ETRs:

- Clearly formulate the main vision and objectives of the respective national model of ETR. It was recognized during qualitative research on public administration bodies that there is no agreement on the main objectives of the ETR in the Czech Republic.

- Define the long-term aspects and outlooks of the ETR. During interviews with business representatives, the most common criticism was that no long-term aspects of the ETR in the Czech Republic have been defined. This gap makes it difficult for business stakeholders to prepare long-term business plans.

- There is a need to create an ETR team and discuss long-term objectives and outlooks of the ETR with the main stakeholders (public administration, businesses, labour unions, NGOs). The fact that there had been no relevant discussion with representative stakeholders was mentioned as a weakness of the ETR in the Czech Republic.

- Prepare a good PR campaign with clearly understood presentations of the basic principles of ETR and results of ex-ante ETR studies. An unsatisfactory level of knowledge about the basic principles of ETR and fiscal neutrality was found in the Czech Republic, mostly among the business sector.

- Present good-practice examples of ETR in other countries (UK, Germany) to avoid scepticism about the practical implementation of ETR in the country concerned.

References

Dresner, S., L. Dunne, and T. Jackson (eds.) (2006), 'Social and Political Responses to Ecological Tax Reform in Europe', *Energy Policy*, 34(8): 895–904.

Dunne, L., and J. P. Clinch (2004), 'The Perception and Attitude of Business to the Environment and Environmental Tax Reform: Some Observations from an Irish Case Study', Planning and Environmental Policy Research Series (PEP), Working Paper 04/02, Dublin: Department of Planning and Environmental Policy, University College Dublin.

EEA (1996), *Environmental Taxes—Implementation and Environmental Effectiveness*, Copenhagen: European Environmental Agency.

——(2008), *Effectiveness of Environmental Taxes and Charges for Managing Sand, Gravel and Rock Extraction in Selected EU Countries*, Copenhagen: European Environmental Agency.

Hadrabová, A. (2002), *Vývoj ekologické politiky*, in V. Spěváček et al., *Transformace české ekonomiky*, Prague: Linde.

Němcová, P., and V. Kotecký (2008), *Ekologická daňová reforma: Impuls pro modernizaci ekonomiky, Infolist*, Brno: Hnutí Duha.

Pearce, D.W. (2001), 'What Have We Learned from the UK's Experience with Market-Based Instruments?' in D. McCoy and S. Scott (eds.), *Green and Bear It? Implementing Market-based Policies for Ireland's Environment*, Proceedings of a conference held on 10 May 2001, Dublin: ESRI.

Pur, L., (2007), *Analýza dopadů návrhu první fáze koncepce ekologické daňové reformy*. Závěrečná zpráva projektu. Praha: Ministerstvo životního prostredí.

Šauer, P. (2007), *Introduction to Environmental Economics and Policy*, Prague: Nakladatelství a vydavatelství litomyšlského semináře.

Ščasný, M., and J. Brůha (2007), *Predikce sociálních a ekonomických dopadů návrhu první fáze ekologické daňové reformy Ceské republiky*, Prague: Centrum pro otázky životního prostředí UK Praha.

Sladovník, K., and D. Rybářová (1990), *Ekologický faktor v daňové reformě*, Prague: Ústav pro životí prostředí.

Zimmermannová, J. (2007), 'Energy Taxation and its Cross-Sectoral Impacts—I/O Methodology', in P. Šauer (ed.), *Environmental Economics, Policy and International Relations*, Prague: Nakladatelství a vydavatelství litomyšlského semináře.

——(2008), *Dopady zdanění elektřiny, zemního plynu a pevných paliv na odvětví výroby a spotřeby v Ceské republice*, Prague: Katedra ekonomiky životního prostředí, VŠE Praha.

7

The Effect of the German and UK Environmental Tax Reforms on the Demand for Labour and Energy

Paolo Agnolucci

7.1 Introduction

As noted in Chapter 5, a number of European countries have introduced Environmental Tax Reforms (ETRs), a policy originally promoted by the Scandinavian governments and later adopted in the Netherlands, the UK, and Germany. This chapter focuses on the ETRs of Germany and the UK.

The German approach to ETR consisted of increases in existing energy taxes and the introduction of a new electricity tax. Exemptions and reductions were provided for the industrial, agricultural, fishing, and forestry sectors. Revenues from the taxes were used to decrease employers' and employees' contributions. The British approach to ETR consisted of the introduction of the Climate Change Levy (CCL), a tax on commercial and industrial energy consumption. Revenues have been recycled back by decreasing employers' social security contributions.

The aim of this chapter is to present a quantification of the effects of the German and the UK ETRs by adopting a simple econometric approach normally used in studies assessing the substitution of input factors. Estimation of the substitution possibilities among production inputs is motivated by policy considerations, such as reducing energy consumption and CO_2 emissions or, more generally, maintaining a socially acceptable level of employment and capital utilization, while pursuing policies aimed at changing relative prices (Arnberg and Bjørner 2007 and Christopoulos and Tsionas 2002). As our aim is to assess the impact of ETRs, the focus of the estimation will be on price elasticities rather than the elasticities of substitution normally discussed in the literature.

This chapter is structured as follows. Section 7.2 deals with the analysis of the impact of the German and British ETRs. In particular, we present a survey of the ETRs introduced in these two countries as well as a succinct discussion of the concept of ETR and of the literature assessing this policy, before moving on to describe our methodological approach and empirical results. Section 7.3 discusses these results in the context of other findings from the literature. Section 7.4 presents the conclusions which can be drawn.

7.2 The Evaluation of Environmental Tax Reforms

From the analysis of Chapter 4, we can conclude that policies like ETRs can be applied to the industrial sector as a whole without taking into account the peculiarities of particular industrial sectors. In this chapter we present an analysis of the impact of the German and British Environmental Tax Reforms (ETRs). In order to provide some background, we present a succinct summary of the German and British ETRs. A more detailed discussion can be found in the references listed below. However, before describing these two policies, the next section clarifies the concept of ETR for the purposes of this chapter, and gives a brief survey of the effects which have been estimated in the literature.

7.2.1 Environmental Tax Reforms: Definitions and Evidence in the Literature

As discussed in the economic literature, uniform environmental taxes enable the achievement of a given environmental standard at minimal abatement cost because the uniform tax rate enforces equal marginal abatement costs across polluters (Baumol and Oates 1971). From the perspective of the government, environmental taxes also have the desirable property of raising revenues. However, environmental taxes tend to be opposed by polluters who, in addition to sustaining costs to abate emissions, need to pay tax on the residual amount of pollution. When not introduced as part of a wider tax reform, environmental taxes redistribute wealth away from polluters. Lobbying from these sectors and concern that the competitiveness of national industries may be affected explain the reluctance of policy makers to introduce environmental taxes (Gee 1997). The concept of ETR, i.e. increasing environmentally related taxes while reducing distortionary taxes on other production inputs, which was originally proposed in Binswanger et al. (1983), can be considered an approach to reduce the extent of the redistribution away from polluters, and therefore the opposition to the increases in the price of natural resources caused by the taxes. Basically, an ETR is a shift in the tax burden from economic 'goods' to environmental 'bads', i.e. from what is socially desirable to what is socially undesirable, such as pollution, resource depletion, and waste (Bosquet 2000 and EC 1993). Taxing natural resources and using the revenues to reduce taxes on labour, income, or investment provides incentives to reduce consumption of materials and energy, while increasing demand for labour or capital (McNeill and Williams 2007). It is worth stressing that the neutrality of ETRs with regard to the revenues accruing to the government and those recycled back is supposed to hold at the macroeconomic level, not at the level of productive sectors or individual taxpayers. However, it is no easy matter even to achieve revenue-neutrality of ETRs at the macro level, as discussed in Speck (2006).

As already noted in Chapter 5, ETRs create a potential for a 'double dividend', i.e. an environmental improvement coupled with an economic benefit (Pearce 1991). This hypothesis has been the cause of an intense academic and political controversy in recent years—see Bosquet (2000), Jackson (2000), Jacobs (1994), McEvoy et al. (2000), OECD (2004), and Patuelli et al. (2005). This debate has highlighted the importance of the way in which the redistribution of the revenues takes place. Extensive analysis and surveys can be found in De Mooij (2000), Ekins and Barker (2001), and Kratena (2002). While the exact nature of the effects depends on the degree of competitiveness in the markets, on the functional forms chosen, and on the values of parameters (Kratena 2002), in the presence of tax distortions efficiency is generally enhanced if revenues from environmental taxation are used to finance cuts in distortionary taxes rather than being recycled as a lump-sum payment. In fact, the existence of welfare gains from recycling schemes reducing existing distortionary taxes, i.e. the *weak* double-dividend hypothesis, is more or less undisputed (Goulder 1995). The occurrence of other versions of this hypothesis, e.g. the strong double dividend, is more uncertain, mainly because tax-interaction effects can lead to a decrease in households' disposable income (Parry and Oates 2000). The environmental-economic literature has normally interpreted the recycling of revenues in ETRs as an opportunity to reduce the cost of labour, an alternative input to the production process, although other forms of revenue-recycling are possible (Patuelli et al 2005). Reducing the cost of labour is an interesting proposition, especially in countries where unemployment is high.

Substantial empirical evidence exists on the predicted effect of ETRs and in particular of ETRs where the environmental tax component is levied on energy consumption or CO_2 emissions. On the basis of about 140 simulations discussed in Bosquet (2000), the author concludes that reductions in carbon emissions can be significant. Marginal gains in employment and marginal gains or losses in activity may be recorded in the short to medium term. Levels of investment and of prices tend to moderately decrease and increase, respectively. In particular, when revenues are redistributed to cut distorting taxes on labour, environmental quality improves, and small gains tend to be registered in the number of jobs and in the output of non-polluting sectors. Results are more ambiguous in the long run, as ETRs may cause some harm to energy-intensive sectors. However, Bosquet (2000) comments that reductions in the output from these sectors may be needed to make the economy more energy-efficient and to achieve the desired reductions in energy and carbon emissions. Also OECD (2004) concludes that an employment dividend can be achieved if revenues are recycled through lower taxation on labour. The larger the amount of recycled revenues, the greater the employment impact, although the magnitude of the effect is typically quite small (OECD 2004). As the environmental effect of ETRs is consistently evident in terms of CO_2 emissions reductions, Patuelli et al. (2005) conclude that ETRs where revenues from a carbon/energy tax are recycled through reductions in labour taxes continue to be a valid model. This confirms the conclusions in McEvoy et al. (2000).

Before discussing German and British policies, it is worth mentioning that the effect of ETRs will depend on the conditions of the economy at the introduction of the policy, in particular with regard to existing taxes, inflationary pressure on prices, and the employment level (McNeill and Williams 2007). Similarly, the results of ex-ante and ex-post studies will ultimately depend on the assumptions incorporated in the CGE and econometric models used to estimate them, in particular on the values of the coefficients relating to the labour market and energy demand, an issue which is mentioned by, among others, Ekins and Etheridge (2006).

7.2.2 German and British Environmental Tax Reforms

Launched in April 1999 as part of a more general overhaul of the tax system, the German ETR was largely motivated to facilitate the allocation of production processes and demand towards technological innovation, and the creation of additional jobs (Beuermann and Santarius 2006). Over the previous 30 years, the share of taxes on labour had increased by 66%, while environmental taxes and charges had fallen considerably (Hey 2005). The ETR concept had been gaining momentum since the early 1990s. Beuermann and Santarius (2006) identify the phases in the debate and two pivotal events, namely the publication of a report by the German Institute for Economic Research (DIW) and the election of the so-called Red-Green coalition. The report concluded that energy consumption and unemployment would considerably decrease as a result of the introduction of an ETR in Germany, while no significant adverse effect on inflation or GDP growth would take place. The election of the Red-Green government in 1998 marked the start of the last phase in the debate, with the discussion now focused on the details of the tax (Beuermann and Santarius 2006 and Hey 2005).

The German ETR has been implemented through the introduction of two laws, which endorsed five energy tax increases over a period of five years. In the first step on 1 April 1999, uniform rates on the consumption of heating oils and road fuels were introduced. An electricity tax was also launched, while the existing tax on light heating oil and natural gas was increased. The consumption of coal remained not subject to energy taxation. The subsequent four steps of the ETR (2000–3) entailed increases in the taxes on electricity and road fuels. No further annual tax increases have been planned. However, an increase in the tax on natural gas and a reduction in the exemptions originally granted to the industrial sector were implemented in 2004. The majority of the revenues from the taxes were used to reduce employers' and employees' social security contributions. The reduction is applied equally to the two groups, i.e. according to a 50–50 ratio.

Originally, all firms in the industrial, agricultural, fishery, and forestry sectors were entitled to an 80% reduction in the tax rates provided that their consumption was above a minimum threshold. Firms in the industrial sector could also apply for a 100% refund on the ETR burden, which was 1.2 times higher than the reduction in statutory pension contributions. In 2003, industry reductions were cut to 40%. The net compensation was also modified, i.e. only 95% of the tax burden above the reductions in decreased statutory pension contributions would be refunded. Further details can be found in Speck (2006). Among other tax reductions in the German ETR one should mention those applied to the consumption of electricity and mineral oil in public transport (50% discount), and of mineral oils and natural gas in power stations (80% discount). Special exemptions for environmentally efficient technologies were also introduced. By 2003, 1.7% of the German tax revenues had been shifted towards resource use and pollution in this way, compared to 1998 levels. Annual energy tax revenues had increased by €18 billion. Despite its controversial nature, the German ETR seems politically well established, probably due to the unpopularity of the other options to finance reductions in social security contributions (Hey 2005).

In the UK, the most important stumbling block to the introduction of an ETR has been the attitude of the public[1] (Dresner et al. 2006). It is therefore not

---

[1] The introduction of VAT on household energy consumption provides a clear example of public opposition to environmental taxes in the UK. In 1993 the Conservative government announced its intention to raise VAT on domestic energy, which had been zero-rated, to 8% and later to 17.5%. Following public opposition and a backbench rebellion, the government was defeated in its attempt to pass the second rise, although it managed to lift VAT to 8%. VAT was reduced to 5%, the minimum rate allowed under EU law, immediately after the Labour Party won the 1997 election.

surprising that the Climate Change Levy (CCL), an energy tax announced in March 1999 and implemented in April 2001, was designed as a downstream tax from which household energy use was exempt. The tax applies only to business energy consumption, i.e. consumption in industry, agriculture, public administration, and the service sectors. Revenues were recycled back mainly through a 0.3% cut in employers' national insurance contributions, i.e. a payroll tax, but also through energy efficiency schemes.

After the tax announcement in 1999, intense lobbying from the industry led to a reduction in rates, and to higher discounts to firms in energy-intensive sectors (initially defined in terms of the IPPC regulations) which signed an energy efficiency agreement. The so-called Climate Change Agreements (CCAs) set out targets on energy consumption or carbon emissions over a decade, comprising a final target in 2010 and interim targets every two years, starting in 2002. The CCL on the sites with a CCA was set for the first target period (to April 2003) at 20% of the tax rate. If a sector met their interim target, all sites in the sector were entitled to the reduced CCL rate for the next two years. If the target was not met, only complying sites were entitled to the discount while other sites had to pay the full rate on their energy consumption in the next target period. The targets were specified relative to a base year, normally 1999 or 2000.[2]

As described in Defra (2003), at the end of the first target period most CCA sectors significantly over-achieved compared to their targets, leading to aggregate absolute savings of 4.3 mtC. The CCAs were expected to save only 2.5 mtC by 2010 (DETR 2000). Although the government presented this as a success, it really meant that the agreed targets had been too easy (Dresner et al. 2006). As savings of 2.6 mtC came from the steel sector, arising largely from output contraction, by 2002 the other CCA sectors reduced carbon emissions by 1.7 mtC. In the absence of other information, Ekins and Etheridge (2006) conclude that it is not unreasonable to attribute these savings to the CCAs. Overall, the savings achieved in the industrial sector point to the existence of substantial cost-effective improvements in energy efficiency, opportunities that might have been unknown to energy managers before the process of negotiating the CCAs.

---

[2] The targets, which were negotiated with each sector by the UK government's Department for the Environment, Food and Rural Affairs (Defra), were set on the basis of the improvements in energy efficiency which the sector would be likely to achieve by 2010 in a business-as-usual (BAU) scenario, i.e. excluding the CCL and CCAs, and the improvements which would arise from the implementation of all cost-effective energy efficiency measures (the ACE estimate). The outcome of the negotiations was a target somewhere between the BAU and ACE estimates (Ekins and Etheridge 2006).

7.2.3 Econometric Approach

In this chapter we adopt a translog cost function to assess the effect of the German and UK ETRs. Our approach is similar in spirit to the general framework described in Kratena (2002), with the difference that we adopt a translog function rather than a generalized Leontief function and that we do not address the effect of ETRs on consumption and on the level of output from the productive sectors. Other functional forms used in the estimation of demand systems are succinctly described in Diewert and Wales (1987). Zarnikau (2003) advocates the use of a non-parametric approach instead of the functional forms normally used in empirical studies. However, using the same data set but a different model selection criterion, Xiao et al. (2007) obtained a completely different result. In any case, as mentioned in Zarnikau (2003), the use of non-parametric methods in a time-series setting is normally precluded by the relatively low number of observations. The econometric approach is described in some technical detail in the Technical Appendix to this chapter, where it can be seen that the demand system estimated is given by

$$s_i = \beta_i + \beta_{iT}t + \beta_{iy}\ln y_t + \sum_j \beta_{ij} \ln \frac{p_{jt}}{p_{\mathrm{cap},t}} \quad i = \mathrm{lab, ene, mat, ser} \qquad (7.1)$$

where lab, ene, mat, and ser stand for labour, energy, materials, and services, respectively.

The choice of sectors assessed in this study was influenced by the availability of data, in particular those related to capital and labour. The sectors modelled cover almost the whole spectrum of manufacturing activity—see Table 7.1 for the list of the sectors, the NACE (Statistical Classification of Economic Activities in the European Community) identifier, and their acronym. Two sub-sectors from the commerce sector have also been modelled. For the sake of brevity, in the tables below we will use acronyms rather than the names of sectors. As one can see from the table, six sectors are analysed in each country. In order to allow international comparisons, three of these sectors are assessed

Table 7.1. Industrial sectors assessed in this study

Acronym	Sector	NACE Taxonomy	Assessed in
FT	Food and Tobacco	15–16	UK
TXT	Textiles and Leather	17–19	Germany
PPP	Pulp, Paper and Printing	21–22	Germany
RP	Rubber and Plastics	25	Germany and UK
NMM	Non-Metallic Minerals	26	Germany and UK
MAC	Machinery	29	UK
ELE	Electrical and Optical Equipment	30–33	Germany and UK
TRA	Wholesale and Retail Trade	G	Germany
FIN	Financial intermediation	J	UK

in both Germany and the UK. However, when using the EU KLEMS data set, comparison across countries should be interpreted with caution as the definitions of inputs as well as the structure of the industries can vary (Timmer et al. 2007b). The estimation was implemented in Eviews by using seemingly unrelated regression (SUR), also known as multivariate regression, or Zellner's method. This method estimates the parameters of the system, accounting for heteroscedasticity and contemporaneous correlation in the errors across equations.

7.2.4 Empirical Results

Tables 7.2a and 7.2b present the coefficients and relative t-statistics, in bold if the coefficient is statistically significant at the 95% confidence level, from the estimation of equation (7.1). The coefficients are grouped on the basis of the equation from which they have been obtained. The first group of coefficients has been estimated from the energy cost-share equation, the second, the third, and the fourth from the labour, materials, and services cost-share equations, respectively. In Tables 7.2a and 7.2b, it will be seen that output and the linear trend, which is used as a proxy for technology, are statistically significant in about half the sectors. Likelihood ratio tests, available upon request, on the linear trend, output, and on the linear trend and output (tested simultaneously), are statistically significant at the 97.5% confidence level or higher. This shows the importance of introducing a linear trend into the equation, i.e. a term which is not always present in the specifications seen in the literature. Tables 7.2a and 7.2b also present the adjusted R^2 for each equation in (7.1). Among the British sectors (see Table 7.2a), the demand for labour is the equation which is best explained by the specifications adopted in this study. The demand for materials (see the third group of coefficients in the table) is also explained rather well, with the exception of the Rubber and Plastics and Non-Metallic Mineral sectors. Overall, the cost-share system explains about 65% of the variance of the data for the energy demand equation. In the case of the German sectors, one can notice that the specifications in Table 7.2b explain very little of the variance of energy demand for the Textiles and Leather, and Electric and Optical Equipment sectors—notice the negative adjusted R^2. In all other sectors, the performance of our approach in explaining the energy demand is markedly better.

In Table 7.2, one can also assess the effect of technological change, modelled as a linear trend, and of output on the input demands, conveyed by the coefficients with an index ending in T and Y, respectively, for example β_{ST} and β_{SY}. One can conclude that technological change tends to increase the consumption of energy and reduce the consumption of labour. This confirms the findings of Allen and Urga (1999) for the British manufacturing sector. In the

Table 7.2a. Coefficients and t-statistics (in bold if significant at the 95% level) of the British sectors

	FT	RP	NMM	MAC	ELE	FIN
β_E	0.085(0.768)	0.853(**4.406**)	1.871(**11.513**)	0.059(0.408)	0.236(1.203)	−0.296(−1.413)
β_{EE}	−0.001(−0.372)	0.006(0.717)	0.038(**5.897**)	−0.001(−0.471)	0.002(0.260)	0.010(**2.674**)
β_{EL}	−0.004(−1.058)	−0.005(−0.561)	−0.043(−**3.805**)	0.016(1.592)	0.003(0.291)	0.007(0.908)
β_{EM}	0.024(**3.754**)	0.053(**4.155**)	0.011(0.477)	−0.005(−0.508)	−0.021(−1.260)	−0.014(−1.006)
β_{ES}	−0.015(−**2.528**)	−0.065(−**4.482**)	−0.021(−1.337)	−0.013(−1.835)	0.011(0.616)	−0.002(−0.192)
β_{EY}	−0.010(−1.054)	−0.097(−**4.894**)	−0.192(−**11.402**)	−0.005(−0.355)	−0.017(−0.824)	0.029(1.484)
β_{ET}	0.001(**3.737**)	0.003(**4.748**)	0.003(**6.630**)	0.000(0.210)	0.000(−0.353)	−0.001(−1.598)
Adj R²	0.58	0.54	0.98	0.71	0.67	0.42
β_L	1.011(**2.413**)	−0.048(−0.151)	1.480(**3.297**)	−2.061(−**1.964**)	1.788(**2.988**)	−3.201(−**2.325**)
β_{LL}	0.117(**6.928**)	0.179(**8.845**)	0.037(0.988)	0.156(**2.124**)	0.019(0.508)	0.095(**2.072**)
β_{LM}	−0.115(−**4.977**)	−0.124(−**5.522**)	0.036(0.696)	−0.101(−1.681)	0.156(**3.504**)	−0.162(−**4.314**)
β_{LS}	0.021(0.918)	0.006(0.266)	0.028(0.685)	−0.010(−0.218)	−0.107(−**2.339**)	0.103(**2.077**)
β_{LY}	−0.063(−1.686)	0.050(1.528)	−0.133(−**2.813**)	0.242(**2.326**)	−0.168(−**2.729**)	0.304(**2.411**)
β_{LT}	0.000(0.096)	−0.009(−**7.168**)	−0.002(−1.457)	−0.007(−**3.274**)	0.002(0.716)	−0.014(−**5.356**)
Adj R²	0.93	0.90	0.74	0.92	0.61	0.79
β_M	−3.306(−**3.653**)	1.126(**2.119**)	4.470(**3.313**)	1.310(1.339)	−0.686(−0.732)	6.764(**6.451**)
β_{MM}	0.239(**4.047**)	0.074(1.698)	−0.315(−**2.182**)	−0.009(−0.125)	−0.239(−**2.662**)	0.083(0.878)
β_{MS}	−0.059(−1.380)	−0.020(−0.618)	0.259(**2.315**)	0.093(1.815)	0.065(0.826)	0.108(1.356)
β_{MY}	0.328(**4.139**)	−0.077(−1.429)	−0.430(−**3.037**)	−0.078(−0.787)	0.136(1.329)	−0.603(−**5.986**)
β_{MT}	−0.003(−**2.019**)	0.008(**4.483**)	0.006(**2.355**)	0.004(1.812)	−0.005(−0.988)	0.009(**4.900**)
Adj R²	0.80	0.35	0.49	0.80	0.88	0.83
β_S	4.528(**6.696**)	−0.274(−0.585)	−3.710(−**3.120**)	3.279(**3.733**)	−0.770(−0.707)	0.452(0.249)
β_{SS}	0.025(0.529)	0.123(**2.903**)	−0.227(−**2.272**)	−0.049(−0.885)	0.064(0.648)	−0.179(−**2.080**)
β_{SY}	−0.399(−**6.592**)	0.046(0.944)	0.403(**3.214**)	−0.323(−**3.788**)	0.087(0.751)	0.014(0.084)
β_{ST}	0.003(1.955)	−0.006(−**3.584**)	−0.007(−**3.464**)	0.001(0.484)	−0.002(−0.352)	0.004(1.142)
Adj R²	0.55	0.37	0.25	0.80	0.36	0.81

Note: As symmetry is imposed, coefficients for any two inputs are shown only once. For example, the coefficient for energy and labour in the energy demand equation, i.e. β_{EL} is equal to that in the labour demand equation, i.e. β_{LE} which is not shown in the table.

156

Table 7.2b Coefficients and t-statistics (in bold if significant at the 95% level) of the German sectors

	TXT	PPP	RP	NMM	ELE	TRA
β_E	0.108(0.435)	0.576(**2.459**)	0.024(0.240)	0.860(**2.579**)	0.089(0.988)	0.253(**2.441**)
β_{EE}	−0.005(−0.153)	0.009(0.465)	0.019(**2.225**)	0.065(**2.585**)	0.001(0.118)	0.016(**2.616**)
β_{EL}	0.002(0.127)	−0.071(−**5.033**)	−0.039(−**3.041**)	−0.023(−1.532)	−0.033(−**2.549**)	−0.017(−1.700)
β_{EM}	0.015(0.351)	0.084(**4.195**)	−0.015(−0.992)	0.053(**2.720**)	0.038(**2.985**)	0.033(**5.584**)
β_{ES}	−0.016(−1.224)	0.002(0.098)	0.032(**2.797**)	−0.054(−**3.123**)	−0.004(−0.336)	−0.029(−**2.467**)
β_{EY}	−0.010(−0.440)	−0.052(−**2.233**)	0.008(0.826)	−0.071(−**2.138**)	−0.011(−1.303)	−0.012(−1.315)
β_{ET}	0.000(0.068)	0.001(**2.442**)	−0.001(−1.360)	−0.001(−1.677)	0.002(**2.783**)	0.001(**3.185**)
Adj R^2	−0.29	0.84	0.84	0.78	−0.02	0.41
β_L	0.886(**4.036**)	0.686(**2.070**)	0.102(0.363)	1.149(**2.951**)	0.104(0.254)	2.857(**14.797**)
β_{LL}	−0.020(−0.926)	0.101(**5.207**)	0.042(1.177)	0.073(1.159)	0.013(0.213)	0.136(**3.361**)
β_{LM}	0.012(0.371)	−0.023(−1.308)	−0.039(−1.164)	−0.075(−1.926)	0.074(1.432)	−0.030(−**2.001**)
β_{LS}	0.028(**2.313**)	0.047(**2.311**)	0.056(**1.978**)	0.040(0.875)	−0.019(−0.549)	−0.044(−0.990)
β_{LY}	−0.054(−**2.756**)	−0.044(−1.416)	0.015(0.561)	−0.077(−**2.093**)	0.007(0.193)	−0.204(−**12.515**)
β_{LT}	−0.004(−**4.555**)	−0.004(−**7.473**)	−0.002(−**2.187**)	−0.003(−**2.758**)	−0.004(−1.176)	0.001(0.913)
Adj R^2	0.97	0.91	0.42	0.80	0.81	0.92
β_M	−0.504(−0.881)	−0.930(−**2.877**)	0.208(0.525)	−1.326(−**3.681**)	−0.131(−0.340)	−0.187(−1.732)
β_{MM}	−0.043(−0.610)	0.074(**2.468**)	0.305(**6.144**)	0.076(1.594)	−0.089(−1.634)	−0.028(−**2.451**)
β_{MS}	0.042(1.425)	−0.095(−**4.355**)	−0.163(−**5.896**)	−0.009(−0.266)	−0.005(−0.158)	0.031(1.657)
β_{MY}	0.103(**2.014**)	0.127(**4.044**)	−0.014(−0.368)	0.157(**4.734**)	0.068(1.865)	0.028(**3.036**)
β_{MT}	−0.001(−0.567)	−0.003(−**4.798**)	0.002(1.147)	0.000(0.030)	−0.004(−1.443)	−0.002(−**4.690**)
Adj R^2	0.19	0.93	0.71	0.57	0.84	0.94
β_S	0.168(0.345)	0.622(**2.203**)	0.171(0.671)	−0.233(−0.723)	0.532(1.850)	−2.213(−**8.661**)
β_{SS}	−0.047(−1.895)	0.029(0.926)	0.074(**2.382**)	0.020(0.442)	0.040(1.227)	0.081(1.468)
β_{SY}	−0.019(−0.436)	−0.038(−1.400)	0.015(0.591)	0.031(0.991)	−0.042(−1.533)	0.198(**9.329**)
β_{ST}	0.003(**2.893**)	0.003(**5.965**)	0.000(−0.127)	0.002(**2.620**)	0.005(**2.675**)	−0.003(−**2.532**)
Adj R^2	0.75	0.97	0.94	0.94	0.93	0.90

Notes: see note to Table 7.2a

case of the sectoral output, an increase in the level of this variable tends to decrease energy consumption, therefore counterbalancing the effect of technological change mentioned above. Among the three sectors present in both countries, namely Rubber and Plastics, Non-Mineral Metals, and Electrical and Optical Equipment, the level of output tends to increase demand for services, in both German and British sectors, while its effect on energy is unequivocally negative. In these three sectors, the technological trend always reduces the demand for labour, with the exception of the British Electrical and Optical Equipment sector. For all other production inputs, the direction of the effect of the technological trend and of output varies somewhat in the sectors which are observed in both countries.

Tables 7.3a and 7.3b display the own- and cross-price elasticities obtained from the parameters in Tables 7.2a and 7.2b and the cost shares of production inputs. With the exception of the elasticity for capital in the German Wholesale and Retail Trade, for services in the British Rubber and Plastic sectors, and materials in the British Financial sector, all other own-price elasticities have the expected negative sign. Among the own-price elasticities, one can observe rather high values, for example in the case of the elasticity for materials and services elasticity in the British Non-Metallic Mineral sector, for services in the British Machinery sector, and for energy and services in the German Textiles sector, as well as the elasticity for materials in the German Wholesale and Retail Trade sector. Among the cross-price elasticities, one can observe the very high values of the elasticity between energy and labour, and between energy and materials in the German Electric and Optical Equipment sector. High values can also be noticed in the case of the elasticities between services and materials in the British Non-Metallic Minerals sector, and between materials and labour, and materials and services in the British Financial sector, as well as for the elasticity between energy and materials in the British Rubber and Plastic sector.

The fact that cross-price elasticities do not have the same value when appearing in different equations, for example the cross-elasticity between energy and labour in the energy demand equation and that for labour and energy in the labour demand equation, is caused by the presence of the cost share in the formula—see (7.5).

With regard to the estimates we could find in the literature, the own-price elasticities for energy and materials in the German Paper, Pulp and Printing sector compare well with those estimated for the same sector in the USA by Roy et al. (2006), namely -0.80 for energy and -0.38 for materials. The value of labour price elasticity in Roy et al. (2006), i.e. -0.79, is about twice the value presented in Table 7.3b. The arithmetic average of the own-price elasticities in Table 7.3 can also be used to compare our results with those from studies estimating a translog cost specification for the manufacturing sector as a

Table 7.3a. Price elasticities for the British sectors

FT	cap	ene	Lab	mat	ser
cap	−0.09	−0.02	0.01	−0.30	0.41
ene	−0.11	−1.02	−0.02	1.81	−0.67
lab	0.00	0.00	−0.19	−0.06	0.25
mat	−0.06	0.06	−0.02	−0.02	0.03
ser	0.30	−0.09	0.34	0.12	−0.68
NMM	cap	ene	Lab	mat	ser
cap	−0.24	0.22	−0.19	0.37	−0.16
ene	0.32	−0.43	−0.24	0.43	−0.08
lab	−0.07	−0.06	−0.57	0.41	0.28
mat	0.14	0.11	0.44	−1.77	1.07
ser	−0.09	−0.03	0.47	1.63	−1.97
ELE	cap	ene	Lab	mat	ser
cap	−0.33	0.05	−0.37	0.81	−0.17
ene	0.46	−0.85	0.52	−1.20	1.07
lab	−0.15	0.02	−0.66	1.04	−0.25
mat	0.19	−0.03	0.61	−1.05	0.28
ser	−0.13	0.09	−0.49	0.93	−0.40

RP	cap	ene	lab	mat	ser
Cap	−0.22	0.13	−0.24	0.60	−0.27
Ene	0.47	−0.76	0.10	2.30	−2.12
Lab	−0.09	0.01	−0.09	0.00	0.16
Mat	0.15	0.15	0.00	−0.39	0.10
Ser	−0.20	−0.43	0.33	0.29	0.01
MAC	cap	ene	lab	mat	ser
Cap	−0.15	0.06	−0.51	0.75	−0.14
Ene	0.23	−1.05	1.17	0.20	−0.55
Lab	−0.12	0.07	−0.19	0.13	0.11
Mat	0.12	0.01	0.10	−0.58	0.35
Ser	−0.08	−0.08	0.25	1.11	−1.21
FIN	cap	ene	lab	mat	ser
Cap	−0.26	0.01	0.00	−0.02	0.26
Ene	0.17	−0.22	0.81	−1.03	0.27
Lab	0.00	0.04	−0.38	−0.46	0.81
Mat	−0.04	−0.16	−1.68	0.10	1.78
Ser	0.08	0.01	0.52	0.32	−0.93

Note: The fact that cross-price elasticities do not have the same value when appearing in different equations, e.g. the cross-elasticity between energy and labour in the energy demand equation and that for labour and energy in the energy demand equation, is caused by presence of the cost share in the formula—see (7.5).

Table 7.3b. Price elasticities for the German sectors

TXT	Cap	ene	Lab	mat	ser
cap	-0.09	0.09	-0.07	0.09	-0.02
ene	0.16	-1.11	0.36	0.95	-0.36
lab	-0.02	0.04	-0.79	0.55	0.20
mat	0.01	0.06	0.31	-0.57	0.19
ser	-0.01	-0.11	0.55	0.91	-1.34
RP	Cap	ene	Lab	mat	ser
cap	-0.01	0.06	0.12	-0.33	0.15
ene	0.21	-0.38	-0.89	-0.02	1.09
lab	0.05	-0.10	-0.57	0.29	0.33
mat	-0.09	0.00	0.20	0.15	-0.25
ser	0.13	0.26	0.69	-0.75	-0.33
ELE	Cap	ene	Lab	mat	ser
cap	-0.21	-0.02	-0.01	0.28	-0.04
ene	-0.19	-0.89	-3.12	4.50	-0.31
lab	0.00	-0.08	-0.61	0.67	0.03
mat	0.06	0.09	0.51	-0.74	0.07
ser	-0.05	-0.03	0.12	0.40	-0.44

PPP	cap	ene	lab	mat	ser
Cap	-0.08	-0.14	-0.14	0.06	0.31
Ene	-0.39	-0.76	-1.22	2.14	0.22
Lab	-0.07	-0.21	-0.36	0.28	0.35
Mat	0.02	0.28	0.21	-0.43	-0.08
Ser	0.22	0.06	0.54	-0.16	-0.66
NMM	cap	ene	lab	mat	ser
Cap	-0.01	-0.26	0.17	-0.09	0.20
Ene	-0.31	-0.22	0.07	0.87	-0.40
Lab	0.06	0.02	-0.46	0.07	0.30
Mat	-0.03	0.26	0.07	-0.44	0.14
Ser	0.13	-0.23	0.55	0.26	-0.71
TRA	cap	ene	lab	mat	ser
Cap	0.12	-0.02	0.02	0.01	-0.13
Ene	-0.07	-0.20	-0.28	1.66	-1.11
Lab	0.00	-0.01	-0.22	0.02	0.21
Mat	0.01	0.45	0.13	-1.29	0.69
Ser	-0.04	-0.08	0.37	0.18	-0.43

Note: See note to Table 7.3a.

whole. Our results for the German and British industrial sectors are rather similar to the elasticities in Christopoulos and Tsionas (2002) for labour and energy in the Greek manufacturing sector, i.e. -0.60 and -0.80 respectively. The average of the labour elasticities is -0.56 for the German industrial sectors in Table 7.3b, and -0.34 for the British sectors in Table 7.3a. The average of the energy elasticities is -0.67 in the German sectors and -0.82 in the British sectors. It is worth mentioning that our average of labour elasticities from the British sectors is identical to the value estimated for Sweden by Enevoldsen et al. (2007), and very similar to the value, i.e. -0.31, in Hisnanick and Kyer (1995) for the US manufacturing sector. The value for own-price energy elasticity in Enevoldsen et al. (2007) is about half the value we have estimated for the German and British sectors.

Finally, following Christopoulos and Tsionas (2002), we have performed unit root tests on the residuals from the four equations comprising the cost-share system (7.1). More precisely, we have run ADF unit root tests with the lag selected by the Schwarz Information Criterion. The residual series from the estimation of the cost-share system are likely to be considered non-stationary if there is no structural relationship among the variables in the equations. As the test statistics in Tables 7.4a and 7.4b are much higher than the 5% critical value, there is no doubt that the residuals are stationary. This finding supports the point of view that the relationships in (7.1) are structural, i.e. the variables are co-integrated.

7.2.5 Impacts of the Environmental Tax Reforms (ETRs)

The impact of the German and the British ETRs can be evaluated on the basis of the elasticities in Tables 7.3a and 7.3b, as the effect of the policies on the demand for energy and labour can be easily computed by multiplying the impact of the policies on prices by the own and cross-price elasticities in the table. It is worth mentioning that in this analysis the output from the sectors is assumed constant. In the case of the German policy, the percentage changes in the energy and labour prices attributable to the ETR have been obtained by dividing the increase in energy costs and the reduction in

Table 7.4a. Results from tests run on the residuals for the British sectors

	FT	RP	NMM	MAC	ELE	FIN
Energy	−3.25	−2.78	−4.16	−4.23	−3.34	−3.27
Labour	−4.11	−3.19	−3.38	−2.55	−4.22	−2.92
Materials	−2.92	−2.78	−2.48	−3.15	−3.78	−2.36
Services	−3.92	−2.66	−1.99	−4.14	−3.22	−3.54

Note: The 5% critical value of the ADF statistics for a series with no deterministic terms is −1.96.

Table 7.4b. Results from tests run on the residuals for the German sectors

	TXT	PPP	RP	NMM	ELE	TRA
Energy	−4.57	−4.04	−4.18	−4.58	−5.47	−3.95
Labour	−4.31	−2.52	−3.62	−3.09	−2.68	−3.62
Materials	−4.26	−4.44	−3.48	−5.02	−4.15	−3.59
Services	−4.40	−2.72	−4.14	−3.35	−2.83	−4.30

Note: see note to Table 7.4a.

national insurance contributions from Bach (2005) by the expenditure on these two production inputs, which has been obtained from the EU KLEMS database. In the case of the UK, we obtained the percentage decrease in the cost of labour from the change in the rate of national insurance contributions caused by the policy. The percentage change in the energy price was obtained by weighting the fuel price with and without the CCL rate (obtained from BERR 2008) by the fuel consumption of the sectors assessed in this study, which has been obtained from ONS (2008). It is worth mentioning that in both Germany and the UK, our computation does take into account the consumption and, when applicable, the effect of ETR on the price of diesel and petrol fuels.

The impact of the German and British ETRs can be seen in Table 7.5, which shows the percentage changes in the demand for energy and labour compared to the demand which would have occurred if the policies had not been introduced. It is worth mentioning that the figures are related to the energy and labour consumption in 2003, a choice dictated by the availability of the data in Bach (2005). However, it is worth mentioning that from 2003 onward, only minor changes have been introduced in the German and British ETRs.

The figures in the tables are the percentage changes compared to the demand for energy and labour if the ETRs had not been introduced.

Table 7.5. Impact of the ETR on the demand for energy and labour in the British and German sectors assessed in this study.

	British Sectors			German Sectors	
	Energy	**Labour**		**Energy**	**Labour**
Food and Tobacco	−3.75	0.07	Pulp, Paper and Printing	−3.03	−0.82
Rubber and Plastics	−3.58	0.08	Rubber and Plastics	−1.18	−0.05
Non-Metallic Minerals	−2.28	−0.13	Non-Metallic Minerals	−0.73	0.40
Machinery	−3.36	0.26	Wholesale and Retail Trade	−2.82	−0.04
Electrical and Optical Equipment	−3.93	0.32			
Financial intermediation	−2.05	0.45			

Note: The figures in the tables are the percentage changes compared to the demand for energy and labour had the ETRs not been introduced.

In the case of the British sectors, as one can see from the table, the decrease in energy consumption caused by the ETR in the sectors assessed in this study has been estimated to be from as low as 2% in the Financial sector to as high as 4% in the Electrical and Optical Equipment sector. The high value of the energy reduction in this sector is due to a combination of high own-price energy elasticity and to the fact that labour is a substitute for energy in the energy demand equation. The reduction in the energy demand of the Food and Tobacco, and Rubber and Plastic sectors is mainly due to the value of the own-price elasticity, as the substitution pattern between energy and labour is not very strong. In the case of the Machinery sector, the effect of the energy price is compounded by strong substitution patterns between labour and energy in energy demand. The lowest change in the energy demand among the sectors in the table, namely in the Financial sector, is due to the low energy elasticity. In fact, as the firms from this sector did not benefit from the discounts in the Climate Change Agreements, the rise in the energy price has been much higher than those observed in the other sectors. With regard to its effect on employment, the British ETR had a much smaller impact than it did on energy demand due to the moderate changes in the labour price brought about by the policy. The highest impact of the policy among the sectors we modelled can be observed in the Financial sector, an increase of about 0.45%. Smaller increases can be observed in the case of the Electrical and Optical Equipment, and the Machinery sectors. It is worth mentioning that the highest labour elasticities can be observed in the case of the Non-Metallic Minerals, and the Electrical and Optical Equipment sectors. The decrease in labour demand in the former is caused by the response of labour to the increase in the energy price, the effect of which reverses the gains brought about by the decrease in the labour price.

In the case of the German sectors, we report results only for four sectors, because of the values of the adjusted R^2 in the case of the Textiles and Leather, and the Electrical and Optical Equipment sectors. In the best case, the ETR impact in these two sectors would not be corroborated by a strong statistical model. In the case of the Electrical and Optical Equipment sector, we also find it difficult to believe the results of the labour price elasticity in the energy demand equation. Among the remaining four sectors, we can observe a strong reduction in the case of energy demand in the Pulp, Paper and Printing, and the Wholesale and Retail Trade sectors. In the latter, this change is due to a considerable increase in the energy price, while in the former it is caused by a high own-price energy elasticity, which is compounded by strong complementarity between labour and energy in energy demand. The effect of the ETR in the other two sectors is markedly smaller, mainly due to the size of the own-price energy elasticities. With regard to the effect of the German ETR on labour demand, one can observe from Table 7.5 that in three instances the effect is negative, although the decrease is marginal in the Rubber and Plastic, and the Wholesale and Retail Trade sectors. This negative effect is related to the complementarity of energy in the labour demand equation. As the cross-price elasticity is smaller than the own-price elasticity, the decrease in labour demand is ultimately caused by the fact that the increase in the energy price is much higher than the change in the price of labour.

7.3 Discussion

Before discussing the limitations of our approach, it is worth comparing our results with those found in the literature. Overall, in the case of the British sectors, our results compare well with those in Cambridge Econometrics et al. (2005) and Barker et al. (2007). Although the authors do not report detailed energy reductions caused by the British ETR in the sectors assessed in this chapter, the decrease in the energy demand from the Mineral Products sector reported in Cambridge Econometrics et al. (2005), i.e. 3.8%, is comparable to that in Table 7.5. The authors also mention that the ETR is estimated to have reduced total final energy demand by 1.8% in 2002, i.e. a figure which validates our results in Table 7.5 if one bears in mind that energy consumption in the transport and domestic sectors, which are not affected by the tax, is included in total consumption. Barker et al. (2007) report similar figures. Also our results for the impact of the German ETR on energy consumption are validated by the figures seen in the literature. Ex-ante estimates discussed in Bach et al. (2002) which were obtained by two different models, i.e. LEAN and PANTA RHEI, pointed at reductions in CO_2 emissions of more than 2% in 2005, a percentage which is comparable to the energy reductions we obtained for the four sectors in the table. However, Barker et al. (2007) reports a higher 4% reduction for 2003, i.e. a percentage slightly higher than those reported in Table 7.5.

With regard to the effects of the ETR on the labour market, our results differ from some of those seen in the literature. In the case of the British sectors, the increase in employment caused by ETRs is higher than those presented in Cambridge Econometrics et al. (2005) and Barker et al. (2007), which are obtained by using MDM-E3 and E3ME (Cambridge Econometrics 2007 and <http://www.camecon.com/ModellingTraining/suite_economic_models/E3ME. aspx>), two models originating from the Cambridge Multisectoral Dynamic Model (Barker and Peterson 1987). The authors forecast a change in the workforce due to the British ETR of a mere 15,000 units, i.e. about 0.05% of the workforce. As one can see in Table 7.5, in one sector we estimated negative impacts on employment, and in two sectors our estimates are similar to the percentage reported by Cambridge Econometrics et al.

(2005). However, in the Machinery, Electrical and Optical Equipment, and in the Financial sectors, the estimated impact of ETR on employment is much higher. Also in the case of the German ETR, the effect of the policy estimated by this study differs from some of the results seen in the literature. Running PANTA REI, Bach et al. (2002) forecast an increase of about 220,000–250,000 jobs in 2003. Running LEAN in the same report showed a more conservative increase of 176,000 in 2008. Considering a 43 million workforce (DeStatis 2008), the range from PANTA REI implies an increase of 0.50–0.60%, i.e. figures which are difficult to reconcile with those in Table 7.5. More positively, Barker et al. (2007) report an increase of about 0.20%, which falls within the range presented in the table.

The difference between our estimates and those derived from the models mentioned above could result from the characterization of the labour market, energy demand, international trade, and of the impact of the policy on the output level. In fact, our approach does not take into account the effect of the ETRs on the level of output and on the level of consumption. In the terms of Kratena (2002), we left out macroeconomic closure. This implies that all model analysis is carried out under the restriction of a constant demand side. In fact, the method of analysis via derivatives which is used in this study is only viable under this assumption. In models like PANTA RHEI or E3ME, the ETRs are allowed to influence, positively or negatively, the level of sectoral output which in turn affects the level of employment. Since, in our study, ETRs are not allowed to influence the level of output, this analysis should probably be framed in a short-run perspective. However, one can argue that the effect so far of ETRs implemented on sectoral output is likely to be small and, consequently, the advantage of modelling this effect explicitly is also likely to be small. Another limitation of our analysis is related to the fact that it does not take into account the interrelationships among sectors and economies. In E3ME and GINFORS, a model related to PANTA RHEI, each country is linked to the others through international trade.[3] In such models, sectoral demand for goods and services from other sectors which are required for current production is calculated using input-output coefficients, although these parameters are fixed exogenously. In contrast, our approach does not model these interdependencies explicitly.

---

[3] In E3ME, the demand for a sector of a given country is related to the weighted demand in all other EU countries, economic activity in markets external to the EU, and relative prices. In GINFORS, each sector of each country receives the demand for exports to each of the other regions, and also receives the corresponding vector of import prices from these regions. The trade share of the country depends on the import and export price as well as a time trend. The import price is determined on the basis of a weighted average of the export prices of its trading partners (Lutz et al. 2010).

With regard to the labour market, Kratena (2002) surveys three possible regimes: a competitive labour market, i.e. typically used in CGE models, search regimes, and union wage-bargaining regimes, a version of which is implemented in E3ME. E3ME's labour market consists of a set of sectoral employment, wage, hours worked, and participation-rate equations. Sectoral employment equations assume a costly adjustment procedure of the level of actual employment to the target level, which depends on output, the real cost of labour, hours worked, the energy price, and an index of technological change. In GINFORS, the level of sectoral employment depends on the level of production, real wages, and a trend. The wage in the economic sectors is determined on the basis of the average wage in the economy, which depends on labour productivity, the consumer price index, and the rate of unemployment (Lutz et al. 2010). Finally, sectoral energy demand is determined in GINFORS by the energy price, the level of output, and a linear trend. A similar characterization can be found in E3ME, with the exception that the linear trend is substituted by a number of variables representing investment and R&D expenditure. In other words, both models adopt an ordinary demand specification where energy consumption is constrained by price, stimulated by an increase in economic activity, and influenced by the level of equipment used in conjunction with energy. The fact that our estimates do not differ markedly from those obtained by E3ME/MDM and GINFORS, despite the fact that we do not allow sectoral output to be influenced by the ETR, can be taken as evidence that: (i) either the impact of the two ETRs on output has not been strong, or that (ii) the presence of the price of the other production inputs in the energy demand can proxy for the effect of ETR on output and the consequent change in the input-output coefficients. Either way, it seems convenient that the estimates of complicated models like E3ME and GINFORS, requiring remarkable intellectual and data-collection investment, can be replicated by a simple econometric approach which can be run with any econometric package by using freely available data. Finally, with regard to labour demand, we tentatively attribute the difference between our results and those of PANTA RHEI to the fact that labour demand in this model does not seem to be influenced directly by the prices of other inputs, such as those in our share system. We conjecture that the results obtained from MDM and E3ME are more similar to ours, because of the presence of the energy price in the equation determining the employment level. As one can see in Table 7.3b, in three out of the four German sectors, the energy price has a negative effect on the level of employment, i.e. the two inputs are complements. The fact that the effect of the energy price on labour demand is not explicitly modelled in PANTA RHEI can explain why the impact of ETR on employment is considerably higher than the impact estimated in this study and in Barker et al. (2007).

7.4 Conclusions

The aim of this chapter was to assess the impact of the British and German ETRs on energy and labour demand. Quite conveniently, our simple econometric approach produced estimates of the energy reductions caused by the ETRs which are similar to those obtained from more complicated multi-sectoral econometric models like those in Barker et al. (2007), Cambridge Econometrics et al. (2005) and Bach et al. (2002). Confirming the findings of Bosquet (2000) from a review of ex-ante simulations of ETRs affecting energy demand, we concluded that the effect of ETRs on energy consumption and therefore carbon emissions can be substantial. With regard to the effect of the ETRs on labour demand, we attributed the difference between our results and those of models like GINFORS to the fact that in the latter the price of energy is not allowed to influence directly the demand for labour. In the case of Germany, our results are more similar to those discussed in Barker et al. (2007). However, in the case of British policy, the impacts we estimated are higher than those reported by Barker et al. (2007). Overall, we once again agree with Bosquet (2000) and OECD (2004) on the fact that the effects of ETRs on employment are small overall and can be positive. This leads us to conclude that ETRs are a convenient policy framework to reduce energy and CO_2 emissions, while leaving the level of employment qualitatively unchanged.

Before closing, it should be mentioned that the validity of our results is more likely to apply in the short rather than the long term, due to the fact that the level of output in our model is not influenced by the ETR itself. While it would seem preferable to have a model where the sectoral output is affected by the policy, the fact that our approach does not have this feature does not seem too much of a shortcoming, as a number of articles have concluded that the effect of ETRs on output and other economic variables is small. This is further corroborated by the fact that our estimates are rather similar to those obtained from more complicated multi-sectoral econometric models where ETRs affect sectoral output. As these models require remarkable intellectual and data-collection investments, while our approach can be implemented with any econometric package by using freely available data, the similarity of our results to those from more complicated models seems a rather convenient feature.

TECHNICAL APPENDIX

Translog demand systems assume a general indirect cost function and apply the Shephard's lemma to determine the demand functions and the share equations.[4] Following Christensen et al. (1975), the non-homothetic translog cost function at time t can be written as

$$\ln C_t = \alpha_0 + \sum_i \beta_i \ln p_{it} + \beta_y \ln y_t + \beta_T t + \sum_i \beta_{iT} t \ln p_{it} + \beta_{yT} t \ln y_t +$$

$$\sum_i \beta_{iy} \ln p_{it} \ln y_t + 0.5 \sum_i \sum_j \beta_{ij} \ln p_{it} \ln p_{jt} + 0.5 \beta_{yy} (\ln y_t)^2 + 0.5 \beta_{TT} t^2 \qquad (A7.1)$$

where C_t indicates the cost, p_{it} the price of the ith input factor, y_t the value of the output, and the term t is used to capture gradual changes in the cost production function. The equation for the cost share s_i, which can be obtained via Shephard's lemma, is

$$s_{it} = \beta_i + \beta_{iT} t + \beta_{iy} \ln y_t + \sum_j \beta_{ij} \ln p_{jt} \forall i = 1, 2, \ldots, n \qquad (A7.2)$$

The parameter β_i measures the autonomous cost shares, i.e. the value of the cost shares irrespective of the value of the variables in the right-hand side of (A7.2). The substitution parameters β_{ij} measure the influence of the input prices on the cost shares. The parameter β_{iT} measures the technology bias or non-neutral technological change, while β_{iy} measures the output composition bias, i.e. the effect of output on the cost shares. The cost function above must be homogeneous of degree 1 in price and satisfy the properties and well-behaved cost functions, while the system of cost shares needs to satisfy the adding-up conditions. These conditions imply the following restrictions:[5] $\sum_i \beta_i = 1$, $\sum_i \beta_{ij} = 0$, and $\sum_i \beta_{iy} = \sum_i \beta_{iT} = 0$ $\forall i = 1, 2, \ldots, n$, while symmetry requires $\beta_{ij} = \beta_{ji}$. The hypothesis that the cost shares are not influenced by technological change or by the level of output can be assessed by testing $\beta_{iT} = \beta_{iy} = 0$ $\forall i = 1, 2, \ldots, n$, or one can test the two components of this joint hypothesis separately. After estimating the cost shares, the substitution parameters in (A7.1) and the cost shares can be used to compute the price elasticities of demand:

$$\eta_{ii} = s_i \sigma_{ii} \text{ and } \eta_{ij} = s_j \sigma_{ij} \text{ with } i \neq j,$$

where σ_{ij} indicates the Allen elasticities, measuring the partial elasticity of substitution between input factors when output is assumed constant. The parameter η_{ii} measures the change in the demand for the ith input brought about by a change in its price, while η_{ij} measures cross-price elasticities. The two input factors are substituted if $\eta_{ij} > 0$ while they are complements if $\eta_{ij} < 0$.

The system of cost shares has been estimated after dropping one equation and dividing the price of the input factors in the remaining equations by the price of the

---

[4] More technically, the translog is a first-order approximation of any demand system, as this functional form has enough parameters so that at any single point the first and second derivatives can be set equal to those of any arbitrary cost function. The translog cost function allows expenditure shares to vary with the level of total expenditure and permits a great variety of substitution patterns (Christensen et al. 1975).

[5] Considering the symmetric restriction $\beta_{ij} = \beta_{ji}$ for all i and j, it is also the case that $\sum_i \beta_{ij} = 0$ that $\forall j = 1, 2, \ldots, n$ (Deiwert and Wales 1987: 36).

input factor, whose cost share is explained by the dropped equation. As we dropped the equation explaining capital cost share, the demand system we estimated is

$$s_i = \beta_i + \beta_{iT}t + \beta_{iy} \ln y_t + \sum_j \beta_{ij} \ln \frac{p_{jt}}{p_{\text{cap},t}} \; i = \text{lab, ene, mat, ser} \qquad (A7.3)$$

where lab, ene, mat, and ser stand for labour, energy, materials, and services, respectively. Following common practice in the literature, all variables in (A7.3) are in real terms. In particular, we used the output deflator to deflate output and the intermediate inputs deflator to deflate the expenditure of production inputs. Data from the EU KLEMS data set were used in the estimation. More information on this data set can be found in Timmer et al. (2007a). Our sample covers the 1978–2004 period. As far as we are aware, this is the first study using data for expenditure on services to assess price elasticities in industrial sectors. All other articles in the literature use data on expenditure on capital, labour, energy, and materials (the so-called KLEM database), at the risk of obtaining biased coefficients from the estimation.

References

Allen, C., and G. Urga (1999), 'Interrelated Factor Demands from Dynamic Cost Functions: An Application to the Non-Energy Business Sector of the UK Economy', *Economica*, 66: 403–13.

Arnberg, S., and T. B. Bjørner (2007), 'Substitution Between Energy, Capital and Labour within Industrial Companies: A Micro Panel Data Analysis', *Resource and Energy Economics*, 29: 122–36.

Bach, S. (2005), *Be- und Entlastungswirkungen der Ökologischen Steuerreform nach Produktionsbereichen*, Berlin: DIW Berlin.

—— M. Kohlhaas, B. Meyer, B. Praetorius, and H. Welsch (2002), 'The Effects of Environmental Fiscal Reform in Germany: A Simulation Study', *Energy Policy*, 30: 803–11.

Barker, T., S. Junankar, H. Pollitt, and P. Summerton (2007), 'The Macroeconomic Effect of Unilateral Environmental Tax Reforms in Europe, 1995–2012', Paper presented at the Eighth Global Conference on Environmental Taxation Innovation, Technology and Employment: Impacts of Environmental Fiscal Reforms and Other Market-Based Instruments, 18–20 October 2007, Munich, Germany.

—— and W. Peterson (1987), *The Cambridge Multisectoral Dynamic Model of the British Economy*, Cambridge: Cambridge University Press.

Baumol, W. J., and W. E. Oates (1971), 'The Use of Standards and Prices for Protection of the Environment', *Swedish Journal of Economics*, 73: 42–54.

BERR (Department for Business Enterprise and Regulatory Reform) (2008), *Quarterly Energy Price*, London: BERR.

Beuermann, C., and T. Santarius (2006), 'Ecological Tax Reform in Germany: Handling Two Hot Potatoes at the Same Time', *Energy Policy*, 34: 917–29.

Binswanger, H. C., H. Frisch, and H. G. Nutzinger (eds.) (1983), *Arbeit ohne Umweltzerstörung. Strategien für eine neue Wirtschaftspolitik*, Frankfurt am Main: Fischer.

Bosquet, B. (2000), 'Environmental Tax Reform: Does it Work? A Survey of the Empirical Evidence', *Ecological Economics*, 34: 19–32.

Cambridge Econometrics (2007), 'E3ME Manual Cambridge', Cambridge: Cambridge Econometrics.

—— Department of Applied Economics, and Policy Studies Institute (2005), *Modelling the Initial Effects of Climate Change Levy*, London: HM Customs and Excise.

Christensen, L. R., D. W. Jorgenson, and L. J. Lau (1975), 'Transcendental Logarithmic Utility Functions', *American Economic Review*, 65(3): 367–83.

Christopoulos, D. K., and E. G. Tsionas (2002), 'Allocative Inefficiency and the Capital-Energy Controversy', *Energy Economics*, 24: 305–18.

DeStatis (Federal Statistical Office) (2008), *National Accounts*, Berlin: DeStatis.

De Mooij, R. A. (2000), *Environmental Taxation and the Double Dividend: Contributions to Economic Analysis*, Shannon: North Holland.

Department for the Environment, Food and Rural Affairs (Defra) (2003), *Climate Change Agreements and the Climate Change Levy: First Target Period Results*, London: Defra.

Department for the Environment, Transport and the Regions (DETR) (2000), *Climate Change: The UK Programme*, London: DETR.

Diewert, W. E., and T. J. Wales (1987), 'Flexible Functional Forms and Global Curvature Conditions', *Econometrica*, 55: 43–68.

Dresner, S., T. Jackson, and N. Gilbert (2006), 'History and Social Responses to Environmental Tax Reform in the United Kingdom', *Energy Policy*, 34: 930–39.

Ekins, P., and T. Barker (2001), 'Carbon Taxes and Carbon Emissions Trading', *Journal of Economic Surveys*, 15: 325–76.

—— and B. Etheridge (2006), 'The Environmental and Economic Impacts of the UK Climate Change Agreements', *Energy Policy*, 34: 2071–86.

Enevoldsen, M. K. E., A. V. Ryelund, and M. S. Andersen (2007), 'Decoupling of Industrial Energy Consumption and CO_2-Emissions in Energy-Intensive Industries in Scandinavia', *Energy Economics*, 29: 665–82.

European Commission (EC) (1993), *Growth, Competitiveness and Employment*, Brussels: European Commission.

Gee, D. (1997), 'Economic Tax Reform in Europe: Opportunities and Obstacles', in T. O'Riordan (ed.), *Ecotaxation*, London: Earthscan, 81–105.

Goulder, L. H. (1995), 'Environmental Taxation and the "Double-Dividend": A Reader's Guide', *International Tax and Public Finance*, 2: 157–83.

Hey, C. (2005), *Sustainable Development and National Budgets: Ecological Tax Reform—Germany*, presented at the EU Sustainable Development Networking Event, 14–15 July 2005, Windsor, UK.

Hisnanick, J. J., and B. L. Kyer (1995), 'Assessing a Disaggregated Energy Input', *Energy Economics*, 17: 125–32.

Jacobs, M. (1994), *Green Jobs? The Employment Implications of Environmental Policy* Brussels: WWF.

Jackson, T. (2000), 'The Employment and Productivity Effects of Environmental Taxation: Additional Dividends or Added Distractions?' *Journal of Environmental Planning and Management*, 433: 389–406.

Kratena, K. (2002), *Environmental Tax Reform and The Labour Market: The Double Dividend in Different Labour Market Regimes*, Cheltenham: Edward Elgar.

Lutz, C., B. Meyer, and M. I. Wolter (2010), 'The Global Multisector/Multicountry 3-E Model GINFORS: A Description of the Model and a Baseline Forecast for Global Energy Demand and CO_2 Emissions', *International Journal of Global Environmental Issues*, 10(1–2): 25–45.

McEvoy, D., D. Gibbs, and J. Longhurst (2000), 'The Employment Implications of a Low-Carbon Economy', *Sustainable Development*, 81: 27–38.

McNeill, J. M., and J. B. Williams (2007), 'The Employment Effects of Sustainable Development Policies', *Ecological Economics*, 64: 216–23.

OECD (2004), *Environment and Employment: An Assessment Working Party on National Environmental Policy*, Paris: OECD.

Office for National Statistics (ONS) (2008), *United Kingdom Environmental Accounts*, London: ONS.

Parry, I. W. H., and W. E. Oates (2000), 'Policy Analysis in the Presence of Distorting Taxes', *Journal of Policy Analysis and Management*, 19: 603–13.

Patuelli, R., P. Nijkamp, and E. Pels (2005), 'Environmental Tax Reform and the Double Dividend: A Meta-analytical Performance Assessment', *Ecological Economics*, 55: 564–83.

Pearce, D. W. (1991), 'The Role of Carbon Taxes in Adjusting to Global Warming', *Economic Journal*, 101: 938–48.

Roy, J., A. H. Sanstad, J. A. Sathaye, and R. Khaddaria (2006), 'Substitution and Price Elasticity Estimates Using Inter-country Pooled Data in a Translog Cost Model', *Energy Economics*, 28: 706–19.

Speck, S. (2006), 'Overview of Environmental Tax Reforms in EU Member States', in M. S. Andersen, T. Barker, E. Christie, P. Ekins, J. F. Gerald, et al. (eds.) (2006), *Competitiveness Effect of Environmental Tax Reforms (COMETR)*, Final Report to the European Commission, DG Research and DG Taxation and Customs Union, National Environmental Research Institute, University of Aarhus, 19–83.

Timmer, M. P., M. O'Mahony, and B. van Ark (2007a), 'EU KLEMS Growth and Productivity Accounts: An Overview', available online at <http://www.euklems.net>.

—— T. van Moergastel, E. Stuivenwold, G. Ypma, M. O'Mahony, and M. Kangasniemi (2007b), 'EU KLEMS Growth and Productivity Accounts Version 1.0 PART I Methodology', available online at <http://www.euklems.net>.

Xiao, N., J. Zarnikau, and P. Damien (2007), 'Testing Functional Forms in Energy Modeling: An Application of the Bayesian Approach to U.S. Electricity Demand', *Energy Economics*, 29: 158–66.

Zarnikau, J. (2003), 'Functional Forms in Energy Demand Modelling', *Energy Economics*, 25: 603–13.

Part III
A European ETR for Growth and Sustainability

8

Models for Projecting the Impacts of ETR

Terry Barker, Christian Lutz, Bernd Meyer and Hector Pollitt

8.1 Introduction

With any modelling exercise, it is important to be aware of the approach, the underlying assumptions and the simplifications that are being made. This is because these all play a large role in determining the nature, magnitude, and direction of the results. With the two models used for this exercise of modelling ETR, the model parameters for behavioural relationships are estimated empirically over historical time-series data for the regions being modelled, rather than by imposing parameters drawn from the literature or assumptions, such as markets being in equilibrium (which is a usual assumption of computable general equilibrium (CGE) models), derived from neoclassical theory. The way such issues as technological progress and the labour market are treated also influences the results.

This chapter describes the main models, E3ME and GINFORS, which were used to provide a quantitative analysis of the effects of a large-scale European ETR. It outlines the similarities between the two models, for example their structure based on the national accounts and long-run econometric equations, while also discussing the differences between the models and their relative advantages, such as E3ME's ability to model short-run (annual) dynamic effects in Europe, and GINFORS' global coverage.

This chapter is a precursor to the detailed scenario analysis of Chapter 9 and serves to identify areas in which the models' results are likely to differ, particularly with regard to the intended impacts of ETR: energy demand and emissions (the environmental effects) and labour demand (the welfare effects). The chapter considers how the treatment of revenues from environmental taxes and charges affects the results of modelling ETRs.

All models explicitly or implicitly recycle the revenues from taxes or charges through the economy. The form of recycling can be by lump-sum transfers (normally in equal amounts) to consumers, a form chosen to minimize the theoretically assumed effects of the transfer on the economy (this is the form of recycling often employed in CGE analysis), or by the reduction of a so-called 'distortionary' tax or charge, such as employers' social-security charges. The form of revenue recycling has been shown to be a crucial factor in reducing the estimated macroeconomic costs of climate change mitigation (Barker et al. 2009a, 2009b).

The next section of this chapter discusses the key relationships likely to be important in the models in the analysis of ETRs in the European Union. In Section 8.3, the model characteristics of E3ME and GINFORS are described and are presented side by side. A brief discussion of the differences and similarities between the models is then offered. Section 8.4 then gives a detailed description of the properties of the models. In Section 8.5, some conclusions are drawn.

The models themselves are very briefly described in the Appendix to this chapter, and it is suggested that readers of this chapter start there. For more detailed documentation of the GINFORS model, the reader is referred to Meyer et al. (2005, 2007), Lutz et al. (2010), and Lutz and Meyer (2009a, 2009b). More information about the E3ME model, including the full online manual, can be found on the model website at ⟨http://www.e3me.com⟩.

8.2 Likely ETR Effects in E3ME and GINFORS

The possible effects of introducing a revenue-neutral ETR, first not using and then using revenues to reduce employment taxes, given the underlying structure and approach of E3ME and GINFORS, can be summarized as follows.

PRICES Pollution taxes are very likely to raise the prices of goods and services according to their pollution content, especially if the main polluting producers (e.g. of electricity generated by coal without any CO_2 capture) are operating in competitive and unregulated markets.

WAGE RATES Without any recycling of revenues, increased prices are expected to lead to increases in wage rates, depending on the treatment of the labour market. When the labour market is characterized in terms of the 'real wage bargaining' model, as is the case in both models, with market power on both sides of the labour market, i.e. employers and trade unions, wage rates will rise. With recycling, the main factor determining the extent to which an efficiency dividend will arise is whether or not the reduction of employers' social-security taxes, combined with higher wage costs, leads to lower or higher overall labour costs per unit of output. The social-security component of unit labour costs will fall, but the wage payments to employees per unit of output will rise, because the higher price inflation will lead to higher wage inflation.

EMPLOYMENT E3ME and GINFORS have different characteristics in relation to employment. With E3ME, the outcome for employment will depend on the stock of available labour resources, i.e. the rate of unemployment. If there are unemployed resources (which is usually the case), then employment will unambiguously increase, through both the substitution effects and firms' falling relative labour costs. Higher employment will probably mean that overall labour productivity in the economy becomes lower. However, as the economy approaches full employment, workers have a stronger bargaining position and there is more likely to be a larger increase in nominal wages and a smaller increase in employment. The knock-on effects on inflation may mean that there is little overall increase in real incomes.

The model GINFORS underlines the importance of the supply side. If labour demand is significantly dependent on the real wage rate, there is a first effect that depends on whether wage or price inflation is stronger, which depends on the situation in the labour market. If there is high unemployment, wages may rise slower than prices and there will be a fall in the real wage rate which will tend to increase employment. Very important for the effect on employment is the use of the revenues of the environmental tax. If it is used to reduce employers' social-security contributions, it will reduce labour costs and increase employment.

Whether there is an effect on the demand side of the economy depends on two parameter constellations in the country models. The first concerns the magnitude of the elasticity of the labour demand functions with respect to the real wage rate. If a fall in the real wage rate is combined with rising employment, a rise in real labour income will occur, if the elasticity is higher than one in absolute terms. But this is only a necessary but not sufficient condition for a rise in consumption demand. Additionally, the marginal propensity to consume must be higher for wage income than for profits. This second condition certainly holds; but the first—that the elasticity of labour demand in respect of real employment be greater than one in absolute terms—is more unlikely. A direct effect on consumption demand, and therefore an indirect effect on employment, arises if the revenue from the tax is used to reduce income taxes.

OUTPUT The higher prices of pollution-intensive products will lead to a loss in price competitiveness on export markets and some loss in the share of domestic markets to imports from other countries. This loss of price competitiveness will be offset by gains in labour-intensive sectors if real wage costs per unit of output have fallen in the ETR through recycling of revenues to reduce employers' taxes. Any improvement in non-price competitiveness will also raise exports. The extra employment will raise incomes, raising consumption and output. There may be an overall increase in output, with the structure changing such that the output of pollution-intensive industries is reduced relative to that of other industries. But since there are countervailing effects, the effect on output may also be slightly negative. It will be seen that the two models, E3ME and GINFORS, give different results in this respect.

TRADE Trade in pollution-intensive products will be reduced, depending on the strength of any rebound effect (the response of the economy to income and output increases following the ETR; the higher incomes, for example, could be spent on road and air travel, increasing use of imported pollution-intensive fuels). Net trade in other products may also be reduced, for the reasons given above.

8.3 General Properties of E3ME and GINFORS

8.3.1 Architecture

E3ME This is a dynamic simulation econometric model, not a CGE model, combining the features of an annual short- and medium-term sectoral model. The detailed nature of the model allows the representation of fairly complex scenarios, especially those that are differentiated according to sector and to country. Similarly, the impact of any policy measure can be represented in a detailed way.

The model is split into three modules: (1) the economy, solved as an integrated regional model; (2) energy, which has a two-way linkage with the economy module and which also feeds into (3) the environment module, which calculates air pollution from end-use as well as energy industry primary use and feeds back into the economy module, through, for example, emission taxes or trading schemes. A module for the sectoral use of materials has been added more recently.

GINFORS This is also not a CGE model. Rather it is based on an evolutionary philosophy with imperfections and allowances for bounded rationality. GINFORS is an integrated system that adds economics to industrial ecology and thus favours policy realism. GINFORS is a global model, and the link between economic activity in the countries is given by international trade, which is the result of global competition in deep sectoral disaggregation.

Each country model consists of a macro-model, an input-output model, an energy model, and a materials model, which are linked with each other. Whilst macro-models by GINFORS are at hand for all countries, input-output models are available for 21 countries only. The economies of the remaining countries are represented solely by a macro-model. GINFORS also contains energy and emission modules for all countries.

Both models are pioneering in that they are based on the 'new economics' or 'complexity economics' (Beinhocker 2006), which looks to institutional, evolutionary, and chaos theory rather than the traditional equilibrium-rationality theory of mainstream economics as represented in CGE models. Both models are multi-country/multi-sector integrated economy-energy-environment models. Combining these attributes is necessary to analyse the implications of long-term energy policy and carbon mitigation options. The explicit modelling of countries is useful, since policies are always related to specific countries and their individual structural properties. The sector approach, including inter-industry relations, is necessary since relations between the environment and the economy are sector specific, with different issues arising for different sectors.

The models differ in country coverage. E3ME is a European model, which explicitly models all 27 EU countries plus Switzerland and Norway. Activity elsewhere in the world is treated as exogenous. The closely related global model, E3MG (Barker et al. 2006; Barker and Scrieciu forthcoming), is less detailed in its treatment of EU institutions, but covers 20 world regions.

GINFORS is a global model covering all EU-27 countries, all OECD countries, and their major trade partners, including all important emerging economies. The system includes a total of 50 countries and two regions, 'OPEC' and 'Rest of the World' (ROW). The 50 explicitly modelled countries and the OPEC region account for around 95% of world GDP and CO_2 emissions. The 21 countries with input-output models cover about 80% of world GDP.

Both E3ME and GINFORS simultaneously find solutions for all countries, but in both systems, single-country solutions may also be calculated.

8.3.2 Parameterization

E3ME has a complete specification of the long-term solution for each main stochastic variable in the form of an estimated equation that has long-term restrictions imposed on its parameters. Economic theory (for example, the recent theories of endogenous growth) informs the specification of the long-term equations and hence the properties of the model; dynamic equations that embody these long-term properties are estimated by econometric methods to allow the model to provide forecasts. The method utilizes developments in time-series econometrics, in which dynamic relationships are specified in terms of error-correction models (ECM) that allow dynamic convergence to a long-term outcome. The specific functional form of the equations is based on the econometric techniques of cointegration and error correction, particularly as promoted by Engle and Granger (1987) and Hendry et al. (1984). Generalized instrumental variable estimation is used and heterogeneity assumed.

GINFORS combines econometric-statistical analysis with input-output analysis, embedded in a complete macroeconomic framework. Nearly all parameters of GINFORS are estimated econometrically using international time-series data. The parameters are estimated by OLS (Ordinary Least Squares).

Both models are econometric models combining regression estimates with input-output coefficients and bilateral trade shares. E3ME extends the formal econometric methods to the estimation of private consumption in total and by function (e.g. housing), fixed investment by industry, exports, imports, their prices, product prices, employment, and wage rates (29 sets of equations in all) by country and sector. In general, GINFORS has the same flexibility, but relies on fixed shares of macro-aggregates for the structure of consumption for energy on the one side, and consumption for non-energy use on the other side. The relation between consumption for energy use and for non-energy use is endogenous. The parameter estimation of E3ME is based on the econometrics of cointegration and error correction, with a shrinkage technique applied to compensate for the short time series in the 12 countries that have joined the EU since 2004.

For GINFORS, the OLS method of econometric estimation was chosen. More adequate estimators could not be used for two reasons: in many countries, the length of the time series is relatively short; and for the automatic estimation of the large number of variables (e.g. price elasticities for 70,304 trade shares), a robust and simple estimation technique is needed.

8.3.3 Data

For E3ME, data must be consistent across countries, and in the same units and definitions. These data are updated as and when new releases become available. For each set of the model variables, the possible data sources are ranked.

The Eurostat National Accounts data set, which establishes a comparable basis across member states, is always the preferred choice. Even where Eurostat data are incomplete or believed to be of poor quality, the Eurostat definitions are adopted and the data are improved via other sources. Eurostat data are further disaggregated using the OECD's STAN database. Data from the AMECO database are used in order to make the Eurostat total consistent with an accepted macroeconomic total, and also to provide limited sectoral information. When Eurostat data are not available or need to be improved, other internationally available sources such as the International Monetary Fund (IMF) are consulted. Once these international data sources have been exhausted, national statistical agencies and other data sources are used to update the remaining missing series and gaps in the data.

The database of GINFORS is supplied by five international sources: OECD, IMF, Eurostat, UN COMTRADE databanks, and the International Energy

Agency (IEA). Furthermore, for two significant countries (China and Taiwan), national statistics are evaluated. The trade data resulted from a merging of OECD and UN data. The data for the macro-model are based on the OECD's *National Accounts of OECD Countries, Detailed Tables* and the IMF's data set *International Financial Statistics*. Since a coherent level of data is necessary for the model, gaps within the data sets are filled by calculations by the model owners. In the majority of cases, the input-output tables are taken from OECD publications and Eurostat. For material-input models, the data supplied by the Sustainable Europe Research Institute (SERI) form the database.

Both models are based on international sectoral National Accounts data, using Eurostat or OECD data as a first choice. The default currency is the Euro in E3ME and the dollar in GINFORS. Other data sources are the UN, Eurostat, the AMECO database, and the IMF. National data sources have only been used when it was unavoidable. The models both use energy data provided by the IEA.

8.3.4 Technical Progress

The approach to constructing the measure of technological progress in E3ME is adapted from that of Lee et al. (1990). It adopts a direct measure of techno-logical progress by using cumulative gross investment, supplemented by data on R&D expenditure, thus forming a quality-adjusted measure of investment. In E3ME, there are two technical progress indicators, one measuring technical progress related to Information and Communication Technologies (ICT) investment in the new economy, and one related to all other investment. The construction of the two indicators is similar, with investment split into ICT and non-ICT related investment. Investment is central to the determina-tion of long-term growth and the model embodies a theory of endogenous growth which underlies the long-term behaviour of the trade and employ-ment equations. The two technical progress indicators can appear together in the stochastic equations and separate long- and short-term parameters are estimated for each one. In E3ME, energy-related investments feed into the model's energy-demand sub-model. Investment in renewables feeds into the model's Energy Technology Model (see Anderson and Winne, 2004 and Barker et al. 2007).

In GINFORS, technical progress is implicitly modelled. The technology is depicted in a two-stage approach. In the first stage, capital, labour, energy, and materials are factors of a limitational technology. But the input coeffi-cients are not constant. The sectoral factor demand functions for labour, capital, energy, and materials in the first stage depend on the relationship between the factor price and the sector price, which is interpreted as the effect of cost-push-driven technical progress. Additionally, time trends reflect autonomous progress. In the second stage, the energy input is divided into the demand for the 11 different energy carriers, assuming price-dependent substitution.

Thus, E3ME explicitly models technical progress endogenously (through a function of accumulated investment enhanced by R&D spending) by industrial sector, and estimates its impact on the economy and energy demand through effects on trade, prices, and employment, all at a sectoral level. In GINFORS, in contrast, technical progress is modelled implicitly. It is assumed that relative prices are cost-push determinants of technical progress. This reduced-form approach is chosen, since R&D data are not available globally at the sectoral level. But nevertheless the direct and indirect effects of technical progress are also depicted.

8.4 The Model Structure in Detail

8.4.1 Trade

In E3ME, all trade is treated as if it takes place through a European 'pool', i.e. a transport and distribution network, into which each region supplies part of its production and from which each region satisfies part of its demand. The export and import volume equations are divided into those going to the internal single market and those going to markets external to the EU. They represent each region's exports into the internal and external pools and imports from them.

The demand for a region's exports of a commodity is related to four factors: demand in the export markets, using their GDP weighted by economic distance; own prices; competitor prices, also using distance weights; and technology indicators. Economic distance is measured by a special distance variable. For a given region, this variable is normalized to be one for the home region and takes values of less than one for external regions. The economic distance to other regions is inversely proportional to trade between the regions. In addition, measures of innovation (including spending on R&D) have been introduced into the trade equations to pick up an important long-term dynamic effect on economic development. Trade volume is separated into intra-EU and extra-EU trade flows. For exports, income is determined separately for the EU and the rest of the world, and price effects are split into three: export prices, export prices in other EU countries, and a 'rest of the world' price variable. In the case of imports, domestic activity is modelled by sales to the domestic market and the three price effects are: import price, price of sales to the domestic market, and the relative price of the currency (the Euro exchange rate). Long-run price homogeneity is imposed for both imports and exports and technical progress measures are included to allow for innovations in trade performance. A synthetic variable to take account of the Internal Market programme is also included.

The basic model of trade prices used in E3ME assumes that the EU regions operate in oligopolistic markets and are each small economies in relation to the total market. Certain commodities such as oil have their prices set in global markets and are therefore treated exogenously, but the majority are set by producers as mark-ups on costs. Alongside the unit cost variable, there are four price terms included in each regression to deal with developments outside the region in question. They are an 'other EU' price, a 'rest of the world' price, a world commodity price variable, and the Euro exchange rate. The measures of technical progress are also included to cope with the quality effect on prices caused by increased levels of investment and R&D.

At the centre of the GINFORS system is a trade model. For 25 commodities as well as the service trade, bilateral trade matrices for 50 countries, including all EU-27 and OECD countries and its major trade partners (emerging economies), are provided. The coefficients of the trade matrices—the trade shares—are endogenous variables derived from the relation between the price of the commodity of the exporting country and the average price of the imports of that commodity in the importing country. Via this trade context, both quantities and prices are properly allocated to the countries.

The countries appear as independent actors within the trade model. Every national model provides import vectors and export price vectors; and receives export vectors and import price vectors in its interaction with the trade model. Values from the country models are given in national currency. These values must be converted to US dollars before being passed to the trade model and the output from the trade model converted back into national currencies.

The aggregates are calculated in the following way: import demand is an aggregate of sectoral imports, which depend on domestic demand and price relations between imports and domestic production. If the country has no input-output model, an aggregated import function is estimated, with GDP and the relative import price serving as determinants. The vector of import prices in US dollars is given by the trade model. By aggregation, a price for total imports can be calculated.

The main exchange rates between the Eurozone, the USA, China, Japan, and the UK are kept constant. For some countries, exchange rates are related to the exchange rate of the regionally leading economy (such as in Europe). For some countries with high inflation rates, they are estimated as a function of the GDP deflator of the respective country and the GDP deflator of the USA. This generally yields good results, with elasticities ranging close to one which implicitly means constant real exchange rates—a robust hypothesis that allows for long-run projections of exchange rates up to 2020.

In the input-output models, production prices are determined by companies via a mark-up calculation from unit costs. Exceptions only occur when, due to the homogeneity of commodities in relation to the global market, companies are price takers, not price leaders. This is typically the case in primary commodity markets where a coherent global market has evolved. Export prices implemented within the bilateral trade model are basically identical to production prices.

In summary, within E3ME, international trade is not modelled on a bilateral basis but by means of a European pool and global pools or networks. The export- and import-volume equations describe each region's exports into and imports from these pools, with relative weights (or 'economic distance') determined by OECD bilateral trade data. GINFORS, in contrast, has a bilateral trade model that connects the countries directly. The share of exports of a delivering country in the imports of a receiving country for a specific good is dependent on relative prices and trends. Imports and export prices by sector are determined in the country models. As the bilateral imports of one country equal the bilateral exports of another, exports and import prices are then given by definition.

Both models allow for imperfectly competitive price structures—producers set prices as a mark-up on unit costs. Trade in commodities that exist in coherent global markets are taken to have an exogenously set price.

8.4.2 Input-Output Structures

The accounting structure for the 42 products and industries in E3ME is based on the Eurostat System of Accounts 1995 (ESA95; Eurostat 1995). Nearly all of the functional classifications can be identified with accounts in the ESA95, and one of the characteristics of the ESA and E3ME is the disaggregation of economic variables.

For the latest version of E3ME, a new set of input-output tables was obtained from Eurostat, the OECD, and the Global Trade Analysis Project (GTAP) database. For each region, an input-output table for 2000 was estimated if this was not already available. The input-output (IO) coefficients implicitly determine the production process of each of the 42 industries. IO coefficients for energy products and material inputs are determined endogenously by the equation results; other IO coefficients change over time to capture the effects of price changes and technological progress. They are typically fitted to a logistic trend line that is treated as exogenous by the model. For consumers' expenditures, which are estimated by functional category, the IO tables provide 'bridge matrices' for converting the functional consumer categories into the IO products.

The input-output models of GINFORS contain 41 sectors. They obtain the vector of export volumes and import prices from the trade model and aggregated private and public consumption figures from the macro-models and distribute them to 41 sectors. From the energy models they receive prices for the energy carriers. The input-output models calculate the vectors by industry of gross production, intermediate demand, the vector of imports, and vectors for the different components of primary inputs. The input-output models further estimate the vector of unit costs and the vector of prices. Since there is only a single table giving the input-output (IO) structures, non-energetic input coefficients cannot be endogenized and are treated as exogenous variables. The input coefficients of the energy rows of the input-output table are fully endogenous, driven by the energy demand of the sector which is calculated in the energy model.

GINFORS uses private household consumption data published by the OECD to analyse consumption patterns, but the absence of bridge matrices makes disaggregating consumption by sector problematic. Energy demand can, however, be inferred and converted into monetary units. The non-energy demand is then derived as the remaining total private consumption that is unaccounted for. The structure of government consumption and capital investment is kept constant or projected in scenarios by exogenous performance targets. The structure of composite commodities for exports and imports is determined by world trade data, so that import functions can be calculated. The exports are generated by the trade model.

In both systems, the input-output models are mainly based on IO tables from international sources. In general, all input coefficients apart from those for energy, which are driven by the energy models, are exogenous.

E3ME has a variable household consumption structure, depending on relative prices and demographic factors. GINFORS has this variability only between energy demand and all other consumption. Consumption structures between energy carriers are price dependent. Both systems convert investment into demand for goods and services. The structure of investment demand is variable in both models, depending on expected activities in the investing industries. In both models, investment is estimated and solved for each industry and country as a function of relative prices and expected output. Both systems explain the prices of goods by unit costs and other variables. Prices for fossil fuels are exogenous in both models, since they depend on the world market. Taxes and other energy price components are also considered.

8.4.3 The Energy Models

The energy sub-model in E3ME is constructed, estimated, and solved for 19 fuel users, 12 energy carriers (also termed fuels for convenience below), and 29 countries. Aggregate energy demand in tonnes of oil equivalent (toe) is determined by a set of cointegrating equations, in which the main explanatory variables are economic activity for each fuel user, their average real fuel prices, and technological progress indicators. Fuel-use equations are estimated for four fuels—coal, heavy oils, gas, and electricity—and the four sets of equations are estimated for fuel users in each country. These equations are intended to allow substitution between these energy carriers by users on the basis of relative prices, although overall fuel use and the technological variables are allowed to affect the choice. The remaining fuels are determined as fixed ratios to similar fuels or to aggregate energy use. The final set of fuels used must then be scaled to ensure that it adds up to aggregate energy demand (for each fuel user and each country). E3ME also incorporates a bottom-up representation of energy technologies to model the take-up of a number of energy-supply options, including an array of low-carbon technologies. Learning curves, relating technology costs to experience and investment, allow for new technologies to become more competitive over time.

The energy-emission models in GINFORS show the interrelations between economic developments, energy consumption, and emissions. For this purpose, the variables of the corresponding macro-model and of the IO model—if available—are used as drivers. Vice versa, the expenditure for energy consumption has a direct influence on economic variables. The final energy consumption of a sector is explained by output, trends, and the relationship between the aggregate energy price—an average of the different carrier prices weighted by their shares in the energy consumption of that sector—and the sector price. If a country does not have an input-output model, GDP is used instead of the sector's output and the sector price is replaced by the GDP deflator.

The final demand of energy carrier i can be calculated by definition, multiplying the share of carrier i in the energy demand of sector j with the final energy demand of sector j and summing over all sectors. For residential, services, manufacturing, and steel production, these shares depend on the relation between the carriers' price and the aggregated energy price of that sector or of relative energy carrier prices. Conversion from primary energy into final energy takes place for electricity and petroleum products. The demand of carrier i for conversion is given by multiplying the production of the secondary energy carrier in question by the input coefficient of primary energy carrier i.

The energy models obtain the vector of gross production by industry and final demand by branches, as well as industry prices and energy import volumes, from the input-output models. The trade model provides energy import prices and energy export volumes to the energy models. Based on energy import prices, the energy models further determine wholesale and retail prices for the energy carriers, which are used in the input-output models.

Both systems use the energy balances of the IEA as the database for their energy models. The structure of the models is very similar. In the first step, final energy demand is estimated for 19 demand sectors. The explanatory variables are the activity variables of the demand sector and the relative energy price of the sector, and in the case of E3ME, the technology variable. The carrier structure of energy demand for 12 energy carriers partly depends on relative carrier prices and has constant structures.

Both models use energy price data from the IEA and use exogenous projections of prices. Chapter 9 describes how two sets of assumed prices were used to account for the increase in energy prices in 2008.

8.4.4 The Emission Models

Emissions may be the result of fuel combustion or other economic activities. E3ME's emissions sub-model calculates air pollution generated from end-use of different fuels and from primary use of fuels in the energy industries themselves, particularly electricity generation. The model computes emissions to the atmosphere of carbon dioxide (CO_2), sulphur dioxide (SO_2), nitrogen oxides (NOx), carbon monoxide (CO), methane (CH_4), black smoke (PM10), volatile organic compounds (VOC), nuclear emissions to air, lead emissions to air, chlorofluorocarbons (CFCs), and four other greenhouse gases: nitrous oxide (N_2O), hydrofluorocarbons (HFC), perfluorocarbons (PFC), sulphur hexafluoride (SF_6). These last four gases, together with CO_2 and CH_4, constitute the six greenhouse gases (GHGs) monitored under the Kyoto Protocol. Using estimated damage coefficients, E3ME may also estimate ancillary benefits relating to reduction in associated emissions, for example, PM10, SO_2, NOx (Barker and Rosendahl 2000).

Emissions data for CO_2 are available for fuel users of solid fuels, oil products, and gas separately. The energy sub-model estimates of fuel by fuel user are aggregated into these groups (solid, oil, and gas) and emission coefficients (tonnes of carbon in CO_2 emitted per tonne oil equivalent) are calculated and stored. The coefficients are calculated for each year when data are available, then used at their last historical values to project future emissions. Other emissions data are available at various levels of disaggregation from a number of sources and have been constructed carefully to ensure consistency.

In GINFORS, the energy models calculate primary and secondary energy demand for 11 carriers in detail, the conversion of energy and CO_2 emissions of the different fossil energy carriers. The energy-emission models are based on the energy balances of the International Energy Agency (IEA) and are, therefore, available for all countries and regions as well. They feature energy consumption structured by the relevant energy carriers. The CO_2 emissions are linked with the fossil energy carriers by constant carbon relations. Since the explicitly given 50 countries plus the OPEC region of the model cover 95% of world CO_2 emissions, the missing 5% are linked to the region 'Rest of the World' so that global coverage of CO_2 emissions is given. The emissions of the other greenhouse gases are modelled by scenario. GINFORS therefore has global endogenous coverage for CO_2 emissions, and scenario estimations for the other greenhouse gases.

8.4.5 The Material Models

E3ME's sub-model of material inputs comprises seven equations, for food, feed, forestry, construction minerals, industrial minerals, ores, and water. In a similar manner to the fuel equations, the independent variables include an economic activity indicator, a price level, and a measure of innovation, and use the standard ECM methodology employed in E3ME's stochastic equations.

Following the template of the energy demand equations, the activity indicator is defined as sectoral gross output converted into 14 material users. In the modelling, the price variable is determined by prices in the sector that produces the material (e.g. water supply for water), with historical data taken from commodity indices where possible. Innovation is determined by levels of investment and R&D, again converted from the 42-sector industrial classification to the material-using groups. As described above, sectoral gross output and investment/R&D in each sector affect the material demands of each material-using group, and price changes affect demand for each material. However, just as important is how changes in material demands feed back to the wider economy through the industries that produce the materials. With the exception of water, the materials are almost exclusively inputs into the production processes of various industries and so are part of intermediate, rather than final, demand. In E3ME, intermediate demands are determined by input-output relationships and it is the coefficients in the input-output table that adjust to reflect changes in demand. The relationship is fairly straightforward, with a 10% increase in demand for a particular material leading to roughly a 10% increase in IO coefficients, although in some cases it would be necessary to apply a correction for heterogeneous output in a given industry (e.g. forestry makes up only a small part of the agriculture industry). The same principle can be applied to consumer demand for water, with a direct link between household demand for water and consumption of water.

In GINFORS, the modelling of material extraction for coal, crude oil, gas, biomass, ores, and other materials has to guarantee that the global economic drivers are linked to resource extraction in the different countries. It is only necessary to distinguish the demand for materials from export and from domestic demand. If this is done, international trade and domestic production, which is also linked with trade, will drive material extraction in a globally consistent way following global economic development. In the MOSUS project, the GINFORS model system was extended by material input models in physical (mass) units. For this task, the first global database on domestic extraction of natural resources was compiled by the Sustainable Europe Research Institute, Vienna, covering 188 countries in a time series from 1980 to 2002 (Behrens et al. 2007). Material input data was collected following the categorization and methodological standards for economy-wide material flow accounting (MFA), as described in the MFA handbook by the European Statistical Office (Eurostat 2001) and then aggregated to the 52 countries and world regions of the GINFORS model. Results have been presented up to 2030 (Giljum et al. 2008; Lutz and Giljum 2009).

In the course of the PETRE project, the material extraction database has been updated until 2005 (<http://www.materialflows.net>). The database now covers more than 200 countries. For each country or each region of GINFORS, material extraction is listed separately according to the categories *used* and *unused extraction*. Furthermore, extraction is divided into the following material-input categories: agricultural products and fish, forestry products, coal, crude oil, natural gas, iron ores, non-ferrous metals, industrial minerals, and construction minerals. Each of the nine material groups was linked to the GINFORS model through drivers, i.e. variables, which explain the development of extraction of a particular resource.

For countries without sectoral detail, GDP in constant prices is the driver. However, the treatment for countries with sector models based on monetary input-output tables is more detailed, with sectoral drivers of the flows between the relevant sectors (Table 8.1). For example, for resource extraction in agriculture, grazing and fish, the intermediate input from the agriculture, forestry and fishing sector to the food sector in constant prices is the chosen driver. Additionally, decoupling factors (representing increases in resource productivity) between biomass extraction and sector output were applied, based on historical evidence from 1991 to 2005. Thus, historic productivity trends are extended into the future. The same approach is applied to forestry and industrial minerals. For fossil energy, resource extraction is linked to production data in tonnes of oil equivalent, which is calculated for all countries in the energy models using data from the IEA energy balances. Results in units of oil equivalent were translated into mass units. The energy models are described in more detail in Lutz et al. (2010). For iron ore, monetary production in constant prices of the iron and steel sector (12) drives iron and steel demand in tonnes. Iron and steel production in the oxygen steel furnace is based on iron ore inputs, whereas electric arc furnaces use scrap metal. The share of electric steel production is extrapolated from historic developments. The iron ore demand for oxygen steel can be satisfied domestically or by imports. Iron

Table 8.1. Explanatory parameters for nine material categories in the material input models in GINFORS

	Material category	Sub-model	Driver
1	Agriculture, grazing, fish	IO model	Sector 1 (agri.) to sector 3 (food)
2	Forestry	IO model	Sector 1 (agri.) to sector 5 (wood)
2	Forestry	IO model	Sector 1 (agri.) to sector 6 (paper)
3	Coal	Energy model	Production of coal in toe (row 1 of the energy balance)
4	Oil	Energy model	Production of crude oil in toe (row 1 of the energy balance)
5	Natural gas	Energy model	Production of gas in toe (row 1 of the energy balance)
6	Iron ores: (1) iron and steel demand	IO model	Production of sector 12 (iron and steel)
6	Iron ores: (2) ore extraction	Trade model	Physical trade balance in t
7	Other metal ores	IO model	Sector 2 (mining & quarrying) to sector 13 (Non-ferrous metals)
8	Industrial minerals	IO model	Sector 2 (mining & quarrying) to sector 11 (Other non-metallic mineral products)
9	Construction minerals	IO model	Sector 2 (mining & quarrying) to sector 26 (Construction)

ore production and trade data (UNCTAD 2007) clearly show that iron ore extraction is concentrated in a few countries. Brazil, China, Australia, India, and Russia accounted for 77% of world iron ore production in 2006. The demand of the different countries is translated into iron ore production using constant physical trade shares of 2006 (UNCTAD 2007). The development of non-ferrous metal ore extraction is explained by a separate model covering global production and demand for metals. Global non-ferrous metal ore extraction is then distributed among all metal-extracting countries, taking into consideration (a) changes in the geographical distribution of non-ferrous metal ore extraction between the different world regions over the past 25 years and (b) the historical trend of increasing recycling of these metals.

Several categories of material extraction are linked to economic drivers, which illustrate the delivery of primary extraction to the first stage of processing (e.g. deliveries from agriculture to the food sector or from forestry to the wood sector). This approach was selected for two main reasons: first, we aimed to disaggregate a maximum number of material categories within the given sectoral structure of the IO models. As, for example, only one sector on biomass extraction (covering agriculture, grazing, fish and forestry) is identified in the OECD IO tables, no separation of agriculture from forestry would be possible at the point of extraction. In order to keep agriculture separate from forestry, specific drivers needed to be identified, which explain the extraction of specific material categories (i.e. delivery of the biomass sector to the food sector explains extraction of agricultural products, grazing and fish; delivery of the biomass sector to the wood and papers sectors explains the extraction of forestry products). The same approach was implemented for deliveries of the mining sector to the non-ferrous metal, the industrial minerals and the construction sectors.

The second main reason is that a mis-assignment of different types of material extraction in early stages of the production process would lead to larger errors than a biased allocation at a later stage, as the processing of materials in the early stages of production follows rather specific processes with particular input relations, whereas in later production stages, the original raw materials are mixed into semi-finished and finished products and distributed over a much larger number of sectors (Schoer 2006). This again calls for the separation of a maximum number of specific materials, which are delivered to different sectors for further processing.

8.4.6 Treatment of Macro Variables

E3ME does not have a macroeconomic component as such. The main macro-aggregates (GDP, and its expenditure components, such as gross investment) are formed by summing the sectoral variables, with the exception of aggregate consumption, which is related to real disposable income by country. Other macro variables are used as signals in sectoral equations: the rate of inflation, the rate of interest in the Eurozone, the level of global oil prices, the various currency exchange rates in the model. Real personal disposable income is formed from wage income, other factor income (rents, dividends), social-security transfers (pensions, unemployment benefits), less taxes, all deflated by the consumer price index.

The macro-models in GINFORS aggregate primary income, import volumes, and prices derived from input-output models. They show the redistribution of income between the government, households, enterprises, and foreign countries and calculate the disposable income for these institutions, which is an important determinant of private and public consumption. The macro-models further depict monetary markets and calculate the interest rate and other determinants of investment. The accounting system of the macro-models further contains the balance of payments. The macro-model for each country consists of five modules: the balance of payments, final demand, the monetary market, the labour market, and the System of National Accounts (SNA). First, the balance of payments consists of monetary transactions between home citizens and foreigners. All flows of the current account, such as goods exports and imports and income paid and received, as well as transfers paid and received, are endogenous. The balance of foreign exchange payments is assumed to be zero and the balance of capital transactions can be calculated as a residual.

All components of final demand are endogenous variables and are mainly explained by income figures. Interest rates play only a minor role. Population, next to GDP, is one important determinant of public consumption. Prices of the different components of final demand are estimated by aggregated prices from the input-output model. If there is no input-output model, aggregated labour unit costs explain aggregated macro prices. The structure of government consumption is kept constant or projected in scenarios by exogenous performance targets. With respect to the monetary market, a reduced form of equilibrium is estimated in which the government bond yield is explained by the discount rate and GDP. The discount rate is explained by the rate of inflation. For the countries of the Euro area, interest rates are exogenous, since there are not enough observations for econometric estimations.

The supply of labour is linked to the rate of population growth, taken as exogenous from the 2005 UN forecast. Labour demand can be calculated by dividing real GDP by labour productivity, which is dependent on the real wage rate and technological trends. The modules for the SNA display the macroeconomic accounting of a country. Their prime objective is to ascertain available income and financial accounts for the private sector and government. Available income, being a determinant of demand for consumption, is a significant variable, as is net lending for the calculation of budgetary constraints.

Both models include aggregated final demand functions, such as consumer expenditure, where the disposable income of private households is the main explanatory variable. In E3ME, there is no accounting system with payments and receipts, which would enable disposable income to be derived from primary income, so the difference between wages and disposable income (corrected for taxes and benefits) is therefore estimated by a regression. In GINFORS, a complete accounting system is included for the most important EU countries of the model. For the other countries, a constant relation between primary income and disposable income is assumed. The balance of payments is represented for all countries.

Global macroeconomic closure in GINFORS is given in the following way: investment functions and savings are independent in the countries. Gaps between investment and savings in a country are closed by the current account balance. Since, globally, exports equal imports and transfers paid equal transfers received, it is guaranteed that globally, investment equals savings. It is assumed for the region ROW (Rest of the World) that the trade balance is zero, which means that imports follow exports from ROW, which are endogenously determined in the trade model. For the other transactions of the current account—international transfers—world totals are zero, so that the balances of ROW equal with opposite sign the totals of the balances of the

50 countries and the OPEC region, which are explicitly part of the system. Further, the difference between the savings and investment of ROW equals the sum of the balances of transfers of the 50 countries. This kind of global closure is a Keynesian feature. A rise in investment in one country will raise income in that country, induce imports, and in this way increase income in other countries. The system attains a global equilibrium with higher investment and higher savings.

8.4.7 Wages and Labour Demand and Supply

Sectoral labour demand measured by number of employees depends in both models on gross production, real wages per head, and other variables. Wages per head are explained in both models using Phillips curve specifications.

Employment in E3ME is modelled as a total headcount number for each industry and country as a function of industry output, wage costs, average hours worked, technological progress, and energy prices (exogenous world oil prices). Industry output is assumed to have a positive effect on employment demand, while the effect of higher wages and longer working hours is assumed to be negative. The effects of technical progress are ambiguous, as investment may create or replace labour. In the income loop, industrial output generates employment and incomes, which leads to further consumer expenditure, increasing total demand. The changes in output are used to determine changes in employment as well as changes in real wage costs. With wage rates explained by price levels and labour market conditions, the wage and salary payments by industry can be calculated from industrial employment levels.

Hours worked is a simple equation, where average hours worked by industry and region are a function of 'normal hours worked', technological progress, and the level of output compared to expected 'normal' output, which takes into account cyclical effects. It is assumed that the effects of technical progress gradually reduce average hours worked over time as processes become more efficient. The resulting estimate of hours worked is an explanatory variable in the employment equation. Wages are determined by a complex union bargaining system that includes both worker productivity effects and prices and wage rates in the wider economy. Other important factors include the unemployment rate, available benefits, and cyclical effects. Generally, it is assumed that higher prices and worker productivity will push up wage rates, but rising unemployment will reduce bargaining power and therefore wages. A single average wage is estimated for each country and sector. These estimates are a key input to both the employment equations and the price equations in E3ME. In the absence of growing output, rising wages will increase overall unit costs and industry prices. These prices may get passed on to other industries through the input-output relationships, building up inflationary pressure.

In determining labour supply, equations for the participation of male and female persons are estimated, the latter as a rate between 0 and 1 for various age bands of male and female populations. Labour market participation is a function of industry output, real retained wage rates, unemployment rates and benefits, average working hours, and skills levels. Participation is assumed to be higher when output and wages are growing, but falls when unemployment is high, or when benefits create a disincentive to work. In addition, there is an economic structure variable which measures the relative size of the service sector of the economy; this has been found to be important in determining female participation rates. The participation rates determine the stock of employment available. This is an important factor in determining unemployment, which in turn feeds into wages and back to labour market participation.

At the level of sectors, in GINFORS labour demand and the respective wages are ascertained for six combined economic sectors. For this purpose, the necessary explanatory factors from the input-output model are combined by aggregation in order to form these six economic sectors. The wages in the economic sectors, defined as the annual wages per employee, result from a 'shift-share' regression with the average wage, which again is the result of a Phillips curve with reference to the labour market situation.

The number of employees depends on production, real wages, and an autonomous trend for technological progress.

The labour input coefficients are given by definition as quotients of employment and gross production, whilst the sum of wages results from the multiplication of the annual wage per employee by the number of employees. In the labour market, supply—measured as labour force—is dependent on the development of population, which is exogenous according to the UN projection. Labour productivity, defined as the ratio of real GDP and employment, is dependent on the real wage rate and technological trends. The aggregated wage rate is dependent on labour productivity and the development of consumer prices.

8.5 Conclusions

Both models are pioneering in that they look to institutional, evolutionary, and chaos theory rather than to the traditional equilibrium-rationality theory of mainstream economics as represented in CGE models. Both models are multi-country/multi-sector models. Both models transmit effects between countries through flows of import and export volumes and import and export prices. The multi-country approach that explicitly models different countries is necessary, since countries and not 'regions' are the relevant policy units. The sectoral focus is necessary, since economy-environment relations are different at the sector level and the economies have different sector structures. Both models are empirically based, using econometric methods for the estimation of the parameters.

A comparison of simulation results is facilitated by the fact that the models have central common properties. On the other hand, there are differences in the specification and parameter estimation of the models, which may yield different simulation results. For example, E3ME models technical progress explicitly, whereas GINFORS does so implicitly. E3ME focuses on Europe, whereas GINFORS is a global model. Trade in E3ME flows to and from a common pool, while GINFORS uses a bilateral trade model with price-dependent trade shares. GINFORS has, compared with E3ME, a less flexible structure of consumption and investment. GINFORS provides macro-models with full SNA structures for the most important countries, whereas E3ME has a simplified accounting tool for the redistribution of income. For the estimation of the parameters, E3ME uses error-correction methods, whereas GINFORS is based on OLS estimations.

The identification of the impacts of these differences on the simulation results is one major outcome of the project. Since the sets of endogenous and exogenous variables are not identical in the models, the formulation of the assumptions and scenarios has to be done very carefully so that identical model experiments can be guaranteed. Comparison of the results and discussion of the differences expand our knowledge about ETR and provide a check, given the two approaches and the common framework. Furthermore, new ETR instruments like the EU ETS, with auctioning and recycling of the auction revenues, can be discussed on a broad modelling base.

APPENDIX

E3ME Model Overview

This section briefly describes the E3ME model which is compared in this chapter with the GINFORS model, and which was used to carry out the ETR and household distributional analysis in Chapters 9 and 10. For a more comprehensive description of the E3ME model, the reader can find additional information, including the online technical manual, on the model website at ⟨http://www.e3me.com⟩.

E3ME is a large-scale model of Europe's economies, energy systems, and environment. A key feature of the model is its high level of disaggregation, which allows for the analysis of detailed policy measures and enables the model to produce a detailed set of results. The main model classifications in version 4.6 of E3ME are:

- 29 countries (the EU-27 plus Norway and Switzerland);
- 19 energy-using groups;
- 12 fuels;
- 42 economic sectors;
- 41 household spending categories.

E3 Interactions

E3ME is intended to meet an expressed need of researchers and policy makers for a framework for analysing the short and long-term implications of Energy-Environment-Economy (E3) policies. The model incorporates two-way linkages, with feedback effects between the economy, energy demand/supply, and environmental emissions (see Figure A8.1). These linkages are a clear advantage over many other models, which may either ignore the interaction completely or only assume a one-way causation, leading to a bias in results.

Version 4.6 of the model also includes a sub-model of materials consumption, which is required to assess the impact of the materials tax in the scenarios. Its structure is similar to that of the energy sub-model, with two-way links to the economy. It is described in more detail in Pollitt (2008).

The economics of E3ME

The economic structure of E3ME is fully consistent with the structure of the National Accounts, as defined by ESA95 (Eurostat 1995), and the definitions used by Eurostat.

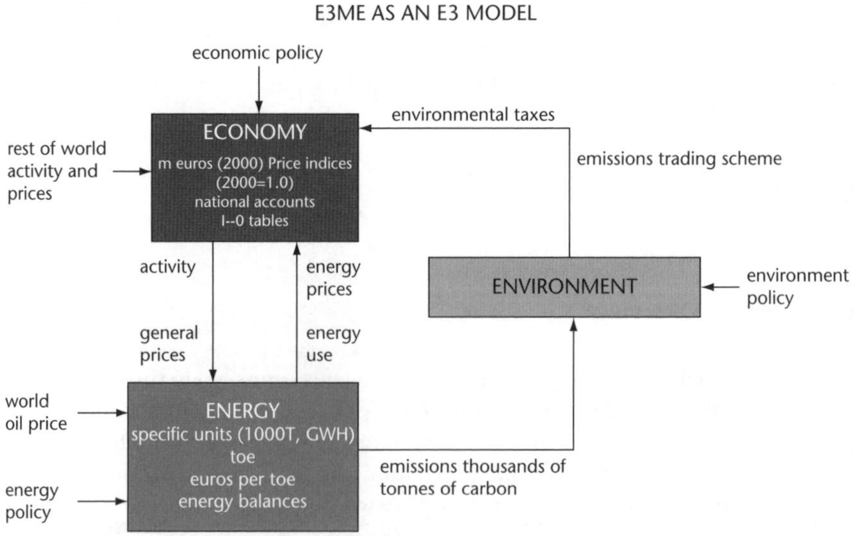

E3ME AS AN E3 MODEL

Figure A8.1 E3ME as an E3 model

The sectors are linked through input-output tables, while the countries are linked through estimated trade equations.

Figure A8.2 shows how the economic module is solved as an integrated EU regional model. Most of the economic variables shown in the chart are at a 42-industry level. The whole system is solved simultaneously for all the industries and all 29 countries, although single-country solutions are also possible. Figure A8.2 shows interactions at three spatial levels: the outermost area is the rest of the world; the next level is the European Union outside the country in question; and, finally, the inside level contains the relationships within the country.

Figure A8.2 shows three loops or circuits of economic interdependence: the export loop, the output-investment loop, and the income loop.

Econometric specification

Within the structure of the National Accounts, E3ME contains around 30 stochastic sets of equations with behavioural parameters estimated using econometric techniques. These equation sets cover the components of final demand, prices, and the labour market, plus energy and material demands. Each equation set is disaggregated by sector and by country; for example, there are 42×29 equations in the set for employment.

Equation parameters are estimated independently for each of these equations, with no cross-sectoral or cross-regional restrictions (i.e. no panel data techniques) imposed on the estimation. The exception to this is the newer member states, with data series

E3ME46 AS A REGIONAL ECONOMETRIC
INPUT-OUTPUT MODEL

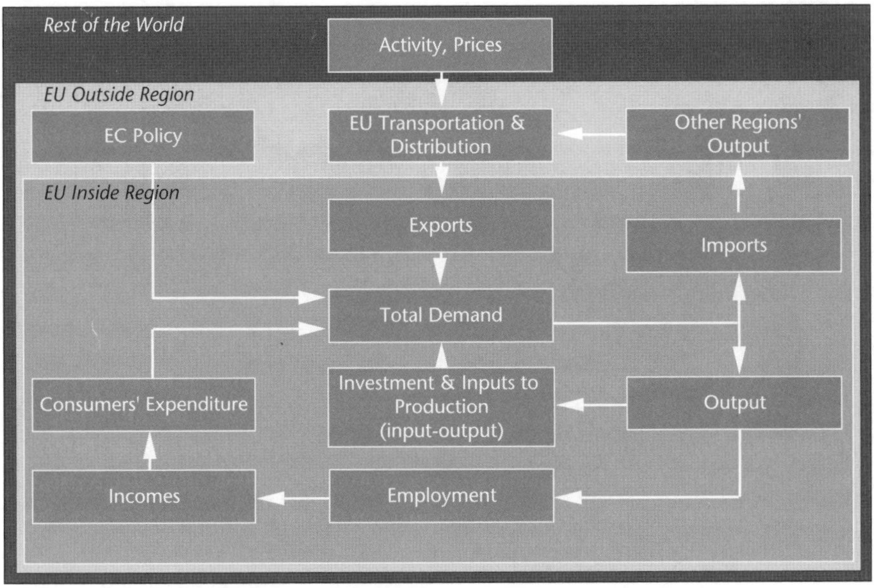

Figure A8.2 E3ME model description

197

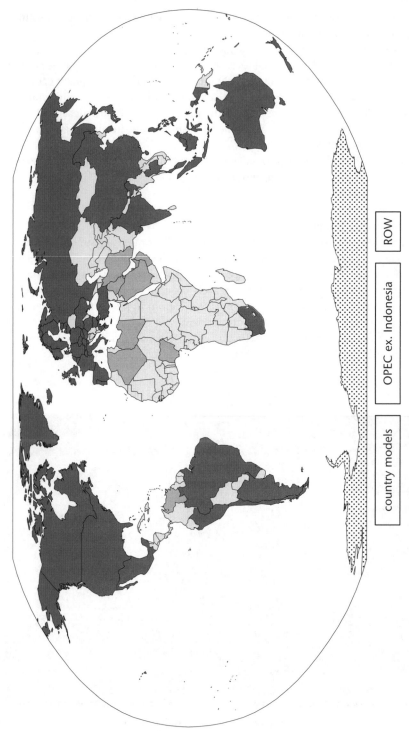

country models | OPEC ex. Indonesia | ROW

Figure A8.3 Country coverage of GINFORS

starting in 1993 or later, where it is not appropriate to estimate long-run relationships on data from a period of transition; for these countries, long-run parameter coefficients are set to match EU-15 averages using a shrinkage technique (Spicer and Reade 2005).

The method of estimation is based on the theories of cointegration and error correction (see Engle and Granger 1987, and Hendry et al. 1984). Essentially this is a two-step method of estimation that allows for short-term dynamic effects, moving towards a long-term outcome (often regarded as equilibrium), and the model is able to capture transition effects as well as longer-term impacts. Due to the simultaneous nature of many of the model's relationships (for example, prices and quantities), the estimation technique used is instrumental variables. The instruments used are based on the previous year's data.

The software used to carry out the parameter estimates is based on the Ox programming language (see Doornik 2007).

GINFORS Model Overview

The model GINFORS (**G**lobal **In**ter-industry **FOR**ecasting **S**ystem) has been developed to allow for a global analysis of the economic-environmental interdependencies as a tool for concrete policy planning (Lutz et al. 2010). It is based on the experience of developing the global energy-economy-environment model COMPASS (Meyer and, Lutz 2002a, 2002b; Meyer and Uno 1999). GINFORS is an economy-energy-environment model with global coverage. All EU-25 countries, all OECD countries, and their major trade partners are explicitly modelled. The model is based on time series of international statistics data from 1980 to 2004. Behavioural parameters are derived from econometric estimations assuming bounded rationality of agents with myopic foresight. Due to the large number of equations, the simple and robust ordinary least squares (OLS) estimation method is applied. The model ensures global consistency. For instance, energy use anywhere in the world is only possible after extraction of some energy carriers. The imports of one country are the exports of another. The whole system is consistently linked and simultaneously solved at the global level.

The model combines econometric-statistical analysis, with input-output analysis embedded in a complete macroeconomic framework. The link between the economic developments in the countries is given by international trade, which is the result of global competition in deep sectoral disaggregation. Nearly all parameters of GINFORS are estimated econometrically using international time series data sets from the OECD, the IEA, and the IMF.

A good impression of the country coverage of the model is provided by Figure A8.3. The black areas are those countries that are explicitly part of the system. The grey areas correspond to the OPEC countries (without Indonesia, which is explicitly modelled) and the white areas represent the rest of the world, ROW. This group consists of economies in Central and South America, in Asia, in Africa, and very few in Europe that play a minor role concerning GDP, trade, and environmental pressure. The model can be extended to further countries.

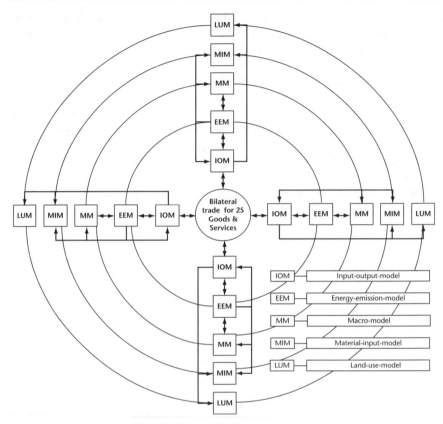

Figure A8.4 The wheel of GINFORS

Figure A8.4 provides a survey of the complete model. The central part of the model is the trade model. Bilateral trade matrices are provided for 25 commodities as well as service trade covering all OECD countries, the EU-25, and 16 further major trade partners. Via this trade context, both quantities and prices are properly allocated to the countries. Each spoke of the wheel stands for the model structure of a certain country. The economic core of the model consists of the macro-model (MM) and the input-output model (IOM). Whilst macro-models by GINFORS are at hand for all countries, input-output models are available for 21 countries only. The economies of the remaining countries are solely displayed by a macro-model. The energy-emission models (EEM) are based on the energy balances of the IEA and are therefore available for all countries and regions. They feature energy consumption structured by the relevant energy carriers. CO_2 emissions are linked with the fossil energy carriers by constant carbon relations.

For all the countries displayed in GINFORS, material consumption structured by six categories is determined. Those are linked either with the input-output model, or, for countries lacking an input-output model, with the macro-model. For the projection of those extractions associated with fossil energy carriers, refer to the results of the energy-emission model. The rings connecting the model segments, land use (LUM), material input (MIM), macro-model (MM), and energy emission (EEM), signify the global identity of these factors. Regarding the balance of payments, itself part of the macro-model, this identity can be explained particularly well. Global imports and exports, at least when calculated according to the same price convention (i.e. 'free on board' or 'cost, insurance and freight'), have to be identical. This requires consistency of global trade and national models, a demand met by GINFORS.

The GINFORS database uses five basic sources: (1) the OECD, (2) the IMF, (3) Eurostat, (4) the COMTRADE data banks of the UN, and (5) the IEA. Furthermore, for two significant countries (China and Taiwan), national statistics are evaluated. The trade data are the result of merging OECD and UN data. The data for the macro-model are based on the OECD's *National Accounts of OECD Countries, Detailed Tables* and the IMF's data set *International Financial Statistics*. Since a coherent level of data is necessary for the model, gaps within the data sets are filled by own calculations. In the majority of cases, the input-output tables were taken from OECD publications. The energy models exclusively correspond to the energy balances published by the IEA. The material input models are based on data provided by the Sustainable Europe Research Institute (SERI) during the PETRE project.

References

Anderson, D., and S. Winne (2004), 'Modelling Innovation and Threshold Effects in Climate Change Mitigation', Working Paper No. 59, Tyndall Centre for Climate Change Research.

Barker, T., S. De-Ramon, and H. Pollitt (2009a), 'Revenue Recycling and Labour Markets: Effects on Costs of Policies for Sustainability', in V. Bosetti, R. Gerlagh, and S. Schleicher (eds.), *Modeling Transitions to Sustainable Development*, Cheltenham, UK: Edward Elgar.

——P. Haoran, J. Köhler, R. Warren, and S. Winne (2006), 'Decarbonising the Global Economy with Induced Technological Change: Scenarios to 2100 using E3MG', *Energy Journal*, 27: p143–60.

——S. Junankar, H. Pollitt, and P. Summerton (2009b), 'The Effects of Environmental Tax Reform on International Competitiveness in the European Union: Modelling with E3ME', in M. S. Andersen and P. Ekins (eds.), *Carbon-Energy Taxation: Lessons from Europe*, Oxford: Oxford University Press.

——O. Løfsnaes, and H. Pollitt (2007), 'The ETM in E3ME43', Cambridge Econometrics Working Paper, available online at: <http://www.camecon.com/Libraries/Downloadable_Files/ETM.sflb.ashx>.

——and K. E. Rosendahl (2000), 'Ancillary Benefits of GHG Mitigation in Europe: SO$_2$, NOx and PM10 reductions from Policies to Meet Kyoto Targets Using the E3ME model and EXTERNE Valuations', in OECD (ed.), *Ancillary Benefits and Costs of Greenhouse Gas Mitigation*, Paris: OECD.

Barker, T., and S. Scrieciu (forthcoming), 'Low Stabilisation within a "New Economics" Macro-Econometric Framework: Insights from E3MG', *Energy Journal*, Special Issue on low-stabilization scenarios.

Beinhocker, E. (2006), *The Origin of Wealth*, Boston: Harvard Business School Press.

Behrens, A., S. Giljum, J. Kovanda, and S. Niza (2007), 'The Material Basis of the Global Economy: Worldwide Patterns of Natural Resource Extraction and their Implications for Sustainable Resource Use Policies', *Ecological Economics*, 64: 444–53.

Doornik, J. A. (2007), *Ox: An Object-Oriented Matrix Language*, London: Timberlake Consultants Press.

Engle, R. F., and C. W. J. Granger (1987), 'Cointegration and Error Correction: Representation, Estimation and Testing', *Econometrica*, 55: 251–76.

Eurostat (1995), *European System of Accounts (ESA95)*, Luxembourg: Statistical Office of the European Union.

——(2001), Economy-Wide Material Flow Accounts and Derived Indicators: A Methodological Guide, Luxembourg: Statistical Office of the European Union.

Giljum, S., A. Behrens, F. Hinterberger, C. Lutz, and B. Meyer (2008), 'Modelling Scenarios towards a Sustainable Use of Natural Resources in Europe'. *Environmental Science and Policy*, 11: 204–16.

Hendry, D. F., A. Pagan, and J. D. Sargan (1984), 'Dynamic Specification', in Z. Griliches and M. D. Intriligator (eds.), *Handbook of Econometrics*, vol. II, Amsterdam: North-Holland.

Lee, K., M. H. Pesaran, and R. G. Pierse (1990), 'Aggregation Bias in Labour Demand Equations for the UK Economy', in T. Barker and M. H. Pesaran (eds), *Disaggregation in Econometric Modelling*, London: Routledge, chapter 6.

Lutz, C., and S. Giljum (2009), 'Global Resource Use in a Business as Usual World Until 2030: Updated Results from the GINFORS Model', in R. Bleischwitz, P. Welfens, and Z. Zhang (eds.), *Sustainable Growth and Resource Productivity: Economic and Global Policy Issues*, Sheffield: Greenleaf Publishers, 30–41.

——and B. Meyer (2009a), 'Economic Impacts of Higher Oil and Gas Prices: The Role of International Trade for Germany', *Energy Economics*, 31: 882–7.

————(2009b), 'Environmental and Economic Effects of Post-Kyoto Carbon Regimes: Results of Simulations with the Global Model GINFORS', *Energy Policy*, 37: 1758–66.

————and M. I. Wolter (2010), 'The Global Multisector/Multicountry 3E-Model GINFORS: A Description of the Model and a Baseline Forecast for Global Energy Demand and CO_2 Emissions', *International Journal of Global Environmental Issues*, 10 (1–2): 25–45.

Meyer, B., and C. Lutz (2002a), 'IO, Macro-finance, and Trade Model Specification', in K. Uno (ed.), *Economy-Energy-Environment Simulation: Beyond the Kyoto Protocol*, Dordrecht: Kluwer Academic Publishers, 55–68.

————(2002b), 'Endogenized Trade Shares in a Global Model', in K. Uno (ed.), *Economy-Energy-Environment Simulation: Beyond the Kyoto Protocol*, Dordrecht: Kluwer Academic Publishers, 69–80.

——————P. Schnur, and G. Zika (2007), 'Economic Policy Simulations with Global Interdependencies: A Sensitivity Analysis for Germany'. *Economic Systems Research*, 19(1): 37–55.

——————and M. I. Wolter (2005), 'Global Multisector/Multicountry 3-E Modelling: From COMPASS to GINFORS', *Revista de Economia Mundial*, 13: 77–97.

——and K. Uno (1999), 'COMPASS—Ein globales Energie-Wirtschaftsmodell', *ifo-Studien*, 45: 703–18.

Pollitt, H. (2008), 'Combining Economic and Material Flows Analysis at the Sectoral Level: Development of the E3ME Model and Application in the MATISSE Case Studies', Matisse deliverable 8.6.1 for European Commission, DG Research, April 2008.

Schoer, K. (2006), 'Calculation of Direct and Indirect Material Inputs by Type of Raw Material and Economic Activities', Paper presented at the London Group Meeting, 19–21 June, Wiesbaden: Federal Statistical Office Germany.

Spicer, M., and J. Reade (2005), 'Incorporating New EU-Member Economies in a Multisectoral, Multi-region Dynamic model: Applying Shrinkage Estimation to E3ME', Cambridge Econometrics Working Paper.

UNCTAD (2007), *Iron Ore Statistics 2007*, Geneva: UNCTAD.

9

Modelling an ETR for Europe

Terry Barker, Christian Lutz, Bernd Meyer, Hector Pollitt and Stefan Speck

9.1 Introduction

This chapter describes how the E3ME and GINFORS energy-environment-economy (E3) models (see Chapter 8) were applied to evaluate the effects of a large-scale ETR in Europe and presents the results from this application. Section 9.2 describes the scenarios that were set up and the baselines to which they were compared. The results from the models are shown in Sections 9.3–9.5, focusing on the aggregate productivity effects and the aggregate and sectoral impacts on environmental and economic indicators. Section 9.6 compares and contrasts the results from the two different models that were used in the analysis. An overall summary of the results is provided in Section 9.7.

A more detailed description of the results from both models may be found in Pollitt and Chewpreecha (2009) and Lutz and Meyer (2009b).

9.2 Baselines and Scenarios

9.2.1 Introduction

This section describes the baseline projections that were used in the analysis and the scenarios that were constructed to incorporate the various elements of the ETR. As much as possible, the same baselines and scenarios were used in E3ME and GINFORS so that a comparison could be made between the results from the two models.

9.2.2 The baseline projections

THE ROLE OF THE BASELINES

The scenarios in the PETRE project are *ex ante*, meaning that they provide an assessment of future developments under different sets of input assumptions. So that the effects of the different inputs can be interpreted, a scenario without ETR, i.e. with no additional inputs, is provided. This is referred to as the baseline case. Results from the other scenarios are reported as (usually percentage) difference from this baseline, allowing an easy interpretation of the impacts of the scenario assumptions.

The baseline itself is not part of the analysis but is important for presentational purposes. As most of the models' relationships are log-linear and the results are presented as percentage difference from base, the levels in the baseline do not usually impact greatly on the final results. For example, if the model suggests that a 50% increase in petrol prices leads to a 10% fall in demand, the results will report a 10% fall, whether the baseline price is 75 or 150 cents per litre.

However, there are cases where this rule does not hold. These are usually in cases where the model's relationships are not log-linear, for example when they are simple linear functions. Some examples are:

- unemployment is the difference between labour supply and labour demand;
- GDP and output are the sum of their components;
- final energy prices are the sum of the raw inputs plus excise duties and other energy taxes.

The last point is particularly relevant to the PETRE scenarios, as they include taxes on energy products. Effectively, this means that the relative impact of the energy taxes is dependent on the baseline energy prices. For example, if the price of petrol is €1 per litre, a 20c/litre tax would mean a 20% increase in prices. However, if the baseline price is €2/litre, then the increase would only be 10%.

Clearly there is a high level of uncertainty over the development of future international energy prices, so an alternative baseline was provided with higher prices (see below).

The baseline also plays an important role in determining the scenario results when fixed targets are met. In the PETRE scenarios, greenhouse gas emissions are reduced by 20% or 30%, compared to 1990 levels, by 2020. This target becomes more difficult to meet if the business as usual (BAU) case includes a 10% increase in emissions than if it suggests there is already a 10% reduction.

The conclusion from this is that the baseline can play a role in determining the results from the scenarios and it is therefore important that a robust and credible baseline is used.

ENERGY AND TRANSPORT: TRENDS TO 2030

One option for forming the baseline would be to create a baseline projection using one of the models included in the study. This would ensure a degree of consistency in all the variables, and in particular between Europe's economies and energy systems, as it would be produced by the model's own internal structure, based on the system of national accounts and the model's own energy/economy linkages. However, the reception of the study by politicians might be more complicated since they are familiar with forecasts which they themselves have ordered.

Therefore a pre-existing published projection was used to form the baseline. This is presented in EC (2008a) and is commonly referred to as the 'PRIMES' forecast, after the model that produced the detailed energy results. This projection is the result of a modelling exercise at the European level and is consistent across Member States. It also provides a consistent view of economic development, energy demands, and CO_2 emissions, a requirement for use with integrated E3 models. The projection, along with its underlying assumptions, is published on the European Commission (DG TREN) website (EC 2008a). The input assumptions for E3ME and GINFORS, including international energy prices, are set to match those of this EC projection.

As this exercise was carried out in mid-2008, it did not take into account the financial crisis and subsequent recession in the second half of 2008 and in 2009.

FURTHER PROCESSING

Several further steps need to be taken before the published projection can be used with either of the two models:

- annual results are estimated, using a simple interpolation algorithm;
- sectoral output is estimated in a way that is consistent with the published aggregate totals;
- economic variables that are not included in the baseline are estimated in a consistent manner.

The process for estimating the other economic variables is to match the growth rates to a similar variable, for example gross and net output. The PRIMES baseline covers the period up to 2030, but in these scenarios only the period up to 2020 is used, as this is the relevant year for the EU's targets on emission reduction and also the final year of Phase 3 of the EU's Emissions Trading Scheme (ETS).

MATCHING THE PUBLISHED FORECAST

The models' results are set to match the PRIMES baseline using an internal scaling mechanism. The same scaling factors are applied to the baseline and each of the scenarios, so that the scenario results represent a difference from base, while also being consistent with the published baseline. For further information about the models, the reader is referred to the model manuals and published documentation (see Chapter 8).

HIGH OIL PRICES

During the PETRE project, international oil prices reached a record high of $146/barrel in mid-2008. This price is significantly different from the forecast prices used in the PRIMES baseline (which has around $60/barrel in 2010 current prices). Prices then fell sharply in response to the global financial and economic crisis to around $35/barrel at the end of 2008 before recovering in 2009. It is clear that there is a lot of uncertainty about future oil prices, for example the extent to which a global economic recovery would be accompanied by a return to high oil prices.

The literature (for examples, see Longo et al. 2007, and Chevillon and Rifflart 2008) produces a wide range of possible outcomes for energy prices so cannot provide much help in answering this question. The solution was therefore to run an additional baseline, which features higher oil prices. They are close to the expectations of IEA (2008a). This baseline is an endogenous solution of the models, with all inputs the same as the main baseline except for input energy prices. The values for energy demand and economic growth are determined by the models' own estimated parameters (i.e. it is solved as if it was a scenario). The main ETR scenario is also run with both sets of oil prices so that the results can be viewed as a difference from base in a situation with low prices and with high prices. A range of possible outcomes is therefore given; these results are shown later in this chapter.

9.2.3 The ETR scenarios

THE BASIC STRUCTURE

To investigate the impacts of an ETR for Europe, six separate scenarios were designed to understand a variety of tax reform options. Each scenario is identified by an acronym. The first letter indicates the baseline to which it is compared with L for low energy prices and H for high energy prices.

The scenario analysis allows for an understanding of different revenue-recycling methods and various scales of ETR in order to meet different greenhouse gas emissions targets. All the scenarios were examined in both E3ME and GINFORS. The scenarios are:

- BL: Baseline (low energy prices, as in the PRIMES projection);
- BH: Baseline sensitivity with high oil price;
- Scenario LS1: ETR with revenue recycling (low oil price) designed to meet unilateral EU 2020 GHG target (20% reduction from 1990 levels);
- Scenario HS1: ETR with revenue recycling (high oil price) designed to meet unilateral EU 2020 GHG target (20% reduction from 1990 levels);
- Scenario HS2: ETR with revenue recycling (high oil price) designed to meet unilateral EU 2020 GHG target, with 10% of revenues spent on eco-innovation measures;
- Scenario HS3: ETR with revenue recycling (high oil price) designed to meet the 'international cooperation' EU 2020 GHG target (30% reduction from 1990 levels).

In all the scenarios the EU targets are met by emissions reductions in the EU, rather than buying emissions reductions from abroad (for example, through the Clean Development Mechanism). In no scenario is there any feedback to the international energy price from the demand response to the ETR.

Each of the ETR scenarios has the same key taxation components:

- a carbon tax is introduced on all non-EU ETS sectors, the rate of which is equal to the carbon price in the EU ETS, with the combination of the two delivering an overall 20% reduction in greenhouse gas emissions (15% CO_2 reduction) by 2020; in the international cooperation scenario this is extended to a 30% GHG (25% CO_2) emissions reduction;
- aviation is included in the EU ETS at the end of Phase 2 (2012);
- the power-generation sector's EU ETS allowances are 100% auctioned in Phase 3 of the EU ETS;
- all other EU ETS allowances are 50% auctioned in 2013, increasing to 100% in 2020;
- the taxation of materials covers consumption of all material inputs (biomass and minerals) covered by the Eurostat definition, apart from energy products; materials taxes are additional to any existing taxes and are introduced at 5% of total price in 2010, increasing to 15% by 2020 for all EU countries in E3ME and for 16 EU countries for which IO data are available from the OECD in GINFORS.

It may be noted that the treatment in the scenarios of auctioning in the EU ETS was decided before the plans for Phase 3 of the EU ETS were agreed by the EU, and therefore it differs somewhat from them. In the event, the agreed auctioning plans envisage a slightly lower level of auctioning by 2020 than that modelled here. The scenarios are summarized in Table 9.1.

Table 9.1. Summary of ETR scenarios

Scenario	LS1	HS1	HS2	HS3
Energy prices	Baseline	High	High	High
CO_2 reduction, 2020	−15%	−15%	−15%	−25%
Materials tax, 2020	15%	15%	15%	15%
Revenue recycling	Employment taxes and income taxes	Employment taxes and income taxes	Low-carbon investment, employment taxes, and income taxes	Employment taxes and income taxes
Other				International cooperation

Note: CO_2 reductions are in comparison to 1990 base.
Sources: Cambridge Econometrics, GWS.

MORE DETAILED SPECIFICATION

Scenario variants

The ETR which forms the main scenario was LS1, the main features of which, as shown in Table 9.1, may be summarized as:

- the EU meeting its 2020 GHG reduction targets;
- a tax on material inputs;
- a corresponding reduction in employers' social security contributions and income taxes.

The other scenarios represent small changes in specification from LS1, allowing the modelling to address some of the key issues of environmental taxation.

HS1 is identical in design to LS1, except it is analysed in the context of higher international energy prices. In HS1, world oil prices are $113/barrel in 2010, rather than $60/barrel in the baseline and LS1 (both nominal prices). The same growth rates are used thereafter. Results from this scenario should be compared to the alternative baseline (which has the same energy prices), but also give an interesting comparison with LS1. For example, a lower carbon price is required to meet the emission-reduction targets in HS1 than is required in LS1.

The prices of non-oil energy inputs are set to grow at the same rate as the headline oil price. This makes results easier to interpret (as direct effects may otherwise be obscured by fuel switching), but also reflects the fact that gas contracts are often linked to oil prices and that transportation costs make up a large share of coal prices.

The prices for non-energy material inputs are set to increase at current trend rates in the baseline. The materials taxes are added on to these base prices; as there are no price data for the models' aggregate materials categories, the treatment is to use implicit indices based on the available economic data, meaning that the changes are always measured in percentages, rather than explicit units such as euros per tonne.

HS2 is identical to HS1 except that revenue-recycling mechanisms are adjusted. The same split between income and employers' taxes is estimated, but 10% of the total revenues are directed towards eco-innovation.

Many studies have attempted to define 'eco-industries' (for example, see Jänicke and Zieschank 2008 and GHK et al. 2007), but these are usually much too detailed to fit into modelling frameworks, or the available data from the National Accounts. Therefore, for the modelling, the revenues were split evenly three ways, between:

- subsidies for renewable electricity generation;
- investment in efficient household appliances;
- investment in efficient transport equipment.

The take-up of more efficient machinery and vehicles can lead to more efficient energy use in all sectors but particularly affects transport sectors and those that use heavy machinery. It might be expected that in this scenario the carbon price required to meet the emission-reduction targets will not be as high as in HS1, because there are simultaneous increases in energy efficiency. This means that the same reductions are achieved at a lower cost.

The final scenario, HS3, considers the effects of ETR in the context of the EU commitment to pursue higher domestic cuts in emissions—specifically a 30% reduction in greenhouse gas emissions by 2020 compared to 1990—provided that 'other developed countries commit themselves to comparable emission reductions' and that 'economically more advanced developing countries commit themselves to contributing adequately according to their responsibilities and capabilities' (EC 2008c: 2). In this 'international cooperation' scenario, therefore, the GHG emission-reduction target is 30% rather than 20% (and, as shown in Table 9.1, the corresponding CO_2 target 25% rather than 15%), all of which are reductions in domestic emissions.

Emission reductions

When the analysis was carried out, the European Commission had not yet suggested how its greenhouse gas reduction target should be met, beyond a basic ETS and non-ETS share, so the models assume a single price instrument that is applied equally to all sectors (including those inside and outside the ETS). Effectively this means that the non-traded sectors face a carbon tax equal to the ETS price, with the number of ETS allowances being continuously adjusted until the targets are met. The carbon tax is additional to any existing taxes. The carbon tax is put in place in 2010, but the revisions to ETS allowances do not start until 2013 to reflect the Phase II agreements that already exist. All action is assumed to be through domestic effort, with JI/CDM (Joint Implementation/Clean Development Mechanism) payments, permissible under the Kyoto Protocol, excluded from the modelling.

As shown in Table 9.1, in scenarios LS1, HS1, and HS2, the 20% GHG target translates into a 15% reduction of energy-related CO_2 emissions compared to 1990 as other emissions, such as methane and nitrous oxide, have already been reduced. The target is reached by higher ETS prices and carbon taxes.

The ETR taxes fall on energy outputs, i.e. the final use of energy, and are based on the carbon content of each fuel. Carbon prices are assumed to be fully passed on to consumers of energy. All carbon taxes are in addition to any existing unilateral carbon taxes before 2009. The CO_2 reductions in the different EU Member States (MS) will be those produced by the same carbon tax increase across the EU.

Revenue recycling

In line with the definition of ETR (for discussion, see NERI et al. 2007), the reforms are assumed to be directly revenue neutral, that is, the increased revenues from environmental taxes are matched by reductions in other taxes. The higher ETS prices affect business directly, although of course businesses may be able to pass these costs on, depending on the degree of competition in the markets for their products. The carbon tax affects both businesses and households. Revenue recycling is designed to recognize that both businesses and households are affected by the higher energy costs and the revenues are allocated to employers and households respectively.

In scenarios LS1, HS1, and HS3, environmental tax revenues are recycled through reductions in income tax rates and employers' social security contributions (which are treated as a tax on employment in the modelling) in each of the Member States, such that there is no direct change in tax revenues in any one country. The scenarios may therefore be considered directly revenue neutral, in the sense that the revenues from the increases in carbon taxes are matched by revenue reduction from reduced income and labour taxes. It should be noted, however, that traditional energy tax revenues, for example from excise duties, will be lower compared to the baseline, as the tax base (energy consumption) is reduced, and these other taxes are not adjusted to compensate for this. So although the scenarios themselves are revenue neutral, this does not mean that they achieve budget neutrality for the economy overall.

The proportion of the tax raised by industry is recycled into a reduction in employers' social security contributions, which in turn reduces the cost of labour. Revenues raised from households are recycled through reductions in the standard rate of income tax. The materials taxes mostly fall on business, so the revenues are recycled through lower employers' social security contributions.

Eco-innovation

In scenario HS2, 10% of environmental tax revenues are recycled through spending on eco-innovation measures, with the remaining 90% recycled through the same measures as in the other scenarios.

Due to differences in definitions, the revenue recycling through eco-innovation is slightly different in E3ME and GINFORS.

In GINFORS, the share of renewables in electricity production is increased due to the additional investment. The rest of additional investment goes to household energy-efficiency spending. The investment needed for a certain increase in renewables or efficiency improvement is based on German and Austrian experience (Lehr et al. 2008 and 2009; Grossmann et al. 2008; Lutz and Meyer 2008). This assumption is quite conservative, as parameters for other countries can be assumed to be more positive. In comparison to the pioneers Germany and Austria, less money for renewables installation or energy-efficiency gains will be needed in most other EU countries.

In E3ME, the revenues are split evenly between investment in more fuel-efficient vehicles, new machinery, and renewable electricity generation. The model's own parameters are used to determine the effects of investment in vehicles and machinery, and the effects of renewables investment are determined by the model's detailed sub-model for power generation (see Anderson and Winne 2004, 2007 and Barker et al. 2007).

International cooperation

Scenario HS3 is used to investigate the effect that international cooperation would have on competitiveness and resources. In this scenario, we assume that the rest of the world takes action towards reducing carbon emissions. International action is expected to reduce the loss of competitiveness that the EU would face if it embarked on unilateral action. However, in this scenario, the carbon price is higher and the tax levied is greater, in order to reduce EU greenhouse gas emissions by 30% in 2020, rather than 20% in the preceding scenarios.

Other than the higher target, and action outside the EU, HS3 is similar in design to HS1. In GINFORS, the ETS and ETR are modelled in the major non-EU OECD countries with CO_2 prices in these countries equal to EU prices. Emerging economies introduce a CO_2 tax that is recycled via income tax reductions, but the tax rates are only 25% of EU (OECD) prices in 2020. The lower tax rates of emerging economies take into account the idea of common but differentiated responsibility (a lower historic burden, lower GDP per capita) that was used for a project for the German Ministry of Economy in

2007 (Lutz and Meyer 2009a), to explore possibilities for the post-Kyoto period, after 2012.

As in the other scenarios, the EU reduction in emissions is assumed to be domestic only, without trying to take account of JI/CDM transactions that could be on top of the extra EU carbon reduction.

E3ME is a European model, so is not able to model international action explicitly. However, in determining the trade effects, E3ME incorporated the non-European results from GINFORS so that the analysis could be carried out on a consistent basis.

9.3 Productivity Impacts

9.3.1 Introduction

One of the main aims of this study was to assess the productivity effects of ETR. We consider three types of productivity:

- carbon productivity (GDP/CO_2 emissions);
- materials productivity (GDP/Domestic Material Consumption);
- labour productivity (GDP/employment).

Employment is measured on a headcount basis in both models; average working hours could be taken into account but, as they do not change by much in the scenarios, they are not included in the results.

9.3.2 The model results

RESULTS FROM E3ME

The E3ME model shows a large increase in carbon and material productivity or, alternatively, a reduction in intensity, as a result of the shift in taxation (see Figure 9.1 for results from LS1). Labour productivity falls, but this is due to higher employment levels rather than falling output from existing employees (see below).

RESULTS FROM GINFORS

The GINFORS model also shows large increases in carbon productivity, increases in material productivity, and a decrease in labour productivity, as shown in Table 9.2.

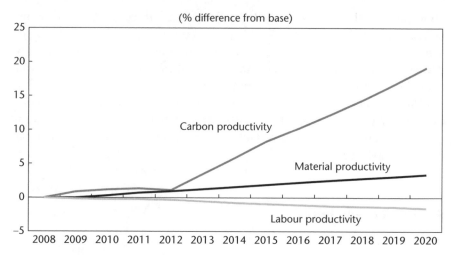

Figure 9.1 Productivity results from E3ME , LS1 scenario
Note: Productivity results, EU-27.
Source: E3ME.

9.3.3 Interpretation of the model results

CARBON PRODUCTIVITY
Carbon productivity, defined by GDP per unit of CO_2 emission, is mainly determined by the emissions targets that are imposed in the scenario specification (although GDP is still endogenously calculated). The carbon prices required to achieve the reductions in emissions are discussed in Section 9.4.

MATERIALS PRODUCTIVITY
The increase in materials productivity (GDP per unit of material consumption) is due to the materials tax that is levied in the scenario. The reduction is quite large for the scale of the tax, with results being dominated by efficiency gains in the construction sector.

Table 9.2. Productivity results from GINFORS (% difference from base, 2020)

Scenario	Material productivity	Labour productivity	Carbon productivity
HS1	0.91	−0.93	8.59
HS2	0.84	−0.71	8.99
HS3	1.78	−2.61	21.35
LS1	1.97	−3.02	17.17

Note: Figures show changes in productivity in 2020, compared to respective baseline.
Source: GINFORS.

LABOUR PRODUCTIVITY

Labour intensity also increases, meaning that average labour productivity falls. This is a trade-off with the reductions in unemployment. The primary effect of lowering the cost of labour (by reducing employers' taxes) means that employment levels rise and, although in E3ME GDP increases (see below), it is not by as much as employment, meaning that average labour productivity therefore falls. Another way of presenting this change is that, as the marginal cost of labour falls, the marginal revenues of additional employees will fall, reducing the average per worker.

9.4 Environmental Outcomes

9.4.1 Impact on carbon prices and CO_2 emissions

CARBON PRICES

The scenarios require a single instrument, a European price for carbon, to cause the reductions in GHG emissions described in Section 9.2. The prices required to achieve the targets are shown in Table 9.3.

These prices are relatively high and considerably above the prices seen so far in the EU ETS. There are four principal reasons for this:

- the targets include sectors of the economy where emissions are still increasing, for example road and air transport; it is assumed that there are no major changes in technology (e.g. electric vehicles), even in the scenarios with high carbon prices;
- the relatively short time period in which to meet these targets, meaning that they are quite ambitious in nature;
- the modelling does not include any accompanying regulatory changes (for example, in order to reach the EU 20% energy efficiency target) which, in reality, would quite likely be implemented;
- there are no assumptions about the EU's 20% renewables target being met.

Table 9.3. Carbon prices in the ETR scenarios, E3ME and GINFORS (in euro, 2008 prices)

	Scenario			
Model	LS1	HS1	HS2	HS3
E3ME	142	59	53	204
GINFORS	120	68	61	184

Note: Figures show a summary of carbon prices (in euro 2008 prices) per tonne of CO_2 for each scenario in 2020.
Sources: E3ME and GINFORS.

The carbon prices should therefore be regarded as a maximum possible outcome, where a single instrument is used to meet an ambitious target. With accompanying regulation, for example on fuel-efficiency standards or shares of renewables, the carbon price required to meet the targets would be lower.

Carbon prices are particularly high when we assume that international energy prices are low (LS1), or when a higher GHG reduction target is set (HS3). In both cases, this is because a larger relative reduction in GHG emissions is required. However, when there are high international energy prices, this already discourages fuel consumption, making the targets easier to achieve (meaning a lower carbon price is required). In addition, if some of the revenues from the carbon taxes and auctioned allowances are used to promote investment in low-carbon technologies (HS2), this also reduces fossil-fuel dependence and a lower carbon price is required.

IMPACT ON EMISSIONS

The emission reductions are given by the targets defined in the scenarios and both the E3ME and GINFORS models assume that these targets are met in 2020, following a smooth path of reduction.

9.4.2 Impact on energy demand

The ETR causes an increase in energy productivity as well as in carbon productivity (or, alternatively, a decrease in energy intensity). However, as one of the impacts of the carbon pricing is a shift from carbon-intensive energy carriers, such as coal, to cleaner fuels, the reduction in energy demand is relatively less than the reduction in carbon emissions.

For example, the GINFORS model predicts an increase of energy productivity of 15% in HS1 in 2020, compared to an increase in carbon productivity of 21%. E3ME shows similar results; Figure 9.2 shows the results by energy carrier in LS1 (other scenarios have similar results). One point that is interesting to note is that the initial reductions in energy demand are not weighted towards coal; this is because it takes several years to build replacement power stations that use alternative fuels.

9.4.3 Impact on material use

The material taxes are initially imposed at a relatively low rate but increase over the forecast period. As it is not possible to obtain detailed price information for the aggregate material categories used in the modelling, the price increase must be implicit. In 2020, the materials tax is therefore defined as 'high enough to raise the prices of raw materials by 15% in 2020'.

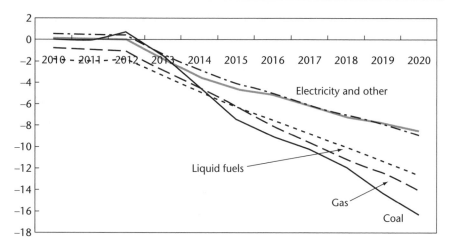

Figure 9.2 Impact of ETR on energy demand, E3ME, LS1 scenario
Note: Y-axis units are percentage difference from baseline (BL).
Source: E3ME.

The results from GINFORS suggest that material consumption could fall by up to 5% compared to the baseline in 2020 as a result of this tax and a slight fall in GDP (see Section 9.5). E3ME shows a similar aggregate reduction, with the largest falls in the use of construction minerals and ores.

9.4.4 Sectoral impacts

One of the advantages of both the E3ME and GINFORS models is the relatively high degree of sectoral disaggregation, allowing an assessment of sectoral impacts. Both models estimate and solve separate equations for energy demand by each of the main sectors (aggregated to 15–20 in total). The treatment for material demands is similar.

The responsiveness of CO_2 emissions from each sector to an increase in energy prices mainly depends on:

- its estimated price elasticities, i.e. by how much the sector reduces energy use in response to higher prices;
- options for switching between fuel inputs, for example from coal to gas;
- existing tax rates in the sector (lower tax rates mean the carbon price has a higher relative impact on total fuel costs).

Table 9.4 shows the sectoral reductions in CO_2 emissions in LS1 in E3ME compared to the baseline (the pattern is similar across the other scenarios). Although power generation has the most scope for a large-scale reduction in emissions, long lead times and a relatively short time period in Phase 3

Table 9.4. EU-27 change in CO_2 emissions, 2020, E3ME (% difference from base in LS1)

Sector		Sector	
Power generation	−15.7	Engineering etc	−21.0
Other energy own use	−17.3	Other industry	−23.9
Iron & steel	−26.1	Rail transport	−17.9
Non-ferrous metals	−30.8	Road transport	−16.3
Chemicals	−32.7	Air transport	−19.6
Non-metallic minerals	−18.0	Other transport	−16.6
Ore-extraction	−26.3	Households	−9.9
Food, drink & tobacco	−15.7	Other final use	−12.7
Textiles & clothing	−20.1	Non-energy use	0.0
Paper & pulp	−34.2	Total	−15.6

Note: Figures show percentage change in EU-27 CO_2 emissions by sector in 2020, compared to the baseline.
Sources: E3ME, Cambridge Econometrics.

(2013–20) of the EU ETS mean that there is only limited decarbonization in the sector. It is some of the energy-intensive industrial sectors, particularly those that can move away from coal, that have the largest reductions. Households and commerce, which have low elasticities and (in most EU countries) already pay higher tax rates on energy, tend to show the smallest reductions in CO_2 emissions.

9.5 Economic Outcomes

9.5.1 Introduction

This section presents the economic results from the E3ME and GINFORS models. As described in Chapter 8, each model includes a fully specified representation of Europe's economies at Member State level, which is integrated with national energy markets and extraction industries. This makes them very well suited to carry out this sort of assessment, with a wide range of economic indicators, at aggregate and sectoral levels, available in the results.

9.5.2 Carbon pricing and higher oil prices

E3ME shows that the effect of a sustained increase in world oil prices (in BH) reduces European GDP in 2020 by around 5% (it is around 3% in GINFORS), outweighing by far the positive gains from the ETR in the ETR scenarios. (This result is not included in the following tables as the presented differences show only the effects of the ETR against their respective baselines.)

The scenarios focus on international energy prices as an exogenous input that is outside the control of European policy makers. However, it should be noted that these scenarios could also be shown as a comparison between the effects of high international energy prices and domestic taxation. Both have similar effects on energy use, but, while domestic taxation raises revenues that can be recycled into the domestic economy, higher international energy prices benefit the energy-producing and exporting countries. In summary, the following results will show that ETR leads to only a small change in GDP in Europe, but higher energy import prices are likely to lead to a much larger reduction.

Finally, it is worth noting that, in the long run, reductions in fossil-fuel use will reduce the exposure of Europe's economies to high and volatile international energy prices.

9.5.2 Tax revenues and revenue recycling

The models estimate that the ETRs will raise very large sums of revenues, up to 7.5% of Europe's GDP in the highest scenario (HS3, see Table 9.5). As described above, this is matched by tax cuts on employers' social security contributions (SSCs) and income taxes elsewhere to achieve revenue neutrality across both businesses and households. Clearly, such a large shift of revenues has the potential to have major economic impacts so this analysis is a key part of the evaluation of the ETRs. The difference in tax revenues between the models stems in part from the different carbon prices, but mainly from a different tax base for the materials taxes, which is higher in E3ME compared to GINFORS.

The revenues raised by the EU ETS amounts to about 0.65% of GDP, which is quite comparable to the result (0.58% of EU GDP) of the impact assessment of the energy and climate package (EC 2008b).

The following analysis looks in more detail at some of the country results for tax revenues and fiscal structure to convey some of the differences between EU Member States and the need, therefore, in the implementation of any real-life ETR to consider the specific contexts and situations of the countries in question. The analysis focuses on the HS1 scenario as modelled by GINFORS.

Table 9.5. Tax revenues, as a percentage of GDP, 2020, E3ME and GINFORS

Scenario	E3ME	GINFORS
LS1	6.6	4.1
HS1	3.3	2.2
HS2	3.1	2.1
HS3	7.5	5.4

Note: Figures show tax revenues as a share of GDP in 2020, current prices.
Sources: E3ME and GINFORS.

Table 9.6. Revenues generated by the ETR in 2020 for selected EU Member States, as a percentage of GDP, scenario HS1, GINFORS

	carbon price revenue to GDP (%)	carbon price and materials tax revenue to GDP (%)
Czech Republic	1.9	3.5
Denmark	1.4	2.6
Estonia	1.4	1.4
Germany	1.9	2.3
Netherlands	2.1	2.9
Spain	1.9	3.6
Sweden	0.9	1.5
United Kingdom	1.7	2.0
EU 27	1.7	2.2

Table 9.6 shows the revenues from the ETR of scenario HS1 in selected EU Member States.

For a better understanding of the magnitude of the revenues accrued, Table 9.7 provides an overview of the fiscal structure of selected EU Member States. The data on different tax-to-GDP ratios reveal large differences between the Member States in terms of both their fiscal structure and their various tax ratios. The last columns of Tables 9.6 and 9.7 show that the ETR revenues in terms of the percentage of GDP in 2020 are comparable to, or even exceed in some countries, the 2005 level of environmental taxes. This scale of ETR is very much larger than those so far implemented in Europe, and briefly discussed in Chapter 5 (for example, the German ETR implemented during the period 1999–2003 raised about 0.8% of GDP).

Table 9.7. Fiscal structure of selected EU Member States, 2005

	total tax incl. SSC	personal income tax	SSC (employer)	SSC (total)	environmental taxes
	as % of GDP	as % of GDP	as % of GDP	as % of GDP	as % of GDP
	Fiscal structure as of 2005				
Czech Republic	37.1	4.6	10.3	16.1	2.7
Denmark	50.8	24.9	0.0	1.1	6.0
Estonia	30.9	5.6	9.9	10.3	2.3
Germany	38.8	8.6	7.0	16.3	2.5
Portugal	35.1	5.3	7.3	11.4	3.1
Romania	27.9	2.3	6.4	9.7	2.0
Sweden	49.6	15.5	9.8	12.8	2.8
United Kingdom	36.1	10.2	3.7	6.7	2.5
EU 27	39.2	7.7	6.7	11.0	2.8

Source: Eurostat (2009).

Table 9.8. Effects of the HS1 ETR (GINFORS) on various tax-to-GDP percentages of selected EU Member States

	total tax incl SSC	personal income tax	SSC (employer)	SSC (total)	environmental taxes
	in % of GDP	in % of GDP	in % of GDP	in % of GDP	in % of GDP
	Fiscal structure of 2020 based on the fiscal structure of 2005 and ETR				
Czech Republic	37.1	4.3	7.1	12.9	6.2
Denmark	50.8	24.5	-2.1	-1.0	8.6
Estonia	30.9	5.5	8.6	9.0	3.7
Germany	38.8	8.2	5.1	14.4	4.8
Portugal	35.1	4.9	5.7	9.8	5.1
Romania	27.9	2.1	5.3	8.6	3.3
Sweden	49.6	15.3	8.5	11.5	4.3
United Kingdom	36.1	9.7	2.2	5.2	4.5
EU 27	39.2	7.3	4.9	9.2	5.0

Source: Eurostat (2009) and own calculations based on results of scenario S1H (GINFORS model).

Table 9.8 shows how the recycling measures affect various tax-to-GDP ratios. The analysis assumes that the overall fiscal structure in 2020 is the same as in 2005 (i.e. column 2 in Table 9.8 is the same as column 2 of Table 9.7, an assumption that is justified by the relative stability of these ratios in most EU Member States). It can be seen that the recycling measures lead to a reduction in both the personal income tax-to-GDP ratio and the SSC-to-GDP ratio. The relative reduction is higher with regard to SSC, which is not surprising, since a larger part of the ETR's revenues are paid by industry (including nearly all the materials taxes) and recycled back via the reduction of employers' SSC.

Some of the results from Tables 9.8 and 9.9 (which show the percentage changes in revenues for various taxes under the HS1 ETR) deserve additional attention. For example, the adopted recycling scheme is clearly not appropriate for Denmark where social security contributions play only a marginal role in the overall fiscal system. Table 9.8 shows that after ETR, instead of paying SSC contribution Danish employers would receive a subsidy, as would the SSC system overall. Table 9.9 shows the large percentage changes in SSC from recycling the Danish environmental tax revenues in this way. The tables also show that the ETR would lead to a very substantial increase in the revenues from environmental taxes, i.e. an increase in the EU ratio of environmental taxes to GDP from 2.8% to 5.0% (Tables 9.7 and 9.8), and a nearly 80% increase in environmental tax revenues (Table 9.9).

Table 9.9. Percentage changes in revenues from different taxes after the HS1 ETR (GINFORS)

	personal income tax	SSC (employer)	SSC(total)	environmental taxes
	percentage change in revenues after ETR implementation			
Czech Republic	−7.1	−30.9	−19.8	130.2
Denmark	−1.6	−6278.5	−194.7	42.6
Estonia	−2.1	−13.3	−12.8	62.2
Germany	−4.3	−27.3	−11.7	91.0
Portugal	−7.3	−22.1	−14.1	64.4
Romania	−8.5	−17.6	−11.6	66.2
Sweden	−1.3	−13.7	−10.5	55.3
United Kingdom	−4.5	−40.4	−22.3	78.3
EU 27	−5.2	−27.0	−16.5	79.2

Source: Eurostat (2009) and own calculations based on GINFORS results, scenario HS1.

It is also interesting to note that a substantial part of the additional tax revenues come from the materials tax, as shown in Table 9.6. The modelling shows that the share of materials tax revenues in total ETR revenues could easily reach and exceed 40% in some countries (e.g. Denmark, Sweden, and Spain). This finding is important in that the revenues generated from taxes levied on energy products and from carbon pricing—including the auctioning of EU emission allowances—may decline in the long term as carbon emissions are reduced by climate policy (in the short and medium terms, they are likely to be maintained by the increasing carbon prices that will be necessary to meet carbon reduction targets). Broadening the tax base with a materials tax will help to maintain revenues from environmental taxes in a largely decarbonized economy. It would also increase EU material and resource productivity and resource security, as discussed further in Chapter 11.

9.5.3 The economic impacts of ETR

Figure 9.3 displays a simplified representation of how the main economic indicators may be affected by the introduction of a large-scale ETR. Even in this representation, however, it is clear that there are several paths of causality through which aggregate indicators, such as GDP and household consumption, may be affected. Some of the most important mechanisms, which relate to the environmental taxes and revenue recycling, are described below. As these have a mixture of positive and negative impacts on aggregate GDP, the final outcomes from the scenarios may also be positive or negative. This is also the case for other economic indicators, including employment.

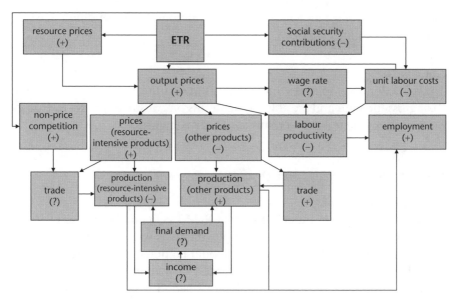

Figure 9.3 Diagram of main economic effects in the models

Higher prices and lower real incomes

The ETR will make energy and materials more expensive, reducing households' real incomes. If manufacturers face higher input costs they may pass a share of their higher input costs on to final consumers, again lowering real incomes. The result is lower household spending, in real terms, and lower GDP.

Loss of competitiveness

Higher unit costs force domestic producers to increase their prices. The result is that they lose competitiveness both in export markets and domestically, meaning, in real terms, that we would expect to see lower exports, higher imports, and a reduction in GDP.

Loss of output in the energy/material sectors

As less energy and materials are consumed, the sectors that produce these goods face a fall of output. These effects are limited, partly because most of these sectors are relatively small in economic terms, but also because Europe imports a large share of its energy and raw materials, so impacts on domestic production are reduced.

Lower labour costs

The reduction in employers' social security contributions means that labour costs are reduced and total employment may increase as a result. With fewer unemployed, average incomes are higher and household spending increases. This leads to an increase in GDP.

Lower income taxes
The reduction in employees' income taxes means that workers keep more of their gross incomes and are able to spend this on consumer products. Household spending increases as a result, and GDP is higher.

9.5.4 Aggregate impacts on GDP and employment

RESULTS FROM E3ME
Results from the E3ME model show that the ETRs defined in Section 9.2 can lead to increases in both GDP and employment, as well as to environmental benefits (see Table 9.10). However, it should be noted that in each case the impacts on GDP are very small. The largest change in GDP, in HS2, is less than 1%, cumulated over the entire forecast period. This equates to less than 0.1 percentage points (pp) on annual growth rates over this time.

LS1 and HS3
The largest increases in employment are in scenarios LS1 and HS3 (the 2.7% increase in HS3, in an EU labour force of about 230 million, amounts to about 6 million jobs). These scenarios also have the highest carbon prices and therefore the highest revenues, through taxes and auctioned allowances, to reduce employers' and income taxes. In both cases, there is a boost to GDP of around 0.5% that arises principally through household consumption, as a combination of higher employment rates and lower income taxes makes households relatively better off (and outweighs the effects of higher prices).

Table 9.10. Aggregate impacts on GDP and employment (% difference from base in 2020), E3ME

Model	Variable	Scenario			
		LS1	HS1	HS2	HS3
E3ME	GDP	0.6	0.2	0.8	0.5
	Employment	2.2	1.1	1.1	2.7
	Consumption	1.3	0.6	0.7	1.4
	Investment	−0.4	−0.3	0.3	−0.7
	Exports	−0.1	−0.2	0.8	−0.3
	Imports	0.0	−0.2	0.2	−0.1
	Price level	1.6	0.8	0.7	1.8

Note: Figures show percentage changes in EU-27 main indicators in 2020, compared to the relevant baseline for each scenario.
Sources: E3ME, Cambridge Econometrics.

In both these scenarios, the ETR has a small negative impact on Europe's trade balance, but this is relatively minor compared to the change in consumption. Investment falls in response to the materials taxes, which make the main components of investment goods, for example metals and cement, more expensive.

HS1

The results from HS1 are essentially a scaled-down version of LS1. As the higher oil price carries out some of the reduction in emissions, the required carbon price is lower, meaning that the price level increases by less and there are reduced revenues to recycle. The impacts are typically halved in magnitude.

HS2

The highest increase in GDP occurs in HS2. The difference between HS2 and the other scenarios is the boost to investment from the revenue recycling into eco-innovation measures. This makes HS2 the only scenario where investment increases. Higher investment leads to an increase in quality, which boosts non-price competitiveness and leads to an increase in exports. Therefore, even though the increase in household consumption is similar to that in HS1, there is a larger increase in GDP.

RESULTS FROM GINFORS

The results from the GINFORS model (see Table 9.11) show that the ETRs will lead to a small reduction in GDP, but an increase in employment. The highest increase can be observed in scenario HS3. In scenario LS1, there is no change in employment because the reduction of labour costs due to ETR balances the GDP reduction. The trade effects depend, among other things, on the carbon

Table 9.11. Aggregate impacts on GDP and employment (% difference from base in 2020), GINFORS

		Scenario			
Model	Variable	LS1	HS1	HS2	HS3
GINFORS	GDP	−3.0	−0.6	−0.3	−1.9
	Employment	0.0	0.4	0.4	0.8
	Consumption	−2.9	−0.7	−0.5	−2.2
	Investment	−1.9	−0.3	0.8	1.5
	Exports	−5.4	−1.4	−1.3	−5.3
	Imports	−4.3	−0.8	−0.4	−2.7
	CPI	3.0	0.9	1.1	4.1

Note: Figures show percentage changes in EU-27 main indicators in 2020, compared to the relevant baseline for each scenario.
Source: GINFORS, GWS.

price. It is also important, mainly on the import side, whether competing countries face the same carbon prices (HS3) or not. International action will reduce GDP in the major economies compared to the baseline. So Europe will only partly profit from international cooperation, which will clearly change the composition of international trade towards low-carbon goods.

Investment will increase in comparison to the baseline in scenario HS2 due to higher investment in renewables and energy efficiency. In scenario HS3, additional investment will be needed to decarbonize the economies.

The Consumer Price Index (CPI) in Table 9.11 shows that prices significantly increase because of the carbon and material taxes, and this is not offset by the reduction in income taxes and labour costs.

9.5.5 Sectoral impacts

The E3ME and GINFORS models are able to show sectoral impacts at a relatively detailed level, with around 40 economic sectors defined in each case. This allows us to look at the main macroeconomic results in more detail. Not unexpectedly, there are sectors that gain and sectors that lose from the reforms.

RESULTS FROM E3ME

The results from E3ME show that the main sectors that lose out from ETR are those that produce and distribute energy (mining and utilities) and material inputs (agriculture and mining) and some of the more energy-intensive sectors (non-metallic mineral products, metals and metal goods, and air transport).

The sectors that gain are those that are not intensive users of energy and materials but benefit from the revenue-recycling measures. In particular, these include distribution and retail, which benefit from higher rates of consumer spending, and business services, which has lower labour costs.

There is little overall impact on construction as the sector gains from lower labour costs but faces higher material costs.

Table 9.12 summarizes the sectoral results from E3ME in LS1. The other scenarios show similar patterns, with the only difference being in HS2, where higher investment through revenue recycling boosts output in sectors that produce investment goods, such as construction and engineering.

RESULTS FROM GINFORS

The pattern of the sectoral results from GINFORS is similar, although most sectors are slightly more negative, reflecting the lower outcome in aggregate GDP. Figures 9.4 and 9.5 show the sectoral changes in output for the UK and Germany in scenario HS1 (again the pattern is the same across scenarios), with

Table 9.12. Percentage change in sectoral output, LS1 scenario, 2020, E3ME

Sector		Sector	
Agriculture	−1.2	Other manufacturing	0.3
Mining	−0.4	Utilities	−1.5
Food, drink and tobacco	0.4	Construction	0.2
Textiles & clothing	0.6	Distribution & retail	0.8
Wood & paper	0.0	Hotels & catering	0.3
Chemicals	0.5	Land transport	0.4
Non-metallic minerals	−1.4	Air transport	−1.0
Metals & metal goods	−1.0	Other transport	−0.5
Engineering	−0.4	Business services	1.2
Transport equipment	−0.3	Government services	0.3

Note: Figures show percentage change in EU-27 sectoral output in 2020 in LS1, compared to the baseline.
Source: E3ME.

the main sectors that lose out being those that produce energy goods and raw materials.

GENERAL TRENDS

Both models show that, not unexpectedly, the sectors that tend to lose out from the ETR are those that produce the energy and material products that are taxed under the scheme, and those that are the most intensive users of these products. The sectors that gain are the more labour-intensive ones which benefit from lower employment costs and, to a lesser extent, the ones that produce consumer goods and therefore benefit from lower income tax rates.

The sectoral results from both models are generally consistent with the pattern from previous model-based studies that considered higher energy

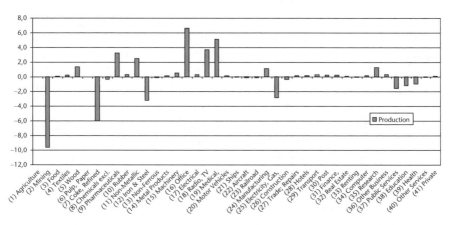

Figure 9.4 Sectoral change in output, Germany, 2020, scenario HS1, GINFORS
Note: Y-axis units are percentage difference from baseline (BH).

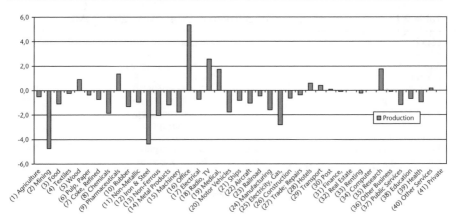

Figure 9.5 Sectoral change in output, UK, 2020, scenario HS1, GINFORS

Note: Y-axis units are percentage difference from baseline (BH).

and material costs (for examples, see Barker et al. 2009; Pollitt 2008; Lutz and Meyer 2009a).

9.5.6 The impact of the ETR carbon price on end-user prices

Current taxes levied on energy products vary very widely both between EU Member States and across different energy products. Moreover, EU Member States implementing an ETR in the past have regularly granted special tax provisions to industrial sectors out of concern for industrial competitiveness (Ekins and Speck 2008). Under these circumstances, a single carbon price across the EU will have very different relative effects on the end-user prices of different fuels in different countries.

Table 9.13 shows that the carbon price in the HS1 ETR scenario as modelled by GINFORS was €68 (2008)/tCO$_2$, and this is the price that has been used to analyse the price impacts of the ETR, with the model outputs being converted (by Stefan Speck) into price changes of energy products in normally used units. The analysis shows by how much a carbon price of €68 (2008)/tCO$_2$ would increase the end-user prices of 2008.

As both the transport fuel prices (petrol and diesel) and the energy/carbon taxes levied on these fuels are the highest when compared to prices and taxes levied on other energy products, it is not surprising that the smallest increase in end-user prices occurs for these fuels. An additional CO$_2$ tax of €68/tCO$_2$ would add around €160 per 1,000 litres (excl. VAT) to the end-user price of unleaded petrol and around €180 per 1,000 litres (excl. VAT) for diesel. Table 9.13 shows that the relative increases in end-user prices from such a

Table 9.13. Price increases in 2020 for various fuels due to a €68/tCO$_2$ carbon price in selected EU Member States (in % of 2008 end-user prices)

	petrol unleaded	diesel	heating gas oil
Czech Republic	13	14	20
Denmark	11	13	14
Estonia	14	15	21
Germany	11	13	20
Portugal	11	14	18
Romania	14	15	18
Spain	13	15	20
Sweden	11	13	14
United Kingdom	11	12	23

Sources: EC (2009a), prices as of 1 September 2008, and own calculations based on GINFORS results, scenario HS1.

tax are rather modest and similar throughout EU Member States, ranging between 10% and 15% for petrol and between 12% and 16% for diesel.

The spread in the increases in relative end-user prices is larger for heating gas oil (14–23%), which is not unexpected, as the final end-user prices differ widely between EU Member States, as a result, among other factors, of the large differences in the energy/carbon taxes levied on heating gas oil. Tax rates levied on heating fuel oil range between €21 per 1,000 litres (Latvia and Lithuania) up to about €400 per 1,000 litres (Italy and Sweden). These different tax rates greatly increase the pre-tax differential in end-use prices in Member States.

A different picture emerges from the effect of the carbon price on natural gas and electricity end-user prices (with 2007 end-user prices being the most recent available for comparison). This assessment needs to differentiate between industrial and household end-user prices for these energy products, as the prices paid by households are regularly much higher than those paid by industry. In some countries (Sweden, Latvia, and France), the household electricity price is twice that of industry, while in others (for example, Denmark and Germany) households pay more than twice the natural gas price paid by industry.

A carbon price of €68/tCO$_2$ implies a tax of around €3.8 euro/GJ for natural gas. The resulting price increase for households would be rather modest in EU Member States with current high natural gas prices and taxes—about 12% in Denmark, 14% in Sweden, 16% in Germany—but much higher in a country like the UK (29%), where household gas prices are relatively low (see Table 9.14). The carbon price would also lead to rather large increases in end-user prices for households in the new EU Member States with increases of about 50% in Estonia and Hungary.

The relative increase in natural gas prices would be higher for industry in all EU Member States (see Table 9.14), with the lowest increase in industrial

Table 9.14. Price increases in 2020 for natural gas due to a €68/tCO$_2$ carbon price in selected EU Member States (in % of 2007 end-user prices)

	Industry	Households
Czech Republic	62	34
Denmark	68	12
Estonia	113	57
Germany	34	16
Hungary	46	51
Sweden	n.a.	14
United Kingdom	42	29

Source: EC (2009b), prices as of 2007, and own calculations based on GINFORS results, scenario HS1.

energy prices found in Germany (34%) and the UK (42%), and the highest in Latvia, Bulgaria, and Estonia (113%). These are average price increases. The actual increases will vary across industrial sectors, because the prices industries actually pay for natural gas differ and depend on the location and the scale of their consumption.

The effect of a carbon price on electricity prices is not straightforward to assess as it depends on the energy mix of the electricity generation sector, and the extent to which the carbon price is passed through to electricity prices. In the calculations that follow of the price increases caused by the carbon price of €68/tCO$_2$, a full (100%) cost pass-through is assumed, and the 2005 CO$_2$ intensity of the electricity generation sectors (IEA 2008b) has been used. The price increases vary widely, ranging from about 3 euro/MWh (Sweden) and 6.3 euro/MWh (France) up to about 53 euro/MWh in Greece and Cyprus and even 58 euro/MWh in Malta. Therefore it is not unexpected that the least increase in relative electricity prices can be found in Sweden and France where households would face an increase of only 2% (Sweden) and 5% (France) (see Table 9.15). The relative increases are also rather low in Denmark (8%) and Germany (15%), as household electricity prices are already rather high in these countries. The highest relative change in household electricity prices would happen in countries with rather low electricity prices and carbon-intensive electricity generation, i.e. Greece and Estonia with a 62% increase, Malta (46%), and Poland (39%). The percentage increases in average industrial electricity prices also vary greatly, from 5% in Sweden, but approximately doubling in Greece, Malta, and Estonia. As with natural gas prices, the actual price increases would vary across industrial sectors.

It is interesting to compare the ETR-induced price increases in the tables above with the (pre-tax) end-user price changes of various oil products arising from the changes in oil prices over 2008–9, shown in Table 9.16. Of course the ETR-induced price increases would take place gradually over 2013–20, and so constitute much less of an inflationary shock than the oil price increases over a

Table 9.15. Price increases in 2020 for electricity due to a €68/tCO$_2$ carbon price in selected EU Member States (in % of 2007 end-user prices)

	Industry	Households
Cyprus	53	39
Czech Republic	53	41
Denmark	n.a.	8
Estonia	112	62
France	12	5
Germany	28	15
Greece	90	62
Malta	99	46
Spain	37	24
Sweden	5	2
United Kingdom	43	25

Sources: EC (2009b), and own calculations based on GINFORS results, scenario HS1.

Table 9.16. Price changes (net of any taxes) in the EU of various oil products, 2008–2009

	Jan. 2008	July 2008	July/Jan. 2008	Jan. 2009	Jan.2009/Jan.2008
	€/litre	€/litre	in %	€/litres	in %
Euro super 95	0.528	0.655	+24	0.307	−42
Diesel	0.595	0.799	+34	0.415	−30
Heating gas oil	0.563	0.753	+34	0.408	−28
Crude oil	0.393	0.531	+35	0.207	−47

Source: EC (2009c).

few months. Even so, it can be seen that the ETR-induced price changes are relatively large, especially for the new EU Member States, which tend currently to have lower energy prices than the EU-15 countries. This reinforces the conclusion in Chapter 6 that ETRs in these countries would need to be implemented with considerable sensitivity.

9.6 Comparison of the E3ME and GINFORS Results

9.6.1 Introduction

In Chapter 8, we noted the key similarities and differences between the models, which influence their results. The conclusion was that the basic model structures are very similar and, as shown in Section 9.2, the scenario definitions (including the baselines), that were used in the two models were also very similar. A comparison of the central outcomes will therefore allow the identification of the key issues and uncertainties that are likely to be important in any implementation of ETR.

9.6.2 GDP and employment

Table 9.17 gives the simulation results of both models for scenarios LS1, HS1, HS2, and HS3. Both models calculate very similar effects for the CO_2 price and labour productivity, but there are systematic differences in the GDP and employment impacts: E3ME calculates positive and GINFORS negative GDP effects, both of which increase with energy prices. Comparing the results for LS1 with those for HS1, we see in the case of GINFORS that the higher CO_2 price is connected with a stronger negative effect on GDP, whereas E3ME calculates a more positive effect on GDP in the case of a higher CO_2 price. These differences can be explained by the different model structures: first, E3ME allows for the possibility that higher energy prices and higher amounts of recycled revenues have partly positive effects on exports via increased investment and higher quality production. In GINFORS, a unilateral rise of energy prices in the EU reduces its share in international trade, which diminishes EU exports and GDP. Secondly, labour supply is assumed to be more restricted in GINFORS. The price-wage mechanism in GINFORS may work more towards higher wages and prices, which limits job creation through international competition, whereas in E3ME higher wages create more income and demand, which is produced by additional employees. Even so, in the high energy price (HS) scenarios, the minimum employment increase for the EU-27 as a whole (in GINFORS in HS1 and HS2) is more than 800,000 compared to the corresponding baseline. The maximum employment increase for the EU-27 as a whole (in E3ME in the HS3 scenario) is 6.2 million.

Table 9.17. Summary results in 2020, E3ME and GINFORS

Scenario	CO₂ price	GDP	Employment	Labour productivity
	Euro 2008/t	% change from baseline	% change from baseline	% change from baseline
LS1				
E3ME	142	0.6	2.2	-1.6
GINFORS	120	−3.0	0.0	−3.0
HS1				
E3ME	59	0.2	1.1	−0.9
GINFORS	68	−0.6	0.4	−1.0
HS2				
E3ME	53	0.8	1.1	−0.3
GINFORS	61	−0.3	0.4	−0.7
HS3				
E3ME	204	0.5	2.7	−2.1
GINFORS	184	−1.9	0.8	−2.6

Note: Figures are for 2020 and show the carbon price and a summary of the main economic results from each model.
Source: E3ME and GINFORS.

Comparing HS2 with HS1, both models show the same reaction: the tax revenue in HS2 is now partly used for pushing investment in renewable energies. In response, both models calculate a lower CO_2 price to meet the targets, and there is a positive effect in both models on GDP (GDP in HS2 is higher than in HS1).

In scenario HS3, in the context of international action, both models calculate a higher CO_2 price, because the reduction target is now 30% instead of 20% in HS1. The effects on EU trade shares are much lower than in HS1. But in this case there are negative effects on the GDP of all other countries, which reduces their imports and thus EU exports and GDP. This explains why GINFORS calculates far higher GDP reductions in HS3 than in HS1. In the case of E3ME, the higher CO_2 price in HS3 will induce more investment and GDP as in HS1, but this is compensated by the export reductions that had been taken from the GINFORS results, so that there is only a slight difference in GDP compared to HS1.

Both models project that the GHG reduction targets of scenarios HS1 and HS2 can be reached with only small influences on GDP. E3ME calculates a slightly positive, GINFORS a slightly negative effect. The deviations from the relevant baseline are less than half of the average growth of one year. Over a period of ten years the annual average growth rate will be affected by less than 0.1 percentage points, which is in the range of 'white noise'.

In HS1, the tax revenues are used to reduce social security payments, which reduces labour costs. Both models estimate a plausible reduction in labour productivity against the baseline. For E3ME ,the result is −0.9, for GINFORS −1.0, which is nearly identical. In HS2, only 90% of the tax revenue is recycled through reduced social security contributions. Both models project an increase of labour productivity (E3ME from −0.9 to −0.3, GINFORS from −1.0 to −0.7). So the differences in the results for employment are driven not by labour productivity, but mainly by GDP.

9.6.3 Conclusions

Carrying out the analysis with two different models was a fairly novel aspect of this analysis. In other studies, it is often difficult to compare model results because of different model structures and underlying assumptions, both in economic theory and in model inputs. However, in the PETRE project two models with very similar structures were provided with inputs that were as far as possible identical. The differences in results can therefore be attributed with confidence to the remaining differences in model specification.

Summarizing the modelling differences in respect to GDP effects, it can be argued that E3ME has the more optimistic, GINFORS the more pessimistic, structure for this type of analysis. Since both models are empirically evaluated, the modelling results mark the range between which the 'true' effects on GDP may lie, but the uncertainty concerning the effects on GDP is small.

Since both models produce nearly identical results concerning labour and resource productivity, both models give the same message: an environmental tax reform which meets the 20% GHG emissions reduction target will raise employment, lower resource consumption, and have only small effects on GDP. Since the specification of the models and their parameterization is based on empirical estimations, this result may be considered to be quite robust.

References

Anderson, D., and S. Winne (2004), 'Modelling Innovation and Threshold Effects in Climate Change Mitigation', Working Paper No. 59, Tyndall Centre for Climate Change Research.

—— —— (2007), 'Energy System Change and External Effects in Climate Change Mitigation', *Environment and Development Economics*, 12(3): 359–78.

Barker, T., S. Junankar, H. Pollitt, and P. Summerton (2009), 'The Macroeconomic Effects of Unilateral Environmental Tax Reforms in Europe, 1995–2012', in J. Cottrell, J. E. Milne, H. Ashiabor, L. Kreiser, and K. Deketelaere (eds.), *Critical Issues in Environmental Taxation*, vol. VI, Oxford: Oxford University Press.

—— O. Løfsnaes, and H. Pollitt (2007) 'The ETM in E3ME43', Cambridge Econometrics Working Paper, available online at: <http://www.camecon.com/Libraries/Downloadable_Files/ETM.sflb.ashx>.

Chevillon, G., and C. Rifflart (2008) 'Physical Market Determinants of the Price of Crude Oil and the Market Premium', *Energy Economics*, 31(4): 537–49.

EC (European Commission) (2008a), 'Energy and Transport: Trends to 2030 (2007 update)', Directorate General for Energy and Transport, European Commission, available on DG Energy web pages.

—— (2008b), 'Impact Assessment Document accompanying the Package of Implementation Measures for the EU's Objective on Climate Change and Renewable Energy for 2020', Commission Staff Working Document, 23 January, SEC(2008)85/3, Brussels.

—— (2008c), 'Decision on the Effort of Member States to Reduce their Greenhouse Gas Emissions to Meet the Community's Greenhouse Gas Emission Reduction Commitments up to 2020' (COM(2008)17 final).

—— (2009a), *Oil Price Bulletin*, Brussels.

—— (2009b), *Statistical Pocketbook 2009*, DG Energy and Eurostat, Brussels.

—— (2009c), *Evolution of Oil and Petroleum Product Prices and Taxation Levels during the Year 2008 in the European Union*, available at <http://ec.europa.eu/energy/observatory/oil/doc/prices/oil_price_in_2008.pdf>.

Ekins, P., and Speck, S. (2008), 'Environmental Tax Reform in Europe: Energy Tax Rates and Competitiveness', in N. Chalifour, J. Milne, H. Ashiabor, K. Deketelaere, and L. Kreiser (eds.), *Critical Issues in Environmental Taxation*, vol. V, Oxford: Oxford University Press, 77–105.

Eurostat (2009), *Taxation Trends in the European Union—Data for the EU Member States and Norway Edition 2009*, Luxembourg: Eurostat.

GHK, Cambridge Econometrics, and IEEP (2007), 'Links between the Environment, Economy and Jobs', Final Report submitted to DG Environment, European Commission, November.

Grossmann, A., U. Lehr, C. Lutz, and M. I. Wolter (2008), 'Gesamtwirtschaftliche Effekte der Umsetzung der EU Ziele im Bereich Erneuerbare Energien und Gebäudeeffizienz in Österreich bis 2020', Studie im Auftrag des Lebensministeriums, Vienna, May.

IEA (International Energy Agency) (2008a), *World Energy Outlook 2008*, Paris: IEA.

—— (2008b) *CO_2 emissions from combustion*, Paris: IEA.

Jänicke, M., and R. Zieschank (2008), 'Structure and Function of the Environmental Industry: The Hidden Contribution to Sustainable Growth in Europe', Working Paper submitted for the PETRE Project, available at <http://www.petre.org.uk/pdf/Janicke_Zieschank.pdf.>

Lehr, U., J. Nitsch, M. Kratzat, C. Lutz, and D. Edler (2008), 'Renewable Energy and Employment in Germany', *Energy Policy*, 36: 108–17,

—— M. I. Wolter, and A. Grossmann (2009), 'Economic Impacts of RES Obligations in Austria: An Application of the Macro-econometric Model e3.at', GWS Discussion Paper 2009/1, Osnabrück.

Longo, C., M. Manera, A. Markandya, and E. Scarpa (2007), 'Evaluating the Empirical Performance of Alternative Econometric Models for Oil Price Forecasting', Fondazione Eni Enrico Mattei Working Papers.

Lutz, C., and B. Meyer (2008), 'Beschäftigungseffekte des Klimaschutzes in Deutschland: Untersuchungen zu gesamtwirtschaftlichen Auswirkungen ausgewählter Maßnahmen des Energie- und Klimapakets', Forschungsbericht 205 46 434, Dessau-Roßlau.

—— —— (2009a), 'Environmental and Economic Effects of Post-Kyoto Carbon Regimes: Results of Simulations with the Global Model GINFORS', *Energy Policy*, 37: 1758–66.

—— —— (2009b), 'PETRE—Results from GINFORS', PETRE Working Paper, June.

NERI (University of Aarhus), Cambridge Econometrics, ESRI, IEEP (University of Economics, Prague), PSI, and WIIW (2007), 'Competitiveness of Environmental Tax Reforms', Final Report to the European Commission, DG Research and DG Taxation and Customs Union, available online at: <http://www2.dmu.dk/cometr/COMETR_Final_Report.pdf.>

Pollitt, H. (2008), 'Combining Economic and Material Flows Analysis at the Sectoral Level: Development of the E3ME Model and Application in the MATISSE Case Studies', Matisse deliverable 8.6.1 for European Commission, DG Research, April.

—— and U. Chewpreecha (2009), 'Modelling Results from E3ME: Final Results from the Petre Project', PETRE Working Paper, June.

10

Implications of ETR in Europe for Household Distribution

Daniel Blobel, Holger Gerdes, Hector Pollitt, Jennifer Barton, Thomas Drosdowski,
Christian Lutz, Marc Ingo Wolter, and Paul Ekins

10.1 Introduction

Equity issues are regularly used as an argument against the further introduction of ETR, because increases in environmental taxes are often thought to fall disproportionately on low-income and rural households. This chapter analyses the household distributional implications of environmental tax reform (ETR).

The chapter is in three sections, which have different authorship. First, there is a literature review (mainly by Blobel, Gerdes, and with some contributions by Drosdowski, Lutz, and Wolter), which reviews theoretical and empirical findings on the distributional effects of environmental taxes and tax reforms in their various facets, as well as policy options to mitigate, or reverse, undesired distributional effects.

The next two sections describe two modelling studies which were undertaken to help gain an understanding of the impacts of an ETR on the distribution of income across individuals and households. One of the two studies was carried out by Cambridge Econometrics (Pollitt, Barton), and this analyses the implications at European level, i.e. covering all 27 EU Member States, of a broad-based ETR for households (split by income, employment status, and location). The third section (by Drosdowski, Lutz, and Wolter) consists of a study by GWS (Institute for Economic Structures Research, Germany), which analyses the implications of an ETR in a single country (Germany) in more detail.

The chapter is derived from a report from the recent ETR project commissioned by the European Environment Agency.[1] It has been edited into its current form by Paul Ekins.

10.2 Literature review

The distributional effects that need to be considered in relation to ETR have various facets:

(1) The distributional effects of the environmental taxes themselves: here, the central problem is that excise taxes have often been found to have a regressive effect, i.e. poorer population groups pay more in relation to their income than richer population groups.

(2) The distributional effects of any tax reductions or revenue distribution associated with the ETR. The tax reductions (or other uses of the environmental tax revenues) may vary, but the typical concept of ETR involves lowering of labour taxes. When analysing the distributional effects of an ETR, one needs to look at the *net* distributional effects.

(3) There are other effects that arise from the broader economic and environmental impacts of ETR. These include price changes of goods and services as a result of the environmental taxes and tax reductions or revenue redistributions, and macroeconomic effects, such as impacts on employment levels.

(4) As a fourth category, one may add the effects of exemptions and other specific provisions that may have been made in the tax design for various purposes (e.g. competitiveness, social concerns, or environmental considerations). These can be seen as part of (1) or (2), but should be recognized specifically, because they constitute deviations from the basic ETR design.

(5) The distribution of the environmental improvements brought about by the ETR. For example, if environmental burdens are disproportionately experienced by low-income households, and ETR reduces these burdens, these changes should be taken into account in the distributional analysis.

The review first looks at theoretical and empirical findings on the distributional effects of environmental tax reforms, along the lines described above:

---

[1] 'Tax reform in europe over the next decades: implications for the environment, for eco-innovation and for household distribution', European Environment Agency, Copenhagen, forthcoming.

the distributional effects of the taxes alone, the net effects when including the revenue redistribution side, and the wider social and environmental implications. It then discusses possibilities that have been implemented or suggested to mitigate, or reverse, negative distributional effects. The final section of the review presents conclusions, which are also intended to serve as a springboard for further discussion.

10.2.1 Distributional effects of environmentally related taxes and ETR

DIRECT DISTRIBUTIONAL EFFECTS

A considerable literature has analysed the distributional effects of environmental taxes in the household sector. Meta-analyses are provided, inter alia, by OECD (1995), Speck (1999), Speck et al. (2006), Leipprand et al. (2007), Peter et al. (2007). A broad international discussion is found in Serret and Johnstone (2006).

In general, energy taxes have been found to have regressive implications, in contrast to taxes on labour or income. However, this general statement may need to be modified when taking account of the specific circumstances. A number of studies have demonstrated that regressive effects are the largest in the area of household energy, with the lowest-income groups bearing the largest tax burden relative to their income. In contrast, motor fuel taxes tend to put the highest relative burden on middle-income groups. This is because the proportion of car ownership is lower in low-income households, and households without cars are not directly affected by motor fuel taxes. There are also country- and region-specific factors, such as overall distribution of income, energy supply structure, energy-efficiency characteristics of domestic fuel use, and reliance on car transport.

The distributional effects of transport-related taxes are examined in detail in a Norwegian study (Aasness and Larson 2002). The authors do not analyse any specific taxes, or taxation schemes, but examine elasticities of household expenditure on various transport-related items and relate this to the environmental effects of different modes of transport. They distinguish between 'high-pollution luxury modes' of transport, such as aviation and taxis, on the one hand, and 'low-pollution necessary modes' of transport, such as buses, bicycles, and mopeds. They conclude that imposing higher taxes on the former and lower taxes on the latter would serve both environmental and equity objectives. With regard to individual car transport, they observe that a high taxation of petrol is desirable from an environmental point of view, but it also increases inequality (a conclusion which somewhat differs from those of the studies cited above). By contrast, they argue that higher vehicle taxes may serve equity purposes better: while petrol offers little variation in quality, the quality of automobiles shows large variation from basic to luxury versions, which leads to a much higher elasticity of expenditure. Railway passenger transportation was found to be distributionally neutral.

Leipprand et al. (2007) examined the distributional effects of environmentally related taxes and charges in five European countries: the Czech Republic, Germany, Spain, Sweden, and the United Kingdom (UK) (Figure 10.1). The analysis included energy taxes as well as charges on water services and refuse collection. The amount paid for these taxes and charges was related to the average disposable household income of different income classes (deciles for most countries), as well as other categorizations of household groups (according to activity and employment status, household size and structure, age, number of active persons, degree of urbanization). In the case of energy taxes, the tax burden was calculated by converting expenditure statistics into physical consumption estimates, and relating the amounts of physical consumption to the tax rate applied in each country. For water services and refuse collection, expenditure data were taken directly as a proxy for charge levels, since in these areas, charges are difficult to separate from prices, and charging systems vary regionally and even locally. An admitted shortcoming of the methodology was the static analysis—it was only based on current expenditure without taking into account dynamic effects, i.e. the incentives provided by price signals to change consumption patterns, which may in turn reduce the tax/charge burdens on individual households in absolute terms.

In the Czech Republic, there is evidence for regressive impacts. Although differences are moderate in general, the difference between the lowest-income group and the others is greater than among the other income groups.

In Germany, evidence for regressive impacts can be found, but mostly for those tax instruments that constitute a relatively small share of the total tax and charge burden. When total sums are considered, these regressive elements are masked by the dominant role of motor fuel taxes. The bulk of tax revenue is generated from the transport sector (fuel taxes on petrol and diesel), while regressive effects are largest in the area of household energy (i.e. relating to the electricity tax and the petroleum tax on heating fuel).

In Spain, significant distributive impacts exist in water charging. In the sum of taxes and charges, these impacts are masked by the more progressive distribution of motor fuel taxes.

There is almost no evidence for regressive impacts of environmental taxes in Sweden. The self-employed seem to be the group that is most affected by disproportionate tax burdens. Yet there seems to be no particular cause for concern with respect to other vulnerable groups, such as the unemployed or families with single parents.

In the UK, the sum of environmental taxes and charges clearly has a regressive impact on households, the payments relative to income decreasing consistently with increasing income levels. A strong regressive impact for water charges

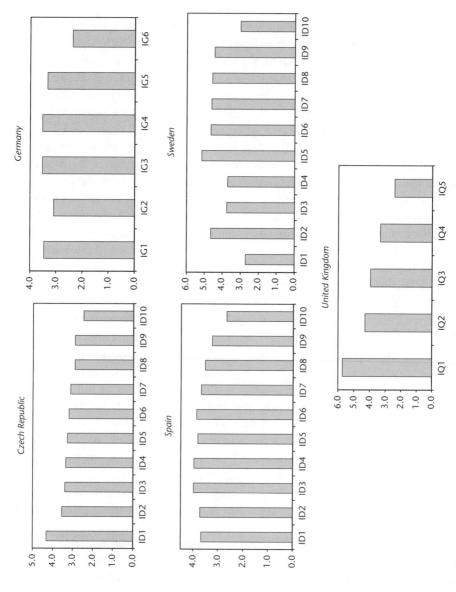

Figure 10.1 Sum of selected environmentally related taxes and charges as a percentage of average disposable household income, by income groups
Note: Deciles for the Czech Republic, Spain, and Sweden; sextiles for Germany; quintiles for the UK Source: Leipprand et al. (2007).

determines the overall trend of the total sum, while motor fuel taxes follow the usual pattern, with middle-income groups paying most in relation to their income. The regressive effect of water charges is essentially the result of charges that are usually not related to the actual quantity of water that is consumed.

In the 1990s, several studies examined the distributional effects of introducing energy or carbon taxes. An early comprehensive study was undertaken by Smith (1992). The study relied on EU household expenditure surveys for six countries. The analysis was static, assuming no indirect effects, no induced changes in demand patterns, and the passing on of taxes to prices to a full extent. Under these assumptions, the ratio of regressivity was calculated for 11 countries. The conclusion was that carbon and energy taxes were weakly regressive for most countries, but more strongly regressive for the UK and Ireland. The regressive effect for the UK and Ireland, as well as (West) Germany, was confirmed by Barker and Köhler (1998), who presented the first comprehensive long-term projection of distributional impacts of an ETR in 11 EU countries until 2010, using their econometric E3ME model (the same model used for the analysis in Section 10.3). Under a set of assumptions (see ibid. 378–80) they estimate the change in expenditure of various low-to-middle-income consumer groups on 'environmentally-sensitive goods and services' induced by taxes imposed on these products. Furthermore, they consider the use of revenues from the reform to reduce social security contributions. Looking at cross-sectional data for 1988, the authors first reveal that the percentage of total expenditure of households on domestic fuels is diminishing with rising household expenditure, i.e. the poor spend a higher share of their income on fuel than higher-income groups. A diametrically opposed situation is found with respect to expenditures on transport, whose share is increasing with higher income.

Their simulation results indicate that in 2010 all socio-economic groups would gain in terms of disposable income in constant 1988 prices, while the income distribution would become moderately more regressive. The authors use a regressivity measure developed in Smith (1992), which is the ratio of tax payments as a percentage of total household expenditure of the poorest quartile over the same share of the richest quartile. Among the countries considered, the regressivity of the distribution would be relatively highest in Germany. This weak regressivity would emerge due to the increased tax burden for domestic energy, affecting mostly the lowest-income brackets and welfare and pension recipients. However, if the reform only included road fuels, the results would indicate a progressive outcome. While the ETR has positive net effects on households' incomes, due to compensating reductions in social security contributions, the authors conclude that additional policy measures must be implemented to correct the regressive effects, which markets cannot achieve. As solutions, they suggest tax reductions for employers employing lower-paid labour, using tax revenues to improve the energy efficiency of fuel use for poorer groups, and raising their incomes directly via social security payments. The crucial importance of the way in which revenues are recycled is also discussed in Johnstone and Serret (2006) and Serret and Johnstone (2006).

Similar results were found by Symons et al. (1997, cited in Speck 1999), who examined the income-distributional impacts in Germany, Italy, Spain, and the UK, based on a static modelling approach. The study found that a CO_2 tax would be regressive for Germany and the UK, as would as an energy tax, with energy taxes slightly less regressive than a CO_2 tax. The impact of the taxes was found to be less regressive in Italy, and even slightly progressive in Spain. The Spanish outcome was attributed to an increasing proportion spent on petrol throughout the income distribution. In contrast, a later article by the same authors (Symons et al. 2002) found regressive effects for Germany and France, to a lesser extent for Spain, a nearly neutral effect for Italy, but a progressive effect for the UK. They explain this unusual finding by the specific expenditure category weights applied in the statistical expenditure data on which the analysis was based—an example of how subtle changes in assumptions and underlying data can influence results to a considerable extent.

Interestingly, by looking at the effects of removing subsidies for energy products in Poland, Freund and Wallich (1997) have shown that middle- and high-income households spent, in relative terms, a larger share of their budget on energy products than low-income households. The findings are not transferable to other Member States due to historic (post-socialist) and country-specific conditions, but they show that the negative correlation between household income and the income proportion spent on energy is not always valid.

The distributional impacts of energy taxation have been analysed in particular depth for the UK, which has also been found to be one of the countries where the associated problems are greatest. As mentioned in this section's introduction, household energy and motor fuels merit being studied separately.

Regarding *household energy*, Ekins and Dresner (2004) concluded that a flat carbon tax on the entire population (both rich and poor), without providing compensation for the poorer segment of the population, would be very regressive and increase the already present price burden on the aforementioned poorer segment. In addition to poorer households paying a larger percentage of their income for electricity, they are less able and willing to switch to energy-efficient appliances due to financial restraints and the fact that many rent their accommodation. This means that low-income households use a larger percentage of 'dirty fuels'. Another problem is that there is variation within income groups, which increases the difficulty of compensating certain segments of the population. Similarly, a study by McNally and Mabey (1999) demonstrated that a tax on domestic energy consumption would be financially regressive for lower-income households, as domestic energy is a necessity good. Crawford et al. (1993), estimate that, while the average consumption of all UK households would fall by nearly 6%, energy consumption in the bottom income quintile would fall by 9% on average, while the consumption of the richest quintile would be reduced by only 1% on average. This means that the financial impact, as well as the reduction of energy consumption, would fall primarily on low-income households.

According to the studies by both Ekins and Dresner (2004) and McNally and Mabey (1999), *motor fuel taxes* are generally considered progressive because they affect the portion of the population who possess cars and not the poorer section who generally do not. However, this is untrue for many of the poorer households in rural areas who travel further, use more fuel, and have less access to public transportation. As a result, McNally and Mabey (1999) have concluded that poor rural households would suffer the most. In addition, urban low-income households owning a car will be less able or willing to switch to a more fuel-efficient car. Therefore, although fuel tax is mainly progressive, a minority of low-income motorists would be disadvantaged.

A clear disadvantage for inhabitants of rural regions was also found to be associated with environmental taxes in Sweden (Speck et al. 2006; Leipprand et al. 2007; Peter et al. 2007). This outcome was found in both an academic study simulating the effects of doubling the CO_2 tax (Brännlund and Nordström 2004), and an ex-post assessment carried out by the Swedish government (Regeringens proposition 2004). Peter et al. (2007) relate this finding to the Swiss situation and comment that, in comparison to Sweden, Switzerland has a better developed public transport system, so the distributional effects of energy or CO_2 taxation between Swiss urban and rural regions would be less pronounced. This points to the importance of behavioural alternatives to avoid burdening certain population groups excessively. Peter et al. (2007) nevertheless emphasize that adverse distributional effects of energy taxes on rural regions remain an important issue, which has also been examined in more depth in earlier studies for Switzerland (e.g. INFRAS/ECOPLAN 1998). It has to be kept in mind that rural households not only tend to have a higher demand for motorized transport, but also consume more household energy (Wier et al. 2005; Speck et al. 2006). A Danish study (Wier et al. 2005) distinguishes between direct and indirect CO_2 tax payments (the latter resulting from price effects in the purchase of energy-intensive goods and services when CO_2 taxes are imposed on industry). It concludes that in Denmark, the higher direct tax burden on rural households is partly offset by their lower indirect tax payments. A net disadvantage for rural household remains, but is fairly small (around 0.04 percentage points related to the share of CO_2 tax payments in disposable income).

The distinction made by Wier et al. (2005) between direct and indirect CO_2 taxation of households is also interesting in a broader sense. They conclude that the regressive effect of indirect CO_2 taxation is generally less pronounced than the effect of direct CO_2 taxation.

The German ETR, which started in 1999 and involved a gradual introduction of measures until 2003, spawned a new wave of research, mostly not concerned with distributional matters (for exceptions, see Bach et al. 2001 and 2002; Grub 2000). Bach et al. (2001, 2002) combined a micro-simulation model (the 'Potsdamer' model) with a structural econometric model (PANTA RHEI; see Section 10.4) estimating short-term future impacts until 2003.

The 'Potsdamer' micro-simulation model was used to analyse the effects of an ETR at household level (micro level). It is based on detailed information on the socio-economic conditions of private households in Germany such as direct and indirect taxes, social security contributions, and transfers. The model differentiates between fossil fuel taxes on gasoline and diesel, fuel oil, natural gas and liquefied gas, and includes data on the consumption behaviour of private households regarding gasoline and diesel. By the time of the analysis, no time-series data were available, so that the data used were random samples from 1993, which were adjusted to 1998 (the base year), taking account of changes in the tax assessment base. In the reference scenario, the fiscal law from 1998 was assumed to be valid until 2003, whereas the ETR was implemented in a second scenario.

The effects of the ETR, obtained by the comparison of the baseline scenario with the ETR scenario, were analysed for five different household sizes and eight different household types for 18 different income groups. They turned out to be rather moderate in size, confirming earlier insight. Moreover, the studies confirmed that the total net burden was generally decreasing with disposable income (again increasing only in the highest-income brackets due to lower impacts of reduced social security contributions for these groups). Concentrating on household size, it showed that the net tax burden in 2003 with the ETR would be higher for all but the single-occupier households in the middle-income range.

Taking account of socio-economic status, only households of middle-income employees without children benefit from the implementation of the ETR. The net burden is also shown to be increasing with the family size. Additionally, the studies take into account the German income tax reform for the years 1999, 2000, 2003, which together with the ETR could be perceived as one big reform package. In general, the combined results show a mitigation of or even overcompensation for the regressivity induced by the ETR. More detailed results can be found in Bach et al. (2001: 108–22).

The same micro-simulation model was used after the actual ETR (Bork 2006), relying on official statistical data until 2003 that replaced the forecast time series from PANTA RHEI. The results are very similar to the previous versions, the only notable exception being that single-occupier households with middle incomes are now also negatively affected by the ETR, due to higher pension contributions than in the forecast versions. In addition, the author confirms that the tax burden associated with energy decreased with income, while showing that the burden associated with motor fuels had an inverted U-shaped pattern in income, i.e. first increasing, then decreasing.

Possibly the newest publication to give some results concerning the distributional effects of the German ETR in 2003 (the most recent year for Income and Consumption Survey data) is Bach (2009), which confirms that these effects are moderate. According to Bach (2009), the energy tax revenues account for 0.75% of disposable income. The ETR burden relative to equivalence-weighted household income is highest for low-income households and decreasing with income, i.e. the burden is regressively distributed. However, the inclusion of adjustments in pension payments leads to mitigated impacts, so that only the poorest households and families with children are negatively affected.

NET DISTRIBUTIONAL EFFECTS

Peter et al. (2007) compare the effects of energy taxes in various European countries (Denmark, Finland, Germany, the Netherlands, Norway, Sweden, the United Kingdom), based on a review of country-specific evaluations. The analysis includes distributional effects, along with environmental and economic effects. The analysis of distributional effects includes revenue redistribution within environmental tax reforms.

The study confirms the generally regressive effect of energy and CO_2 taxes on households. It also found that in most of the countries analysed, the energy tax burden on households was greater than the burden on industry. This is not only due to the tax exemptions granted to energy-intensive industries for competitiveness purposes, but also to the lower demand elasticity in the household sector. The authors also point out that price increases resulting from higher energy prices tend to be passed on from industry to households. Therefore, when considering macroeconomic effects, there is a more pronounced distributional shift of the tax burden to households from industry than when only looking at the direct financial effects.

When including the redistribution side and the specific tax design in the analysis, Peter et al. (2007) found that the regressive effect of the ETR was nearly neutralized in the Netherlands and Sweden. This was achieved in very different ways in the two countries. In the Netherlands, a certain tax-free basic amount of electricity consumption is granted per year to each household, whereas in Sweden, most of the revenue was recycled via income tax reductions and only a smaller part was used to reduce employers' labour taxes.

In *Sweden*, distributive impacts were a major concern from the outset of the introduction of the Green Tax Shift, and it was stated that consideration would be given to effects on income distribution, regional effects, and effects on industrial competitiveness. Generally, the tax shift has led to a change in the distribution of the tax burden and relief between households and firms, with households experiencing a net tax reduction and service firms experiencing a net increase in taxation (Leipprand et al. 2007).

In 2004, the government itself evaluated some actual effects of the Green Tax Shift for the period of 2001–3 (Regeringens proposition 2004). Importantly, the question is more who has benefited more from the green tax shift (rather than who has lost out), since households were generally benefiting. The net effect was relatively small for all social groups: less than 1% of disposable income in all groups. It was positive for almost all groups.

- Income decile: all deciles had a net increase (ranging from 130 to 300 SEK), except for the lowest (190 SEK decrease) and highest deciles (60 SEK decrease).
- Type of household: households with multiple incomes and no children had the largest net increase.
- Regional distribution: the net tax burden decreased in all regions both relatively and absolutely. Households in Gothenburg and Stockholm gained the most, while rural areas gained less.
- Type of housing: the biggest differences in distributive effects can be seen for different types of housing.

Most studies evaluating the distributional effects of the German ETR concluded that the household sector was a net loser from the reform, whereas energy-intensive industries benefited from it (Hillebrand 2000; Bach et al. 2001; GBG 2004; Bach 2005). The reason for this is that certain industries were granted extensive tax exemptions but profited from the revenue distribution in the form of reduced pension payments to the full extent. However, more recent research came to a different conclusion and found that for the household sector as a whole, the net effect of ETR was nearly neutral (Bach 2009). The main reason for this revised assessment was that the new analysis—which was undertaken ex post for 2003—took into account not only the relief from lower social security contributions but also the effect of pension adjustments induced by the ETR: owing to the particular rules governing the adjustment of pensions, the reduction in pension contributions led to increased pension payments. This again confirms the observation that subtle changes in the design of analysis may influence conclusions on distributional effects significantly.

Although the new study showed the net financial effect of the ecotax on the households sector as a whole to be nearly neutral, it still showed a slight regressive effect, although it can be argued that the financial burden after revenue redistribution is not too significant in absolute terms, with the lowest-income decile experiencing the highest net financial burden in relation to income (0.13% of disposable household income compared to 0.02% for the average of households). However, when applying a further differentiation according to the structure of households, negative distributional effects are more pronounced for certain groups. Families with children are affected the most by an ecotax. Single parents and parents with more than two children lose up to 0.5% of their available income. Single people and married couples without children, on the contrary, experience positive effects from the ecotax (see Table 10.1).

In general, households of jobholders experience positive or little negative cumulative effects from the ecotax, while households of unemployed persons and pensioners experience no change in the cumulative tax burden. Households of self-employed profit only to a small extent from reduced pension contributions. Civil servants and non-working persons receive hardly any benefit from reduced pensions contributions or adjusted social transfers (Bach et al. 2001; Bach 2009).

WIDER SOCIAL AND ENVIRONMENTAL IMPLICATIONS OF ETR

On a positive note, the German ETR has helped stabilize and even lower *pension contributions*. From yearly ecotax revenues of approximately 18 billion euro, around 90% are being used to finance pensions. Although pension contributions rose again in the years after 2002, they are at present still lower (19.9% of gross salary) than they were before the introduction of the ETR in 1999 (20.3%). Without ETR, their level would be 1.7% percentage points higher, i.e. 21.6%. In discussions, it has often been stressed by proponents, as well as opponents, of ETR that the pension-stabilizing function of the German ETR has been its main guarantee for survival in a changing political environment, as it has convinced fiscal politicians despite all ideological differences that there was no alternative to keeping this instrument.

Job creation has been an official goal of many environmental tax reforms. In the German case, as modelled by Kohlhaas (2005), the biggest employment effect was achieved in 2003, with 250,000 additional jobs, equal to 0.75% above the reference scenario without ETR. In 2010, the job effect was predicted to decrease to 0.5% additional employment. According to this analysis, reduced non-wage labour costs have been the main factor by which the ETR contributed to the creation of jobs, in addition to more short-term job effects associated with energy-saving investments induced by the rise in energy taxes. The positive effect on job creation is expected to partially offset the potentially

Table 10.1. Net income effects for private households' due to the German ETR in 2003 (percentage of disposable household income)

Deciles net equivalent household income	Single households	Single parents		Married and unmarried couples				Other households	House-holds total	Ecotax alone[1]
		with 1 child	with 2 and more children	without child	with 1 child	with 2 children	with 3 and more children			
1st decile	+ 0.02	− 0.20	− 0.35	− 0.16	− 0.27	− 0.28	− 0.48	− 0.38	− 0.13	− 1.05
2nd decile	+ 0.16	− 0.21	− 0.28	− 0.13	− 0.25	− 0.31	− 0.50	− 0.15	− 0.10	− 0.98
3rd decile	+ 0.22	− 0.10	− 0.25	− 0.01	− 0.25	− 0.27	− 0.39	− 0.00	− 0.05	− 0.94
4th decile	+ 0.17	− 0.11	− 0.48	+ 0.04	− 0.15	− 0.23	− 0.32	+ 0.04	− 0.05	− 0.94
5th decile	+ 0.27	− 0.04	− 0.31	+ 0.08	− 0.15	− 0.17	− 0.25	+ 0.02	+ 0.01	− 0.86
6th decile	+ 0.22	− 0.00	− 0.21	+ 0.04	− 0.10	− 0.18	− 0.23	− 0.04	− 0.02	− 0.85
7th decile	+ 0.15	− 0.16	− 0.29	+ 0.06	− 0.05	− 0.12	− 0.18	+ 0.05	− 0.00	− 0.80
8th decile	+ 0.11	− 0.14	− 0.35	+ 0.03	− 0.03	− 0.10	− 0.16	− 0.02	− 0.01	− 0.73
9th decile	+ 0.05	− 0.10	− 0.22	+ 0.03	− 0.03	− 0.05	− 0.14	− 0.03	− 0.00	− 0.66
10th decile	− 0.02	− 0.15	− 0.17	+ 0.03	− 0.03	− 0.03	− 0.13	− 0.01	− 0.00	− 0.47
Total	+ 0.11	− 0.13	− 0.29	+ 0.03	− 0.08	− 0.13	− 0.24	− 0.03	− 0.02	− 0.75

Note: [1] Income effects without redistribution for comparison purposes.
Source: Modified from Bach (2009).

negative distributional effects of ETR on the unemployed, who may eventually benefit from the job-creating impact of the reform. However, no data are available on which social groups have actually benefited or will benefit from the increase in jobs (Leipprand et al. 2007).

The net distributional effect of environmental taxes can be defined so as also to include the distribution of beneficial effects these taxes have on the *state of the environment*. There are some indications that the environmental effects add a progressive element, since lower-income households tend to suffer more from environmental pollution (cf. Pye et al. 2008), and would therefore benefit more than other groups from pollution reduction. However, there is currently a lack of empirical data that could clarify the relationship between the impacts of environmental taxes and the resulting benefits for different social groups. In addition, it is even theoretically difficult to draw the line between environmental damages occurring at specific places and fiscal instruments that have the general aim of alleviating pressure on the environment (Meyer-Ohlendorf and Blobel 2008). In particular, environmentally motivated energy taxes are in the first place associated with the aim of combating climate change, where cause and effect are very far from each other in time and place.[2] As a further aspect, there is no straightforward way of expressing benefits from environmental protection in monetary terms. The OECD (1994, cited in Leipprand et al. 2007) claims that, although pollution control benefits tend to be progressively distributed when measured in physical units, they may not be when measured in value terms, as lower-income households appear to value environmental benefits less than upper-income households.

A qualitative link, at least, between environmental taxation and the distribution of environmental effects was identified in the study conducted by Luhmann et al. (1998), which estimated the distributional effects of environmental fiscal reform aimed at reducing road traffic emissions in Berlin. It concluded that 'applying tax measures to improve environmental quality associated with the reduction of road traffic may result in a progressive distribution of the benefits and therefore reduce the extent of regressiveness of the distributive function' (Luhmann et al. 1998: 8). As poorer households in Berlin were discovered to be more exposed to road traffic pollution than wealthier households, which posed a correspondingly greater health risk for them, a tax would result in a progressive distribution of benefits in terms of health risk reductions.

---

[2] Energy use and, in particular, the use of fossil fuels also have environmental effects that relate more directly to local pollution. Energy taxes are therefore sometimes differentiated according to certain environmental characteristics of the energy carrier, other than CO_2 (in the case of the German ecotax, a differentiation has been made between leaded and unleaded petrol, as well as according to the sulphur content of fuels).

10.2.2 Policy options to avoid negative distributional effects

The most important insights resulting from the research summarized above are as follows: (1) there is a risk that ETR will be regressive, i.e. the net burden is highest for lowest-income households and decreasing with income, (2) the absolute financial burden is rather small, (3) the regressivity of environmental taxes is clear concerning energy expenditures, less clear regarding personal transport fuel consumption, and (4) where revenue redistribution is made via lowering social security contributions, households not benefiting from reduced social security payments (the unemployed and retirees) often bear the highest burden. This section discusses policy options to mitigate the negative distributional effects, or enhance the positive social effects, of environmental tax reforms. It includes concepts that have actually been applied, as well as suggestions that have been made in the current debate.

The policy options can broadly be structured into two types: (1) measures on the taxation side, and (2) measures related to the redistribution of revenue. As a third category, one could identify other complementary measures that are not part of an ETR package but are nevertheless suited to modifying its distributional effects. However, the distinction between measures inside or outside the ETR package may be more relevant in terms of political communication than in practical terms. All compensation mechanisms normally entail expenditure from the state budget, or forgone tax revenue, whether a formal link to revenue from environmental taxes is drawn or not. A practical difference, however, remains in that in the case of explicit ecotax revenue redistribution, the amount of budget resources spent is more directly linked to the amount of ecotax revenue. Table 10.2 summarizes some policy options according to the structure mentioned above.

MEASURES ON THE TAXATION SIDE
In Germany, certain ecotax reductions were introduced specifically for social purposes and not all of them were sound from an environmental point of view. The environmentally doubtful electricity tax reductions for night storage heating systems (predominantly used in poorer households) were phased out between 2003 and 2007, while a small proportion of ecotax revenue was used to financially support the modernization of heating systems. Reduced ecotax rates for public transport, in contrast, can be seen as a subsidy serving both social and environmental objectives.

Green Budget Germany (GBG 2008) proposes a *progressive electricity tax*: for instance, low total amounts of electricity consumption could be taxed at 0.5 ct/kWh, average consumption at 2 ct/kWh, and high consumption at 4 ct/kWh. Moreover, GBG advocates abolition of the electricity base fee (or standing charge) and apportionment of electricity costs on the price per kWh.

Table 10.2. Policy options to avoid negative distributional effects of ETR on private households

Option	Example / Source
Taxation side	
tax exemptions	reduction in electricity tax for night storage heating (Germany)
	energy tax reductions for public transport (Germany)
progressive taxation	progressive electricity tax (GBG 2008)
	progressive water/wastewater charges (Portugal)
tax-free basic amounts	Netherlands
choose tax base in a way that richer households are more affected	taxes or charges applied on air traffic (Leipprand et al. 2007)
Redistribution side and/or complementary measures	
eco-bonus	Swiss CO_2 tax
	Herlitzius and Schick 2008
income tax reductions / income tax reform	Sweden
	Germany (Bach et al. 2001)
general support measures for vulnerable households (increase in transfer payments)	GBG 2008
specific support measures for vulnerable households: transfer payments to cover energy costs	means-tested benefit for heating costs (Germany)
specific environmentally-oriented support measures: subsidies for energy-saving investments, public transport etc.	subsidies for replacement of night storage heating (Germany)
	GBG 2008
	Ekins and Dresner (2004)
	McNally and Mabey (1999)
	Netherlands until 2003

These measures would, according to GBG, have positive distributional effects, as poor households have lower energy consumption. Thus, they would profit (a) from the abolition of the base fee and (b) from a reduced tax rate for low electricity consumption. Concerning the latter measure, however, the authors concede that the scope for governmental influence on the tariff design of electricity providers would need to be examined. On tax matters, by contrast, the state has undisputed competency, which underlines the role taxation may have in contributing to a more socially equitable price design for environmental resources. As an example of *progressive environmental charges*, Wier et al. (2005) report that progressive charging in the household sector for water consumption and wastewater treatment is being applied in Portugal.

In the Netherlands, a basic energy tax allowance is granted per year for each household connected to electricity. The amount of the allowance is fixed anew annually; in 2008, it was at 199 euro. Before 2001, the tax allowance was granted instead for certain basic amounts of energy use (800 cubic meters of gas and 800 kWh of electricity). This measure was explicitly introduced in order to mitigate adverse affects on poorer households, recognizing that certain amounts of energy use cannot be avoided. In addition, a special tax allowance is granted for older people, taking into account that they tend to need more heating energy (VROM 2004, 2005). From Denmark, in contrast, Wier et al. (2005) report that the Ministry of Taxation considered the administrative effort required for 'personal green allowances' too high and therefore preferred compensation measures in the form of reductions in other taxes. However, the same authors sound a note of caution with regard to this approach. First, they observe that this solution may be better practised in countries like Denmark, with an overall high taxation level and a broad array of applied tax bases, than in countries with different taxation policies. Second, they warn that where there is only a weak link between environmental taxation and compensation measures applied in other areas, such compensation measures may not be an effective tool to counteract the general perception that environmental taxes are socially unfair.

Leipprand et al. (2007) propose to minimize regressive effects by taxing goods and services primarily used by high-income groups. They cite proposals for taxing kerosene or charging airline tickets as one example (an approach that is also supported by the findings by Aasness and Larson 2002, as cited above). Referring to the less regressive effect of motor fuels in comparison with household energy, they nevertheless point to the fact that average figures tend to mask individual hardships.

REVENUE DISTRIBUTION AND/OR COMPLEMENTARY MEASURES

Recently, various groups have discussed the concept of the 'ecobonus' as a means to neutralize the regressive effects of the ecotax (e.g. Herlitzius and Schick 2008 in a discussion paper for the German Green Party). The concept is based on a system in which environmental taxes are combined with per-capita refunds. In this system, the revenues gained from the ecotax would be redistributed over the population. The amount of the ecobonus would be independent of the energy consumption of the individual recipients. This system is currently practised in Switzerland, where it has been applied to the national CO_2 tax since 2008. Here, the revenues are distributed proportionally over the population and enterprises based in the country. Taxes paid by enterprises are redistributed to enterprises, while the sum is proportionally linked to the employees' wages. Taxes paid by citizens are evenly redistributed to the citizens. In the Swiss canton of Basel City, such a bonus system was first implemented in 1999: revenues from a unit-based charge on electricity are redistributed to local residents and domestic industry through a bonus system. Each consumer receives a fixed payment; companies receive a payment for each employee, which increases with wages up to a maximum determined by the contribution ceiling for unemployment insurance (INFRAS 2003). An earlier Swiss study (INFRAS/ECOPLAN 1998), which investigated the economic and social impacts of different energy tax schemes, showed that redistributing revenues in the form of a per-capita bonus is the most progressive option and creates the most beneficial social effects, although it leads to slightly negative effects on economic development, because it forgoes the opportunity to use the revenues to reduce distortionary taxes.

Income tax reductions as a means to achieve a more equitable distribution of ETR effects have already been mentioned above in the discussion of the Swedish case. A somewhat related discussion can be found in the German case. In their comprehensive assessment of ETR effects, Bach et al. (2001) point out that the ETR should be seen as an integral part of a comprehensive reform package that involved reductions in income tax and increases in child allowance. The impacts on different social groups were modelled both for the ETR alone and for the complete reform package. The results suggest that the regressive effects of the ETR are largely removed when the accompanying changes in income tax are taken into account. Workers and households with children are expected to benefit in particular; among the disadvantaged are 'small numbers of singles and couples without children and with low gross incomes' (Bach et al. 2001: 167). Although this sort of evaluation could be dismissed as somewhat arbitrary, since it mixes environmental policy instruments with non-environmentally related policies, it may support the conclusion that overall, fiscal and social policies can help correct negative distributional impacts from environmental taxes, which may be a better solution than building all correction factors into the environmental policy package itself.

In the German context, Leipprand et al. (2007) mention that social welfare recipients receive a means-tested benefit for heating costs, so that increases in the costs for domestic heating are automatically compensated. Although this institution has been created completely independently of the ETR introduction, it can be seen as a measure that alleviates adverse effects on low-income households. However, transfer payments specifically designed to cover energy costs are problematic from both an environmental and a fiscal point of view: they remove the incentive for the recipient to save energy and, by encouraging excess consumption, strain public budgets to an unnecessary extent (Dünnhoff et al. 2006).

In the UK context, Ekins and Dresner (2004) examined a variety of *compensation packages* that had been proposed for poor households in the event of the introduction of a carbon tax on household energy. All proposed compensation packages proved to be progressive on average for the lowest-income deciles. However, due to the large divergence in energy consumption within income deciles, averages conceal big differences in net gains and losses within each decile. No way was found to ensure that, even with compensation, fuel poverty would not be worsened for those it already most badly affects.

Consequently, Ekins and Dresner have developed and researched two alternative approaches. The first approach is only to impose carbon taxes on households after fuel poverty has been addressed through a government-subsidized insulation programme for low-income households. However, although this plan would help mitigate the social impacts to a small degree, it would not effectively meet environmental objectives because it would still allow for a rise in household carbon emissions for a prolonged period. The second approach is to promote energy efficiency by imposing a 'climate change surcharge' on those households that did not install cost-effective energy efficiency measures within a specified time. This would be enforced by energy audits of homes, beginning with those households best able to afford the measures. Medium- and low-income households unable to pay for these improvements would receive low-cost loans and grants. According to the authors' estimations, implementing such a scheme over ten years would save a minimum of 10% of household carbon emissions (about 4 million tonnes). At the same time, households would save close to £20 billion net present value for an initial investment of £6.4 billion. In addition, by contributing to eradicating fuel poverty, the plan would eventually allow for a non-regressive carbon tax to be imposed, which would lead to further emission reductions in the household sector.

Also in the UK context, McNally and Mabey (1999) present the potential results of two options for mitigating the negative effects of energy taxation on fuel-poor households: the joint introduction of a carbon/energy tax and a lump sum to compensate low-income households for any losses, and a government-sponsored home insulation programme for low-income families. While under the former scheme the government would have to pay indefinitely for continued inefficient energy consumption, the latter scheme encourages conservation and reduces compensation payments, which makes it more effective in the long run. In the context of motor fuel taxes, McNally and Mabey (1999) suggest that part of the revenue could be used for public transport schemes, especially in rural areas.

In the Netherlands, until 2003, around 15% of the revenue from the tax on household energy was used for an *energy premium system* rewarding private households for the purchase of energy-efficient appliances (Duscha et al. 2005).

Finally, the GBG (2008) discussion paper proposes an ecotax redistribution scheme for Germany that would combine various concepts. One-third of the revenues would be used to subsidize investments in energy-efficient equipment, such as refrigerators ('climate bonus'). Another third would be divided over the recipients of transfer payments in order to compensate for rising energy prices ('social bonus'). In so doing, the incentive for energy saving would not be reduced. The last third would be divided over the number of social insurance contributors and disbursed to enterprises on a per-employee basis ('employment bonus'). According to GBG, this scheme would result in higher employment effects than a blanket decrease in non-wage labour costs.

10.2.3 Concluding remarks and discussion

It has been clearly demonstrated for most of the European countries examined that environmental taxes often have regressive effects on private households. The actual distributional impact depends, inter alia, on the subject of taxation: notably, taxes on household energy tend to be clearly regressive, while transport-related taxes have mixed distributional results.

Regressive effects may be mitigated by various redistribution and compensation mechanisms. However, even in the presence of such mechanisms, they often remain to some extent.

In the case of energy taxes at least—which have been by far the most commonly applied taxes in environmental tax reforms—the political scope for further increasing the tax burden may be limited if there are energy price rises in the future. In the past, fuel tax increases coinciding with high oil prices have led to massive protests and policy changes (e.g. in the UK and Germany). In the area of household energy in Germany, hardships imposed on poor households by high energy costs have recently become the subject of intensive debate. It has been estimated that each year, around 0.8 million households in Germany are temporarily cut off from the electricity grid because they were not able to pay their bills (Meyer-Ohlendorf and Blobel 2008).

At the same time, energy taxes tend to have a price-stabilizing effect as their amount is not affected by the price volatility in both energy and carbon markets. They are therefore well-suited to providing long-term price signals that may induce behavioural change and investments. VAT, in contrast, exacerbates price fluctuations, as it is applied on a percentage basis to a price, not to physical units.

Keeping the prices for energy and other environmental resources low cannot be considered an appropriate way of making social policy. Instead, social policy goals should be pursued through measures specifically targeted at improving the situation of poor households, while retaining an incentive to save energy and other resources. This can be done, for example, by adjusting other elements of the taxation system (e.g. income and labour taxation) in a way that contributes to a more even distribution of income, or by increasing overall transfer payments for the poor. At the same time, economic instruments of environmental policy will need to be implemented and communicated in a way that takes into account social considerations very carefully.

In fact, the political acceptability of ETR is likely to depend on complementary measures being introduced to ensure that all parts of the population, even the poorest, can meet their basic needs that depend on natural resources. This is currently not the case, even in rich Western European countries (which is exemplified by excess winter mortality associated with fuel poverty in the UK, as well as by the incidence of poor households being cut off from the power grid in Germany). Rather than making energy cheap across the board, policies should aim at ensuring certain minimum standards for access to energy and transport services for the whole population.

In order to enhance social acceptance, as well as the environmental effectiveness of ecotaxes, it can be recommended that part of the revenue is spent on the support of environmentally friendly investments. This enhances the capacity of those taxed to adjust their consumption behaviour, contributes to an environmental restructuring of the economy, and creates employment. It is also very much in line with current proposals for a 'green new deal' in the face of the economic crisis.

In view of the environmental steering function of ecotaxes, as well as a notion of 'environmental justice', it should be noted that empirical analysis has shown a higher per-capita use of environmental resources by high-income groups, while poorer segments of society, due to their lower levels of consumption, cause less harm to the environment (Pye et al. 2008). While there is limited scope for avoiding or substituting certain basic levels of resource use even if prices are high, excess consumption by high-income groups is not very effectively targeted by ecotaxes as long as the latter remain low in proportion to income. This provides arguments for either granting tax allowances for certain basic amounts of consumption, introducing progressive forms of excise taxes (cf. Ott and Schlüns 2008), or shifting the taxation base to certain goods that are especially consumed by high-income groups.

On the revenue redistribution side, the 'ecobonus' concept has been found effective in neutralizing regressive effects. However, this would reduce the function of ecotaxes to an environmental steering instrument, while completely giving up their fiscal, revenue-raising function. It would also mean giving up the 'double-dividend' concept of generating employment by lowering labour costs. In the German context, proponents of the 'ecobonus' solution have argued that while the ETR as currently implemented has been perceived as socially unbalanced, a per-capita redistribution would gain more popular support. However, there may be some reason to doubt this argument: opinion surveys have shown that the redistribution principle of ETR has been very poorly understood by a large majority of the population. First, they are personally much more aware of the taxation side than the redistribution side and second, to the extent that the redistribution concept is known, it has mostly been considered as illogical because of the view that environmental taxes should be directly redistributed for environmental purposes (Beuermann and Santarius 2002). This suggests that it is far from guaranteed that the ecobonus concept would be better understood.

10.3 Distributional Impacts of ETR in the EU

This section reports an assessment of the distributional impacts of ETR carried out at the European level, 'using the Cambridge Econometrics' European model E3ME. The E3ME model includes 13 different socio-economic groups, including five income quintiles, six groups defined by employment status (including retired), and urban and rural splits.

Of the different elements of the distributional impacts of ETR for households listed at the start of Section 10.2, this section assesses the direct effects and the indirect economic consequences of both environmental taxes and the recycling of revenues through a combination of reductions in employers' taxes and income taxes. The distribution of environmental impacts is much more difficult to quantify and requires a more specialized environmental modelling approach that is beyond what is reported here.

A general outline of the E3ME model can be found in the Appendix to Chapter 8. In this section, the method used to model the impact of ETR on income distribution is first explained, followed by a brief recapitulation of the baseline case and the scenarios used, which have already been described in Chapter 9. Then the results from the modelling exercise are presented, followed by the conclusions drawn from them.

10.3.1 Modelling the impact of ETR on income distribution

The analysis of the distributional implications of ETR for households was carried out using a scenario-based approach. The scenarios in the project are ex ante, meaning that they provide an assessment of future developments under different sets of inputs. So that the effects of the different inputs can be interpreted, we also ran a separate model, referred to as a baseline or business-as-usual case, with no additional inputs. Because the scenarios for the assessment are the same as those presented in Chapter 9, the distributional results in this section are consistent with the more macro-level results presented there.

E3ME, as currently specified, has a relatively simple top-down, partial model treatment of the impact of ETR on different socio-economic groups. This treatment shares some of the characteristics of micro-simulation models and is described in detail in an earlier application of E3ME to ETR and its effects on equity (see Barker and Köhler, 1998). However, this earlier treatment relies on data from 1988, 1992, and 1993 and is restricted to 11 EU Member States. The current version of E3ME (version 4.6) makes use of the household spending survey data for 2005 published by Eurostat in spring 2008, and covers all EU-27 countries individually. The model also includes 13 different socio-economic groups, including five income quintiles, six groups defined by employment status (including retired), and urban and rural splits.

The line of causation in the model is as follows:

- Changes in fuel prices due to ETR will in turn affect industry prices (disaggregated by industry and region). Industry prices are also indirectly affected by other factors in the model, such as wage demands.

- A change in industry prices will subsequently affect consumer prices (disaggregated by consumption category and by region). An average consumer price for each region is calculated by taking a weighted average of the disaggregated consumer prices.

- Nominal incomes (which may be disaggregated only by region, or by region and *socio-economic group*) comprise total wage receipts plus other income such as dividends. Real incomes (disaggregated by region, *but not by socio-economic group*) are calculated by dividing total nominal incomes (disaggregated only by region) by average consumer prices. This is a key factor in determining long-term growth in household consumption.

- Once these variables have been estimated, average consumer prices (disaggregated by *socio-economic group* and region) are estimated by taking a weighted average of consumer prices, but with a different set of weights for each group and region.

- Real incomes (disaggregated by *socio-economic group* and region) are then calculated by dividing nominal incomes (disaggregated by region and *socio-economic group*) by average consumer prices in each group.

It should be noted that this top-down treatment has no feedback (either direct or indirect) from the income distribution variables to the rest of the model, including determination of aggregate household consumption. As the primary effects are of energy prices on income distribution, this seems reasonable. Although real incomes are estimated for each socio-economic group, the model relies on the simplifying assumption that the consumption function is identical for all the groups. This is because the time-series data required for estimating separate consumption functions for each socio-economic group are not available at a European (and in most cases national) level (Germany is an exception and so is presented in a separate case study in later sections). Figure 10.2 demonstrates this relationship, with feedback from the aggregate consumption equations, but not from the results of the income distribution analysis. The indirect effects follow from changes to variables calculated in the rest of the model.

The revenue recycling will have further impacts; reductions in employers' social security contributions will lead to people moving from unemployment

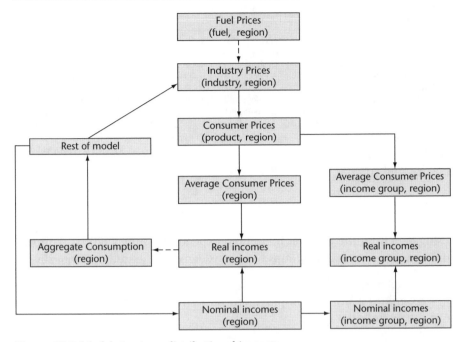

Figure 10.2 Model structure: distributional impacts

Note: A solid line represents a general or identity relationship, a dotted line one that is explicitly estimated using historical time-series data.

to employment (i.e. between socio-economic groups), but is not expected to change the incomes within groups. Reductions in income tax, however, will boost the incomes of all groups where wages make up a share of total income. Nominal incomes (at the foot of Figure 10.2) will therefore increase as a result.

10.3.2 Baseline and scenarios

The baseline is described in Section 9.2.2 of Chapter 9, and will not be further discussed here. The scenarios evaluate the economic and social effects of ETR, with a particular focus on productivity and competitiveness. The four scenarios are designed to highlight these impacts under different sets of background assumptions, described in Section 9.2.3 of Chapter 9. The scenarios are summarized in Table 10.3, which is the same as Table 9.1.

10.3.3 Results

MAIN FINDINGS

This section presents the results from the modelling exercise. The aim of this study was to assess the distributional effects of ETR on household income

Table 10.3. Summary of ETR scenarios

Scenario	LS1	HS1	HS2	HS3
Energy prices	Baseline	High	High	High
CO_2 reduction, 2020	−15%	−15%	−15%	−25%
Materials tax, 2020	15%	15%	15%	15%
Revenue recycling	Employment taxes and income taxes	Employment taxes and income taxes	Low-carbon investment, employment taxes and income taxes	Employment taxes and income taxes
Other				International cooperation

Note: CO_2 reductions are in comparison to 1990 base.
Sources: Cambridge Econometrics, GWS.

using data from the Eurostat household expenditure survey (2005). Thirteen different socio-economic groups were considered in the study, specifically:

- five income quintiles;
- six groups defined by employment status (including retired);
- urban and rural splits.

Real incomes are formed by the combination of nominal incomes and price (inflationary effects), both of which are affected by the scenarios used in the study. In E3ME, incomes are composed of:

- wages;
- non-pension benefits;
- pensions;
- other income (e.g, dividends).

Income taxes and employees' social security contributions are subtracted from this to give a measure of real disposable (i.e. 'take-home') income. The composition of each group's disposable income varies (for example, the retired group are heavily dependent on pensions). However, in the PETRE scenarios, benefits and pensions were index-linked to wages, so gross income in each group tends to grow by the same amount. This is an important assumption as, if benefits are indexed to general prices, groups relying on benefits would gain by less. There is, however, variation in income tax rates.

Following from the PETRE results, there are increases in real incomes in all the groups in all of the scenarios in 2020 at the EU level (see Table 10.4). This increase is in the region of 1.5% in the scenarios with higher carbon prices (in LS1 due to lower oil prices and in HS3 due to a higher carbon-reduction target) where there are larger sums of revenue available for recycling, and up to 1% in the other scenarios. Note that if benefits were fixed in nominal terms, the outcomes would most likely be negative for groups relying on benefits.

Table 10.4. Change in real income—EU results, 2020, E3ME

	LS1	HS1	HS2	HS3
All households	1.46	0.62	0.95	1.58
Expenditure groups				
First quintile	1.51	0.63	0.87	1.70
Second quintile	1.43	0.62	0.92	1.59
Third quintile	1.38	0.60	0.92	1.51
Fourth quintile	1.44	0.63	0.96	1.57
Fifth quintile	1.56	0.68	1.03	1.67
Socio-economic groups				
Manual workers	1.40	0.61	0.95	1.52
Non-manual workers	1.41	0.63	0.98	1.52
Self-employed	1.31	0.58	0.95	1.41
Unemployed	0.79	0.41	0.65	1.03
Retired	1.06	0.49	0.75	1.28
Inactive	0.14	0.13	0.34	0.36
Population density				
Urban	1.60	0.70	1.00	1.75
Rural	1.31	0.57	0.89	1.44

Note: Figures show percentage difference from the respective baseline (i.e. L or H) in real incomes in each group, 2020, EU-27.
Sources: E3ME, Cambridge Econometrics.

It is important to note that these results only show averages for each group. This is as detailed as the survey data go but there could be considerable variation within groups. For example, within one group, different individuals may have more or less efficient central heating systems installed or there may be differences in the level of insulation in their homes. Car ownership within groups may also vary and the size and fuel efficiency of cars may differ, affecting the amount of income that is spent on them. A final point to note is that, depending on whether individuals are on fixed or flexible contracts, the impacts on nominal wages will vary in response to higher inflation rates. Those workers who are on flexible contracts are not tied in for long periods of time so have far more bargaining opportunities than those on fixed contracts, and hence may see larger increases in their real incomes because of this.

The following three sections provide interpretation of the results according to the category of the groups, i.e. the expenditure groups, the socio-economic groups, and population density. The possible reasons for the differences across groups follow those discussed above, and the results are generally consistent.

EXPENDITURE GROUPS

There are several general trends that can be identified within the different scenarios. First, perhaps unexpectedly, it is not the lowest-income groups that lose out relatively to the other groups, it is in fact the middle-income quintiles where real incomes increase by the least. The reason for this is that they spend a larger share of their incomes on heating and transport fuels combined, while the lower-income households do not tend to own cars (and the high-income households spend relatively less on fuel).

The exception to this is HS2, where the lowest-income group is the one that gains the least, and the ETR is slightly regressive across all the income groups. The main factor behind this is that a share of the revenue is recycled into investment in low-carbon technologies, leading to larger gains in vehicle efficiency. This disproportionately benefits the higher-income groups who spend more on transport fuels.

SOCIO-ECONOMIC GROUPS

The trends within the socio-economic employment groups are clearer. In all scenarios, the unemployed and the inactive groups experience the smallest increases in real incomes, whilst the retired also benefit less than other working groups. This result occurs because these groups do not gain anything from lower income tax rates. On the other hand, manual and non-manual workers and the self-employed experience larger increases in real income, with HS3 producing the greatest changes for all groups.

Manual and non-manual workers see similar increases in their real incomes, whereas the self-employed experience slightly less of an increase. This could be due to the effect that higher energy prices might have on business profitability and hence dividends, especially if they cannot completely pass these costs on via increased prices.

POPULATION DENSITY

The results show that urban households see a larger increase in real incomes than rural households in all scenarios. Living in a rural area often means that fuel consumption is higher due to the need to drive further and more frequently to reach amenities, workplaces, schools, and so on. Those living in cities may infrequently use their cars or not own a car at all if it is more feasible to walk, cycle, or use public transport. Furthermore, rural households often spend more on heating homes, due to older, poorer central heating systems or insulation. Rural homes are also larger and more likely to be detached on average than urban dwellings, further increasing heating expenditure.

The smallest difference in the change in real incomes between urban and rural households exists in scenario HS2, reflecting the advantages that revenue recycling for investment in low-carbon technologies would bring to rural households, through improvements in heating systems and, in particular, vehicle fuel efficiency.

VARIATION BETWEEN MEMBER STATES

When considering each individual Member State separately, the results for LS1, which has some of the biggest changes (the broad conclusions would be the same for the other scenarios), show that there is considerable variation in the changes in income between countries. These results are presented in Figure 10.3. It is evident that there is much more difference in the changes in income between countries than within countries. Whilst the changes in income are usually fairly similar for each income group within one country, the differences between countries are often large. For instance, whilst all income quintiles within the UK experience changes in income of around 1%, in Slovakia the changes in income are reported to be around 6.5%.

There are several reasons why the variations in changes in income occur:

• different macroeconomic outcomes in the scenarios;
• different patterns of source of income;
• different expenditure patterns in each group.

In almost all cases, there are increases in real incomes. However, it should also be noted that in Greece, Spain, Ireland, and Hungary, a fall or no change in real incomes is reported in one of the income groups. These results always occur in

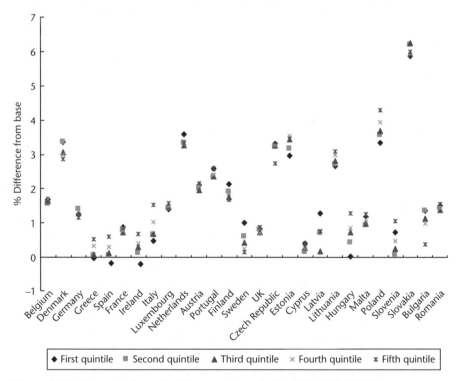

Figure 10.3 Change in household income by quintile, LS1, 2020, E3ME

the lowest-income quintile, mainly because individuals within these groups do not have to pay a large amount of income tax but do spend a large proportion of their income on energy for heating. In these cases the reductions in income tax do not outweigh the negative effects of higher energy prices.

In these particular countries, it is also often the case that the groups are rather spread out in terms of their gains in real incomes, with the highest-income group experiencing the largest increase in their real incomes. This suggests that income distribution becomes more unequal due to ETR. For example, in Hungary, the lowest-income quintile sees no increase in real incomes, yet the highest-income group enjoys an increase of around 1.5%.

10.3.4 Conclusions

The modelling results showed that, at an EU aggregate level, the ETR would generally create a positive change in real incomes for all socio-economic groups and hence encourage employment, supporting the case for future ETR in the EU. In most countries, and at the aggregate EU level, the impacts were not found to be regressive across income groups.

However, the results also show that the different socio-economic groups may gain by different amounts according to their income status, their employment status, or whether they live in an urban or rural area. First, those groups that do not pay income taxes, i.e. the unemployed, the inactive, or the retired, generally see a smaller increase in their real incomes than the employed or self-employed. Those who are not in work will not see very much of an increase in their real incomes as they do not benefit from the reduction in income taxes. Second, a similar divide can be seen between the urban and rural groups. For both groups there is a positive change in real incomes, but in all scenarios the urban population experience greater increases than the rural group due to the smaller amount they spend on both transport and heating fuels. As for the income groups, the middle-income quintiles seem to have the smallest increases in real incomes in most scenarios, due to the larger share of their income which is spent on both transport fuels and heating costs. The highest-income group do not spend as large a proportion of their income on these expenditures, whilst those individuals within the lowest-income group often do not own cars so do not encounter the associated increase in fuel costs.

For all groups, HS3 creates the largest increases in real incomes. In this scenario, there is international cooperation between the EU and other external nations. The EU consequently reduces GHG emissions by 30% via higher carbon prices, whilst other countries make comparable reductions. The revenue that is generated from this version of ETR is recycled via greater reductions in income taxes, leading to the greater increases in real incomes seen in the results. This scenario is particularly attractive therefore, as the so-called 'double dividend', whereby employment is stimulated whilst the environment is improved, is increased.

Prior to investigation, it might be assumed that the lowest-income group would gain the least from any ETR. However, the results show that this is not the case, and that in fact the middle-income groups, particularly the third quintile, see the smallest increase in their real incomes for the aforementioned reasons. These results are broadly consistent with those discussed in the literature review in this report.

Then again, there are several countries in which the lowest-income quintile actually experiences no change or in fact a slight fall in their real incomes, suggesting that the trade-off between decreased income taxes and increased fuel costs is negative. Furthermore, it can be seen that in these particular countries there is a big difference between the gains experienced by the richest and the poorest quintiles, suggesting that ETR could in fact create a less equal distribution of income.

ETR could therefore be challenged by interest groups or the individuals from those groups that lose out from the reforms. Alternative arrangements for support may therefore be required to make ETR politically feasible. Regulatory changes (for example, promotion of electric vehicles) that would reduce energy and material consumption without increasing prices may also be desirable, but neither these nor the impacts of support for particular socio-economic groups are considered here.

The conclusion from this exercise is that it is possible for ETR to stimulate employment, as real incomes could be increased through a decrease in income taxes. There is therefore potential for a double dividend, in which employment is increased and the environment is improved. However, the policy must be carefully formulated in detail so as to minimize the negative impacts of the reforms on particular socio-economic groups.

10.4 Distributional Impacts of ETR in Germany

This section analyses the distributional impacts on households in Germany of an environmental tax reform (ETR), whereby a carbon tax of €68/tCO$_2$ in 2020 is introduced in the non-ETS sector (this is the rate that formed the basis of the end-user price analysis in Section 9.5.6 of Chapter 9), revenues from which amount to around 1% of GDP.

Using the established structural macroeconometric model PANTA RHEI and a socio-economic extension of the underlying INFORGE system called DEMOS, we analyse the repercussions of an ETR for the German economy as a whole, and, in particular, for the consumption patterns of 25 types of households in the year 2020. For each household type in DEMOS, the modelling involves spending on 41 consumption expenditure categories. These categories include expenditures on electricity, gas, and other fuels, as well as transport, and they are immediately affected by the price changes set in motion by the reform and calculated with PANTA RHEI.

The structure of this section is as follows. A short analysis of historical data is followed by a description of the modelling tools, PANTA RHEI and DEMOS. Then come the modelling assumptions and results of the study, and the conclusions drawn from them.

10.4.1 Historical distribution patterns

In order to assess the distributional impacts of ETR, it is useful first to examine historical data describing the income situation of various groups and types of households, as well as their consumption patterns.

Table 10.5 shows the distribution of disposable incomes across household types in 2004, which is the last year for which comprehensive official income data with a breakdown into subcategories of the non-employed group were available at the time of writing. The data indicate the degree of after-tax inequality between different socio-economic groups, living in five groups of households distinguished by size. Household groups are defined by the main source of income accruing to the main income recipient of a given household. There are five categories of households in each group, i.e. households with one person (1 Phh), two persons (2 Phh), three persons (3 Phh), four persons (4 Phh), and five or more persons (5+ Phh).

It may be seen from Table 10.5 that the households whose main income recipients are described as 'self-employed' receive a multiple value of the average income accruing to households (given by the last row of the table). The employees' incomes are more or less similar to the average, especially

Table 10.5. Average disposable incomes for different household types, 2004 (in euros)

	1 Phh	2 Phh	3 Phh	4 Phh	5+ Phh
Self-employed	80200	113400	108100	120900	135500
Employees	23100	41200	46000	52100	54000
Public officials	29700	54700	59900	65100	70400
Salaried employees	24700	44900	50700	58400	61500
Wage earners	17800	31200	37500	41800	44800
Not employed	15500	27600	34600	40900	40200
Unemployed	9700	20700	26300	34100	30400
Retirees (excl. public officials)	15900	26800	38800	46800	52800
Retired public officials	28400	45500	61000	n.a.	n.a.
Welfare recipients	8700	13900	17200	21200	28400
All households	21000	37700	48900	59000	63000

Source: Federal Statistical Office of Germany (2008: 238–9).

those of salaried employees constituting the majority of such households (almost 52% of employee households and 25% of all households). Among employees, wage earners receive the lowest, while public officials the highest remunerations in this group. Independent of size, households of not-employed persons have less income at their disposal than the average. Here, there is a significant difference between retired persons with higher incomes (among the retired, a small group of former public officials receive disproportionately high pensions) and the lower-income groups of unemployed and welfare recipients.

In order to simplify the analysis and make the results more comparable in the international context, the subsequent results and their discussion will refer to only five groups and five household sizes. In DEMOS, nine socioeconomic groups are part of the model, which is important when specific details of the German system are emphasized. The data can later be aggregated as required, as is done here. The groups are the households of self-employed, employees, retirees, unemployed (including welfare recipients), and a residual category called 'others', which consists of not-employed persons receiving the main part of their incomes from dividend payments, rental activities, or relatives, which renders this heterogeneous group hard to interpret but is required for completeness of the analysis.

Table 10.6 shows the relative weight of these household types according to their number. It reveals that the biggest groups of households—employees and retirees—constitute 80% of all households. Interestingly, among the two smallest household sizes, the shares of retiree households are the biggest.

Before the ETR impacts are studied, we also take a look at the consumption structure of the status groups involved, as depicted in Tables A10.1 and A10.2 in the Appendix. The data are from the year 2002, which is the last historical time-point of the consumption modelling for which DEMOS uses original structural data from the German Federal Statistical Office. In Table A10.1, the shares of 41 consumption categories, as well as 13 sub-aggregates in total consumption, of each household group are displayed. Among these categories, the ones most directly affected by the ETR appear in italics. The data

Table 10.6. Percentage shares of household types in total number of households, 2004

	1 Phh	2 Phh	3 Phh	4 Phh	5+ Phh	total
Self-employed	1.6	2.1	1.4	1.4	0.6	7.0
Employees	13.1	12.2	8.7	7.7	2.6	44.4
Retirees	16.4	16.5	2.0	0.5	0.2	35.6
Unemployed	3.8	2.6	1.5	1.0	0.6	9.5
Others	2.1	0.9	0.4	0.2	0.0	3.5
total	37.0	34.2	14.0	10.7	4.0	100.0

show that low-income households, i.e. the retirees and unemployed, spend a disproportionately high share of their consumption expenditure on electricity, gas, and other fuels, whereas the share of the self-employed is close to the average and the share of employees is below average. Therefore, it could be intuitively expected that higher prices for energy would have a regressive impact on household expenditure, i.e. be disproportionately disadvantageous for the poorest households in terms of additional spending relative to income, without additional adjustments. Not quite as clear-cut are the implications of data referring to transport expenditures, especially the category 'operation of personal transport equipment', on which the employed spend an above-average share of their total spending, whereas the poorer households, who do not use automobiles so much, spend a lower share. The category 'operation of personal transport equipment' includes spare parts, accessories, fuels, lubricants, maintenance, repair, and other services related to personal transport equipment.

Table A10.2 presents a different view on household consumption, showing the shares for the respective groups in total consumption of single product groups and their aggregates. For energy consumption, it becomes clear that while employee households consume almost 44% of the total, this share lies below their share of all consumption categories (presented in the last row of the table), which amounts to nearly 49%. Conversely, higher relative shares are spent by poorer households (retirees and unemployed), while the share for the self-employed does not greatly differ from their average spending behaviour, which is also true of the two other relevant consumption categories. Among remaining groups, the spending patterns vary, probably reflecting car ownership and usage across these groups. Consequently, the share of spending on the 'operation of personal transport equipment' is disproportionately high for employees, related to their average share, and also very large in absolute terms (57.1%), while the groups partly excluded from car use, again retirees and the unemployed, devote less than their average consumption share to this category. In contrast, employees use relatively less public transportation, which is reflected in their less-than-average share, while the unemployed spend significantly more on transport services.

10.4.2 Models Used

The ETR modelling in this section relies on two models, PANTA RHEI and DEMOS, which are described in the following subsections.

PANTA RHEI

To quantify ETR effects, the macroeconometric model PANTA RHEI is used. PANTA RHEI is an ecologically extended version (Bach et al. 2002; Lutz et al. 2005: Meyer et al. 2007a: Lutz et al. 2007; Lehr et al. 2008) of the 59-sector

Figure 10.4 Simplified model structure of PANTA RHEI

econometric simulation and forecasting model INFORGE (Meyer et al. 2007b). The INFORGE model, which depicts the German economy in great detail, is linked via detailed housing and transport modules to the German energy balance and related CO_2 emissions. Demographic development, international variables such as energy prices and growth of world trade, and more technical parameters such as heating values are among the exogenous variables.

The extension consists of a deeply disaggregated energy and pollution model, disaggregated according to the energy balance, as shown in Figure 10.4. From the modelling aspects, PANTA RHEI belongs to the class of econometric input-output models. Its advantages are the ability to model bounded rationality decisions and the broad empirical database. PANTA RHEI is built fully integrated and bottom up. The latter principle means that each sector of the economy is modelled in great detail and the macroeconomic aggregates are calculated by explicit aggregation. The model describes inter-industry flows between the 59 sectors, their deliveries to personal consumption, government, equipment, investment, construction, changes in stocks, exports, as well as prices, wages, output, imports, employment, labour compensation, profits, taxes, and so on, and describes income redistribution in full detail. One further strength of the model is its high level of interdependence, for instance between prices and wages or between prices and volumes.

Final demand is determined by the disposable income of private households, interest rates and profits, world trade variables, and the relative prices of all components and product groups of final demand. For all intermediate inputs, imports and domestic origins are distinguished. Given final and intermediate demand, final production and imports are derived. Employment is determined by the production volume and the real wage rate in each sector, which in turn depends on labour productivities and prices.

The effects of a given policy measure are calculated by comparing different simulations of the model, called scenarios, one using a reference development without the measure (the baseline) and one—or more—that include a policy measure. A comparison of the effects on the macroeconomic indicators then shows the net economic effects, for example on the labour market, on GDP etc.

DEMOS

In order to provide a socio-economic extension to the existing INFORGE/ PANTA RHEI models, the DEMOS module has been developed. Its first version was completed in 2004 and focused on labour market disaggregation by formal qualification. In the new version (DEMOS II, see Drosdowski and Wolter 2008), labour market modelling has been extended through the use of more comprehensive time-series data, making deeper analyses possible. However, the main upgrade was the inclusion of detailed household data consistent with the German system of national accounts (SNA).

The system contains differentiated household structures, information about their income generation and distribution, as well as consumption patterns (Figure 10.5). The time-series data used (historically from 1991 to 2004) encompass 45 household categories, combining nine socio-economic groups and five different household sizes. Both demographic and economic developments drive the structural composition of households. At each point in time, every type of household receives specific market income flows (wages, salaries, and profits), is subject to taxation and social security payments, and receives government transfers. The redistributed primary incomes yield disposable incomes that are subsequently devoted to consumption and saving.

Each type of household displays a distinct consumption structure using its disposable income on 41 expenditure categories. The single consumption categories vary over time according to group-specific income developments and price changes, generating structural shifts in consumption and therefore

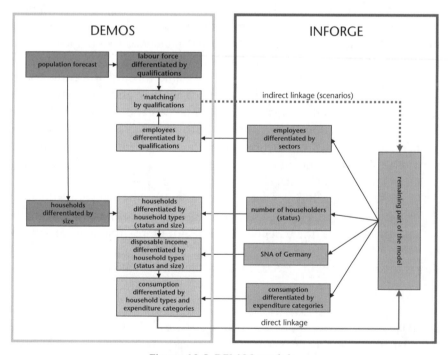

Figure 10.5 DEMOS module

changing consumption patterns across groups. The paths of different consumption items rely on empirically estimated relationships, which amount to almost 2000 in total. Such a complex approach is required in order to adequately capture the varying influences on consumption for heterogeneous groups that do not respond to income or price changes in a uniform way.

Integrated with INFORGE, DEMOS is well-equipped to analyse policy changes by means of simulations. For instance, exogenous politically initiated price changes affect all markets and households simultaneously, leading to changing income and consumption patterns within and between household types over time. In this chapter, however, constant consumption structures for the year 2020, along with a constant distribution of disposable incomes between household types, generated by DEMOS, are used to analyse distributional impacts. In particular, we assume a constant distribution of each consumption expenditure category between household types, analysing the effects of price changes and behavioural adjustments caused by the ETR and given by PANTA RHEI.

10.4.3 Scenario assumptions and results

SCENARIO ASSUMPTIONS
This section uses the same scenarios as described in Section 9.2 of Chapter 9. In one of these scenarios, HS1, a carbon price €68/tCO$_2$ is needed in 2020 to reach the EU unilateral 20% emissions reduction target. This carbon price is used in PANTA RHEI, with the tax revenues recycled through reductions in income tax rates and social security contributions, as described in Chapter 9.

AGGREGATE IMPACTS OF THE ETR IN PANTA RHEI
The overall macroeconomic impact of the introduction of a carbon tax in the non-ETS sector increasing to €68/tCO$_2$ in 2020 is very small. Table 10.7 shows that the price increase in carbon-intensive products leads to an overall increase in the consumer price index (CPI). Among prices for consumption expenditure categories, the price for 'electricity, gas and other fuels' increases by 21%, while the price for 'operation of personal transport equipment' increases by 15%. As ETR revenues are recycled via reductions in social security contributions, labour costs decrease, which is the main driver for the additional employment of 152,000 in 2020 against the baseline. The employment increase is concentrated in trade and service sectors (see Table 10.8).

PROJECTED DISTRIBUTIONAL IMPACTS, DEMOS
In order to study distributional impacts, some structural data from DEMOS for 2020 are taken and combined with information from both PANTA RHEI scenarios (BH and HS1). The burden of the ETR is measured as the relative

Table 10.7. Macroeconomic impacts of scenario HS1 in Germany—deviations from baseline BH in 2020, PANTA RHEI

	absolute values	deviation in %
GDP (Bill. € in 2000 prices)	−0.1	0.0
Household Consumption	3.3	0.2
Government Consumption	2.0	0.4
Equipment	0.6	0.2
Construction	0.2	0.1
Exports	−0.4	0.0
Imports	3.3	0.2
CPI (2000 = 100)	2.25	1.84
Disposable income (nominal)	23.2	1.2
Employment in 1000	152	0.4

Note: Unit of disposable income is € billion.

Table 10.8. Sectoral employment effects of ETR, PANTA RHEI

	absolute values			deviation in %		
	2010	**2015**	**2020**	**2010**	**2015**	**2020**
Employment						
Agriculture, hunting, forestry and fishing	1.1	2.9	4.5	0.2	0.6	0.8
Mining and quarrying	1.2	3.7	6.2	1.4	5.6	12.5
Manufacturing	3.2	1.1	−5.9	0.0	0.0	−0.1
Electricity, gas and water supply	0.8	1.7	2.2	0.3	0.7	1.1
Construction	2.6	4.3	5.5	0.1	0.2	0.3
Wholesale and retail trade, repair	12.5	29.3	39.3	0.2	0.6	0.7
Hotels and restaurants	7.2	17.1	24.3	0.5	1.0	1.4
Transport, storage and communications	5.2	12.3	17.9	0.3	0.7	1.0
Financial intermediation	0.4	0.9	1.1	0.0	0.1	0.1
Real estate, renting and business activities	5.9	13.4	18.4	0.1	0.3	0.3
Public administration and defence, social sec.	13.6	26.3	33.4	0.5	1.1	1.4
Education	3.0	5.4	5.3	0.1	0.3	0.3
Health and social work	0.2	1.0	−0.7	0.0	0.0	0.0
Other community, social and personal services	2.7	6.2	7.7	0.2	0.4	0.4
Private households with employed persons	−1.2	−3.5	−6.7	−0.2	−0.5	−0.9
Total	**58.2**	**122**	**152**	**0.2**	**0.3**	**0.4**

shift of the expenditure share of each household type compared to the aggregate/average household structure. Figure 10.6 presents the total impact of the ETR on household consumption relative to disposable income across household types in relation to the same share for the average household. The zero line represents the percentage-point change in the ratio of total consumption to total disposable income (average share), as a basis for inter-household comparisons. The same normalization will apply to the analysis of single expenditure items discussed below.

The figure clearly indicates that the ETR contributes to expenditure shifts between household types and groups. Poorer households boost their total

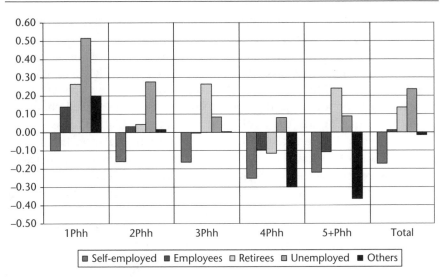

Figure 10.6 Total ETR burden across household types (in percentage points)

energy and transport expenditure shares, in percentage points of disposable income relative to the average, disproportionately highly in comparison with other household types. Overall, the group with the highest burden, particularly among smaller households, is the group of unemployed households, whose additional expenditures are visible for all household sizes. Since on average the household types belonging to the unemployed are indebted (they have consumption shares exceeding one), the indebtedness of these households increases slightly. Retiree households, the second poorest group, also realize the second-highest overall increases. They are highest for three-person households and households with five or more persons. However, retirees living in four-person households have a lower share of additional total spending in their disposable income. Contrary to the unemployed realizing only additional burdens compared to the average, the group of self-employed realizes only relative reductions, i.e. disproportionately low burdens, in their consumption shares in disposable income, leading to higher savings, since the disposable income gains are positive for all household types.

Among employee households, the overall change in expenditure shares relative to the average is declining in household size, being positive for single households and two-person households and negative for bigger ones. Overall, the share for employee households does not deviate from the average household. Finally, the group of 'others' displays large increases among relatively poor single households and large reductions for the two largest household types. As Table 10.5 shows, the smaller households in this group are among the poorest overall, whereas the largest households receive the highest incomes. This difference is probably explained by the heterogeneity of income sources for this particular group.

In order to clarify the result that additional total expenditure (total burden) as a share of disposable income associated with the ETR decreases with income, we ranked the household types according to their average disposable income, from the lowest to the highest, and plotted the ranked change in expenditure share against them (from the lowest to the highest increase). The result showed in Figure 10.7 clearly displays a negative relationship, i.e. the poorest households located on the left-hand side of the income scale realize the highest relative burdens, which is a regressive outcome.

The results suggest that the poorest households may be forced to carry the burden of the ETR by increasing their expenditure shares and thus indebtedness. Now, it is instructive to analyse the expenditure share changes pertaining to the relevant expenditure categories, which are also included in Table A10.4 in the Appendix.

Consequently, Figure 10.8 shows the percentage-point changes of shares of energy expenditures in disposable income across household types relative to the change of the average energy expenditure share in disposable income.

The figure shows that the expenditure shares of energy for the poorer households increase, while the shares for higher-income households decrease, capturing the regressivity of the ETR measures related to energy prices and confirming the empirical evidence found in previous studies. The rising

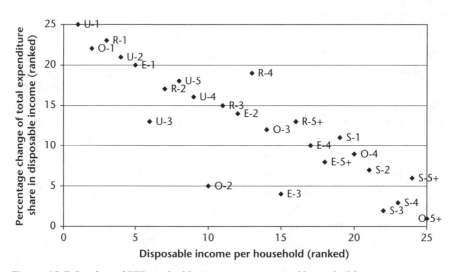

Figure 10.7 Burden of ETR ranked by income position of household types

Note: Letters denote groups (S: self-employed, E: employed, R: retirees, U: unemployed, O: others); digits denote size (e.g. 5+ stands for households with five or more persons). The numbers along the axes indicate rank (from low (0) to high (25)).

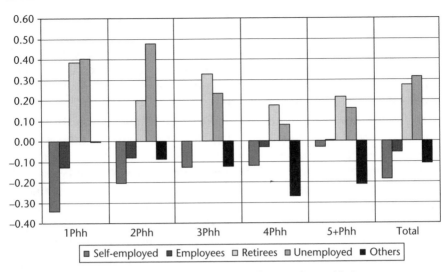

Figure 10.8 Additional energy expenditure as a share in disposable income across households in comparison with the average (in percentage points)

expenditure share of energy partly explains the nature of changes in total consumption as a share of disposable incomes for those groups shown in Figure 10.8. Remember that the shares of energy for poorer households are relatively highest as Tables A10.1 and A10.2 in the Appendix indicate. The ETR increases their share of energy in their consumption structure still more disproportionately as Table A10.3 (in the Appendix) shows. Note that the nominal consumption shares of all expenditure categories (in italics), outside those positively affected by the ETR, decline.

The results for 'electricity, gas and other fuels' from Table A10.3 show that the share increases for the unemployed and retirees are above the average, whereas the additional shares for the other groups are below it. However, the situation is different when the shares of 'operation of personal transport equipment' in comparison with the average share across household groups are considered. Here, the shares for employee households are above the average, the share for the self-employed is close to the average, while the shares for the two poorest groups are below it. The distribution of share gains reflects the initial distribution of consumption spending related to this category, which is skewed towards employee households that operate and own the largest share of cars in society. Not surprisingly, higher prices for this expenditure item affect their consumption disproportionately. At the opposite extreme, household groups owning and using relatively fewer automobiles increase their shares of total expenditure to a more moderate extent. Even though the consumption structure changes, however, the expenditure shares in disposable income of items other than those directly affected by ETR-induced price increases do not significantly decline, as seen in Table A10.4.

Figure 10.9, displaying the difference between percentage-point expenditure changes in disposable income for single-household types and the percentage-point change of consumption in disposable income for the average household, provides additional insight.

The results show that the group of employee households devotes disproportionately more of its disposable income than other household groups to this kind of expenditure. However, unemployed households are also forced to spend a larger share on this consumption category, especially households with five or more persons, three persons, and two persons. The additional burden for the latter is the highest for household groups of this size. Although retiree households spend the highest additional share among the biggest households as well as a significant share among three-person households, they have the biggest share reductions relative to the average among single households. Since the old-age population constitutes the largest group among single households (over 40% in 2004), the share for all retiree households declines. As in the previous case for energy, self-employed households spend less than the average.

The patterns seen in Figure 10.9 do not allow a clear-cut conclusion that the impact of this expenditure category is regressive or progressive, since both low-income and high-income groups are positively or negatively affected. The

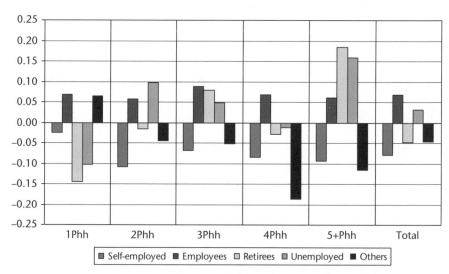

Figure 10.9 Additional expenditure on 'operation of personal transport equipment' as a share of disposable income in comparison with the average share (in percentage points)

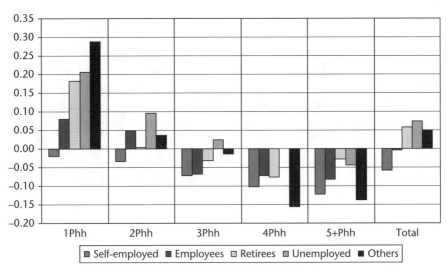

Figure 10.10 Additional expenditure share for transport services in disposable income across households in comparison to the average share (in percentage points)

literature reviewed in Section 10.2 reports mixed results for this category as well.

The last consumption item directly affected by the ETR is the category 'transport services'. As Table A10.3 indicates, the percentage-point change in the structure of all household groups does not differ from the average. However, an analysis of changes of expenditure shares in disposable income shows some distributional shifts, as seen in Figure 10.10.

The additional expenditure shares decline with rising household size, being especially big and positive for poorer single households. Across household groups, the unemployed, the retired, and other non-employees display disproportionately high burdens, while employees and the self-employed spend less than the average. These patterns clearly display the regressivity of the ETR measures.

In order to provide some additional evidence that the ETR implies regressive outcomes, we also present the changes in the share of food consumption in disposable income across household types relative to average change (in percentage points) (Figure 10.11). The food example is chosen, because it is the only relevant spending category besides vehicle purchases that is significantly negatively affected by the ETR in terms of disposable income (see Table A10.4 in the Appendix).

Figure 10.11 shows clearly that the unemployed reduce their disposable income shares of spending on food disproportionately, followed by retirees, who also reduce all their shares, even if not that strongly. On the other hand,

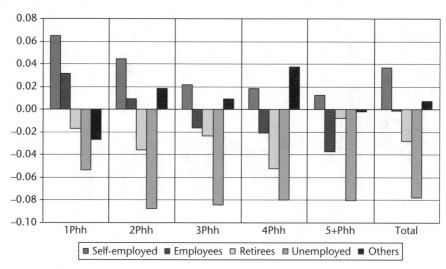

Figure 10.11 Changes in the share of expenditure on food in disposable income across household types relative to average change (in percentage points)

the self-employed, in previous examples always seen to be reducing their shares, now increase their share of consumption in this category. Among employee households, the two smaller categories increase their shares, while the larger household types decrease them. Overall, retirees and the unemployed display consumption reductions, while the self-employed increase their consumption share. Employee households, however, stay put more or less.

In sum, the distributional impact of the ETR is regressive, because poorer households disproportionately increase their expenditure shares on environmentally related goods that they cannot easily avoid. As seen in the food example, they are also forced to consume a smaller amount of basic items, for which they usually spend higher shares of their disposable incomes.

Finally, in order to provide additional intuition, the effects of the ETR across household groups can also be quantified. Table 10.9 shows in euros the additional expenditures on the environmentally related consumption items discussed, along with percentage changes in shares of disposable income included in parentheses and taken from Table A10.4.

It is clear that the additional burden is rather moderate for household groups, even the unemployed and retirees in the case of energy expenditures, especially given the fact that the additional shares of disposable income spent on energy never exceed 1%. Thus, an adequate average compensation of the poorest households would be rather easy and inexpensive. Given this additional insight, it can be stated that the study confirms the main findings of the related literature, demonstrating that on average ETR is only mildly regressive,

Table 10.9. Changes in nominal expenditures across households due to ETR (euros)

	Self-empl.	Empl.	Retirees	Unempl.	Others
Electricity, gas and other fuels	830	350	294	222	172
	(0.5)	(0.6)	(0.9)	(1.0)	(0.6)
Operation of personal transport equipment	556	276	112	101	110
	(0.3)	(0.4)	(0.3)	(0.4)	(0.3)
Transport services	378	157	106	81	102
	(0.2)	(0.3)	(0.3)	(0.4)	(0.3)

Note: The consumption changes in percentage points of disposable income are included in parentheses.

especially concerning energy consumption. It may, however, be far more difficult to identify and compensate high-consuming households among the poorest households.

10.4.4 Conclusions on ETR in Germany

The analysis of an additional ETR in Germany confirms the most important results of related studies for Germany, concluding that such reforms are expected to, or do actually, involve slightly regressive effects on households' expenditure. Accordingly, lower-income groups not benefiting from reduced social security contributions, such as the unemployed and retirees, incur the highest burdens in terms of additional expenditure on environmentally related goods and services whose prices are changed due to the ETR, which is especially true for energy expenditure. Employee households are not particularly affected in their overall consumption in comparison to the average household, even though their nominal expenditure on motor fuels increases disproportionately. On the other hand, the self-employed, which is the highest-income household group of all those analysed, reduce their share of expenditure on energy and transport in disposable income in relation to the average. The analysis also shows that the ETR is associated with higher employment, lower unemployment, and higher disposable income at the macro level. Because the use of revenues from environmental taxes is crucial for the distributional effects of an ETR, part of the additional incomes could be redistributed in order to correct its regressive effects.

10.5 Conclusions on ETR and household distribution

The results indicate that a large-scale ETR in Europe would have the least favourable effects for lower-income households, mainly consisting of the unemployed and retired people. In the E3ME case, where the ETR increases disposable income across Europe, these households experience the lowest proportional increase in income. In the modelling of the German case, the analysis was carried out in terms of expenditure shares in relation to the average household, and showed that poorer households experience the highest increase in expenditure shares on household energy. The effect on middle-income households is close to the average, while the effect on richer households is below the average. However, the distributional effects are different across expenditure categories. While they are particularly clear in the case of household energy expenditure, they are less pronounced in the case of operation of personal transport equipment. Hence it may be concluded that the projected outcome of ETR is regressive.

However, two important qualifications to this conclusion need to be made. The first is that, if (as in both modelled cases) ETR causes average incomes to rise overall, then all households may be made better off in absolute terms—it is just that lower-income households may benefit the least relatively speaking. This is therefore not a policy outcome that makes lower-income households actually worse off.

The second is that the magnitude of the regressive effect is small, with the results from Germany suggesting that the additional expenditure burden for the worst affected social group will not exceed 1% of disposable income.

It is certainly possible to compensate low-income households on average for these effects out of the extra income generated by the ETR, or through a judicious redistribution of some of the environmental tax revenues. However, this compensation may be more difficult for those low-income households that use most energy for transport or for heating their homes.

APPENDIX

Table A10.1. Shares of consumption expenditures across household groups, 2002 (in %)

No.	Category	Self-empl.	Empl.	Retirees	Unempl.	Others	Avg.
		Household group					
1	Food	8.8	10.0	10.6	12.8	9.3	10.1
2	Non-alcoholic beverages	1.4	1.5	1.3	1.8	1.3	1.5
3	Alcoholic beverages	1.4	1.7	1.8	1.9	1.5	1.7
4	Tobacco	1.5	2.3	1.2	3.8	1.8	1.9
5	Clothing	5.1	5.1	4.5	3.9	4.3	4.8
6	Footwear	0.9	0.9	0.8	0.9	0.8	0.9
7	Actual rentals for housing	5.0	6.6	7.8	14.6	9.5	7.2
8	Imputed rentals for housing	10.7	8.7	10.7	6.1	8.7	9.5
9	Maintenance and repair of the dwelling	0.7	0.6	0.9	0.5	0.9	0.7
10	Water supply and misc. services rel. to dwelling	2.3	2.2	2.7	2.7	2.5	2.4
11	Electricity, gas and other fuels	3.7	3.4	4.4	4.5	3.4	3.8
12	Furniture and furnishings, carpets etc.	3.2	3.1	2.7	2.8	3.0	3.0
13	Household textiles	0.6	0.6	0.7	0.5	0.5	0.6
14	Household appliances	0.9	0.9	1.2	0.9	0.9	1.0
15	Glassware, tableware and household utensils	0.6	0.6	0.6	0.5	0.6	0.6
16	Tools and equipment for house and garden	0.5	0.7	0.7	0.6	0.5	0.6
17	Goods and services for routine household maintenance	1.6	1.4	1.7	1.5	1.2	1.5
18	Medical products, appliances and equipment	1.2	1.2	2.6	0.9	1.4	1.6
19	Outpatient services	1.9	1.5	2.0	0.7	1.7	1.7
20	Hospital services	0.8	0.8	2.0	0.3	0.8	1.1
21	Purchase of vehicles	5.7	6.0	4.1	3.1	5.3	5.3
22	Operation of personal transport equipment	6.5	7.5	4.6	5.5	5.7	6.4
23	Transport services	2.2	2.1	2.2	2.4	3.1	2.2
24	Postal services	0.2	0.2	0.2	0.3	0.3	0.2
25	Telephone and telefax equipment	0.2	0.2	0.2	0.2	0.2	0.2
26	Telephone and telefax services	2.3	2.3	2.5	3.2	3.0	2.4
27	Audio-visual, photographic and information processing	1.7	2.1	1.5	1.9	2.0	1.9
28	Other major durables for recreation and culture	0.3	0.3	0.1	0.2	0.2	0.2
29	Other recreational items and equipment, gardens and pets	1.9	1.9	1.9	1.9	1.7	1.9
30	Recreational and cultural services	3.2	3.4	3.4	3.1	3.2	3.3
31	Newspapers, books and stationery	1.8	1.9	2.2	2.1	2.2	2.0
32	Package holidays	0.3	0.3	0.4	0.2	0.2	0.3
33	Education	1.0	0.8	0.3	0.6	1.1	0.7
34	Catering services	5.0	4.9	4.4	3.5	5.0	4.7
35	Accommodation services	0.8	0.8	0.8	0.5	0.6	0.8
36	Personal care	1.9	2.0	2.1	2.0	1.9	2.0
37	Personal effects n.e.c.	0.9	0.9	1.0	0.6	0.7	0.9
38	Social protection	1.1	1.2	0.9	1.1	0.8	1.1
39	Insurance	5.6	3.1	2.2	2.0	2.4	3.1

(continued)

Table A10.1. Continued

		Household group					
40	Financial services n.e.c.	3.3	2.7	2.8	2.5	3.8	2.8
41	Other services n.e.c.	1.6	1.5	1.5	1.1	1.9	1.5
1–4	Food, beverages and tobacco	13.1	15.5	14.9	20.3	13.9	15.1
5–6	Clothing and footwear	6.0	6.0	5.3	4.8	5.1	5.7
7–11	Housing, water, electricity, gas and other fuels	22.4	21.5	26.5	28.4	25.0	23.5
12–17	Furnishings, hh. equipment and routine hh. maintenance	7.4	7.2	7.5	6.7	6.8	7.3
18–20	Health	3.9	3.6	6.6	1.9	3.9	4.4
21–23	Transport services	14.3	15.6	10.9	11.0	14.1	13.8
24–26	Communication	2.6	2.7	2.9	3.7	3.4	2.8
27–32	Recreation and culture	9.2	10.0	9.7	9.3	9.6	9.7
33	Education	1.0	0.8	0.3	0.6	1.1	0.7
34–35	Restaurants and hotels	5.8	5.7	5.2	4.0	5.6	5.5
36–38	Personal services	3.8	4.2	3.9	3.7	3.5	4.0
39–40	Finance	8.9	5.8	4.9	4.5	6.2	6.0
41	Other services n.e.c.	1.6	1.5	1.5	1.1	1.9	1.5
	Total	100.0	100.0	100.0	100.0	100.0	100.0

Table A10.2. Household groups' shares of different expenditure categories, 2002 (in %)

		Household group					
No.	Category	Self-empl.	Empl.	Retirees	Unempl.	Others	Total
1	Food	13.7	48.0	29.7	6.6	2.0	100.0
2	Non-alcoholic beverages	15.1	51.0	25.5	6.4	2.0	100.0
3	Alcoholic beverages	12.8	49.2	30.2	6.0	1.9	100.0
4	Tobacco	12.3	57.5	18.0	10.2	2.0	100.0
5	Clothing	16.6	50.9	26.3	4.2	2.0	100.0
6	Footwear	16.0	51.6	25.0	5.3	2.0	100.0
7	Actual rentals for housing	10.9	44.8	30.8	10.6	2.9	100.0
8	Imputed rentals for housing	17.8	44.7	32.1	3.4	2.0	100.0
9	Maintenance and repair of the dwelling	15.9	43.3	33.9	4.0	2.8	100.0
10	Water supply and misc. services rel. to dwelling	15.4	44.8	31.6	5.9	2.3	100.0
11	Electricity, gas and other fuels	15.3	43.5	33.1	6.1	2.0	100.0
12	Furniture and furnishings, carpets etc.	16.8	50.4	25.8	4.8	2.2	100.0
13	Household textiles	14.9	47.1	31.6	4.4	2.0	100.0
14	Household appliances	14.1	44.7	34.2	5.0	2.0	100.0
15	Glassware, tableware and household utensils	15.9	50.8	26.9	4.3	2.2	100.0
16	Tools and equipment for house and garden	13.4	51.6	28.7	4.6	1.8	100.0
17	Goods and services for routine household maintenance	17.2	43.7	32.2	5.1	1.8	100.0

18	Medical products, appliances and equipment	12.2	37.4	45.7	2.8	1.9	100.0
19	Outpatient services	17.5	43.7	34.4	2.3	2.2	100.0
20	Hospital services	11.3	36.1	49.6	1.4	1.6	100.0
21	Purchase of vehicles	17.0	55.6	22.1	3.1	2.2	100.0
22	Operation of personal transport equipment	16.0	57.1	20.5	4.5	2.0	100.0
23	Transport services	15.5	47.8	27.9	5.7	3.1	100.0
24	Postal services	14.8	46.6	29.2	6.9	2.7	100.0
25	Telephone and telefax equipment	14.8	46.5	29.1	6.9	2.7	100.0
26	Telephone and telefax services	14.7	46.6	29.1	6.8	2.7	100.0
27	Audio-visual, photographic and information processing	13.9	55.4	23.2	5.2	2.3	100.0
28	Other major durables for recreation and culture	19.6	57.0	16.7	4.5	2.3	100.0
29	Other recreational items and equipment, gardens and pets	15.7	49.2	28.0	5.0	2.0	100.0
30	Recreational and cultural services	15.3	49.1	28.7	4.8	2.1	100.0
31	Newspapers, books and stationery	14.1	46.1	31.9	5.4	2.5	100.0
32	Package holidays	14.2	44.4	36.9	3.1	1.4	100.0
33	Education	23.3	56.9	11.9	4.5	3.4	100.0
34	Catering services	16.7	50.9	26.2	3.9	2.3	100.0
35	Accommodation services	16.6	48.5	30.0	3.2	1.6	100.0
36	Personal care	14.4	49.1	29.2	5.2	2.1	100.0
37	Personal effects n.e.c.	15.5	48.4	30.6	3.7	1.8	100.0
38	Social protection	15.5	54.7	22.9	5.2	1.7	100.0
39	Insurance	28.0	47.4	19.6	3.4	1.7	100.0
40	Financial services n.e.c.	18.3	46.6	27.7	4.5	2.9	100.0
41	Other services n.e.c.	16.6	48.0	28.7	3.9	2.8	100.0
1–4	Food, beverages and tobacco	13.6	49.6	27.8	7.0	2.0	100.0
5–6	Clothing and footwear	16.5	51.0	26.1	4.4	2.0	100.0
7–11	Housing, water, electricity, gas and other fuels	15.0	44.5	31.9	6.3	2.3	100.0
12–17	Furnishings, hh. equipment and routine hh. maintenance	16.0	48.1	29.1	4.8	2.1	100.0
18–20	Health	14.0	39.5	42.4	2.3	1.9	100.0
21–23	Transport services	16.3	55.0	22.3	4.1	2.2	100.0
24–26	Communication	14.8	46.6	29.1	6.8	2.7	100.0
27–32	Recreation and culture	14.9	49.8	28.2	5.0	2.2	100.0
33	Education	23.3	56.9	11.9	4.5	3.4	100.0
34–35	Restaurants and hotels	16.7	50.6	26.7	3.8	2.2	100.0
36–38	Personal services	14.9	50.5	27.8	4.9	1.9	100.0
39–40	Finance	23.4	47.0	23.4	3.9	2.3	100.0
41	Other services n.e.c.	16.6	48.0	28.7	3.9	2.8	100.0
	Average	15.7	48.6	28.3	5.2	2.2	100.0

Table A10.3. Changes in shares of consumption expenditures across household groups caused by ETR (in %)

No.	Category	Household group					
		Self-empl.	Empl.	Retirees	Unempl.	Others	Avg.
1	Food	−0.16	−0.20	−0.22	−0.28	−0.21	−0.20
2	Non-alcoholic beverages	−0.04	−0.04	−0.03	−0.05	−0.04	−0.04
3	Alcoholic beverages	−0.02	−0.04	−0.03	−0.04	−0.02	−0.03
4	Tobacco	0.00	−0.01	0.00	−0.01	−0.01	0.00
5	Clothing	−0.09	−0.09	−0.08	−0.07	−0.05	−0.08
6	Footwear	−0.01	−0.01	−0.01	−0.01	−0.01	−0.01
7	Actual rentals for housing	−0.04	−0.05	−0.07	−0.11	−0.08	−0.06
8	Imputed rentals for housing	−0.12	−0.11	−0.13	−0.07	−0.11	−0.11
9	Maintenance and repair of the dwelling	−0.01	−0.01	−0.02	−0.01	−0.02	−0.01
10	Water supply and misc. services rel. to dwelling	−0.05	−0.05	−0.06	−0.06	−0.05	−0.05
11	**Electricity, gas and other fuels**	**0.73**	**0.71**	**0.94**	**0.90**	**0.72**	**0.78**
12	Furniture and furnishings, carpets etc.	0.02	0.02	0.01	0.01	0.02	0.02
13	Household textiles	−0.01	−0.01	−0.01	−0.01	−0.01	−0.01
14	Household appliances	−0.02	−0.01	−0.02	−0.02	−0.02	−0.02
15	Glassware, tableware and household utensils	−0.01	−0.01	−0.01	−0.01	−0.01	−0.01
16	Tools and equipment for house and garden	−0.01	−0.02	−0.02	−0.01	−0.01	−0.01
17	Goods and services for routine household maintenance	−0.04	−0.03	−0.04	−0.04	−0.02	−0.03
18	Medical products, appliances and equipment	−0.03	−0.03	−0.06	−0.02	−0.03	−0.04
19	Outpatient services	−0.04	−0.04	−0.05	−0.01	−0.04	−0.04
20	Hospital services	−0.02	−0.02	−0.04	−0.01	−0.02	−0.03
21	Purchase of vehicles	−0.14	−0.15	−0.10	−0.09	−0.12	−0.13
22	**Operation of personal transport equipment**	**0.43**	**0.49**	**0.31**	**0.35**	**0.40**	**0.42**
23	**Transport services**	**0.32**	**0.31**	**0.33**	**0.31**	**0.41**	**0.32**
24	Postal services	0.00	0.00	0.00	0.00	0.00	0.00
25	Telephone and telefax equipment	0.00	0.00	0.00	−0.02	0.00	0.00
26	Telephone and telefax services	−0.06	−0.05	−0.06	−0.07	−0.08	−0.05
27	Audio-visual, photographic and information processing	−0.01	−0.02	−0.01	−0.02	−0.01	−0.01
28	Other major durables for recreation and culture	−0.01	−0.01	0.00	−0.01	0.00	0.00
29	Other recreational items and equipment, gardens and pets	−0.05	−0.05	−0.05	−0.05	−0.04	−0.05
30	Recreational and cultural services	−0.07	−0.08	−0.08	−0.07	−0.06	−0.08
31	Newspapers, books and stationery	−0.04	−0.04	−0.05	−0.05	−0.05	−0.05
32	Package holidays	0.00	0.00	0.00	0.00	0.00	0.00
33	Education	−0.03	−0.03	−0.01	−0.02	−0.03	−0.02
34	Catering services	−0.02	−0.02	−0.02	−0.02	−0.02	−0.02
35	Accommodation services	−0.03	−0.03	−0.03	−0.03	−0.03	−0.03
36	Personal care	−0.04	−0.05	−0.05	−0.05	−0.04	−0.05
37	Personal effects n.e.c.	−0.02	−0.02	−0.02	−0.01	−0.02	−0.02
38	Social protection	−0.04	−0.05	−0.04	−0.08	−0.06	−0.04
39	Insurance	−0.10	−0.06	−0.04	−0.03	−0.04	−0.06
40	Financial services n.e.c.	−0.08	−0.07	−0.07	−0.08	−0.13	−0.07

41	Other services n.e.c.	−0.03	−0.04	−0.04	−0.03	−0.05	−0.04
1–4	Food, beverages and tobacco	−0.23	−0.28	−0.29	−0.37	−0.27	−0.27
5–6	Clothing and footwear	−0.10	−0.10	−0.09	−0.08	−0.06	−0.09
7–11	**Housing, water electricity, gas and other fuels**	**0.51**	**0.49**	**0.66**	**0.64**	**0.46**	**0.55**
12–17	Furnishings, hh. equipment and routine hh. maintenance	−0.07	−0.07	−0.08	−0.08	−0.06	−0.07
18–20	Health	−0.09	−0.09	−0.15	−0.04	−0.09	−0.10
21–23	**Transport services**	**0.61**	**0.65**	**0.53**	**0.58**	**0.69**	**0.61**
24–26	Communication	−0.06	−0.05	−0.06	−0.09	−0.08	−0.06
27–32	Recreation and culture	−0.18	−0.20	−0.20	−0.20	−0.18	−0.20
33	Education	−0.03	−0.03	−0.01	−0.02	−0.03	−0.02
34–35	Restaurants and hotels	−0.05	−0.05	−0.06	−0.05	−0.05	−0.05
36–38	Personal services	−0.10	−0.11	−0.11	−0.15	−0.11	−0.11
39–40	Finance	−0.18	−0.13	−0.11	−0.11	−0.18	−0.14
41	Other services n.e.c.	−0.03	−0.04	−0.04	−0.03	−0.05	−0.04
	Total	**0.00**	**0.00**	**0.00**	**0.00**	**0.00**	**0.00**

Table A10.4. Changes in shares of consumption expenditures in disposable income across household groups caused by ETR (in %)

		Household group					
No.	**Category**	**Self-empl.**	**Empl.**	**Retirees**	**Unempl.**	**Others**	**Avg.**
1	Food	−0,07	−0,11	−0,14	−0,19	−0,10	−0,11
2	Non-alcoholic beverages	−0,02	−0,02	−0,02	−0,03	−0,02	−0,02
3	Alcoholic beverages	−0,01	−0,02	−0,02	−0,03	−0,01	−0,02
4	**Tobacco**	**0,00**	**0,01**	**0,01**	**0,02**	**0,01**	**0,01**
5	Clothing	−0,04	−0,05	−0,05	−0,05	−0,03	−0,05
6	Footwear	0,00	0,00	0,00	−0,01	0,00	0,00
7	Actual rentals for housing	0,00	−0,01	−0,01	−0,02	−0,01	−0,01
8	Imputed rentals for housing	−0,03	−0,04	−0,05	−0,03	−0,03	−0,04
9	Maintenance and repair of the dwelling	−0,01	−0,01	−0,01	−0,01	−0,01	−0,01
10	Water supply and misc. services rel. to dwelling	−0,02	−0,03	−0,04	−0,04	−0,03	−0,03
11	**Electricity, gas and other fuels**	**0,48**	**0,61**	**0,94**	**0,98**	**0,56**	**0,67**
12	Furniture and furnishings, carpets etc.	0,02	0,03	0,03	0,03	0,03	0,03
13	Household textiles	0,00	−0,01	−0,01	−0,01	−0,01	−0,01
14	Household appliances	−0,01	−0,01	−0,01	−0,02	−0,01	−0,01

(continued)

Table A10.4. Continued

		Household group					
15	Glassware, tableware and household utensils	−0,01	−0,01	−0,01	−0,01	−0,01	−0,01
16	Tools and equipment for house and garden	−0,01	−0,01	−0,01	−0,01	−0,01	−0,01
17	Goods and services for routine household maintenance	−0,02	−0,02	−0,02	−0,03	−0,01	−0,02
18	Medical products, appliances and equipment	−0,01	−0,02	−0,04	−0,01	−0,01	−0,02
19	Outpatient services	−0,02	−0,02	−0,03	−0,01	−0,02	−0,02
20	Hospital services	−0,01	−0,01	−0,03	0,00	−0,01	−0,01
21	Purchase of vehicles	−0,07	−0,09	−0,07	−0,07	−0,07	−0,08
22	**Operation of personal transport equipment**	**0,30**	**0,45**	**0,33**	**0,41**	**0,33**	**0,38**
23	Transport services	0,22	0,27	0,33	0,35	0,33	0,28
24	Postal services	0,00	0,00	0,00	0,00	0,00	0,00
25	Telephone and telefax equipment	0,00	0,00	0,00	−0,01	0,00	0,00
26	Telephone and telefax services	−0,03	−0,03	−0,04	−0,05	−0,04	−0,03
27	Audio-visual, photographic and information processing	0,00	0,00	0,00	0,00	0,00	0,00
28	Other major durables for recreation and culture	0,00	0,00	0,00	0,00	0,00	0,00
29	Other recreational items and equipment, gardens and pets	−0,02	−0,03	−0,03	−0,04	−0,02	−0,03
30	Recreational and cultural services	−0,03	−0,05	−0,05	−0,05	−0,03	−0,05
31	Newspapers, books and stationery	−0,02	−0,03	−0,04	−0,04	−0,03	−0,03
32	Package holidays	0,00	0,00	0,00	0,00	0,00	0,00
33	Education	−0,01	−0,02	−0,01	−0,02	−0,02	−0,01
34	**Catering services**	**0,01**	**0,01**	**0,01**	**0,01**	**0,01**	**0,01**
35	Accommodation services	−0,02	−0,02	−0,03	−0,02	−0,01	−0,02
36	Personal care	−0,02	−0,03	−0,03	−0,04	−0,02	−0,03
37	Personal effects n.e.c.	−0,01	−0,01	−0,02	−0,01	−0,01	−0,01
38	Social protection	−0,02	−0,03	−0,03	−0,06	−0,03	−0,03
39	Insurance	−0,04	−0,03	−0,02	−0,02	−0,02	−0,03
40	Financial services n.e.c.	−0,04	−0,04	−0,05	−0,06	−0,07	−0,05
41	Other services n.e.c.	−0,02	−0,02	−0,03	−0,02	−0,02	−0,02
1–4	Food, beverages and tobacco	−0,09	−0,14	−0,18	−0,22	−0,12	−0,14
5–6	Clothing and footwear	−0,05	−0,06	−0,06	−0,06	−0,03	−0,05
7–11	**Housing, water electricity, gas and other fuels**	**0,42**	**0,54**	**0,84**	**0,89**	**0,49**	**0,59**
12–17	Furnishings, hh. equipment and routine hh. maintenance	−0,02	−0,02	−0,04	−0,04	−0,01	−0,02
18–20	Health	−0,04	−0,05	−0,09	−0,03	−0,04	−0,06
21–23	**Transport services**	**0,45**	**0,63**	**0,59**	**0,69**	**0,59**	**0,57**
24–26	Communication	−0,03	−0,03	−0,04	−0,06	−0,04	−0,03
27–32	Recreation and culture	−0,08	−0,11	−0,13	−0,14	−0,09	−0,11
33	Education	−0,01	−0,02	−0,01	−0,02	−0,02	−0,01
34–35	Restaurants and hotels	−0,01	−0,01	−0,02	−0,01	−0,01	−0,01
36–38	Personal services	−0,05	−0,07	−0,08	−0,11	−0,06	−0,07
39–40	Finance	−0,08	−0,07	−0,07	−0,08	−0,09	−0,07
41	Other services n.e.c.	−0,02	−0,02	−0,03	−0,02	−0,02	−0,02
	Total	**0,39**	**0,57**	**0,70**	**0,80**	**0,55**	**0,56**

References

Aasness, J., and E. R. Larson (2002), 'Distributional and Environmental Effects of Taxes on Transportation', Statistics Norway, Research Department, Discussion Paper No. 321, Oslo, Norway.

Bach, Stefan (2005), 'Be- und Entlastungswirkungen der Ökologischen Steuerreform nach Produktionsbereichen. Band I des Endberichts für das Vorhaben: "Quantifizierung der Effekte der Ökologischen Steuerreform auf Umwelt, Beschäftigung und Innovation"', Deutsches Institut für Wirtschaftsforschung (DIW) Berlin, Report commissioned by the German Federal Environment Agency, August 2005.

—— (2009), 'Zehn Jahre Ökologische Steuerreform: Finanzpolitisch erfolgreich, klimapolitisch halbherzig', Deutsches Institut für Wirtschaftsforschung (DIW), Berlin, Wochenbericht des DIW Berlin No. 14/2009, 1 April: 218–27.

—— C. Bork, M. Kohlhaas, C. Lutz, B. Meyer, B. Praetorius, and H. Welsch (2001), *Die ökologische Steuerreform in Deutschland: Eine modellgestützte Analyse ihrer Wirkungen auf Wirtschaft und Umwelt*, Heidelberg: Physica-Verlag.

—— M. Kohlhaas, B. Meyer, B. Praetorius, and H. Welsch (2002), 'The Effects of Environmental Fiscal Reform in Germany—A Simulation Study', *Energy Policy*, 30: 803–11.

Barker, T., and J. Köhler (1998), 'Equity and Ecotax Reform in the EU: Achieving a 10 per cent Reduction in CO_2 Emissions Using Excise Duties', *Fiscal Studies*, 19(4): 375–402.

Beuermann, C., and T. Santarius (2002), 'Reaktionen gesellschaftlicher Akteure auf die Ökologische Steuerreform. Kurzfassung der Ergebnisse und Empfehlungen des Projekts PETRAS "Policies for Ecological Tax Reform: Analysis of Social Responses"', Wuppertal Institut für Klima, Umwelt, Energie.

Brännlund, R., and J. Nordström (2004), 'Carbon Tax Simulations Using a Household Demand Model', *European Economic Review*, 48: 211–33.

Bork, C. (2006), 'Distributional Effects of the Ecological Tax Reform in Germany: An Evaluation with a Microsimulation Model', in Y. Serret and N. Johnstone (eds.), *Distributional Effects of Environmental Policy*, Paris: OECD, and Cheltenham: Edward Elgar, 139–70.

Crawford, I., S. Smith, and S. Webb (1993), 'VAT on Domestic Energy', IFS (Institute for Fiscal Studies) Paper, London: KKS Printing.

Drosdowski, T., and M. I. Wolter (2008), 'Sozioökonomische Modellierung: Integration der Sozioökonomischen Gesamtrechnung (SGR) des Statistischen Bundesamtes in DEMOS II', Institute for Fiscal StudiesGWS Discussion Paper 2008/8, Osnabrück.

Dünnhoff, E., I. Stieß, and C. Hoppenbrock (2006), Energiekostenanstieg, soziale Folgen und Klimaschutz: Endbericht gefördert durch die Hans-Böckler-Stiftung, Institut für Energie- und Umweltforschung (IFEU) und Institut für sozial-ökologische Forschung (ISOE), Heidelberg/Frankfurt am Main, November.

Duscha, M., D. Seebach, B. Grießmann, U. Rath, and S. Thomas (2005), 'Politikinstrumente zum Klimaschutz durch Effizienzsteigerung von Elektrogeräten und -anlagen in Privathaushalten', Büros und im Kleinverbrauch'. Endbericht im Auftrag des Umweltbundesamtes, Institut für Energie- und Umweltforschung (IFEU), Heidelberg, March.

Ekins, P., and S. Dresner (2004), *Green Taxes and Charges: Reducing their Impact on Low-Income Households*, London: PSI paper; York: York Publishing Services Ltd.

Freund, C., and C. Wallich (1996), 'Public-Sector Price Reforms in Transition Economies: Who Gains? Who Loses? The Case of Household Energy Prices in Poland', *Economic Development and Cultural Change*, 46(1): 35–59.

GBG (Green Budget Germany) (2004), 'ECOTAX: GBG Memorandum 2004: Green Budget Germany Demands for Ecotax and Fiscal Reform in Germany from 2005', November.

—— (2008), 'Sozial ausgestaltete ökologische Finanzreform', Discussion Paper.

Grub, M. (2000), 'Verteilungswirkungen der ökologischen Steuerreform auf private Haushalte: Eine empirische Analyse', *Vierteljahrshefte zur Wirtschaftsforschung*, Heft 1/2000: 17–37.

Herlitzius, B., and G. Schick (2008), 'Ökobonus—neues Instrument für Klimaschutz und ökologische Gerechtigkeit', Diskussionsvorlage für den Länderrat, 5 April.

Hillebrand, B. (2000), 'Ökologische Steuerreform 1999–2003—Sektorale Be- und Entlastungen', Rheinisch-Westfälisches Institut für Wirtschaftsforschung (RWI), Essen.

INFRAS/ECOPLAN (1998), 'Soziale und räumliche Verteilungswirkungen von Energieabgaben', Study commissioned by the Swiss Federal Office of Energy.

INFRAS and Plaut (Schweiz) Consulting AG (2003), 'Evaluation des Stromsparfonds Basel', Studie im Auftrag des Bundesamtes für Energie/Energiewirtschaftliche Grundlagen, Schlussbericht, 1 September.

Johnstone, N., and Y. Serret (2006), 'Distributional Effects of Environmental Policy: Introduction', in Y. Serret and N. Johnstone (eds.), *Distributional Effects of Environmental Policy*, Paris: OECD, and Cheltenham: Edward Elgar, 1–19.

Kohlhaas, M. (2005), 'Gesamtwirtschaftliche Effekte der ökologischen Steuerreform. Band II des Endberichts für das Vorhaben: "Quantifizierung der Effekte der Ökologischen Steuerreform auf Umwelt, Beschäftigung und Innovation"', Report commissioned by the German Federal Environment Agency, August 2005.

Lehr, U., J. Nitsch, M., Kratzat, C. Lutz, and D. Edler (2008), 'Renewable Energy and Employment in Germany', *Energy Policy*, 36: 108–17.

Leipprand, A., N. Gavalyugova, N. Meyer-Ohlendorf, D. Blobel, and A. Persson (2007), 'Links between the Social and Environmental Pillars of Sustainable Development: Task 1D: Environmental Taxes', Ecologic, September. (Unpublished contribution to Pye et al. (2008).)

Luhmann, H. J., R. Ell, and M. Roemer (1998), 'Unevenly Distributed Benefits from Reducing Pollutants, Especially Road Traffic Emissions, Via Reducing Road Transport', Working Paper 6—Executive Summary, July 1998, Wuppertal Institute for Climate, Energy and Environment.

Lutz, C., B. Meyer, C. Nathani, and J. Schleich (2005), 'Endogenous Technological Change and Emissions: The Case of the German steel industry', *Energy Policy*, 33(9): 1143–54.

—— —— —— —— (2007), 'Endogenous Innovation, Economy and Environment: Impacts of a Technology Based Modelling Approach for Energy-Intensive Industries in Germany', *Energy Studies Review*, 15(1): 2–18.

McNally, R. H. G., and N. Mabey (1999), *The Distributional Impacts of Ecological Tax Reform*, Godalming: WWF, UK.

Meyer, B., M. Distelkamp, and M. I. Wolter (2007a), 'Material Efficiency and Economic-Environmental Sustainability: Results of Simulations for Germany with the Model PANTA RHEI', *Ecological Economics*, 63(1): 192–200.

—— C. Lutz, P. Schnur, and G. Zika (2007b), 'Economic Policy Simulations with Global Interdependencies: A Sensitivity Analysis for Germany', *Economic Systems Research*, 19: 37–55.

Meyer-Ohlendorf, N., and D. Blobel (2008), 'Untersuchung der Beiträge von Umweltpolitik sowie ökologischer Modernisierung zur Verbesserung der Lebensqualität in Deutschland und Weiterentwicklung des Konzeptes der Ökologischen Gerechtigkeit: Hauptstudie—Modul 1–3', Report commissioned by the German Federal Environment Agency, Ecologic, Berlin.

OECD (1995), *Climate Change, Economic Instruments and Income Distribution*, Paris: Organisation for Economic Co-operation and Development.

Ott, Hermann E., and J. Schlüns (2008), 'Energiearmut, Luxusverbrauch', *Die Tageszeitung*, 11 July.

Peter, M., H. Lückge, R. Iten, J. Trageser, B. Görlach, D. Blobel, and R. Andreas Kraemer (2007), 'Erfahrungen mit Energiesteuern in Europa: Lehren für die Schweiz', Report commissioned by the Swiss Federal Office of Energy, December 2007, Infras/Ecologic, Berlin.

Pye, S., I. Skinner, N. Meyer-Ohlendorf, A. Leipprand, K. Lucas, and R. Salmons (2008), 'Addressing the Social Dimensions of Environmental Policy: A Study on the Linkages between Environmental and Social Sustainability in Europe', AEA Energy and Environment, Ecologic, and University of Westminster, Report commissioned by the European Commission.

Regeringens proposition (2004), Budgetpropositionen för 2004, 2003/04:1, Stockholm, Regeringskansliet.

Serret, Y., and N. Johnstone (2006), 'Distributional Effects of Environmental Policy: Conclusions and Policy Implications', in Y. Serret and N. Johnstone (eds.), *Distributional Effects of Environmental Policy*, Paris: OECD, and Cheltenham, Edward Elgar, 286–314.

Smith, S. (1992), 'The Distributional Consequences of Taxes on Energy and the Carbon Content of Fuels', *European Economy*, Special Edition No. 1: The Economics of Limiting CO_2 Emissions, 241–68.

Speck, S. (1999), 'Energy and Carbon Taxes and their Distributional Implications', *Energy Policy*, 27: 659–67.

—— M. Skou Andersen, H. Ørsted Nielsen, A. V. Ryelund, and C. Smith (2006), *The Use of Economic Instruments in Nordic and Baltic Environmental Policy 2001–2005*, Copenhagen: Nordic Council of Ministers, TemaNord 2006: 525.

Symons, L., S. Speck, and J. Proops (1997), 'The Distributional Effects of European Pollution and Energy Taxes', Paper Presented at the Conference, The International Energy Experience: Markets, Regulations and Environment, 8–9 December, Warwick.

—— —— —— (2002), 'The Distributional Effects of Carbon and Energy Taxes: The Cases of France, Spain, Italy, Germany and UK', *European Environment*, 12: 203–12.

VROM (2004), *The Netherlands' Tax on Energy: Questions and Answers*, The Hague: Ministry of Housing, Spatial Planning and the Environment (VROM), Directorate-General for Environmental Protection.

—— (2005), *Greening the Tax System in the Netherlands*, The Hague: Netherlands Ministry of Housing, Spatial Planning and the Environment (VROM).

Wier, M., K. Birr-Pedersen, H. K. Jacobsen, and J. Klok (2005), 'Are CO_2 Taxes Regressive? Evidence from the Danish Experience', *Ecological Economics*, 52: 239–51.

11

Global Economic and Environmental Impacts of an ETR in Europe

Stefan Giljum, Christian Lutz and Christine Polzin

11.1 Introduction

Given the strong dependence of European production and consumption activities on resource imports from other world regions (see Chapter 2), the introduction of an ETR in Europe and other industrialized countries—and its effects on resource prices—would affect the economies of both the EU and the rest of the world. This chapter will analyse some economic and environmental dimensions of these effects. It includes a quantitative analysis of changing global patterns in economic growth, international trade, material extraction, and energy-related CO_2 emissions. The main research questions which guided this analysis were:

- What are the global consequences of the implementation of an ETR (and thus resource productivity increases) in Europe in terms of worldwide patterns of natural resource extraction, production, trade, and consumption?

- What are the differences between a business-as-usual scenario, a unilateral EU ETR scenario, and a European ETR in combination with wider commitments to emission reductions in other developed countries and economically more advanced developing countries?

- Which European industries would be most negatively affected in their international competitiveness by the implementation of an ETR in Europe?

- What are the policy implications of the global effects of an ETR?

The relevance of these questions is underlined by the current discussions at international climate conferences about the impacts of unilateral versus multilateral policy strategies and on the precise interpretation of 'common but differentiated responsibilities', a principle agreed to in the Kyoto Protocol. This chapter contributes to the discussion on the roles of the industrialized, emerging, and developing countries in dealing with climate change and, more precisely, on the policy impacts of EU versus international environmental tax reforms (see e.g. Helm 2008; Whalley and Walsh 2009).

The main policy conclusion from this chapter is that strong concerted action from the EU, other OECD countries, and emerging countries is needed in order to slow the current growth rate of global CO_2 emissions and resource use in order to achieve more environmentally sustainable economic growth.

The chapter is structured as follows: Section 11.2 provides a brief overview of the Global Inter-industry Forecasting System (GINFORS) model, as well as the scenarios in the context of global impact modelling. Detailed results are presented and discussed in Section 11.3. Policy conclusions are derived in Section 11.4, and Section 11.5 provides conclusions.

11.2 Model description and scenarios

A modelling approach based on the model GINFORS was used to analyse the global impacts of different ETR policy scenarios. As a global economy-energy-environment simulation model, GINFORS can be used to analyse outcomes of different future (policy) scenarios and to show the interactions and interdependencies of different economic and environmental variables. GINFORS links modules for bilateral trade, macroeconomic behaviour, and industrial output from input-output tables and energy use and prices. GINFORS explicitly covers countries accounting for about 95% of world GDP, as well as 95% of global CO_2 emissions. A simplified model for the rest of the world (ROW) ensures global coverage. It also includes a global data set on material extraction which allows the analysis of European and global patterns of resource extraction. In the PETRE project, the GINFORS model was one of the two main simulation models for assessing the implications of the implementation of an ETR in Europe and the only one that allowed analysis of the global implications (see Chapter 8 for a more detailed description of the models).

In the course of PETRE, six scenarios were implemented in GINFORS, based on the proposals which had been discussed at various levels in the EU (EC 2008a), some with different variants, until the year 2020 (see Chapter 9 for more details). Analysis of the global implications of an ETR in Europe focused on the high oil price scenarios BH (baseline scenario with high oil prices), HS1 (ETR with revenue recycling designed to meet the unilateral EU 2020 20% GHG reduction target), and HS3 (ETR with revenue recycling designed to meet the higher 30% EU GHG reduction target for 2020, to be adopted if other countries cooperate on climate change mitigation). Given the current developments regarding the oil price and forecasts by the IEA (2009), the low oil price scenario was not analysed in detail. The HS3 scenario with international cooperation is especially important in the global context as it refers to the objective that the 30% reduction in greenhouse gas emissions by 2020 compared to 1990 would be pursued for the period beyond 2012, provided that 'other developed countries commit themselves to comparable emission reductions' and that 'economically more advanced developing countries commit themselves to contributing adequately according to their responsibilities and capabilities' (EC 2008a: 2).

Note that material and energy prices were assumed to be independent of the measures taken in the different scenarios. It would be reasonable to assume that an ETR in Europe may lead to declining international energy and material prices and thus stimulate additional demand from emerging economies and developing countries. However, as there was no data to indicate possible reactions of oil and material suppliers, such price developments have not been modelled. They could be included as part of a sensitivity analysis in future work (see IEA 2009).

11.3 Scenario results and discussion

11.3.1 Global economic implications

To analyse the global economic implications of an ETR in Europe, model calculations were compared on economic growth and trade (particularly the developments of imports and exports) and on the performance of different industries. The following analysis will largely focus on the EU-27, OECD (non-EU), emerging economies,[1] and the rest of the world (ROW).

IMPACTS ON ECONOMIC GROWTH
In the baseline scenario BH, annual average GDP growth in the EU-27 is expected to remain positive and to fluctuate between 2.2% and 2.5% until 2020 (see Table 11.1). In the non-EU OECD group, growth rates range between 2.0% and 3.0%. Given that the population of emerging and developing countries is projected to increase significantly over the next four decades and that industrialization is expected to continue and broaden, average annual GDP growth rates in the group of emerging economies are between two and three times higher than in the EU and other OECD countries. Growth in the rest of the world largely depends on energy and resource prices, which

---

[1] The group of emerging economies in the GINFORS model comprises the following countries: Argentina, Brazil, China, India, Indonesia, the Philippines, Russia, South Africa, and Thailand.

Table 11.1. GDP development in the baseline scenario BH

Average annual growth rates	1995–2000	2000–2005	2005–2010	2010–2015	2015–2020
	In % (based on US$ PPP, 2004)				
EU-27	3.1	1.9	2.2	2.5	2.2
OECD (non-EU)	3.8	2.6	2.0	3.0	2.9
Emerging economies	6.2	8.0	8.7	8.3	6.8
RoW	3.8	4.9	5.1	3.7	2.9
World	4.2	4.8	4.4	4.9	4.4

Shares in world GDP (PPP 2004)	2000	2005	2010	2015	2020
	In % (based on US$ PPP, 2004)				
EU-27	25.4	22.4	20.4	18.4	16.8
OECD (non-EU)	41.3	37.5	33.8	31.2	29.3
Emerging economies	27.9	31.4	37.0	42.0	46.0
RoW	5.9	9.2	9.5	9.0	8.5
World	100.0	100.0	100.0	100.0	100.0

Note: Regional aggregate economic growth rates are calculated based on GDP expressed in purchasing-power parity (PPP) terms.

are not supposed to be above average after 2010, in line with the expectations of the International Energy Agency (IEA 2008a).

This trend also leads to a shift in global economic weight (in terms of output) away from the traditional industrialized countries. While the EU and OECD countries together accounted for almost 62% of world GDP in 2000, this share is expected to shrink to around 46% in 2020 in the baseline scenario, while emerging and developing countries together will produce around 54% of global GDP. These figures are calculated based on GDP expressed in purchasing-power parity (PPP) terms. When calculating them in market exchange rates, the shares of the OECD (non-EU) countries are higher.

Table 11.2 illustrates the impacts of the implementation of the policy measures in scenarios HS1 and HS3 on GDP in the different regions and in the world as whole.

The impacts of the policy measures on world GDP are limited. As could be expected, the introduction of the policy measures in Europe alone (HS1) reduces world GDP by only US$3 billion compared to the baseline in 2020, mainly due to declines in the EU (- US$92 billion) which would be bigger than the relative gains in the non-EU OECD countries (US$28 billion), the emerging economies (US$53 billion), and the rest of the world (US$6 billion). A more substantial decline in world GDP can be observed in scenario HS3, with a reduction of US$1.3 trillion. However, this is still only 1.4% lower than

Table 11.2. GDP impacts in different world regions, three scenarios (in billion US$ 2000, PPP)

GDP in 2020	Total value of GDP, baseline BH	Absolute deviation of HS1 from BH in 2020	Percentage deviation of HS1 from BH in 2020	Absolute deviation of HS3 from BH in 2020	Percentage deviation of HS3 from BH in 2020
EU-27	15,931	−92	−0.6	−297	−1.9
OECD (non-EU)	27,840	28	0.1	−78	−0.3
Emerging economies	43,699	53	0.1	−688	−1.6
RoW	8,033	6	0.1	−266	−3.3
World total	94,926	−3	0.0	−1,313	−1.4

the baseline BH. It should be noted that HS3 also has positive impacts on some countries' GDP in comparison to BH in 2020—in the EU-27 notably Latvia (+8.6%) and the Slovak Republic (+4%), in the other OECD countries notably Korea (+6.9%) and Australia (+1.3%), in the emerging economies mainly the Philippines (+2.7%) and Argentina (+1.4%), and in the ROW Singapore (+5.9%) and Malaysia (+1.5%). The size of the worldwide reduction in GDP must be compared to the enormous negative externalities related to global warming and environmental degradation. Determining the costs of these externalities to the environment, society and the economy in the absence of policy interventions continues to be a topic of debate (see for example Sterner and Persson 2008).

The regions' relative positions (shares) in the total value of global GDP do not vary significantly between the different scenarios. Shrinking shares of the EU-27 and OECD (non-EU) groups in global GDP are observed in all scenarios in the period from 2000 to 2020: from 66.6% in 2000 to 46.1% (BH), 46% (HS1), and 46.4% (HS3). In contrast, the positions of the emerging countries and of the rest of the world will be stronger. The emerging countries' share of global GDP will increase from 28% to 46% in all scenarios between 2000 and 2020, and the rest of the world will gain between 2.6% (BH and HS1) and 2.4% (HS3).

IMPACTS ON INTERNATIONAL TRADE AND SECTORAL COMPETITIVENESS

Increasing international trade and deeper integration of different world regions in global markets have been central characteristics of globalization. Between 2000 and 2007, world export volumes grew by 5.5% annually, while production only increased by 3.0% a year. Growth in trade was highest for manufactured products (6.5%), followed by agricultural products (4.0%), and fuels and mineral products (3.5%) (WTO 2008).

Table 11.3. Export developments in different world regions, baseline scenario BH

Average annual growth rates	2000–2005	2005–2010	2010–2015	2015–2020
	In % (based on US$, 2000)			
EU-27	3.7	3.1	2.6	2.9
OECD (non-EU)	7.7	5.1	3.1	2.5
Emerging economies	5.1	9.3	5.4	6.1
RoW	8.7	8.3	5.3	5.8

Table 11.4. Import developments in different world regions, baseline scenario BH

Average annual growth rates	2000–2005	2005–2010	2010–2015	2015–2020
	In % (based on US$, 2000)			
EU-27	1.7	2.8	3.6	3.7
OECD (non-EU)	1.6	2.7	4.0	3.9
Emerging economies	14.2	7.6	7.0	6.3
RoW	7.1	7.6	5.2	5.7

In the baseline scenario, the GINFORS results show continuous growth of both exports (Table 11.3) and imports (Table 11.4) in monetary terms across all regions from 2000 to 2020.

The lowest growth of export values is expected in the non-EU OECD region, while the highest growth will occur in the group of emerging countries. For the periods 2010–15 and 2015–20, the growth of imports in the emerging countries can be expected to be twice as high as that in the EU-27 in the baseline scenario BH.

Table 11.5 shows that exports will not change significantly in countries outside the EU (less than 2%) in response to the introduction of HS1 and HS3 policy measures, compared to the baseline situation in 2020. In scenario HS3,

Table 11.5. Export impacts of different scenarios for the four regions

Country group	Total value of exports, 2010 (PPP bn US$)	Total value of exports, BH, 2020 (PPP bn US$)	Absolute deviation of HS1 from BH in 2020 (PPP bn US$)	Percentage deviation of HS1 from BH in 2020	Absolute deviation of HS3 from BH in 2020 (PPP bn US$)	Percentage deviation of HS3 from BH in 2020
EU-27	5144.4	7972.0	−60.1	−0.8%	−264.2	−3.3%
OECD (non-EU)	4044.7	5505.1	14.1	0.3%	−29.5	−0.5%
Emerging economies	6651.4	11036.0	19.8	0.2%	−159.2	−1.4%
RoW	3166.5	4913.9	7.4	0.2%	−73.2	−1.5%

exports in non-EU OECD countries would be 0.5% lower than in the baseline, 1.4% lower in the group of emerging countries, and 1.5% lower in the rest of the world. In the EU itself, exports would slightly decline by 0.8% in HS1 and by 3.3% if HS3 policies were to be adopted. Countries within the groups are affected differently. Resource exporters will have to reduce exports such as fossil fuels. Thus, the largest export reductions in 2020, compared to the baseline scenario, would be experienced by OPEC (−12.7%), Spain (−8.9%), Italy (−8.2%), and Canada (−6.3%). In the emerging economies, exports would decline in China (−3.4%), South Africa (−2.7%), and Russia (−1.7%). In contrast, some Asian countries can increase their trade shares and export more than in the baseline scenario by 2020, especially in scenario HS3, notably Korea (+8.7%), Singapore (+5.5%), the Philippines (+2.8%), Malaysia (+2.5%), and India (+2.3%).

The ETR does not only affect the international competitiveness of different countries but also that of different sectors. ETS and ETR will increase transport costs, which will partly reduce the ongoing globalization process in terms of international trade volumes. Exports and imports will therefore be lower than in the baseline.

Comparing EU export growth rates in the different policy scenarios with the baseline in 2020, all sectors under investigation would experience stronger declines in HS3 than in HS1 (see Figures 11.1 and 11.2). Since the higher costs of fossil fuels lead to a loss in sectoral price competitiveness, especially in

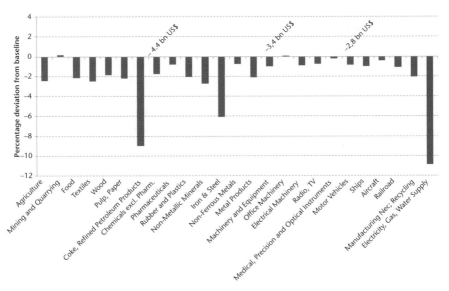

Figure 11.1 EU exports to non-EU countries—percentage deviation of HS1 from baseline in 2020

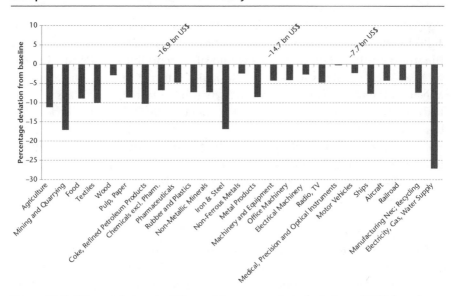

Figure 11.2 EU exports to non-EU countries—percentage deviation of HS3 from baseline in 2020

energy-intensive industries in the short run, the strongest decline rates would be experienced in the utilities and heavy industries, notably Electricity, Gas and Water Supply (HS1: −10.9%, HS3: −27.1%), Coke and Refined Petroleum Products (HS1: −9.0%; HS3: −10.4%), and Iron and Steel (HS1: −6.1%; HS3: −16.8%). Interestingly, export values of the Mining and Quarrying sector would increase by 0.2% in HS1, but decline by 17.0% in HS3 compared with the baseline in 2020. This may be explained by the fact that the exports of Mining and Quarrying depend entirely on the demand of the world market, which GINFORS reflects by fixed supply structures. As the use of coal declines significantly in scenario HS3, the exports of Mining and Quarrying reduce accordingly. Apart from Mining and Quarrying, Office Machinery, as well as Medical, Precision and Optical Instruments, would be least negatively affected in HS1 (experiencing growth rates of 0.05 and −0.2% respectively compared to the baseline in 2020).

The relatively weak negative effects on exports in the emerging countries in HS3 may be due to the fact that many of them have a diversified export market in which the industrialized countries of the EU and OECD are not always the main destination. For example, only 10% of all Chinese exports will be delivered to the EU in 2020 if HS3 policies are implemented, while 67% will go to the rest of the world, 10% to OPEC, and 13% to other emerging countries. In the case of India, 58% of all exports are expected to go to the rest of the world, 25% to the EU, 14% to other emerging countries, and 3% to OPEC by the year 2020 in scenario HS3.

In terms of absolute monetary values, the strongest declines would be experienced in EU exports of Chemicals (excluding pharmaceuticals) (HS1: −US$4.4 bn., HS3: −US$17.0 bn.), followed by Machinery and Equipment (HS1: −US$2.8 bn., HS3: −US$14.7 bn.), and Motor Vehicles (HS1: −US$2.8 bn., HS3: −US$7.7 bn.).

In total, the EU's export markets would not suffer notably by the unilateral introduction of an ETR in scenario HS1. A more significant impact on trade for all country groups can be expected from scenario HS3 with its larger reduction in CO_2 emissions in the EU, and international cooperation to reduce emissions in other countries.

11.3.2 GLOBAL ENVIRONMENTAL IMPLICATIONS

Two core indicators were chosen for the analysis of the environmental impacts of the scenarios—material extraction and CO_2 emissions. The first indicator, material extraction of natural resources, is strongly related to various environmental impacts. Material extraction of mining metals and ores, for example, influences the environment in various ways, including structural changes to the landscape which reduce the value of important ecosystem services, diminished aesthetic values, the loss of biodiversity, increased local demand for water and electricity, the contamination of surface and ground waters, the release of hazardous elements from soil and rocks or from the minerals themselves to the environment (for example, of sulphur-containing substances in brown-coal mining, causing acidification of ground water) (Giljum et al. 2005). Although the GINFORS model does not deliver data on environmental impacts related to material extraction and use, an indirect link between the overall levels of resource extraction and environmental consequences can be established. CO_2 emissions, the second indicator, are widely regarded as the major cause of global warming and thus play a central role in the current climate policy negotiations. Moreover, CO_2 emissions are closely linked to the use of materials (in particular fossil fuels).

Both indicators are production-oriented indicators, in other words, they show the extent of environmental pressures in those countries where they occur. Additional models are needed to analyse consumption-oriented indicators which illustrate the environmental pressures associated with the final consumption of goods and services in a particular country. GINFORS cannot allocate environmental data (such as material extraction) to specific economic variables, such as domestic final consumption or exports, in the country models. This impedes assessment of all direct and indirect (upstream) materials needed for producing specific imported and exported goods. Consequently, a complementary model, called GRAM (Global Resource Accounting

Model), was constructed in the course of the PETRE project, which allows the calculation of comprehensive consumption indicators (for different environmental categories, such as material extraction and CO_2 emissions). GRAM complements GINFORS in terms of determining the resource base of the European economy in a comprehensive manner, fully including the international trade dimension (Giljum et al., 2008b). Please see Chapter 2 for detailed results of the GRAM model. This chapter will only present and discuss the results of the GINFORS model.

Impacts on material extraction

Figure 11.3 presents global used material extraction disaggregated into nine material categories in the baseline scenario. Historical data shows that global used extraction grew at around 1.5% p.a. from 40 billion tonnes in 1980 to 57 billion tonnes in 2005. This trend of increasing extraction continues in the baseline scenario, with total used extraction reaching more than 80 billion tonnes in 2020 and more than 100 billion tonnes in 2030. The figures for extraction in 2020 are thus close to earlier baseline scenario calculations (Giljum et al. 2008a). Growth rates are unevenly distributed among the main material categories. Figure 11.3 clearly illustrates that construction minerals, non-ferrous metals, and iron ores will experience the highest growth rates. By 2030, extraction of construction minerals will be more than twice as

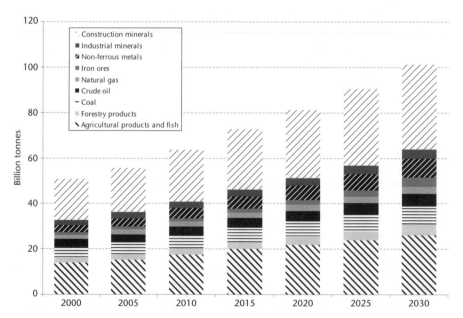

Figure 11.3 Global used material extraction of different material categories, baseline scenario BH

high as in 2000, an indication of the importance of this category of materials for resource-intensive industrial development, especially in emerging markets such as China.

The shift in global material extraction and production patterns is underpinned by Figure 11.4, which shows that shares of EU-25 and other OECD countries will decrease continuously to less than 30% in 2030. At the same time, the emerging countries and the rest of the world will raise their share in global extraction.

Together, Figure 11.3 and Figure 11.4 confirm that a significant reduction in the material throughput of the world economy and the related negative environmental impacts can only be tackled on a global scale. While material extraction is comparatively low in the EU-25,[2] it is important to note that the European Union has larger net imports of resources than any single country in the world economy (see Giljum at al. 2008b). From a consumption perspective, which includes indirect (or embodied) natural resources of traded products, the shares of both the EU-25 and the rest of the OECD countries would thus be bigger than Figure 11.3 suggests. This implies that production of products for final consumption in industrialized countries uses more resources

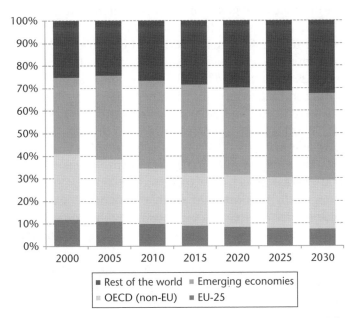

Figure 11.4 Global shares of used material extraction for country groups, baseline scenario BH

---

[2] Owing to a lack of data from Romania and Bulgaria, resource extraction is only analysed for the remaining EU-25. All other data in this chapter refer to the EU-27.

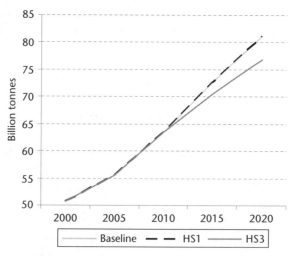

Figure 11.5 Global used material extraction, three scenarios

than those extracted within these countries. Figure 11.5 illustrates the global development of material extraction in the three scenarios.

The figure illustrates that global material extraction continues to grow in all three scenarios. With less than 0.1% reduction, the worldwide effects of the measures implemented in scenario HS1 are negligible (and cannot be discerned in Figure 11.5). HS3 measures lead to a global decrease in material extraction of 5.3% compared to the baseline BH in 2020, but overall levels of extraction still continue to grow. In HS3, the highest growth rates of material extraction between 2000 and 2020 occur in Portugal (+175% compared to 178% in BH), Brazil (+146% compared to 156% in BH), Japan (+110% in both HS3 and BH), and Malaysia (+109% compared to 107% in BH). Throughout the scenarios, the group of emerging countries largely determines the overall growth trend. Brazil is expected to experience the strongest growth in material extraction, especially iron ore, due to large amounts of available resources, agricultural and forestry products, and construction materials (overall growth in material extraction between 2000 and 2020: 156% in BH and HS1, 146% in HS3).

Comparing the effects of policy measures in scenarios HS1 and HS3 with the baseline in terms of material extraction in the year 2020, HS1 policy measures lead to a decrease in material extraction in the EU-25 by 1.47% and in the rest of the world by 0.08% (see Table 11.6). In the OECD (non-EU) and emerging countries, by contrast, material extraction increases slightly by 0.1% and 0.03% respectively. Globally, HS1 policy measures thus lead to a very low decrease of material extraction compared to the baseline (-0.11% or 90 million tonnes). HS3 policies, on the other hand, are expected to reduce global

Table 11.6. Impacts of an ETR on material extraction in HS1 and HS3

Country group	Total extraction, BH, 2020 (in billion tonnes)	Absolute deviation of HS1 from BH in 2020 (in billion tonnes)	Percentage deviation of HS1 from BH in 2020	Absolute deviation of HS3 from BH in 2020 (in billion tonnes)	Percentage deviation of HS3 from BH in 2020
EU-25	6.8	−0.10	−1.47 %	−0.24	−3.6 %
OECD (non-EU)	18.7	0.02	0.10 %	−1.03	−5.5 %
Emerging economies	31.5	0.01	0.03 %	−2.23	−7.1 %
RoW	24.2	−0.02	−0.08 %	−0.79	−3.3 %
Global total	81.2	−0.09	−0.11 %	−4.30	−5.3 %

material extraction by 4.3 billion tonnes (−5.3%) in 2020. In this scenario, material extraction declines most significantly in the emerging countries (−7.1%), followed by the OECD (non−EU) group (−5.5%), the EU−25 (−3.6%), and the rest of the world (−3.3%). It is remarkable that in scenario HS3 material extraction impacts in emerging countries are so much higher than in the EU. This clearly indicates the importance of a global perspective.

Impacts on energy-related CO_2 emissions
Figure 11.6 shows the energy-related CO_2 emissions in the baseline scenario for the four regions.

The figure shows that the expected future emissions of the EU remain almost constant, while those of the three other country groups will grow continuously until 2030. The most notable increase will happen in the emerging countries. In the G5 group (China, India, Brazil, South Africa, and Mexico), for example, energy-related CO_2 emissions will increase by almost 9 billion tonnes, of which more than half will be emitted by China. At the global level, these figures are in line with the Reference Scenario of the 2008 World Energy Outlook (IEA 2008a), in which global energy-related CO_2 emissions are expected to rise from 28 gigatonnes in 2006 to 41 gigatonnes in 2030—an increase of 45%. According to the IEA, three-quarters of the increase in projected annual emissions comes from China, India, and the Middle East, and 97% from non-OECD countries as a whole. Note again that these emissions are territorial, that is, production-oriented.

Figure 11.7 compares the absolute values of energy-related CO_2 emissions in the different policy scenarios.

As with material extraction, the global impact of scenario HS1 is very limited; global reduction only equals −0.8%. In scenario HS3, however, the reductions of CO_2 emissions are substantial, with 15.6% fewer emissions worldwide than in the baseline BH. The measures implemented in HS3 thus

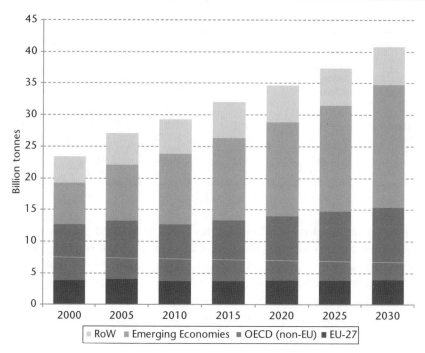

Figure 11.6 Energy-related CO_2 emissions in different world regions, 2000–2030, baseline scenario BH

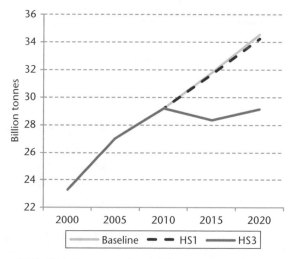

Figure 11.7 Global energy-related CO_2 emissions, three scenarios

Table 11.7. Impacts of an ETR on energy-related CO_2 emissions in HS1 and HS3

Country group	Total energy-related CO_2 emissions in BH, 2020 (in Mt)	Total change in HS1 from BH in 2020 (in Mt)	Relative change in HS1, % against BH in 2020	Total change in HS3 from BH in 2020 (in Mt)	Relative change in HS3, % against BH in 2020
EU-27	3776.3	−318.8	−8.4 %	−722.4	−19.1 %
OECD (non-EU)	10244.6	10.4	0.1 %	−1829.1	−17.9 %
Emerging economies	14835.5	2.3	0.02 %	−2741.9	−18.5 %
RoW	5854.9	0.4	0.01 %	−141.4	−2.4 %
Global	34526.7	−272.8	−0.8 %	−5398.6	−15.6 %

achieve the stabilization of CO_2 emissions between 2010 and 2020 in absolute terms. Table 11.7 presents the detailed numbers for CO_2 emissions in the four world regions.

While CO_2 reduction in the EU is already substantial in HS1 (−8.4%), all other regions are not affected and show slight increases in CO_2 emissions. On the contrary, the measures implemented in scenario HS3 lead to a substantial reduction in CO_2 emissions in all world regions compared to the baseline in 2020, with similar reductions in the EU, the OECD, and the emerging economies. Among the group of emerging countries, the largest CO_2 reductions would result in South Africa (−48%), India (−27.5%), and China (−20.8%). The reduction in the rest of the world is smaller, as the policy measures have not been implemented in these countries. In these countries, emission reductions would only be experienced in the OPEC countries (−9.5%) and Chile (−2.5%), while the other countries may see small increases in CO_2 emissions of between 0.2% (in Hong Kong) and 2.3% (in Singapore).

The fact that the impact on material extraction (Table 11.6) is much lower than on carbon emissions (Table 11.7) is due to the fact that no material taxes are implemented in the major emerging economies in scenario HS3. Coordinated action in the major economies could reduce material extraction much further.

11.4 Policy implications

The results from the modelling exercise support four main conclusions.

From a global perspective, the first conclusion to be derived from this study is that combating climate change can only be successful through global cooperation and global climate treaties. As the large emerging countries will increase their share in global CO_2 emissions (Figure 11.6), ensuring their contribution to a post-Kyoto agreement on climate change must be one of the key objectives in future international climate treaties. As the impacts of scenario HS1 have shown, unilateral action by the EU is insignificant in terms of global environmental sustainability. EU environmental policy objectives, such as the 2°C target for the maximum global temperature increase above pre-industrial levels, can emphatically not be achieved through measures in the EU alone. All OECD countries and the major emerging economies have to join to keep the carbon concentration below 450 parts per million (ppm) (IEA 2008a). Coordinated multilateral policies are also necessary in order to avoid carbon leakage (Bruvoll and Fæhn 2006; IEA 2008b). If only EU-27 members participate, the emissions of non-participating countries could further increase through the migration of emission-intensive industries.

Second, targets in the range of 20–30% reductions of CO_2 emissions are not sufficient to lessen the environmental impacts of our economic activities. Targets are also needed on overall resource use. The scenarios have confirmed that overall resource use will grow steeply at the global level if no measures are taken to further increase resource productivity and to limit resource consumption. Similar to the Kyoto goals on CO_2 reductions, it is thus strongly recommended that goals are set aimed at reducing overall resource use. The results of the scenario analyses suggest that a reduction of the overall level of resources used would be most effective if done in concerted action between the EU and emerging economies. The changes expected in response to the introduction of an ETR in Europe alone (HS1), but also in collaboration with the OECD and emerging economies (HS3), are in line with the results from other studies on this topic (see e.g. IPCC 2008). The focus on CO_2 reductions in most international climate policy negotiations, including the Copenhagen Climate Conference, is too narrow. As the case of biofuels has shown, it is important to consider not just CO_2 but also other greenhouse gases, such as nitrous oxide (Howarth and Bringezu 2009). Otherwise, expensive policy instruments aimed at climate change mitigation by cutting CO_2 emissions, such as biofuel targets, Carbon Capture and Storage (CSS), and nuclear energy, may in fact increase overall levels of resource use and thus indirectly aggravate climate change. As most greenhouse gas emissions are indirectly related to resource extraction and use, particularly the combustion of extracted fossil fuels, it is crucial to address one of the most important contributors to climate change—the unsustainable use of resources such as raw materials, land, and water. This is not only a root cause of climate change, but also a serious environmental threat in a finite world and one which ultimately impacts on people's livelihoods.

Third, given the growing importance of embedded emissions in imports and exports, the integration of environmental aspects into trade policies must play a key part in the implementation of a pathway towards sustainable growth in Europe and globally. Multi-regional input-output models of CO_2 emissions

Table 11.8. Production versus consumption-based CO_2 emissions in different world regions

	Production-based emissions (Mt CO_2)		Consumption-base emissions (Mt CO_2)		CO_2 trade balance (Mt CO_2)	
	1995	2000	1995	2000	1995	2000
OECD	11,229	12,088	12,487	14,037	−1,259	−1,949
Non-OECD	6,469	6,821	5,498	5,687	971	1,134
World Total	19,138	21,757	19,272	22,171	−134	−414

Source: Nakano et al. (2009: 7).

have shown that CO_2 emissions would be significantly higher in the industrialized world if indicators were based on consumption-oriented indicators (Shui and Harriss 2006; Nakano et al. 2009). The consumption-based CO_2 emissions of the OECD overall, for example, were 16.1% higher in 2000 than the conventional measurement of production-based emissions suggests. Those differences even exceed 30% in seven OECD countries (Austria, France, Luxembourg, Portugal, Sweden, Switzerland, and the United Kingdom) (Nakano et al. 2009).

Since the environmental effects of production often occur beyond European borders, effective and globally responsible environmental policies should take a life-cycle perspective in assessing and addressing current challenges; in other words, address the environmental effects of production independently of whether the negative impact occurs within European borders or beyond (see e.g. OECD 2001; Peters 2008). Therefore, the issue of shared responsibility of producers and consumers is likely to remain a prominent topic at global climate negotiations, especially for developing countries which produce a large share of GHG emissions on behalf of industrialized countries ('outsourced emissions'). As recent studies reveal, around one-third of the Chinese GHG emissions are related to the production of exports to the rest of the world (Weber et al. 2008). The findings of this chapter feed into the current discussion on producer versus consumer responsibilities in the world economy (Lenzen et al. 2007; Wiedmann et al. 2007; Rodrigues and Domingos 2008). Whereas most existing accounting frameworks (including the Kyoto Protocol) follow a production or territory accounting principle, it is debatable whether a consumption-oriented accounting approach may also be useful in analysing sustainability-oriented concepts such as the allocation of 'fair shares' of the world's resources to all inhabitants of the planet (see for example Bruckner et al. 2010). An agreement on the distribution of costs to reduce GHG emissions between the producers and the consumers of products in the world economy is a possible step towards the realization of an effective post-Kyoto regime. Alternatively, a global carbon tax could be a solution in sharing the common responsibility of all countries. A carbon tax in China, for example, would decrease their embodied emissions and, by raising their prices to consuming countries, reduce exports. This, in turn, again feeds into the topic of producer versus consumer responsibility.

Finally, the results support an OECD proposal for the joint reform of fiscal and environmental measures which may protect the environment as well as raise revenue and free up resources which can be allocated to poverty reduction efforts (OECD 2005). The trends in all scenarios show a dramatic increase in natural resource extraction which is already beyond sustainable levels in many resource-rich countries and causes substantial social and environmental impacts (see EEA 2005; UNEP 2007). If policies do not tackle these problems, they may exacerbate them. Many of the external EU policy documents, such as the trade strategy 'Global Europe' (EC 2006) and the 'Raw Materials Strategy' (2008), have been criticized because the goals of *access* to and *supply* of raw materials and natural resources prevail over the objective of their *sustainable* and *equitable* use (FoE 2008). Such criticism, along with the long-term trends in resource use and environmental impacts, suggests that Europe should more actively address the potential conflict between economic goals (ensuring access to resources around the globe) and development goals (raising the material standard of living in developing countries). The European Commission is in a strong position to ensure that the causal link between environmental and wider social and economic development goals is better recognized and articulated in development cooperation and that adequate response systems will be developed. In the UN Millennium Development Goals (MDGs), environmental issues do not receive much attention outside of MDG 7 on environmental sustainability. According to the UNDP (2005), the lack of quantifiable targets for MDG 7 has been one reason for its relatively low profile on the global agenda. Apart from ETR, a frequently expressed policy suggestion for developed countries is an increase in technical and financial assistance for measures to reduce emissions and implement adaptation measures in developing countries (Stern 2007). Helping developing countries in their efforts for mitigation and adaptation may also be achieved by placing access to resource-efficient technologies in the public domain, either by removing restrictions related to intellectual property rights on such technologies, or through international public buyouts of the relevant patents.

11.5 Conclusions

This chapter has presented and discussed some of the global economic and environmental implications of the introduction of an ETR in Europe, based on scenario simulations using the GINFORS model.

The results show that the implementation of an ETR could reduce the EU's resource consumption as well as its CO_2 emissions. The worldwide effects of the unilateral ETR scenario (HS1) on the growth trend of used material extraction and energy-related CO_2 emissions are negligible. Resource extraction in the EU would only be reduced by around 1.5% (100 million tonnes) and global CO_2 emissions by less than 1%. Without international cooperation, global material extraction and energy-related CO_2 emissions will continue to grow. This trend is largely led by the group of emerging countries. In an internationally cooperative context, however, the economic impacts of a major ETR in Europe on the rest of the world are small, while the environmental benefits can be quite significant. In scenario HS3, the larger ETR (than HS1) in the EU, in the context of global cooperation, reduces global material extraction by more than 5% and global CO_2 emissions by more than 15%, while reducing world GDP by only 1.4% compared to the baseline scenario in 2020. Thus, an ETR in Europe would be more effective in terms of reducing global CO_2 emissions and material extraction in a context of international cooperation on emission reduction targets.

An increase in international carbon prices will reduce overall exports and impact the international competitiveness of emission-intensive industries. Measured in terms of export growth rates, the negative effects on international competitiveness are especially pronounced in European emission-intensive industries and are smaller in the unilateral ETR policy scenario than in the scenario with multilateral cooperation. The strongest export decline rates would emerge in the EU's utilities and heavy industries (electricity, gas and water supply; coke and refined petroleum products; iron and steel). In terms of absolute monetary values, the strongest declines would be experienced in EU exports of chemicals (excluding pharmaceuticals), machinery and equipment, and motor vehicles. Relatively weak negative effects would be observed on the export growth rates of emerging countries.

Four major policy conclusions can be drawn from this investigation. First, combating climate change is significantly more successful in a context of international cooperation and through strong global climate treaties. Second, targets on CO_2 emissions alone are not sufficient to lessen the environmental impacts of our economic activities. Targets should also be envisaged for other resource use with damaging environmental effects. Third, given the importance of embedded emissions in imports and exports, environmental aspects must be integrated into international trade policies in order to achieve sustainable development. Possible approaches to sharing the common responsibility of all countries may include a fair distribution of costs to reduce GHG emissions between the producers and the consumers of products in the world economy, or agreement on a global carbon tax. Finally, the results call for a stronger recognition of the intricate linkages between economic and environmental objectives in international development cooperation policies, and for adequate responses such as increased technical and financial assistance for mitigation and adaptation, or international public buyouts of patents on expensive resource-efficient technologies.

Future research should first of all further improve the models. This holds for the integration of additional data, and a better representation of the energy supply and upcoming technologies. More and more internationally comparable data are becoming available. The underlying assumptions of bounded rationality have to be crosschecked and combined with new agent-based approaches that are increasingly able to overcome the simplified assumptions of the homo oeconomicus on which most energy models are based. Supply-side developments like crude oil stocks and supply constraints and their medium-term price implications should be taken into account. The understanding of the role of technology has to be further improved, either by linking the models with technology-based bottom-up models or by better incorporation of technology data. This can include such stock data as the power-generation mix with its age structure, or the vehicle fleet, which limits substitution possibilities in the medium term. Future technology options such as renewable energy sources, efficiency potentials, or Carbon Capture and Storage (CCS) should also be analysed. Models should also be expanded to cover additional greenhouse gases and material extraction categories, other environmental impacts, and scarce biocapacity. Otherwise, complex impacts of, for example, an international CCS strategy on energy efficiency, energy consumption, material extraction, and economic conditions and effects will not be fully covered. Combining the results presented in this chapter with environmentally extended multi-regional input-output models, such as GRAM, can substantially improve understanding of consumer and producer responsibility in the context of international negotiations.

References

Bruckner, M., C. Polzin, S. Giljum (2010), 'Counting CO_2 emissions in a globalised world: Producer versus consumer-oriented methods for CO_2 accounting', DIE Discussion Paper, 9/2010.

Bruvoll, A., and T. Fæhn (2006), 'Transboundary Effects of Environmental Policy: Markets and Emission Leakages', *Ecological Economics*, 59: 499–510.

EC (European Commission) (2006), 'Global Europe. Competing in the World: A Contribution to the EU's Growth and Jobs Strategy', EC, DG External Trade, Brussels.

—— (2008a), *Decision on the Effort of Member States to Reduce their Greenhouse Gas Emissions to Meet The Community's Greenhouse Gas Emission Reduction Commitments up to 2020* (COM(2008)17 final), available from <http://ec.europa.eu/environment/climat/pdf/draft_proposal_effort_sharing.pdf>.

—— (2008b), *The Raw Materials Initiative: Meeting our Critical Needs for Growth and Jobs in Europe* (COM(2008) 699), EC, DG Environment, Brussels.

EEA (European Environment Agency) (2005), *The European Environment. State and Outlook 2005*, Copenhagen: European Environment Agency.

FoE (Friends of the Earth) (2008), 'Living beyond its Resources: Impacts of 'Global Europe' on Sustainable Development: Background and Issues', available from <http://www.global-europe.org/docs/GlobalEurope_Conference_Background_Issues_ 241108.pdf>.

Giljum, S., A. Behrens, F. Hinterberger, A. Stocker (2005), 'Scenario Evaluation Component Material Extraction', MOSUS Work Package 5.2 (Environmental Evaluation), SERI, Vienna, available at <http://www.mosus.net/documents/Evaluation%20report_Material%20flows_final.pdf>.

—— —— —— C. Lutz, and B. Meyer (2008a), 'Modelling Scenarios towards a Sustainable Use of Natural Resources in Europe', *Environmental Science and Policy*, 11: 204–16.

—— C. Lutz, A. Jungnitz, M. Bruckner, and F. Hinterberger (2008b), 'Global Dimensions of European Natural Resource Use', First results from the Global Resource Accounting Model (GRAM), SERI Working Paper 7, Sustainable Europe Research Institute, Vienna.

Helm, D. (2008), 'Climate-Change Policy: Why has so Little been Achieved?' *Oxford Review of Economic Policy,* 24: 211–38.

Howarth, R. W., and S. Bringezu (eds.) (2009), 'Biofuels: Environmental Consequences and Interactions with Changing Land Use', Proceedings of the Scientific Committee on Problems of the Environment (SCOPE) International Biofuels Project Rapid Assessment, 22–5 September 2008, Gummersbach, Germany.

IEA (International Energy Agency) (2008a), *World Energy Outlook 2008,* Paris: IEA.

—— (2008b), 'Issues behind Competitiveness and Carbon Leakage: Focus on Heavy Industry', IEA Information Paper, October 2008, IEA, Paris, available at <http://www. iea.org/Textbase/papers/2008/Competitiveness_and_Carbon_Leakage.pdf>.

—— (2009), *World Energy Outlook 2009*, Paris: IEA.

IPCC (2008), 'Further Work on Scenarios Report from the IPCC Expert Meeting towards New Scenarios for Analysis of Emissions, Climate Change, Impacts, and Response Strategies', 19–21 September, 2007, IPCC-XXVIII/Doc.8 (19.III.2008), Noordwijkerhout, the Netherlands, available at <http://www.ipcc.ch/meetings/session28/doc8. pdf>.

Lenzen, M., J. Murray, F. Sack, and T. Wiedmann (2007), 'Shared Producer and Consumer Responsibility—Theory and Practice', *Ecological Economics*, 61(1): 27–42.

Nakano, S., A. Okamura, N. Sakurai, M. Suzuki, Y. Tojo, and N. Yamano (2009), 'The Measurement of CO_2 Embodiments in International Trade: Evidence from the Harmonised Input-Output and Bilateral Trade Database', STI Working Paper 2009/3, DSTI/DOC(2009)3.

OECD (2001), *Extended Producer Responsibility—A Guidance Manual for Governments*, Paris: OECD.

—— (2005), *Environmental Fiscal Reform for Poverty Reduction*, DAC Guidelines and Reference Series, Paris: OECD.

Peters, G. (2008), 'From Production-Based to Consumption-Based National Emission Inventories', *Ecological Economics*, 65: 13–23.

Rodrigues, J., and T. Domingos (2008), 'Consumer and Producer Environmental Responsibility: Comparing Two Approaches', *Ecological Economics*, 66(2–3): 533–46.

Shui, B., and R. C. Harriss (2006), 'The Role of CO_2 Embodiment in US-China Trade', *Energy Policy*, 34: 4063–8.

Sterner, T., U. M. Persson (2008), 'An even sterner review: Introducing relative prices into the discounting debate', *Review of Environmental Economics and Policy*, 2(1), 61–76.

UNDP (2005), Environmental Sustainability in 100 Millennium Development Goals Country Reports. <http://www.unep.org/dec/docs/UNDP_review_of_Environmental_Sustainability.doc> (accessed 14 April 2009).

UNEP (2007), *Global Environmental Outlook – 4*, Malta: Progress Press Ltd.

Weber, C. L., G. P. Peters, D. Guan, and K. Hubacek (2008), 'The Contribution of Chinese Exports to Climate Change', International Input-Output Meeting on Managing the Environment, Seville, Spain.

Whalley, J., and S. Walsh (2009), 'Bringing the Copenhagen Global Climate Change Negotiations to Conclusion', *CESifo Economic Studies*, 55: 255–85.

Wiedmann, T., R. Wood, M. Lenzen, J. Minx, D. Guan, and J. Barrett (2007), *Development of an Embedded Carbon Emissions Indicator—Producing a Time Series of Input-Output Tables and Embedded Carbon Dioxide Emissions for the UK by Using a MRIO Data Optimisation System*, Final Report to the Department for Environment, Food and Rural Affairs by Stockholm Environment Institute at the University of York and Centre for Integrated Sustainability Analysis at the University of Sydney, London: Defra.

WTO (World Trade Organization) (2008), *World Trade Statistics 2008*, Geneva: World Trade Organization.

12

ETR and the Environmental Industry

Martin Jänicke and Roland Zieschank

12.1 Introduction

Industries which reduce pollution, increase resource productivity, or foster a switch to renewable from non-renewable resources are collectively called the 'environmental industry' (EI), which has been perceived as an important sector contributing to sustainable growth in Europe (Ayres and van den Bergh 2005). This chapter presents concepts that define the EI, explores the structure and growth of these industries in Europe, and the extent to which environmental tax reform (ETR)—within a mix of instrument—may play a role in fostering that growth.

The first section considers the structure, function, trends, and governance of the EI, which has until now been largely an 'invisible industry' in terms of statistics and sectoral analysis. Attempts to determine the size of the industry have resulted in grossly differing outcomes, illustrating a lack of consensus on its definition. To get a clearer picture, we differentiate between two subsectors: pollution management—mainly end-of-pipe treatment—and resource management, including clean(er) technology. These two faces of the EI have quite different environmental and economic implications. Whereas resource management typically intends to influence (and increase) resource productivity, pollution control mostly has no positive influence on productivity—or even a negative one. Pollution management has an important impact only on specified pollutants, with the impact on resource use being insignificant or even negative. Efficient resource use, on the other hand, may have lower impacts on specific pollutants but has impacts on a broader variety of environmental stress factors: from mining to transport, from waste to emissions or dissipative losses of all kinds, which are responsible for environmental deterioration.

Efforts to statistically define the environmental industry as a fast-growing 'quasi sector' have estimated that in 2004 it accounted for at least 2.6% of GDP in the EU (see Section 12.2.2) and about 8% in Germany in 2007. This industry, however, has been underestimated in the existing statistics. The German case shows that investment in climate-friendly technologies alone amounted to 5% of the GDP in 2005 (BMU 2009). Beyond statistics, the major importance of the environmental industry can be shown in terms of a functional analysis. To the extent that negative environmental factors, if uncontrolled, may constrain both economic growth and the welfare to be derived from it, the EI, by controlling these factors, may be regarded as a *condition* for sustainable growth. At the same time, the EI is performing well in global markets, and seems well positioned to be of increasing worldwide importance. Where it provides the basis for a competitive exports industry, the EI can also be said to contribute to the general competitiveness of the national economy. The EI therefore is both a condition of and contributes directly to sustainable economic growth. The process is essentially policy driven.

Therefore questions of governance play an important role and are considered in the final subsection of Section 12.2.

The potential for multiple win-win effects from the EI is illustrated in four 'best practice' case studies in Section 12.3: renewable energy, eco-construction, fuel-efficient diesel cars, and industrial waste management/recycling. The section considers their economic impact and how the trends in these sectors have been influenced by environmental policy. 'Policy' in this context does not mean only the use of environmental taxes. Environmental policy—especially if it is oriented towards innovation—typically employs a 'multi-impulse approach' (Klemmer 1999). It will be seen that in all four case studies environmental policy was found to be the clear driving force in Germany.

12.2 Function, structure, dynamics, and governance of the environmental industry

Eurostat and the OECD define the EI as follows: 'The environmental goods and services industry consists of activities which produce goods and services to measure, prevent, limit, minimise or correct environmental damage to water, air and soil, problems related to waste, noise and eco-systems. This includes cleaner technologies, products and services that reduce environmental risk and minimise pollution and resource use.' (OECD and Eurostat 1999).

However, following Ernst & Young (2006; see Boxes 12.1 and 12.2), we also distinguish between enterprises that produce marketable goods and services for both traditional additive pollution management ('clean-up' or 'end-of-pipe

> **Box 12.1** POLLUTION MANAGEMENT
>
> '... sectors that manage material streams from processes (the techno-sphere) to nature ... typically using "end of pipe" technology'.
>
> *Source*: Ernst & Young (2006).

> **Box 12.2** RESOURCE MANAGEMENT
>
> 'sectors that take a more preventive approach to managing material streams from nature to techno-sphere'
>
> *Source*: Ernst & Young (2006).

treatment'), and those concerned with integrated resource management or eco-efficient production and consumption.

This differentiation between pollution management and resource management seems plausible and useful. However, contrary to Ernst & Young and Eurostat, we propose to include 'clean(er) technology' in the resource management sector (see also DTI and Defra 2006). This revised classification would include all 'integrated' environmental technologies in the subclass of resource management. This also would underline the special character of the clean-up/end-of pipe type of environmental technology, which as a rule causes not only additional costs, but in most cases leads also to additional resource use (e.g. the lime input for desulphurization or materials for sound-absorbing barriers). Resource management, on the other hand, means more efficient resource use and thereby also higher productivity (Meyer et al. 2007). Innovations can also take place in the area of pollution management and clean-up technology. Often these technologies are highly effective as far as special pollutants are concerned. Eco-efficient innovations and resource management, however, typically have a broader scope of environmental effects, as well as being more competitive economically.

12.2.1 The Environmental Industry as a Functional Condition of Sustainable Growth

Industrial growth is only sustainable if negative external effects and damage costs are steadily 'neutralized' and environmental impacts remain at a constant or decreasing level. This necessitates a permanent reduction of emissions, waste, or other negative ecological effects relative to the produced unit of GDP, either by pollution management or resource management. The production and innovation of pollution control technologies and ex ante eco-efficient products or investment goods (including the related services) is the function of specialized producers, defined as the 'environmental industry' (which also includes the green technology division of companies). It is a sector producing marketable technical solutions for global environmental needs. The market potential is different from many other products as it is characterized by its global dimensions, a long-term future perspective, and permanent pressure for environmental innovation.

Due to inherent market failures the EI is to a high degree policy driven (Ernst & Young 2006; Jänicke and Jacob 2006). Markets are the most important mechanism for stimulating competitive innovations of clean/cleaner technologies, but their potential comes with qualifications. Markets in general do not have (a) the capability to detect long-term environmental damage, (b) private firms do not have an adequate incentive to develop marketable solutions, and typically markets are (c) unable to create sufficient demand for such solutions—which need high market penetration to be effective in terms of environmental protection.

Here the constitutional obligations and legitimation mechanisms of democratic government become relevant. The role of public policy is especially important when the pressure for change is high and the rate of technical progress too low (e.g. for climate change). Governments, individually or by concerted action, typically translate environmental threats into regulations, particularly if they come under political pressure. Such policy regulations support the demand for marketable solutions. At the same time, they provide standardized information about problems, solutions, and the probable reaction of competitors and clients.

The growth of the EI can be primarily explained by the functional necessity of damage prevention which in the past often has manifested itself by ecological crises or political protest (e.g. Japan, USA, or Germany). Recent examples include China and Southern Europe.

Since pollution sinks are restricted and natural resources limited (or characterized by volatile prices), global industrial growth necessitates ever-increasing eco-efficiency. This causes permanent pressure for environmental innovation (Jänicke 2008). The EI, therefore, is not only a fast-growing but also a highly innovative sector. According to the (then) British Department of Trade and Industry, the EI is highly knowledge-intensive, contributing more than average to the added value and productivity of the national economy (DTI and Defra 2006: 6). Since the EI provides marketable solutions not only for governments but also for enterprises facing the risk of environmental regulation or other kinds of pressure, this sector may also have a modernizing function for the whole economy.

The first function of the EI is to prevent or reduce environmental damage. But there is also a more constructive function, especially in highly developed countries: to improve environmental conditions, to satisfy the increased demand of the growing global middle class for a healthy and 'natural' environment.

So far this is true only for highly developed countries, which play the role of trend-setters, thereby creating lead markets for environmental innovations (Jacob et al. 2005; Beise and Rennings 2003). Successful exports—starting from leading national markets—may be the most plausible test of whether the growth of the sector has a positive impact on sustainable growth in economic terms.

The special characteristics of the EI and eco-efficient innovation such as global and future market potential and their role in the competition for innovation, etc.—may explain why the widely predicted regulatory 'race to the bottom' did not take place. It should be noted in this context that countries with stricter environmental policies on average are more competitive than others (Esty et al. 2006; Jänicke and Jacob 2006). New findings indicate that countries with innovative environmental technologies prove successful in total factor productivity (the efficiency of production with given capital and labour inputs) and therefore in economic growth (Allianz 2008: 33).

12.2.2 Structure of the Environmental Industry

As already noted, the Environmental Industry has no clear statistical status and is not part of the traditional sectoral system. It has a statistically defined core and a more open marginal area. A certain sectoral identity, however, can be discerned not only in terms of the kind of output but also in certain sectorally specific activities such as collective lobby activities. For a long time the EI was defined as the sum of producers of 'end-of-pipe' technology, typically adding clean-up measures to 'dirty technologies' (including related services). Now, however, the EI is usually divided into two parts, concerned with the two different functions of pollution management and resource management.

In their broad empirical study, Ernst & Young (2006) described the EU-25 EI as a sector with a turnover of €227 billion or 2.2% of GDP (2004). If the contributions of omitted sectors are estimated and added in, the total turnover is at least €270 billion (more than 2.6% of GDP; see Table 12.1, although this estimate is still incomplete), and the EU-25 EI provided at least 3.4 million full-time job equivalents.

A more recent publication came to the conclusion that the renewable sector alone provided 1.4 million jobs (which could grow to 2.8 million in 2020; ENDS 2009). Germany, France, and the UK are the dominant EI countries and

Table 12.1. Eco-industry turnover, EU-25, Germany, and the UK, 2004 (€ bn.)

	EU-25	Germany	UK
(A) Pollution Control:	**82.0**	**26.5**	**4.7**
• Waste water treatment	52.2	19.3	1.6
• Air pollution control	15.9	4.5	1.7
• Remediation/Clean up of soil/groundwater	5.2	1.1	0.3
• Noise and vibration control	2.0	0.4	0.1
• Environmental monitoring/instrumentation	1[2]		
• Nature protection[1]	5.7	1.2	1.0
(B) Resource Management:	**168.5**	**75.3**	**14.8**
• Solid waste management and recycling[1]	52.4	14.9	6.4
• Recycled materials	24.3	6.8	3.5
• Renewable energy production	6.1	2.2	0.4
• Water supply	45.7	11.4	4.5
• Eco-construction (estimated)	>40[2]	40 (2005)[2]	
(C) Administration. Management. Research[1]	**19.8**	**4.4**	**2.0**
• General public administration	11.5	4.4	1.6
• Private environmental management	5.8		0.4
• Environmental research and development	2.5[2]		
Total	**>270.3**	**>106.2**	**>21.5**

Notes: [1] Revised classification.
[2] Estimations (not included in the totals in the Ernst & Young study).
Source: Ernst & Young (2006); authors' compilation.

also are characterized by the highest contribution to foreign trade within the EU (Ernst & Young 2006: see also DTI and Defra 2006 and Cambridge Econometrics et al. 2007). According to Roland Berger, the size of the German EI (defined as 'GreenTech') was actually 8% of GDP in 2007 (BMU 2009). Employment in the EI in Germany was at least 1.8 million in 2006, and in 2007/8 in the UK 0.9 million, respectively 4.5% and 3.1% of total employment (BMU and UBA 2009; Innovas 2009).

Figure 12.1 shows different OECD countries' market share of the global EI. It shows that Germany has the largest share among European countries, and its share has increased constantly since 2000, surpassing that of the US in 2003. It is for this reason that the four mini-case studies later in this chapter focus on Germany.

Table 12.1 shows the sectoral breakdown of the EI in the EU-25 according to the classification by Ernst & Young (2006). We use this study to provide a plausible *structure* for the EI, although the empirical picture is incomplete and the *size* of this industry is still underestimated. The classification has been revised as shown: 'Solid waste management and recycling' has been added to the 'resource management' category and 'nature protection' to the traditional 'pollution control' category. Estimates of turnover have been added where available (and mentioned in the EU study). Administration, management, and research have been placed into a separate class, because they have to do with both pollution management and resource management (before they were

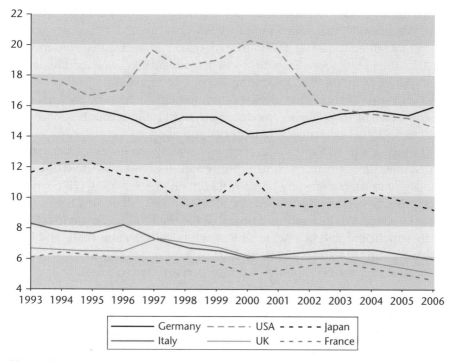

Figure 12.1 Environmental industry—world market share of OECD countries
Source: BMU and UBA (2009).

included in the clean-up sector). Finally, additional aspects of the 'environmental industry' are identified, which are not (or at least not fully) included in the calculations by Ernst & Young, with some estimates for Germany and the UK added by the authors.

Besides the existing problems of statistical classification of the environmental industry, a major difficulty is to define the size of environmental improvement which needs to be delivered by enterprises in order to be included in the EI (Miltner 2008). For example, which kinds of cars or buildings are energy efficient enough to be included? This blurring is one of the factors causing the underestimation of the size of this 'sector'.

Even the study by Ernst & Young follows this pattern of underestimation. Their turnover figure for the British EI is €21.5 billion (in 2004). DTI and Defra have a significantly higher figure of €35 billion in 2005 (DTI and Defra 2006). The figure for the annual turnover of the German EI in Ernst & Young (2006) is €66.2 billion. This is not even half the figure found by Roland Berger (BMU 2007). Some environmentally beneficial technologies and services of relevance are not included in the Ernst & Young calculation, for example, eco-construction, the EU-wide turnover of which the authors have estimated at

€40 billion.[1] In addition, the figure for the renewable energy industry is far too low. For example, the German industry is worth not €2.2 billion as quoted, but €12.3 billion (in 2004). Eco-tourism or 'green' financing (e.g. in Germany neither the public Kreditanstalt für Wiederaufbau (KfW) nor the influential semi-public Deutsche Bundesstiftung Umwelt is included in Ernst & Young 2006). Bio-products or other specified environmentally friendly products (e.g. energy-efficient 'Top Runner' products) are not visibly accounted for in the statistics. All these practices lead to underestimation.

The problem of underestimation becomes even clearer if we consider a study on German investment in climate protection. It shows that investment in climate protection alone amounts to €95 billion or 5% of GDP (2005). If the recent policy package is included, an additional €30 billion or 1.5% of GDP must be added. It is interesting to note that the resulting energy-saving effects of these policies result in a net surplus of several billion euros (BMU and UBA 2009; see also UBA 2007; McKinsey 2007).

In summary, the main points of this section are therefore that:

- The EI has two quite distinct components: industries which supply traditional *pollution control* technologies and services ('end-of-pipe treatment'); and those industries concerned with *resource management* (management of materials and energy). Both components of the EI have contributed to environmental improvement in the EU. Pollution control treatment has a stabilizing function in moderating the environmental impacts of industrial growth and remains a field for possible innovation (e.g. waste incineration). It may, however, increase production costs and material use and therefore reduce resource productivity. On the other hand, more efficient resource use (eco-efficiency) is likely to increase resource productivity and to reduce costs in companies.

- The total calculable turnover of the EU-25 EI is clearly higher than the Ernst & Young study shows (at least €270 billion rather than €227 billion). Figures for renewable energy, for example, are too low, others are not included. The EI is larger if subgroups which are less 'visible' in terms of statistics are included. Taking this into account, it is highly probable that the EU-25 environmental industry (2004) is an industry of not less than 2.6% of the GDP.

- However, a relevant part of the industry remains invisible as eco-efficiency becomes a general trend for the whole of business and industry, expanding beyond the traditional environmental sector. In Germany, the engine-building industry could be seen as an example (Deutsche Bank

---

[1] This is now equivalent to the German investment in energy-efficient buildings in 2005 (BMU and UBA 2009).

Research 2008). Eventually, a general *mainstreaming* of eco-efficiency could finally make the search for a special environmental industry obsolete.

A final point is that, within the EI as here defined, it is resource-efficient (not end-of-pipe) technologies which are characterized by high growth. A recent study of seven OECD countries using a similar dual classification comes to the conclusion that 'cleaner production' today has a larger market share than the 'end-of-pipe' subgroup (Frondel et al. 2007; see also DTI and Defra 2006).

12.2.3 Dynamic: Environmental Industry, a Fast-Growing Sector

According to the EU Commission, the core of the European eco-industry grew by 8.3% per annum between 2004 and 2008, well above the average rate of economic growth, generating a turnover in 2008 of €319 billion (European Commission 2009). The growth rate was higher than the already above average growth between 1999 and 2004 (Ernst & Young 2006). According to Roland Berger, the global market of the Eco-Industry has an average annual growth rate of 6.5%. It could rise from €1,400 billion in 2007 to €3,100 billion in 2020 (BMU 2009). A forecast made by McKinsey shows that the global demand for energy-efficient technologies in energy-intensive sectors alone could rise from €500 billion (2008) to €2,100 billion (2020) (McKinsey 2009).

The growth rate is particularly high in Germany, where the estimated share of GDP was 8% in 2007 and could rise to 14% in 2020 (BMU 2009). A survey of 1,500 German firms producing environmental technology and services provided the following picture (Table 12.2) of this industry, here entitled the 'GreenTech'industry:

In terms of growth, enterprises related to environmentally friendly energy supply and efficiency of energy and material use are clearly dominant. Again, the major importance of the resource management sector is visible. The table also emphasizes the especially high growth dynamics in this sector. In

Table 12.2. Structure and growth of the German 'GreenTech' industry

	German share of greentech world market%	Annual turnover growth 2005–07%	Expected annual turnover growth 2008–10%
Environmentally friendly energy supply	30	29	35
Energy efficiency	12	20	22
Material efficiency	6	21	24
Recycling	24	18	16
Sustainable water supply	10	15	14
Sustainable mobility	18	15	17

Source: BMU (2009).

Germany, this is clearly higher than the growth of the pollution control sector, which is subject to decreased domestic demand and is successful only as an export sector. We can plausibly assume that the growth of the resource management sector is higher also in other highly developed countries where domestic markets for clean-up technologies tend to stabilize (or even decrease). In contrast, the world market for resource-efficient technologies is rapidly expanding. Companies often benefit directly from the cost-saving potential of production-integrated environmental technologies, and related innovations are set to gain enormously in importance worldwide (Allianz 2008: 30). Germany—together with other European countries and especially the UK—has a strong export position in this regard (see ADEME 2007).

A significant additional driving factor seems to be the volatile prices of resources. A survey of German companies on the strategic relevance of aspects of 'Global Change' revealed that more than 80% of companies fear resource scarcity (Biebeler et al. 2008: 14–26).

The rapid growth of resource management technologies in comparison with the growth of the pollution control sector is highlighted when we compare the present real turnover growth of selected eco-efficient technology in Germany (Table 12.2) with the constant demand for pollution control technology. The expenditures of public, private, and privatized public companies on pollution control remained stable in Germany between 1994 and 2005 (€33.9 billion compared to €34.1 billion; Statistisches Bundesamt 2009: 321).

Calculations of the growth of employment in the German EI rely mainly on statistics for traditional, and in the meanwhile slow-growing, end-of-pipe technologies (see Figure 12.2). Again, the development in the total EI is therefore being underestimated.

The growth of employment in the sector of eco-efficient technologies ('GreenTech') is significantly higher, with renewable energy having the highest growth rates (Figure 12.3). In 2009, the sector provided 340,000 jobs (in 2004, 160,000; BMU and UBA 2009; Umwelt 12/2010).

A cross-sectional analysis of economic performance in 15 EU countries points out that investing in more efficient use of energy is a driving factor for economic growth and therefore energy-efficient measures and innovations will play the role of a *key strategy* for sustainable growth in Europe (Allianz 2008: 31). Calculations on the return of investment on a global scale have shown, that—with an average internal rate of return of 17%—the annual investment of $170 billion could result in savings of up to $900 billion annually by 2020 (McKinsey Global Institute 2008: 7–8). In addition, the costs of building new power plants could be avoided. (At a micro-economic level, however, energy-efficient investments will bear costs as well as benefits, depending on the sector, company, or policy instrument; see also BMU and UBA 2009.)

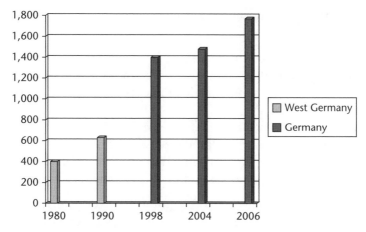

Figure 12.2 Employment in the German environmental industry (in 1,000s)
Sources: Own compilation; BMU (2008).

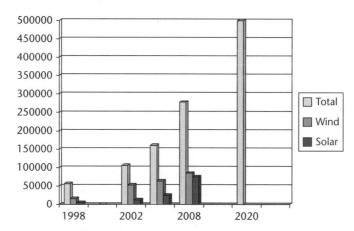

Figure 12.3 Employment in the German renewable energy sector, 2004–2008, forecast 2020
Sources: BMU and UBA (2009).

12.2.4 Governance

We now analyse the relationship between regulation and the growth of the EI. This leads in the next section to four selected case studies that explore the relationship between environmental policy, growth, and innovation.

'Compliance with policy objectives and legal requirements set by the EU and national authorities will be the main drivers of eco-industry growth in the near future' (Ernst & Young 2006: 48). If this is true, then the question of governance arises. In a recent publication, we have argued (Jänicke 2008)

323

that environmental innovation is best supported under the following conditions:

- clear, demanding, and calculable goals;
- a policy mix supporting all phases of the innovation process and providing additional supporting instruments (e.g. labelling or networking of all kinds);
- economic instruments (like eco-tax reforms and/or emission trading) to stimulate a *general tendency* ('Tendenzsteuerung');
- and *specific 'detailed regulation'* ('fine-tuning', 'Detailsteuerung') to use specific innovation potentials and/or to overcome specific obstacles.

Therefore financial instruments like environmental tax reform (ETR), together with specific regulation (e.g. the Japanese Top Runner Programme), are regarded as the most effective approach to environmental innovation. Ekins and Venn (2006) have shown the importance of both instruments in a comparative study. Not least the technological effects of high energy prices in the 1970s and today have confirmed the significant role of the price mechanism. However, it is not easy to find data reliable enough to prove the plausible relationship between changes in relative prices and the growth of the EI in general. Again, it is the two faces of the EI that create the difficulty. There is no plausible positive relationship between resource prices or taxes and the growth of traditional clean-up technologies. However, the correlation between resource prices and resource management (or eco-efficiency) is highly plausible (and taxing the emissions from dirty fuels may provide an additional incentive to shift to cleaner energy sources).

Changes in (relative) resource prices can be effected both by market mechanisms and by government intervention. Government intervention can function as a positive incentive (through subsidies or feed-in tariffs) or as a negative incentive (through taxes or emission trading). Positive incentives give support to a specific innovation. Negative incentives like taxes create economic pressure for innovation in a certain field of technology. The advantage of negative incentives is the openness of the field of innovation and the creation of public revenue. Both kinds of intervention change relative prices, which has the desired steering effects.

The impacts of rising oil prices are also relevant here. However, rising oil (or raw material) prices have a general influence and cannot explain the specifics of particular cases of outstanding national performance.

In the following section, we explore the phenomenon of successful eco-efficient innovation in Germany using four case studies. We illustrate the broad spectrum of influences supporting eco-efficient innovation and the growth in the eco-industry. Both policy regulation and a price mechanism are clearly essential, but the policy mix is different from case to case.

324

12.3 Successful Eco-efficient Innovation: Four Examples from Germany

The four areas of the EI selected for study deliver both environmental and economic benefits. They are also the areas in which the German EI has played a prominent role in Europe. These areas are: (1) low-energy houses, (2) efficient fuel consumption of cars (especially fuel-efficient diesel cars), (3) industrial recycling, and (4) green electricity. These areas illustrate the large potential of resource-efficient innovation stimulated by ambitious environmental policy measures.

We will look at the policy mix and the price mechanism, but also at the outcomes and impacts—the potential co-benefits—of ambitious environmental policy measures. The German eco tax has contributed to innovation and growth in the field of (1) low-energy buildings and (2) fuel-efficient diesel cars (Jacob et al. 2005). In both cases, additional supporting instruments came into effect: energy minimum performance standards for buildings, together with subsidies for energy-saving investments and tax differentiation for new fuel-efficient cars were additional instruments in the policy mix. (3) Recycling is dominated by regulation, but in the case of industrial recycling, the rapid increase in material prices has also stimulated more efficient solutions. Finally, we describe the case of (4) renewable energies, where financial mechanisms—here subsidies as feed-in-tariffs—have caused rapid development. Again, a policy mix with additional instruments was relevant. In addition, we will look at factors like export, job creation, and of course environmental impacts (see Table 12.3).

12.4.1 Energy-Efficient Buildings

A policy to improve the energy efficiency of buildings was part of the climate programme of the SDP/Green coalition government beginning in 1998. The effect of this policy was a reduction in the CO_2 emissions of the residential sector in Germany of 43 million tonnes between 1995 and 2007, while UK residential CO_2 emissions changed little over the same period (Figure 12.4). The policy mix included energy-efficiency standards (insulation, heating system), together with financial mechanisms, of which the most prominent was the eco tax (1999).

Support for energy-efficient construction and re-development is a special activity of the state-owned bank Kreditanstalt für Wiederaufbau (KfW). KfW invested €8.9 billion in 2009—an increase of more then 30% compared to 2008 (KfW 2010). The average energy saving of residential building funded under KfW's CO_2 Building Rehabilitation Programme was about 50%. There

Table 12.3. Eco-industry: four German success stories

	Fuel-efficient diesel Cars	Low-energy Buildings	Industrial Recycling	Renewable Energies
Taxes/Price Mechanism	Eco Tax, Car Tax, Oil Price	Eco Tax, Oil Price	Raw Material Prices	Oil price
Other dominant instruments		Standards, Subsidies	Regulation	Feed-in Tariffs, Subsidies
Growth	++	+	++	++
Employment	+	+		++
Innovation	+	+	++	++
Export	++	+	+	++
Environmental Impacts	+	++	+	++

Note: + = above average; ++ = well above average.
Source: Own judgement.

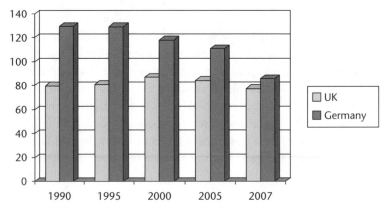

Figure 12.4 CO_2 emissions from the residential sector in the UK and Germany, 1990–2007 (in Mt)

Sources: Ziesing (2009); Defra (2009).

has been a rapidly expanding market for both new and refurbished low-energy houses in Germany since 1999. The creation of more than 14,000 very low-energy new buildings (<4 litres oil/m^2) was supported by the KfW between 1999 and 2007 (KfW 2008). The most energy-efficient subgroup of these buildings, known as passive houses (<1.5 litres oil/m^2), has experienced a similar growth rate, as shown in Figure 12.5. There is no comparable development in the UK, despite part nationalization of the banking sector in 2008.

The cost difference between new standard and passive houses is only around 8%. The subsidy for such houses was increased in 2007, together with a 30% tightening of the efficiency standard, for both new and refurbished houses (which after 2012 will be strengthened again by 30%). The

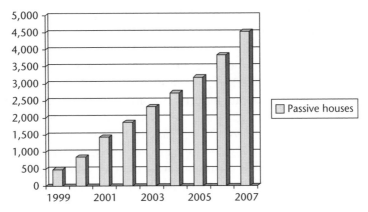

Figure 12.5 Passive houses in Germany, 1999–2007
Source: KfW (2008).

previous energy standard of 2002 was about 7 litres oil/m^2 for single family houses and this was strengthened again in 2007. The average energy consumption of older houses in Germany is 25 litres oil/m^2 (KfW 2008; BMU 2009: 59 ff.).

Investment in new and refurbished energy-efficient buildings in Germany amounted to €40 billion in 2005 (BMU and UBA 2009). The construction industry—after a long recession—in 2008 experienced a revival, mainly due to the new energy and climate policy (Keitel 2008). The market for special components of low-energy houses (e.g. insulation materials) is rapidly increasing. The market for heat pumps was similarly dynamic (a 44% increase in 2006). Germany also has the highest proportion of low-energy houses in Europe, often pre-fabricated. This development puts Germany in a strong position to benefit from the European passive house standard (from 2021 on) for new buildings.

12.4.2 Fuel-Efficient Diesel Cars

It may be surprising to consider diesel cars as part of the EI; but cars with a fuel efficiency double that of the existing car fleet are certainly worth putting in this category.

Diesel cars with a fuel consumption of 3 or 5 litres/100 km came on the market in Germany in 1999. Shortly before (1997), a differentiation in the car tax had been introduced, which explicitly supported fuel-efficient cars with a high tax bonus. This was a de facto bonus for diesel (according to an earlier agreement between state governments and the German car industry). Only diesel cars with fuel injection were able to achieve the supported performance level. Paradoxically, the success of the most energy-efficient 3-litre diesel car produced by Volkswagen was limited, but fuel-efficient diesel cars in general enjoyed rapid growth. This was because the 1997 regulation happened to coincide with the introduction of the eco tax. The eco tax was introduced in 1999 and added to the mineral oil tax which had already been strongly increased in the early 1990s. This led to a successive reorientation of German car drivers, and in turn the auto industry, towards more fuel-efficient vehicles in other segments of the car fleet as well. The result was not only a global market success for fuel-efficient diesel cars, but a general decrease in fuel consumption since 1999. This development, which coincided with the start of the SDP/Green coalition government, also influenced the CO_2 emissions of road traffic in general (see Figure 12.6). In Germany, unlike in the UK, there has been a revised emission trend since 1999. In addition to the car tax and the eco tax, there was also a highway toll for commercial transport vehicles from 1 January 2005 onwards (10–15.5 ct/km). In 2007, increased VAT was added.

The effect of the eco tax was already visible before the oil price increase. Therefore the improved eco-efficiency can be explained to a high degree by this policy intervention, though the later effect of the oil price cannot be ignored.

The economic result was the clear world market success of German diesel cars, with Germany being the lead market, while the US market is seen as an early follower (Figure 12.7).

12.4.3 Industrial Recycling

The strategic role of recycling for sustainable growth is widely acknowledged. But achievements have so far been limited. There is still a limited emphasis on resource productivity, compared with labour productivity. In 2007, 46% of total production costs for German industry were for intermediate material

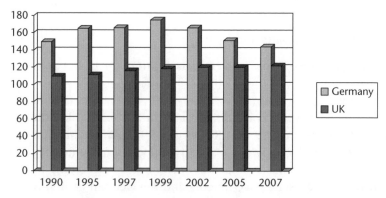

Figure 12.6 CO_2 emissions of road traffic in Germany and the UK, 1990–2007 (in Mt)
Sources: Statistische Bundesamt (2009); Defra (2009).

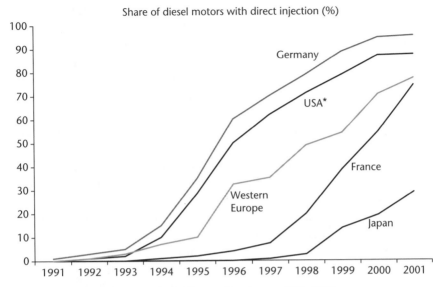

Figure 12.7 Market shares of fuel-efficient diesel cars, 1991–2001

Note: * USA: predominantly light trucks.
Source: Jacob et al. (2005).

goods, with this share increasing due to rising prices for raw materials. The share of direct labour costs, on the other hand, has steadily decreased and now accounts for only 18% (Statistisches Bundesamt 2009). Sustainable growth may need a new understanding of productivity, focusing on resources instead of labour productivity.

More efficient use of material resources has several advantages. It can reduce costs and increase profitability, particularly in times of high prices for raw materials. It can stimulate innovations and create new markets (e.g. for waste separation technologies). In most cases, it will also reduce the environmental impacts at all stages of the production process. Using recycled metal, for example, can cut emissions by four-fifths. Recycling contributes to minimizing material flows from the sphere of production and consumption to nature. All this is underlined by the fact that 'more than 95% of the resources lifted from nature are wasted before the finished goods reach the market. And many industrial products—such as cars—demand additional resources while being used' (Reid and Miedzinski, 2008).

In 1994, Germany introduced an ambitious recycling policy, which was strengthened in 2001 by a regulation which included a target to prevent any landfill without pre-treatment—in the last resort, that means incineration—by 2005. The German sustainable development strategy has set a target to increase German resource productivity by 100% between 1994 and 2020 (Bundesregierung 2004).

Apart from a successful voluntary agreement with the construction industry, German waste policy has been driven by regulation. Töller (2007), in an examination of steering modes in German waste policies during the last 15 years, concludes that, in the case of German waste policies, there is no evidence for a sometimes supposed 'withdrawal of the state', symbolized by deregulation, privatization, or an increased intensity of societal self-regulation. Public policy has caused an increase of recycling rates together with energy recovery from incineration, and it has reduced the rate of final disposal to landfills from 63.5 million tonnes in the year 1998 to 45.7 million tonnes in 2005 (Statistisches Bundesamt 2007: 7). The total use of material resources in 2008 was 10.6% lower than in 1994 (Statistisches Bundesamt 2009). An important environmental benefit is a reduction of greenhouse gas emissions. According to the German Ministry of Environment, 40 million tonnes CO_2 equivalents have been avoided by waste management, mainly by closing down landfill deposition sites (compared with 1990; BMU 2006: 37).

One reason for the trend mentioned is the decrease of construction waste due to the stagnation of the German economy after 2001. The advanced waste management policy (e.g. the phasing out of landfill without pre-treatment), however, also seems to have been a relevant factor. The third most relevant factor is the change in commodity prices in recent years (Destatis et al. 2007: 17), especially the increase for economically important metals and materials.

Figure 12.8 shows a remarkable increase in the recycling rate of industrial waste in the last few years in parallel to the rapid increase in raw material prices (2000–5: +80%; BMU 2007). The most plausible explanation is the immediate pressure of raw material prices on the industry as a hard cost factor. The price signal seems much less visible and relevant for other sectors.

Compared with the UK (and most other EU member states), the German regulation caused a significantly higher share of recycled or incinerated waste, and consequently a significantly lower proportion of waste deposited in landfills.

The economic co-benefits of this policy have been the rapid growth and increased employment in the waste industry and the recycling sector. The Ministry of Environment calculates a turnover for the waste industry of about €50 billion and employment figures of about 250,000 jobs. In addition, there was an annual saving of raw material imports of about €3.7 billion. The recycling sector reached annual growth of turnover and employment rates of 13% and 9% respectively between 2004 and 2006 (BMU 2007: 15, 95–7). German recycling technologies have a 25% share of the global market, with a market share for automatic separation technologies—a fast-growing market—

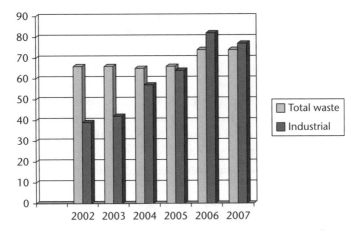

Figure 12.8 Recycling rates in Germany, 2002–2007 (including energy recovery, per cent)

Source: Statistische Bundesamt (2009).

of 64% (ibid. 13, 105). The German Institut der Deutschen Wirtschaft (Biebeler et al. 2008; and Barth 2006) has stressed the rising economic importance of the re-use and recycling of raw materials.

Statistics from Defra also show high growth of the British waste management sector from €6.8 billion (2000) to €11.9 billion (2005). The employment figures are 69,000, including 17,000 jobs in the recycling sector. The share of landfilled municipal waste is higher in the UK, and the proportion of recycling or incineration with heat recovery is lower than in Germany.

12.4.4 Green Power

An ambitious regulation to stimulate renewable energy in the German power sector was introduced by the SDP/Green coalition government (1998). This policy was very effective and has caused a rapid increase in renewable electricity. The original target of a 12.5% share of electricity by 2010 was exceeded in 2007, when it reached about 14.2%. A new target of 30% by 2020 was fixed in 2009. Only one year later it was changed again to now 45%.

The main instrument has been the feed-in tariff (FIT), which changed the relative prices of renewable and conventional power and has also been widely adopted in other countries (Reiche 2005; Mez 2008). The policy instrument already existed through the Electricity Feed-In Act of 1990, but was significantly increased and broadened in 1998 by the Renewable Energy Resources Act (EEG). The EEG guaranteed to generators attractive prices for renewable electricity. In 2005, total tariff payments amounted to €4.19 billion, increasing electricity costs for households by 3% (BMU 2006, 2007).

The increase in renewable power has been remarkable. While from 1991 to 2001 there was a doubling of green power production (from 19 to 37 TWh p.a.), the next doubling took place within only five years, with 73 TWh generated in 2006 and 86.7 TWh in 2007. Figure 12.9 shows this acceleration in the quantity of renewable generation.

The environmental benefit of this policy was considerable: 115 million tonnes CO_2 emissions have been avoided in 2007. No other instrument of German climate policy has been more effective (BMU 2007; BEE 2008). The positive impact on air pollution through other avoided emissions should also be mentioned, with external costs of some €8.6 billion being avoided for the fiscal year 2007.

The turnover in the green power sector was €25 billion in 2007, up from €12.3 billion in 2004. The direct and indirect employment effect in 2008 was 340,000 jobs. The forecast for 2020 (500,000) may already be too pessimistic (BMU 2007, 2009; Umwelt 12/2010).

The additional cost per kWh of the FIT policy, which is paid by all households, was 1 eurocent in 2007; and a total of €8 billion in 2010. In addition, the FIT payments for producers are lowered over time as technologies become more competitive. The financial support through the FIT can also be viewed as an investment in the first-mover advantage of a strong export position for the German photovoltaic (PV) and wind energy industries. It could also be seen as a public investment in a remarkable innovation process. Immediately after 1998, a rapid increase in inventions (patents) in the area of renewable energy could be observed in Germany. In 2009, the findings of an international study showed that 'feed-in tariffs were considered the most effective policy

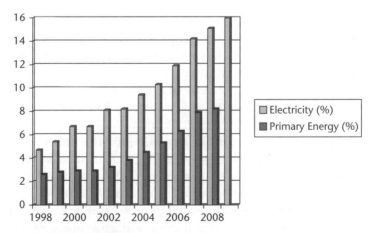

Figure 12.9 Share of renewable energy in Germany, 1998–2009 (per cent)
Sources: BMU (2009); BEE (2009).

framework' in this context (Frankfurt School of Finance and Management and UNEP 2009: 63).

The global market share of Germany for biogas technologies is 65%, for PV 41%, and for wind energy 24% (BMU 2007: 41).

12.4.5 Consequences of a worldwide economic downturn

Parts of the German eco-industry have been confronted with problems in 2009, owing to the impacts of the global financial crisis. The renewable energy sector, especially solar companies, have suffered from cuts in financial flows. This has led to a radical fall in prices of solar companies—as venture capitalists and private equity investors cut back on remaining capital flows. Moreover, public stock markets relating to clean energy also fell through 2008 and 2009, and fundraising for clean energy projects has been very difficult (Frankfurt School of Finance and Management and UNEP 2009). Also some investments in renewable energy power projects slowed down owing to the credit crunch and new conditions for developers and sponsors.

Chinese manufacturers have gained market share as they produce solar panels much more cheaply than many firms in Germany. One result of all this has been that prices for solar panels have fallen by around 30%. While this may boost demand in the long term, it makes short-term operating conditions difficult.

Furthermore, the policy change in Germany to a more conservative and nuclear-friendly government in autumn 2009 could undermine the capacity of the German renewable energy sector to reach former growth rates.

Working in the opposite direction, the global economic crisis has led to an increase of demand for some climate-friendly technologies, as new economic stimulus packages have been applied by national governments and international institutions like the European Commission.

According to Robins et al. (2009), at the end of the year 2008 and in the first months of 2009 stimulus packages made an additional €2,170 billion available worldwide, with €490.1 billion in Europe (see also UNEP 2009). The German stimulus package was calculated to be €81.0 billion, including €10.7 billion of 'green investment', 13.2% of the whole package. Other studies differ, but the package amounts to around more or less 1.4% of German GDP in 2009 (see e.g. Deutsche Bank Advisors 2009; Ecologic 2009; EREF 2009: Saha and von Weizsäcker 2009). The discourse around the concepts of 'green New Deal' or 'green recovery' (UNEP 2009) advocates addressing the ecological or climate crisis and the economic crisis at the same time by investing in energy efficiency, renewable energies, public transport, clean freight vehicles and cars, as well as 'smart grids', efficient use of water, and research and development relating to new environmental solutions of all kinds.

Other factors support the long-term trend of a growing eco-industry. For example, strong growth rates in renewable energies can be observed in countries which have been less affected by financial market problems, like China or India (Roland Berger 2009). In addition, ambitious government goals in important core markets (e.g. Europe, the USA, and once again, China and India) to increase the share of renewable energy may support German companies in the longer run.

12.5 Conclusions

This chapter has focused on the Environmental Industry (EI) and its function, structure, and dynamics, especially in Germany, but to some extent also in the UK and Europe. It has distinguished between the two faces of the EI: more traditional end-of-pipe treatment or 'pollution management' sector, and the newer, fast-growing area of eco-efficiency or 'resource management'. It is clear that the extent and growth of this industry has so far been underestimated, largely due to lack of data and insufficient statistical definitions. To a large extent it is an 'invisible industry' (DTI and Defra 2006). It consists not only of specialized producers of eco-technology but also refers to the *internal* activities of companies, such as the eco-design of products or measures aimed at increasing resource productivity. A recent study of Germany found that the size of the eco-industry is about 8% of total GDP for 2007.

The chapter then explored recent trends in four subsectors of the German environmental industry, which is the most developed in Europe: renewable electricity, low-energy buildings, fuel-efficient diesel cars, and industrial recycling. All these subsectors have been supported by strong environmental policies and illustrate the extent to which such policy can stimulate resource-efficient innovation. In addition to their environmental benefits, innovation in these subsectors has been shown to have delivered increased employment and exports.

The headline conclusions from the case studies are as follows:

- In each case, government intervention, generally through a policy mix of different instruments, was essential to the achievement of the environmental and economic benefits, which, as already noted, included innovation, growth, exports, and employment. Environmentally, German 'green power' in 2007 avoided 115 million tonnes CO_2 emissions, up from 85 million tonnes on 2005. The improvements in waste management have also reduced greenhouse gas emissions, with savings since 1990 of around 40 million tonnes CO_2 equivalents, mainly by closing down landfill sites.

- There is clear evidence that the environmental policy measures stimulated innovation. The cases of energy-efficient buildings and renewable energy show clear feed-back in the innovation cycle from diffusion to invention, suggesting that environmental policy can also enlarge the technical potential and the available options.

- The German eco tax of 1999 seems to have played an important role in the reduction of traffic-related CO_2 and the reduction of heat energy for households. More generally, the change in relative prices—whether through taxes or subsidies (feed-in tariffs)—seems to have been the dominant influence across the case studies. The combination of economic instruments and regulation was also important. Taxation was a strong driver in the first two cases (fuel-efficient cars and buildings). Regulation was important in the case of industrial recycling, but the role of the (market) price mechanism was visible in the case of industrial waste management as well.

Our strongest general conclusion is that relative price changes, whatever their cause, had the strongest steering effects. Though subsidies (including FITs) have proven important as specific market support for certain technologies, ETR, complemented by regulation, seems the best general mechanism to stimulate a broader range of innovations. This is a message which surely has considerable importance at a time when government spending and investment, and the scope for tax cuts, are likely to be constrained, while unemployment calls for measures to reduce the cost of labour. In addition, it is clear from the evidence that the introduction of ETR would foster processes of technological progress, which sometimes cannot be visualized very easily in modelling processes like GINFORS or E3ME, because technical and also social innovations take some time before they show macroeconomic extensions.

CO_2 taxation in ETR seems to have a special role to play—from a political point of view—in providing a further stimulus for renewable energies, as well as discouraging further investment in coal-based power plants, not only in Germany (see SRU 2011). This could result in a major shift in investment, especially if 10% of ETR-generated revenues were to be re-invested in renewable energy technologies. The employment effect of the ETR in Germany was estimated to be 250,000 (SRU 2002).

The structure of the renewable energy industry seems set to change rapidly through current dynamics relating to innovation processes and 'economies of scale'. Expert estimates suggest that in 2012 in southern Germany the reduction of production costs of solar energy will reach the level of €0.15 per kWh (in California €0.11 and in Spain about €0.10 per kWh). If this happens, solar energy will reach 'grid parity' and will be fully competitive with coal-fired power plants, a position that would be enhanced if there was also adequate pricing of CO_2. This would stimulate the emergence of new energy companies: some *solar power companies* are now using their own products and act as final users as well as *energy suppliers* (e.g. Colexon and Q-Cells in Germany or First Solar in the USA). In the longer term, new economic structures will be supported. This is just one possible example of how ETR, by fundamentally changing relative prices to make environmental damage more expensive, might not only make a major contribution to climate protection, but could also address the deeper underlying problem of the conflict between economic growth and the environment more generally.

References

ADEME (Agence de l'Environnement et de la Maîtrise de l'Energie) (2007), 'Comparaisons internationales de l'efficacité énergétique', *Stratégie & études*, No. 6. Angers.

Allianz Dresdner Economic Research and The Lisbon Council (2008), *European Growth and Jobs Monitor: Indicators for Success in the Knowledge Economy*, Special Report: Energy efficiency—A Key Driver of Growth, Frankfurt am Main: Allianz Dresdner Economic Research.

Ayres, R. U., and J. C. J. M. van den Bergh (2005), 'A Theory of Economic Growth with Material/Energy Resources and Dematerialization: Interaction of the Three Growth Mechanisms', *Ecological Economics*, 55: 96–118.

Barth, H. (2006), 'Umwelteffizienz im internationalen Vergleich', *Vierteljahresschrift zur empirischen Wirtschaftsforschung aus dem Institut der deutschen Wirtschaft*, 33(4/2006): 59–68.

BEE (Bundesverband Erneuerbare Energien) (2008), 'Erneuerbare Energie im Jahr 2008', available at <http://www.bee-ev.de/_downloads/publikationen/sonstiges/2009/090107_BEE_Jahreszahlen_2008.pdf>.

—— (2009), *Stromversorgung 2020: Wege in eine moderne Energiewirtschaft. Branchenprognose 2020*, Berlin: Bee.

Beise, M., and K. Rennings (2003), 'Lead Markets for Environmental Innovations', ZEW Discussion Paper 03–01, Mannheim.

Biebeler, H., M. Mahammadzadeh, and J.-W. Selke (2008), 'Globaler Wandel aus der Sicht der Wirtschaft: Chancen und Risiken, Forschungsbedarf und Innovationshemmnisse', *Analysen—Forschungsberichte aus dem Institut der deutschen Wirtschaft*, IW-Analysen, No. 36. Cologne.

BMU (Bundesministerium für Umwelt, Naturschutz und Reaktorsicherheit) (ed.) (2006), *Renewable Energy Sources in Figures—National and International Development*, Berlin.

—— (ed.) (2007), 'GreenTech Made in Germany', *Umwelttechnologie-Atlas für Deutschland*, 1, Studie von Roland Berger Strategy Consultants im Auftrag des BMU, Munich: Vahlen.

—— (ed.) (2008), *Entwicklung der Erneuerbaren Energien in Deutschland im Jahr 2007: Grafiken und Tabellen*, Berlin: BMU.

—— (ed.) (2009), 'GreenTech Made in Germany', *Umwelttechnologie-Atlas für Deutschland*, 2, Studie von Roland Berger Strategy Consultants im Auftrag des BMU, Munich: Vahlen.

—— and UBA (Umweltbundesamt) (2009), *Umweltwirtschaftsbericht 2009*, Berlin: BMU and UBA.

Bundesregierung Deutschland (2004), *Fortschrittsbericht 2004: Perspektiven für Deutschland. Unsere Strategie für eine nachhaltige Entwicklung*, Berlin.

Cambridge Econometrics, GHK, and IEEP (Institute for European Environmental Policy) (2007), 'Links between the Environment, Economy and Jobs', EU Financial Instruments, available at <<http://www.ieep.eu/publications/publications.php>.

Defra (2009), 'E-Digest Statistics Climate Change: Estimated Emissions by Source, Fuel Type and End User 1990–2007'.

Destatis, UBA, and BGR (Bundesanstalt für Geowissenschaften und Rohstoffe) (2007), *Umweltdaten Deutschland. Nachhaltig wirtschaften—Natürliche Ressourcen und Umwelt schonen*, Dessau, Wiesbaden, and Hannover: Statistisches Bundesamt, UBA.

DTI and Defra (2006), 'Bridging the Gap between Environmental Necessity and Economic Opportunity: Environmental Innovation', First Report of the Environmental Innovations Advisory Group, London: Environmental Industries Unit, Department of Trade and Industry.

Deutsche Bank Advisors (2009), 'Global Climate Change Regulation: Policy Developments: July 2008-February 2009', available at <http://www.dbadvisors.com/deam/stat/globalResearch/climatechange_globalpolicydevelopments.pdf>.

Deutsche Bank Research (2008), 'Deutscher Maschinenbau macht Wirtschaft fit für die Zeit nach dem Öl', *Energie und Klimawande—aktuelle Themen*, 435. Frankfurt am Main: Deutsche Bank Research (Report by J. Auer).

Ecologic (2009), 'Economic Stimulus in Europe—Accelerating Progress towards Sustainable Development?' Background Paper, ESDN Meeting, Prague. Berlin: Ecologic-Institute.

Ekins, P., and A. Venn (2006), 'Assessing Innovation Dynamics Induced by Environmental Policy', Report prepared by the Policy Studies Institute, London, for the DG Environment, Brussels.

ENDS (2009), 'EU Renewables Sector to Create 400,000 New Jobs', *ENDS Europe DAILY*, Tuesday 2 June.

EREF (European Renewable Energies Federation) (2009), 'Economic Crisis: Rescue Packages in EU 27 and Renewable Energy', Brussels: European Renewable Energies Federation (Report by D. Fouquet and H. Witdouck).

Ernst & Young (2006), 'Eco-Industry, its Size, Employment, Perspectives and Barriers to Growth in an Enlarged EU', Final report, Brussels: EC, DG Enterprise.

Esty, D. C., A. L. Levy, T. Srebotnjak, A. de Sherbinin, C. H. Kim, and B. Anderson (2006), 'Pilot 2006. Environmental Performance Index'.

European Commission (2009), 'European Industry in a Changing World: Updated Sectoral Overview 2009', Commission Staff Working Document, Brussels, 30 July, SEC (2009) 1111 final.

Frankfurt School of Finance and Management and UNEP (2009), *The Global Financial Crisis and its Impact on Renewable Energy Finance*, Frankfurt am Main: New Energy Finance Limited.

Frondel, M., J. Horbach, and K. Rennings (2007), 'End-of-Pipe or Cleaner Production—An Empirical Comparison of Environmental Innovation Decisions across OECD Countries', in Nick Johnstone (ed.), *Environmental Policy and Corporate Behaviour*, Paris: OECD; Cheltenham, UK and Northampton, MA, USA: Edward Elgar, 174–212.

Innovas (2009), 'Low Carbon and Environmental Goods and Services: An Industry Analysis', Commissioned by BERR, available at <http://www.berr.gov.uk/files/file50253.pdf>.

Jacob, Klaus, M. Beise, J. Blazejczak, D. Edler, R. Haum, M. Jänicke, T. Löw, U. Petschow, and K. Rennings (2005), *Lead Markets for Environmental Innovations*, Heidelberg: Physica Verlag.

Jänicke, M. (2008), *Megatrend Umweltinnovation*, Munich: Oekom.

—— and K. Jacob (2006), 'Lead Markets for Environmental Innovations: A New Role for the Nation State', in M. Jänicke and K. Jacob (eds.), *Environmental Governance in Global Perspective: New Approaches to Ecological Modernisation*, Berlin, 30–50 (= Forschungsstelle für Umweltpolitik, FU Berlin, FFU rep 01–2006, Special edition on the occasion of the 20th anniversary of the Environmental Policy Research Centre).

Keitel, H. P. (2008), 'Ganzheitlich denken—Qualität bauen Klimaprobleme lösen', Speech of the President of the German Construction industry to the German Construction industry Confederation, 26 June 2008, Berlin.

Klemmer, P. (ed.) (1999), *Innovationen und Umwelt*, Berlin: Analytica.

Kreditanstalt für Wiederaufbau (KfW) (2008), Personal information given to Martin Jänicke.

—— (2010), 'Press release—KfW Achieves Record Financing Volume in Germany', available at <http://www.kfw.de/EN_Home/Presse/Our_Current_Work/KfW_achieves_record_financing_volume_in_Germany.jsp>.

McKinsey (2007), 'Costs and Potentials of Greenhouse Gas Abatement in Germany', a Report by McKinsey & Company, on behalf of BDI Initiative—Business for Climate.

—— (2008), *The Case for Investing in Energy Productivity*, San Francisco: McKinsey & Company Inc.

—— (2009), 'Kosten und Potentiale der Vermeidung von Treibhausgasemissionen in Deutschland', Eine Studie von McKinsey & Company erstellt im Auftrag von 'BDI initiativ—Wirtschaft und Klimaschutz', Aktualisierte Energieszenarien und-sensitivitätsanalysen, March 2009. Bundesverband der Deutschen Industrie, Berlin, available at <http://www.bdi.eu/download_content/Publikation_Treibhausgasemissionen_in_Deutschland.pdf.>

Meyer, B., M. Distelkamp, and M. I. Wolter (2007), 'Material Efficiency and Economic-Environmental Sustainability', *Ecological Economics*, 63: 192–200.

Mez, L. (ed.) (2007), *Green Power Markets: Support Schemes, Case Studies and Perspectives*, Brentwood, Essex: Multi-Science Publishing Co. Ltd.

Miltner, A. (2008), 'The Environmental Industry in UK and Germany: Size and Achievements', Policy Studies Institute, London. Working Paper 2008; PETRE project.

OECD and Eurostat (1999), *The Environmental Goods & Services Industry: Manual for Data Collection and Analysis,* Paris: OECD.

Reiche, D. (ed.) (2005), *Handbook of Renewable Energies in the European Union,* 2nd edition, Frankfurt am Main: Peter Lang.

Reid, A., and M. Miedzinski (2008), 'Eco-Innovation: Final Report for Sectoral Innovation Watch', May 2008, available at <http://www.technopolis-group.com>.

Robins, N., R. Cover, and C. Singh (2009), *A Climate for Recovery,* London: HSBC Global Research.

Roland Berger Strategy Consultants (2009), *Wind Energy Manufacturer's Challenges. Using Turbulent Times To Become Fit for the Future.* Hamburg.

Saha, D., and J. von Weizsäcker (2009), 'Estimating the Size of the European Stimulus Packages for 2009: An Update', available at <http://aei.pitt.edu/10549/01/UPDATED-SIZE-OF-STIMULUS-FINAL.pdf>.

SRU (Sachverständigenrat für Umweltfragen) (2002), 'Umweltgutachten 2002: Für eine neue Vorreiterrolle', Berlin: SRU.

—— (2011), 'Sondergutachten 2011: Wege zur 100% erneuerbaren Stromversorgung', Berlin: SRU, available at <http://www.umweltrat.de/SharedDocs/Downloads/DE/02_Sondergutachten/2011_Sondergutachten_100Prozent_Erneuerbare.pdf?__blob=publicationFile>.

Statistisches Bundesamt (2007), *Nachhaltige Abfallwirtschaft in Deutschland,* Ausgabe 2007, Wiesbaden: Statistisches Bundesamt.

—— (2009), *Statistisches Jahrbuch.* Wiesbaden: Statistisches Bundesamt.

Töller, A. (2007), 'Die Rückkehr des befehlenden Staates? Muster und Ursachen der Veränderung staatlicher Handlungsformen in der deutschen Abfallpolitik', *Politische Vierteljahresschrift,* 48(1): 66–96.

'Umwelt' (2010), Journal of the German Federal Ministry for the Environment, Natur Conservation and Nuclear Safety (ed.), issue no. 10/2010, Reinfelden: G+J Corporate Editors GmbH.

UBA (Umweltbundesamt) (2007), 'Wirkung der Meseberger Beschlüsse v. 23. August 2007 auf die Treibhausgasemission in Deutschland im Jahr 2020', Dessau: UBA.

UNEP (2009), 'Rethinking the Economic Recovery—A Global Green New Deal', Report by E. Barbier, available at <http://www.unep.org/greeneconomy/portals/30/docs/GGND-Report-April2009.pdf>.

Part IV
Conclusions

13

ETR for Green Growth: Summary, Conclusions, and Recommendations

Paul Ekins and Stefan Speck

13.1 Introduction

ETR implementation in Europe goes back to the early 1990s, with the early adopters Sweden, Denmark, Norway, Finland, and the Netherlands being followed by the UK and Germany in the late 1990s (EEA 2000, 2005; Andersen and Ekins 2009), as well as some new EU member states more recently. The actual implementation of the rather simple concept of a tax shift differs from one country to another depending on their starting position and political objectives (see Speck and Jilkova 2009). For instance, the Swedish ETR implemented in 1991 was part of a much larger fiscal reform process where the clear political intention was to reduce the tax burden (i.e. the ETR was not revenue neutral) as well as high marginal rates of income tax. The German intention when the ETR was implemented in 1999 was completely different as the government stuck much more closely to revenue neutrality in order to improve the environment, in particular to reduce greenhouse gas emissions, and to reduce employers' and employees' statutory pension contributions in order to reduce labour costs and to increase employment. The UK objectives were similar to those in Germany, while those of Estonia, the first of the new EU member states to implement an ETR, were closer to the Swedish example, as the increased environmental tax revenues were used to counterbalance the loss in revenues caused by the reduction of personal income tax rates.

Until quite recently, the years since 2001 saw a decline in the momentum of ETR in Europe, with only Estonia, and to a lesser degree the Czech Republic, among the new member states, following the example of the early ETR countries. This is probably partly due to higher international energy prices in the first decade of the 2000s, but is also partly due to the emergence of the

EU Emission Trading System (EU ETS), following the failure of the European Commission in the 1990s to persuade member states to introduce an EU-wide carbon/energy tax. The EU ETS is now the main policy at EU level for the reduction of carbon emissions. However, the decision to auction from 2013 the majority (and, by 2027, 100%) of EU ETS emission allowances means that governments will have a new source of environment-related revenues. This has in turn led to a broadening of the concept of ETR to that adopted in this book, along the lines of the World Bank's usage of the term environmental fiscal reform (EFR), which involves the use of 'a range of taxation or pricing instruments that can raise revenue, while simultaneously furthering environmental goals' (World Bank 2005: 1). It seems logical to include in the definition of a possible ETR, as in this book, not only the revenues generated from environmental taxation, in particular, from energy and carbon taxation, but also those resulting from the auctioning of EU ETS emission allowances.

As discussed further below, a combination of increasingly stringent carbon reduction targets, and the need for a number of European governments to increase revenues from taxation to cut public deficits, has led to a resurgence of interest in carbon/energy taxation and ETR, with Denmark, Ireland, and Sweden all introducing new (or redesigning existing) green fiscal instruments in 2009.

13.2 The Direct Impacts of ETR

ETR operates by raising the prices of resource use and pollution through taxing the relevant environmental emissions or resource use, or some proxy for them. To be administratively feasible, taxation should apply broadly to a range of sectors in the economy. It is therefore important, if ETR is to be an appropriate instrument in relation to energy use, that it is likely to be effective across different industrial sectors with very different patterns and levels of energy use, depending on their products and the processes they employ. Research reported in Chapter 4 showed that this was indeed the case.

The project on which this book is based proceeded from a hypothesis that the policy instrument ETR could increase human well-being through three pathways (as shown in Figure 1.6, reproduced here as Figure 13.1): environmental improvement, the generation of economic activity and employment, and the stimulation of green technologies and new environmental industries. Each route could make an important contribution to more sustainable economic growth in Europe. An assessment of the effectiveness of ETR must consider each of the three pathways through the questions: does ETR reduce energy use and pollution (in this case, CO_2 emissions)? Does ETR stimulate

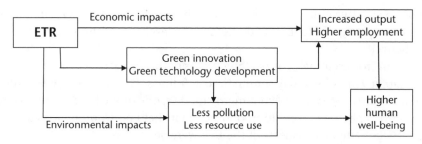

Figure 13.1 Hypothesized paths from ETR to higher human well-being

green innovation and green technology development? Does ETR increase employment and output?

The direct route of environmental improvement is well understood. By increasing the relative prices of pollution and resource use, these are reduced. For those industrial sectors investigated, the research found a price elasticity of energy demand of about -0.6, which is of the same order of magnitude as other estimates in the literature. Moreover, it also found an income elasticity of energy demand of 0.5. This means that, in a context of economic growth, energy demand (and any associated GHG emissions) will increase, unless the underlying growth in energy demand is choked off by simultaneous increases in energy prices. The rationale for environmental taxes in this context is quite clear. It is in fact not clear that the political commitments that have been made to dramatic reductions in energy-related GHG emissions over the next decade can be achieved without them (or an equivalent carbon pricing mechanism, such as emissions trading).

There has already been substantial research to suggest that ETR is both environmentally effective (i.e. it does reduce both energy use and CO_2 emissions) and neutral or beneficial for the wider economy (see e.g. Bosquet 2000; Ekins and Barker 2001; Patuelli et al. 2005). Consistent with the findings of these reviews of the literature, the results from the research in this project suggest that the effect of ETRs on energy consumption and therefore CO_2 emissions can be substantial.

Taxes generate revenues and the ETR approach recommends that these are (mainly) used to reduce other taxes, especially those on the productive factors of labour and capital. Reducing such distortionary taxes may increase labour and output, the direct route of economic benefit from ETR. Moreover, in respect of the economic impacts of ETR, the results here are again consistent with the literature that has found that the effects of ETRs on employment tend to be small and can be positive, depending on the size of the reduction in the labour costs effected by the ETR and the extent to which labour use increases as energy becomes more expensive. The implication is that ETRs are very likely to be an effective policy approach to reducing energy use and CO_2 emissions, while increasing employment and leaving the level of the output qualitatively unchanged.

The macro-econometric modelling results of this project, described in detail in Chapter 9, may be briefly summarized as follows. The modelling was carried out using two large macro-econometric models, one of the EU-27 (E3ME) and one with explicit representation of other countries and world regions as well (GINFORS). The main aspects of the ETR were defined as:

- the 20% reduction 2020 GHG target for the EU being met through a combination of auctioned ETS allowances and carbon taxes;
- a materials tax, starting at 5% of value and increasing to 15% in 2020;
- revenue recycling through reductions in employers' social security contributions and in income taxes.

A set of scenarios was constructed to analyse the key aspects of ETR, with different scenarios showing the key impacts under two sets of international energy prices, a share of revenues recycled through eco-industries, and in the context of international cooperation in carbon reduction. All the scenarios were assessed using E3ME and GINFORS, which were described and compared in Chapter 8. The use of two models provides a check on the robustness of results.

Gains in productivity

The results from both models showed that meeting the GHG reduction targets generates substantial improvements in productivity per unit of carbon, per unit of energy, and per unit of material input. However, the carbon price required to achieve this is higher than any that has been seen previously in the EU ETS. This partly reflects the ambitious nature of the targets and the limited time available with which to achieve them, but also reflects the assumption that there are no policies complementary to the ETR, such as regulation, or renewable energy strategies, which in some circumstances could achieve carbon reductions at lower costs. Costs could also be reduced by purchasing credits from international offsetting mechanisms such as the Clean Development Mechanism (CDM). The carbon prices from the models are therefore likely to be at the upper end of those actually required.

Labour productivity falls as a result of the reforms, but this should not necessarily be viewed as a negative outcome. As the cost of labour falls from the revenue recycling, it becomes cost-effective for firms to employ less ef-ficient workers meaning that there is an increase in total employment, although average productivity falls.

Revenues

An issue that always arises with taxes that are intended to change behaviour is whether such taxes generate stable revenues, or whether the induced behaviour change will cause the revenues to decline over time.

The first point to note is that a number of taxes that are intended to affect behaviour have in fact provided stable revenues over long periods. For example, tobacco, alcohol, and fuel taxes certainly cause people to smoke, drink, and drive less than they would otherwise, and this is part of their purpose, but also have provided substantial revenues to many countries over a considerable period. There is therefore no automatic contradiction between behavioural, including environmental, taxes, affecting behaviour and generating stable revenues.

The second point is that, when behavioural taxes are raised, the effect on the revenues will depend on the proportion of the tax in the price of the affected product(s) and the price elasticity of demand (the proportional change in demand caused by a change in the price). If the price elasticity of demand is between 0 and -1, as mostly seems to be the case for energy products, then an increase in the tax on the products will yield an increase in revenue, because the proportional increase in the tax rate will be higher than the proportional fall in demand, so that the product of the tax rate and the quantity of the product, which gives the revenues, will increase.

Even if the price elasticity of demand is more negative than -1, so that demand falls by proportionally more than the tax rate increases, if the tax is a relatively small part of the price of the taxed product, then tax revenues could increase.

Furthermore, given the positive income elasticity of energy demand, economic growth will tend to increase the demand for energy and offset the price effect of the tax. This is of course one reason why an escalating tax is so necessary if energy demand and associated emissions are to be substantially reduced. Without a continually increasing energy price, growing incomes and the rebound effect from energy-efficiency improvements are likely to result in increasing energy use in the future, as they have in the past.

Finally, while the revenues raised from carbon taxes may fall towards the middle of this century, if industrial economies succeed in achieving the radical decarbonization targets that seem likely to be required to avoid the worst impacts of climate change, there is a good case for taxing energy as well as carbon (because all energy sources have negative environmental impacts and energy efficiency is subject to widespread market failures), and energy of some kind is always going to be a core input to the economy. Moreover, as shown in Chapter 9, materials taxes can also be a significant source of revenues, and demands for materials are expected to remain substantial, even in the context of decarbonization.

There is therefore no firm basis for thinking that the high levels of environmental tax revenues resulting from the ETR scenarios modelled here (up to 7.5% of GDP, as shown in Table 9.5) are unstable and would necessarily decline. On the contrary, further reductions in carbon emissions might easily require even higher carbon taxes, and gradually over 2020–50 energy taxes could be increased instead of carbon taxes, and materials taxes could be increased to achieve further improvements in resource productivity, so that total environmental tax revenues could easily stay on a rising trajectory, permitting other taxes to be lower. In the context of an ageing European population, it may even be that this would be a more secure source of revenue than the taxes on employment that currently yield a large share of tax revenues in most European countries. At the very least, it would seem prudent to take opportunities to diversify away from this tax base, such as by increasing the currently rather small, and falling, share of revenues coming from carbon/energy and materials taxes (the share of environmental tax revenues in both GDP and total tax revenues has fallen since 1999; Eurostat 2009: 109).

Macroeconomic outcomes

Both models show that the ETR will lead to an increase in employment and a decrease in unemployment. Although the size of the increase varies between the two sets of model results, the results suggest that the increase could be quite substantial: up to 2.7% higher than otherwise.

The effect of ETR on aggregate GDP is ambiguous, with E3ME suggesting a slight increase by 2020 but GINFORS a slight decrease. The main reason for the difference is the different specifications for the models' trade equations and treatment of technological change, but both models suggest that the impacts will be very small, particularly when put in the context of annual growth rates or related to the economic effects of international energy price increases.

Sectoral impacts

As with every reform, ETR will create winners and losers. It is not surprising that the main sectors that lose out are those that produce energy and raw materials and the most intensive users of these products. The sectors that are likely to gain are those that are intensive users of labour, whose costs fall under the reforms, and those that produce goods and services for consumers, who benefit from lower income taxes and a resulting increase in household spending.

If a share of the revenues is used for investment in low-carbon technologies, this will benefit the sectors that produce investment goods, such as engineering and construction. Many parts of these sectors have available spare capacity following the financial and economic crisis in 2008/9.

Direct policy implications

These results show that ETR could result in long-term economic as well as environmental benefits and that there is a clear case for future ETR in Europe. The results suggest that the ETR outlined in this report could lead to a net gain in welfare and the creation of 1–6 million additional jobs.

However, the ETR should if possible be coordinated at the European level, as trade between member states could be important in determining the competitiveness effects. As shown in the 'international cooperation' scenario, an even better outcome would be possible if Europe's main trading partners entered into a similar agreement as this would reduce the competitiveness effects further. This would give scope for Europe to cut its domestic carbon emissions by more and would provide more revenues for tax cuts elsewhere.

13.3 Impacts on Innovation: the Low-Carbon Transition

Perhaps even more important than the direct effect of ETR on output is the indirect effect, through its stimulation of green innovation and environmental industries. There is strong evidence that policies that induce relative price changes between resource-using and resource-saving technologies will stimulate innovation in the direction of the latter. Moreover, the EU results in scenario HS2 showed that investment in green technologies could significantly reduce both the carbon price and potential GDP loss in reaching the 20% target.

Detailed work on the expanding environmental industries (EIs) sector in Germany suggests that German environmental policy has been successful in stimulating green innovation across a range of environmental industries, with strong economic gains in terms of output, employment, and exports, with even stronger benefits likely to be generated in the future as the technologies are taken up as part of global industries. There is strong suggestive evidence that the growth of the environmental industries in Germany, in particular, and a number of important innovations that either are contributing strongly to German economic performance, or are likely to do so in the future, have been driven by the financial incentives that have been implemented, including feed-in tariffs, reduced-rate loans for energy efficiency in buildings, and the previous German ETR. The UK, in contrast, has been much less successful in stimulating the EIs in these sectors. The effectiveness of the incentives apart from ETR are a strong argument for using some of the ETR revenues to deploy and develop new low-carbon technologies, as part of a portfolio of policies that tackle various barriers to these technologies.

The environmental industries not only mitigate or prevent the costs of environmental damage generated by industrial growth. They also make a double contribution to that growth, both as a fast-growing part of the national economy themselves, and by improving the productivity of other sectors by reducing the costs of resource use. Where the demand for green technologies is increasing globally, this can lead to new comparative advantages, industries, and export markets, further stimulating employment and output. They thereby promote European competitiveness and generate economic welfare, as well as environmental improvements, which are all necessary characteristics of sustainable, or green, growth.

13.4 The Global Promise of ETR

EU economic activity and environmental impacts are a relatively small, and declining, share of global totals, so that if the EU introduces ETR by itself, while the economic and environmental impacts in Europe may be substantial, the impact on both the environmental and economic global totals is small. However, where the ETR is undertaken in a context of global cooperation on climate policy, the global impact on both CO_2 emissions and resource consumption is significant. The modelling in Chapter 11 showed that the global impacts from the European ETR are insignificant in the unilateral scenario (HS1), but substantial in the scenario of global climate cooperation (HS3), when global CO_2 emissions are effectively stabilized by 2020, and are 15.6% below the baseline, and global resource consumption has also dropped by more than 5%. Global GDP, meanwhile, is about 1.4% below the baseline in HS3. This is comparable to the estimates in the Stern Review (Stern 2007) and far below the Review's estimates of the costs of unabated climate change.

This provides a strong motivation for considering ETR as part of the policy mix in international climate negotiations and any resulting international climate agreement.

13.5 Complementary Policies to ETR

There are two important reasons for implementing ETR in conjunction with complementary policies, rather than as a stand-alone instrument.

The first is that, despite their advantages in many contexts, market-based instruments are not the only possible choice in environmental policy. It may well be that the environmental effectiveness of ETR may be enhanced by complementing it with a judicious choice of other instruments: regulation, voluntary agreements, or information. An effective ETR to address climate change might therefore be embedded in a more general package including stronger regulation for carbon and energy efficiency, for example, for buildings, vehicles, and power stations. Chapter 12 showed that the German ETR was supported by a range of complementary instruments which were effective at stimulating the development of environmental technologies. If this approach can enhance the environmental effectiveness of ETR in this or other ways—for example, modelling work (Barker et al. 2008) suggests that regulation can supplement carbon prices to achieve more stringent targets at lower carbon prices—then, as already noted, it can achieve a given environmental improvement at lower cost than ETR by itself. This provides a reason for thinking that the carbon prices estimated in Chapter 9 (with no complementary policies) as necessary to reach the EU carbon reduction targets for 2020, are at the upper end of the necessary range. They could very possibly be significantly reduced if other instruments were introduced to increase their impact.

The other reason for not implementing ETR by itself is political. One inevitable result of ETR focusing on carbon emissions is price increases of fossil fuels (that is part of their purpose). In the HS1 scenario, these amount to up to about 30% for electricity, for a high-carbon electricity mix, 25–30% for natural gas, and somewhat less for road fuels (11%), because they are relatively highly taxed already. While with ETR these price increases would be offset by reductions in other taxes, the promise of tax reductions may not have public credibility and even if it does, it may not fully offset the unpopularity of energy price rises.

ETR is likely to be opposed by sectors that lose out from the reforms. The higher the reductions in carbon emissions and materials consumption, the more these sectors are likely to lose out in economic terms (although other sectors and households will gain). Arrangements for supporting vulnerable sectors in the context of an ETR are discussed in detail in Andersen and Ekins (2009) and need not be rehearsed here, except to say that, because losing sectors may have political influence, such arrangements may be required to make strong ETR politically feasible. The challenge is to introduce them in ways that do not undermine the environmental effectiveness of the ETR. Increasingly, it seems desirable that competitiveness issues related to particular vulnerable sectors should be addressed through sectoral agreements at the global level, rather than through distortions of the price signal at the regional (e.g. EU) and national levels, as has been the main approach so far. As with the global implementation of ETR, this will depend on further progress being made at the global level on agreement to reduce greenhouse gas emissions in order to mitigate climate change.

Vulnerable sectors are not the only political reason for complementary measures in the implementation of ETR. As was stressed in Chapter 10, there is also the issue of the fair treatment of vulnerable households. This is an issue that should always be given close consideration when an ETR is being considered, planned, or introduced. It is not possible, however, to generalize as to how different countries should address the issue, because their internal situations, fiscal systems, and political contexts are so different, a point that applies to a number of the implementation issues related to ETR.

13.6 Tailoring ETR to Different Country Contexts

The context for the implementation of ETR differs widely across countries. Fiscal systems are a complex and deeply embedded part of a country's institutional structure, and proposals for fiscal reform will inevitably interact with a range of other important issues—most obviously business competitiveness and distributional impacts on household expenditure, as discussed in the previous sub-section—which are politically very sensitive. Countries will, therefore, wish to approach and implement ETR in very different ways, and would be well advised to do so in a way that was well informed by analysis of political, institutional, and cultural, as well as economic, factors.

The modelling results in Chapter 9 clearly show that the ETR considered there would lead to a considerable reduction in employers' social security contributions (SSC)—assuming that other factors do not change—and to an increase in employment. So far, the experience of the ETRs implemented in the UK and Germany during the last decade have shown that the reduction in SSC has never been a long-lasting effect, as governments have increased SSC rates again—although it can be argued that without the ETRs the SSC would be higher still.

Although it is outside the scope of this book, the level of social security contributions should of course also be considered in the context of the discussion about the ageing population in Europe, because of the associated need for higher public expenditures in the fields of pension, health care, and long-term care in the future (EC 2009). However, like ETR itself, issues associated with ageing EU populations affect member states rather differently. The projections regarding future age-related public expenditure are heavily dependent on projected spending on public pensions. However, pension schemes differ between EU member states, and public pension expenditure in countries, such as Poland, Estonia, and Latvia, which reformed their pension scheme by switching from a publicly funded scheme to privately funded schemes, is projected to decrease in the future. This obviously affects the extent to which countries would wish to reduce SSC, as opposed to other taxes, as part of an

ETR. Again, different country contexts rule out simple generalizations, but it may be freely admitted that the ETR framework described in Chapter 9, which applies (for reasons of simplicity and ease of modelling) the same recycling policy for all EU member states irrespective of the differences in their overall national fiscal structure, is unlikely to be the best approach in practice. In the real world, there is no 'one size fits all' approach to ETR, because of the substantial fiscal, political, and economic differences between countries. However, this does not mean that there are no opportunities for implementing a coordinated ETR at the European level, a brief discussion of the prospects for which takes this book towards its close.

13.7 An ETR for Europe? Challenges, Opportunities, and Straws in the Wind

The analysis presented here suggests that ETR is conceptually still a very attractive policy instrument with which to address environmental issues, especially climate change, with a minimum negative, and perhaps even an overall positive, economic outcome. Moreover, there are recent signs that, after a period in which ETR seemed to have lost political purchase, governments are now rediscovering an interest in it. In Denmark and Sweden, the governments announced further ETRs during 2009. In France, an ETR centred on a carbon tax was due to be introduced in January 2010, but the tax was struck down by the constitutional court because there were too many exemptions. In Ireland, a carbon tax was introduced at €15 per tonne (equivalent to €0.042 per litre of petrol) in the 2010 Budget at the end of 2009. This was not matched by tax reductions, but was part of a new taxation package to reduce Ireland's budget deficit.

The emergence of the EU ETS as a decisive environmental policy tool at the EU level, with its opportunities for raising substantial revenues from the auctioning of allowances, and the need for many EU countries to address large budget deficits, argues for a broadening of the ETR concept from a simple exercise in tax shifting (although such a concept may still be appropriate in certain circumstances). It may become more appropriate to speak of environmental fiscal reform (EFR), which is already being promoted by the OECD and World Bank and which, as noted above, emphasizes the revenue-raising potential of environmental taxation, which, in the current context of fiscal deficits that need to be addressed, could reduce the need to increase other taxes, such as income and capital taxes.

The imperative of emission reduction in the EU

Fiscal deficits are not the only current circumstance in the EU arguing for increased carbon-energy taxes. The scientific imperative for strong action on climate change is strengthening inexorably, and seems likely to continue to do so. The achievement of the EU's climate package, involving a 20% reduction in greenhouse gas emissions, a 20% share of renewable source in final energy demand, and a 20% improvement in energy efficiency, by 2020, is far from certain, and may well become more stringent as the need to reduce emissions still further becomes more apparent.

Carbon-energy taxes are the only measure that would promote progress towards all three of the EU's 20% reduction targets. The IEA (2007: 31) stresses the importance of energy prices in promoting energy efficiency. In the EU, the goal of improving energy efficiency by 20% should reduce the total energy bill by some €100 billion (EC 2008). ETR would be a low-cost way of seeking to realize these cost and energy savings.

The auctioning of ETS allowances

The impending auctioning of EU ETS allowances means that there is in prospect a source of revenues at the European level from a European environmental instrument. It has long been recognized that an auctioned environmental trading scheme has much in common with an environmental tax. Having implemented the former, the European Council may be prepared to re-consider the latter, especially where it can strengthen and make more effective the EU ETS; or auctioning in the ETS may be supplemented by a carbon-energy tax in the non-ETS sectors, as was proposed by France.

The whole question of a carbon-energy tax at the EU level has received fresh impetus from the continuing weakness of the carbon price in the EU ETS, which is perceived to be well below the level required to stimulate significant investment in low-carbon technologies. It would be perfectly possible to combine the EU ETS with a carbon tax (see Ekins 2009), which would then have the effect of putting a floor on the carbon price and reduce the uncertainty surrounding the economic effectiveness of future investments.

The Energy Tax Directive

Moreover, there is also a potential role for the EU Energy Tax Directive, which sets minimum levels for energy taxes. These are currently far too low to be significant in either environmental or fiscal terms, but the European Commission is bringing forward a revision to the Energy Tax Directive, proposals for which include a differentiation between the tax rates on energy and carbon.

Were this proposal to be accepted, there would then be in place an instrument at EU level which could gradually raise the level of energy/carbon taxes in all EU countries, bringing about a harmonized ETR across the EU of the kind that this book has proposed.

Such a development remains only a tantalizing possibility. At present, it is clear that the radical differences in historical background, current context, and public perception between different European countries, combined with the fact that taxation is an issue which requires unanimity in the European Council, make the prospects for a European ETR seem rather remote.

The Challenge of Broader Dematerialization

Much of the detailed work described here has had decarbonization as its focus. This is quite simply because the data on carbon emissions and their relation to economic activity are much better than for other material flows. However, the results from both models showing increased material productivity as a result of the materials tax show that ETR is a relevant and effective policy approach for broader dematerialization, as well as for reducing carbon emissions. A major challenge for future research and policy is to develop the data and evidence base to enable ETR to be more widely used to reduce material flows apart from emissions of carbon.

Time for EU Leadership

In summary, there has now been substantial experience in Europe of ETR on a relatively small scale. The evidence presented here suggests that ETR is appropriate, as a broadly based instrument, to apply across different economic sectors. The results of the research reported here are consistent with other studies that show ETR to be beneficial for the environment, and to be either neutral or marginally positive for employment. It improves the environmental performance of an economy by reducing pollution and the use of resources, and can improve its economic performance, through two routes: the reduction of distorting taxes on capital and labour, and the stimulation of eco-innovation. Improved environmental performance, and improved economic performance, should both contribute to improved human well-being.

Less positively, the evidence also suggests that a European ETR will not be a politically straightforward policy instrument to introduce. At the EU level, its introduction would need to be by consensus across the EU-27, which will be anything but easy to achieve. Its relationship to the EU Emissions Trading System (ETS) would need to be carefully thought through. At the national level, its implementation would need to be very sensitive to the different national contexts, some of which, as in the Czech case study in this research, do not seem particularly auspicious for the introduction of ETR.

However, the results in this book suggest that a broadly based ETR across Europe could play a very important and cost-effective role in meeting the EU's emission reduction targets for 2020, especially in a context of global cooperation on climate policy. It can also be used to increase resource efficiency more broadly. Certainly it is not clear that there is any other policy which would perform as well both economically and environmentally across countries as diverse as the EU. The recent science of climate change has established the urgency of finding an immediate and effective means of achieving large-scale reductions in GHG emissions.

ETR therefore represents a great policy opportunity to address global and regional environmental challenges in a way that is both cost-effective (the property of environmental economic instruments), and supportive of employment, technological innovation, and the creation of new industries that can contribute significantly to long-term economic development. These are large benefits from public policy.

Finally, there are good arguments, to do with the necessary institutional structures for implementation, for preferring a carbon tax to emissions trading at the global level, at least in the short term and perhaps as a transitional instrument to a global trading scheme, and these arguments are increasingly being rehearsed in the context of post-Kyoto negotiations and, in particular, how to include emerging and developing economies appropriately in a post-Kyoto agreement.

The economic, as well as the environmental, benefits of a European ETR are great and argue strongly that ETR should be an essential part of the policy mix that will be required to achieve steep cuts in GHG emissions. It is surely up to the politicians and policy makers to find a way of addressing the political challenges of ETR in order to realize its benefits on behalf of the EU as a whole.

13.8 ETR and Green Growth

The title of this book claims that ETR is a policy for green growth, that is, environmentally sustainable economic growth in Europe and elsewhere, and the book now concludes with some reflections on this claim, in the light of the evidence that has been presented.

The relationship between economic growth and the environment is a topic that emerges periodically at times of perceived environmental stress, stimulates a flurry of debate, often of a fairly unconstructive kind between environmentalists and economists, and then disappears from view. The first cycle was sparked off in the 1970s by the Club of Rome publication, *The Limits to*

Growth (Meadows et al. 1972), the second coincided with the Earth Summit in 1992 (Meadows et al. 1992). The whole debate to the end of the century was reviewed in Ekins (2000). The Meadows team produced a '30-year update' in 2005 (Meadows et al. 2005), which presaged a third round of debate, running at the moment (e.g. Victor 2008; Jackson 2009), in which a larger role is played by concerns about climate change and, to a lesser extent, biodiversity loss. So far the debate has had practically no impact on the priority in public policy that is accorded to economic growth, and each time the cycle comes round it is clear that, while there have been important environmental improvements in mainly richer countries related to local environmental issues, at the global level, since the previous cycle, there has been substantial further environmental deterioration, which gives greater cause for serious environmental concern.

The growth-environment debate may be roughly characterized as follows. Those on the 'limits' side of the argument, who were initially on the margins of broad economic opinion, have asserted fairly consistently that:

1. The Earth and its resources are physically finite;

2. There are limits to the extent that humans can exploit the environment without undermining its ability to continue to perform the environmental functions, or provide the ecosystem goods and services, on which the human economy and society depend.

3. In several areas, these limits are now being exceeded, and in due course this will have serious detrimental effects on human ways of life.

4. Economic growth is a major cause of this exceeding of limits, not least because it has more than offset the increases in material and energy productivity which have been achieved.

5. There is little evidence on the big issues that 'absolute decoupling' on the necessary scale for environmental sustainability (e.g. in respect of global warming, a maximum 2°C global average temperature rise) can be achieved between economic growth and environmental damage; and therefore

6. Rich countries at least should cease in their pursuit (or at least their unremitting prioritization) of economic growth and learn to manage a low-growth or even a no-growth (also called a steady-state) economy. At the same time, it is generally acknowledged that growth is both necessary and desirable to reduce poverty in emerging economies and developing countries.

7. Most recently, as briefly discussed in Chapter 1, the argument has emerged that a low or no-growth economy need not imply low or declining welfare, because there is very little evidence that recent growth in rich countries has substantially increased welfare among the general population.

357

Those on the other side of the debate started off the 1970s by contesting each of these assertions. Most recently, practically everyone now accepts the first three points, especially in respect of climate change and biodiversity loss. Beyond that, there is now a wider range of opinion in the mainstream, exemplified by the Stiglitz-Sen report (2009) commissioned by the French government,[1] the 'Beyond GDP' conference (2007), and the Communication[2] (2009) of the European Commission, and the ongoing initiative that also involves the OECD, Club of Rome, and the WWF.[3] The UK Sustainable Development Commission contributed to the debate with its report *Prosperity without Growth*,[4] which resulted in a book of the same name (Jackson 2009), which was cited by the *Financial Times* (28 November) as 'one of the best books of 2009'. The UK government's Sustainable Development Strategy of 2005[5] has 'living within environmental limits' as one of its fundamental objectives, and more recently Rockström et al. (2009) considers that humanity is operating well beyond the limits on three out of nine environmental issues (climate change, biodiversity loss, the nitrogen cycle).

At the same time, there has been a resurgence of interest in, and work on, the concept of 'green growth', partly in response to the financial crisis, with UNEP calling for a 'Global Green New Deal' and launching a Green Economy Initiative,[6] and partly out of the perceived need to address environmental problems in ways that reinforce growth and competitiveness rather than undermining it.[7]

An important argument in the current round of debate, as noted under point 5 above, is that the extent of decoupling between economic growth and environmental impact is now so great, if environmental limits (especially in respect of climate change) are to be respected, and the historical evidence shows that such decoupling is so difficult to achieve, that it should now be concluded that economic growth and environmental sustainability are in fact incompatible (see Jackson 2009, chapter 5, pp. 67 ff). The claim that ETR can be a policy for environmentally sustainable economic growth, or green growth, in a rich economic region like Europe, is therefore not uncontroversial.

The evidence in this book suggests that, with ETR and complementary policies, global greenhouse gas (GHG) emissions could certainly be stabilized

---

[1] 'Report of the Commission on the Measurement of Economic Performance and Social Progress', <http://www.stiglitz-sen-fitoussi.fr/documents/rapport_anglais.pdf>.

[2] <http://eur-lex.europa.eu/LexUriServ/LexUriServ.do?uri=COM:2009:0433:FIN:EN:PDF>.

[3] <http://www.beyond-gdp.eu/>.

[4] <http://www.sd-commission.org.uk/pages/redefining-prosperity.html>.

[5] <http://www.defra.gov.uk/sustainable/government/publications/uk-strategy/>.

[6] <http://www.unep.org/greeneconomy/>.

[7] For OECD work in this area, see <http://www.oecd.org/document/10/0,3343,en_2649_37465_44076170_1_1_1,00.html>. For that of the UN Economic and Social Commission of Asia Pacific (UNESCAP), see <http://www.greengrowth.org/focus.asp>.

by 2020, at a cost to GDP in that year of no more than 2% (see Chapter 9), which amounts to a reduction in the annual growth rate of less than 0.1%. This is a small fraction of the global average GDP growth of about 3% per annum experienced over the first seven years of this century.

Clearly, after 2020, there will need to be large further reductions in GHG emissions if global average temperature change is to be kept within 2°C, as the science suggests is desirable. However, even the most pessimistic estimates of the costs of large-scale reductions in these emissions do not suggest that they bring economic growth to a halt; the maximum GDP cost of a 90% emissions reduction in the review of modelling estimates in Stern (2007: 270) is 15% by 2050, which implies that, at an underlying 3% rate of growth, the economy in 2050 will be 2.8 times its size in 2010, rather than 3.3 times. This is significantly less, to be sure, but it still only implies a loss of about 0.5% growth per annum (i.e. the growth rate falls to 2.5% per annum), which is a far cry from growth stopping altogether.

Of course, as has been stated throughout this book, climate change is only one of the environmental challenges facing humanity, although one of, if not the, most important. Addressing other challenges will require improvements in resource efficiency in the use of practically all materials, and absolute reductions in the use of many of them. Some of the other most pressing challenges involve achieving sustainable use of renewable resources, and stemming the loss of biodiversity. This last will require humans to become far more aware of the needs of other species to have space for their habitats, and to constrain accordingly the human appropriation of this space and the primary production that comes from it. It may be that these further constraints add to the reduction in economic growth arising from the reduction of greenhouse gas emissions, although analysis comparable to the work on carbon reduction does not yet exist to say with any confidence how large any such further constraint on growth might be.

Moreover, it is also worth stating that, without drastic improvements in carbon and wider resource productivity, and resulting large-scale reductions in environmental deterioration, it is most unlikely that the 2–3% per annum rates of economic growth, routinely assumed in economic modelling exercises, will actually materialize. It may seem trite to say that, by definition, unsustainable economic growth, such as that being currently experienced, *cannot* be projected indefinitely into the future, but most economic models and future projections do just that. In reality, therefore, far from carbon reduction, improvements in other material productivities, and biodiversity conservation resulting in lower economic growth than would otherwise occur, they will actually increase it. If the more pessimistic projections of 'business-as-usual' environmental impacts prove to be close to the mark, then it may be that stringent environmental measures will actually prevent the global economy from going into precipitate decline. This is what was meant in Chapter 12 by the remark that such measures, and the industries they promote, are a *condition* for sustainable growth, as well as a contributor to it.

Economic growth comes about through innovation driven by increased knowledge. It was this process that resulted in humans learning how to use fossil fuels on a large scale from about 1700 (the fossil fuels themselves had existed much longer than humans), and much economic growth was doubt-less the result of this (Ayres and Warr 2009). It will be this process that drives innovation to decarbonize human energy use, if humans are wise, in response to the threat of climate change. The decarbonization transition may be bumpy, because fossil fuels are very convenient and human societies have become very dependent on them, but there is no reason to imagine, given the current availability of low-carbon energy sources and technologies, and the exponentially growing stock of scientific knowledge of all kinds, that the deployment of these energy sources and technologies will bring economic growth to a halt (although they will certainly change its direction and have an effect on the lifestyles that people live). In fact, provided that the policies required for this deployment are economically sensible, there is rather every reason to imagine that it, and the knowledge that will go with it, will generate new industries that will provide an engine for economic growth in the future. And what is true for low-carbon economic development may be true for more resource-efficient development of all kinds.

This book suggests that ETR is an economically sensible policy to help to bring about the low-carbon transition. Conceivably, the transition could be contrived without it, but almost certainly at significantly higher cost. Certainly other policies can support and reinforce an ETR to make it even more effective. But ETR emerges from the evidence as a crucial element in the policy mix to permit an economic growth that is compatible with climate stability, and, by analogy, with environmental sustainability more generally.

References

Andersen, M. S., and P. Ekins (eds.) (2009), *Carbon-Energy Taxation: Lessons from Europe*, Oxford: Oxford University Press.

Ayres, R., and B. Warr (2009), *The Economic Growth Engine: How Energy and Work Drive Material Prosperity*, Cheltenham: Edward Elgar.

Barker, T., T. Foxon, and S. Scricieu (2008), 'Achieving the G8 50% Target: Modelling Induced and Accelerated Technological Change Using the Macro-econometric Model E3MG', *Climate Policy*, 8, Special Issue on 'Modelling Long-Term Scenarios for Low-Carbon Societies', S30–45.

Bosquet, B. (2000), 'Environmental Tax Reform: Does it Work? A Survey of the Empirical Evidence', *Ecological Economics*, 34: 19–32.

EC (European Commission) (2008), *20 20 by 2020 Europe's climate change opportunity*, Communication from the Commission to the European Parliament, the Council, the European Economic and Social Committee and the Committee of the Regions, COM (2008) 30 final, Brussels, 23 January.

EC (European Commission) (2009), *2009 Ageing Report: Economic and Budgetary Projections for the EU-27 Member States (2008–2060)*, Joint Report prepared by the European Commission (DG ECFIN) and the Economic Policy Committee (AWG), European Economy 2/2009, European Communities 2009, available at <http://ec.europa.eu/economy_finance/publications/publication14992_en.pdf>.

EEA (European Environment Agency) (2000), *Environmental Taxes: Recent Developments in Tools for Integration*, Copenhagen, Denmark.

—— (2005), 'Market-Based Instruments for Environmental Policy in Europe', EEA Technical Report No. 8/2005, Copenhagen.

Ekins, P. (2000), *Economic Growth and Environmental Sustainability: The Prospects for Green Growth*, London and New York: Routledge.

—— (2009), 'Carbon Taxes and Emissions Trading: Issues and Interactions', in Andersen and Ekins (2009), 241–55.

—— and T. Barker (2001), 'Carbon Taxes and Carbon Emissions Trading', *Journal of Economic Surveys*, 15(3): 325–76.

Eurostat (2009), *Taxation Trends in the European Union Data for the EU Member States and Norway*, Report by Eurostat and EC Directorate General for Taxation and Customs Union, Luxembourg: Office for Official Publications of the European Communities.

IEA (International Energy Agency) (2007), *Energy Use in the New Millennium: Trends in IEA Countries*, Paris: IEA.

Jackson, T. (2009), *Prosperity without Growth: Economics for a Finite Planet*, London: Earthscan.

Meadows, D. H, D. L. Meadows, J. Randers, and W. Behrens (1972), *The Limits to Growth*, a report commissioned by the Club of Rome, New York: Universe Books.

—— —— —— (1992), *Beyond the Limits: Global Collapse or a Sustainable Future*, London: Earthscan.

—— J. Randers, and D. L. Meadows (2005), *The Limits to Growth: The 30-Year Update*, London: Earthscan.

Patuelli, R., P. Nijkamp, and E. Pels (2005), 'Environmental Tax Reform and the Double Dividend: A Meta-analytical Assessment', *Ecological Economics*, 55: 564–83.

Rockström, J., W. Steffen, K. Noone et al. (2009), 'A Safe Operating Space for Humanity', *Nature*, 461, 24 September: 472–5.

Speck, S., and J. Jilkova (2009), 'Design of Environmental Tax Reforms in Europe', in Andersen and Ekins (2009).

Stern, N. (2007), *The Economics of Climate Change*, Cambridge: Cambridge University Press.

Victor, P. (2008), *Managing without Growth: Slower by Design, not by Disaster*, Cheltenham: Edward Elgar.

World Bank (2005), *Environmental Fiscal Reform: What Should be Done and How to Achieve it*, Washington: World Bank.

Index

363

Index